PENGUIN C

THE PILLOW BOOK

SEI SHŌNAGON (?966–?1017) was a gentlewoman in the court of Empress Teishi, in what is now Kyoto, Japan. *The Pillow Book* is her 'journal' of anecdotes and observations based on her life at court. It was probably completed in the first years of the eleventh century.

MEREDITH McKINNEY gained a Ph.D. in medieval Japanese literature from the Australian National University in Canberra, where she presently teaches in the Japan Centre. She lived and taught in Japan for twenty years, and now lives near Braidwood, New South Wales. Her other published translations include *Ravine and Other Stories* by Furui Yoshikichi (1997) and *The Tale of Saigyō* (1998).

SEI SHŌNAGON

The Pillow Book

Translated with Notes by MEREDITH McKINNEY

PENGUIN BOOKS

PENGUIN BOOKS

Published by the Penguin Group
Penguin Books Ltd, 80 Strand, London WC2R ORL, England
Penguin Group (USA) Inc., 375 Hudson Street, New York, New York 10014, USA
Penguin Group (Canada), 90 Eglinton Avenue East, Suite 700, Toronto, Ontario, Canada M4P 2Y3
(a division of Pearson Penguin Canada Inc.)
Penguin Ireland, 25 St Stephen's Green, Dublin 2, Ireland (a division of Penguin Books Ltd)
Penguin Group (Australia), 250 Camberwell Road, Camberwell, Victoria 3124, Australia
(a division of Pearson Australia Group Pty Ltd)
Penguin Books India Pvt Ltd, 11 Community Centre, Panchsheel Park, New Delhi – 110 017, India
Penguin Group (NZ), cnr Airborne and Rosedale Roads, Albany, Auckland 1310,
New Zealand (a division of Pearson New Zealand Ltd)
Penguin Books (South Africa) (Pty) Ltd, 24 Sturdee Avenue,
Rosebank, Johannesburg 2196, South Africa

Penguin Books Ltd, Registered Offices: 80 Strand, London WC2R ORL, England

www.penguin.com

This translation first published in Penguin Classics 2006

036

Grateful acknowledgement is made for permission to reproduce
the illustrations by Sugai Minoru, from 'Makura no Sushi',
Shogakukan Inc., 1997

Copyright © Meredith McKinney, 2006
All rights reserved

The moral right of the translator has been asserted

Set in 10.25/12.25 pt PostScript Adobe Sabon
Typeset by Rowland Phototypesetting Ltd, Bury St Edmunds, Suffolk
Printed and bound in Great Britain by Clays Ltd, Elcograf S.p.A.

ISBN-13: 978-0-140-44806-1
ISBN-10: 0-140-44806-3

www.greenpenguin.co.uk

Contents

Acknowledgements

I would first like to thank The Australian National University's Japan Centre, where I was able to work on this translation as a Visiting Fellow from 2002 to 2005. I also wish to thank the Australian Government's Asialink programme, which enabled me to spend three precious months in Japan during 2005 while I completed the translation.

Friends have been invaluable to me throughout this time, both in their warm support and in their immensely helpful reading and comments on some or all of the translation at various stages. I am particularly grateful to dear friends Timoshenko Aslanides, Nicola Bowery, Julian Davies, David Farrah, Stephanie L'Heureux and Simon Patton, as well as to Naomi Fukumori for her long-distance professional help and comments.

I also owe a deep debt of gratitude to Royall and Susan Tyler, who have helped and supported me in countless ways throughout this undertaking, and most particularly to Susan, whose meticulous and deeply informed editorial assistance has been of immense value to me.

My gratitude to Sugai Minoru for his illustrations, taken from details found in various early scrolls, and to Shōgakukan Publishing Company for making them available.

Finally, I would like to thank Penguin Classics editor Lindeth Vasey for her wonderfully friendly and sensitive editorial assistance throughout this project.

Chronology

*Main background events are included. Names are given in the
Japanese order, family name first.*

966? Sei Shōnagon born. Father Kiyohara Motosuke, mother's
name unknown.

967 Emperor Murakami, Ichijō's grandfather, dies. Inter-
regnum for two years.

969 Enyū (b. 959), Ichijō's father, succeeds to the throne.

975 Princess Senshi (964–1035) becomes Kamo High Priestess
(until 1031).

977 Fujiwara Teishi born. Father Fujiwara Michitaka (b. 953),
mother Takashina Kishi (d. 996).

978 Fujiwara Senshi (962–1001), daughter of Fujiwara Kaneie,
becomes Empress of Emperor Enyū.

980 Ichijō born. Father Emperor Enyū, mother Fujiwara Senshi.

984 Emperor Enyū retires and takes Buddhist orders. Succeeded
by Kazan (968–1008), eldest son of Emperor Reizei.

986 Emperor Kazan retires and takes Buddhist orders. Succeeded by Ichijō.

990 Teishi becomes High Consort to Emperor Ichijō. Fujiwara
Kaneie, Michitaka's father, becomes Chancellor.

991 Retired Emperor Enyū dies; Empress Dowager, Fujiwara
Senshi, takes the tonsure.

993 Fujiwara Michitaka becomes Chancellor. ?Sei Shōnagon
becomes a gentlewoman in Teishi's court.

994? Fujiwara Korechika (974–1010), Michitaka's son, presents Empress Teishi with the paper Sei Shōnagon will use
for her *Pillow Book*.

995 Chancellor Fujiwara Michitaka dies. Michitaka's brother
and rival, Fujiwara Michinaga (966–1027), increases his
power.

996 Teishi's brothers Korechika and Takaie (979–1044) attack
Retired Emperor Kazan; they are arrested and forced to leave
the capital. ?Governor of Ise Minamoto Tsunefusa visits Sei
Shōnagon and discovers and circulates the early draft of *The
Pillow Book*. Teishi gives birth to a daughter, Princess Shūshi.

997 Korechika and Takaie are allowed to return to the capital.

999 Major fire at Imperial Palace. Teishi gives birth to a son,
Prince Atsuyasu.

1000 Michinaga's daughter Shōshi becomes High Consort to
Emperor Ichijō, replacing Teishi in his favour. Teishi gives
birth to a daughter, Princess Kyōshi, and dies two days later.
Sei Shōnagon leaves the court.

1011 Emperor Ichijō dies. Succeeded by Sanjō.

1017 Last reference to Sei Shōnagon.

Introduction

A thousand years ago, in a world in many ways unimaginably different from ours, a lady at the imperial court of Japan settled herself in front of a precious bundle of paper and began to write the extraordinary work later called *Makura no sōshi*, known to English readers as *The Pillow Book*. In it she wrote about her world, in a voice so vividly alive that we find ourselves in the presence of a woman we recognize as we would a friend.

The world Sei Shōnagon lived in and wrote for was the intimate world of the court – instantly recognizable to her and her audience, but so opaque to us that often we have only her words to guide us. As we read her apparently crazy quilt of vignettes and opinions and anecdotes, we find ourselves deep inside this world, and feel her responses along our own nerves. But the modern reader's compelling sense of intimacy with Sei Shōnagon and her world, which is one of the great achievements of her writing, is of course based on an illusion. We do not know that world, and before we enter it with her it is best to learn a little about it.

SEI SHŌNAGON AND THE BACKGROUND TO HER WORLD

Sei Shōnagon lived at the height of the Heian period. 'Heian' roughly translates as 'peace and tranquility', and nicely expresses the nature of this long, sunny period in Japanese history, stretching from 794 to 1186, when Japanese culture flowered and came into its own. This flowering grew from the fertilizing contact of the native culture with that of China, but by Sei Shōnagon's time the direct impact of that powerful foreign civilization had largely been absorbed and contact with China had virtually ceased, although its culture was still a potent presence in civilized Japanese life.

The city in which Sei Shōnagon lived, Heian-kyō (present-day Kyoto), was usually known simply as 'the capital'. Around and beyond, in wider Japan, lay the provinces, which for those people in Heian-kyō constituted a kind of outer darkness against which the cultured life of their capital glowed the more brightly. At the glowing centre of this world was the Emperor and his court. Heian-kyō was modelled on the Chinese capital Ch'ang-an, with a large imperial palace in the north of the city and a grid of streets to the east, west and south of it. The walled palace-grounds were in turn divided into the outer imperial palace, which held the buildings of the governmental bureaucracy, and, within another wall, the smaller inner complex of gallery-connected buildings that housed the Emperor and his various consorts, as well as some administrative buildings. (See 'The Inner Palace' in Appendix 1.)

This world – of the capital, more specifically of the inner palace area, and most particularly of the household of Empress Teishi where Sei Shōnagon served as gentlewoman – is that of *The Pillow Book*. Small though it may seem from our perspective, it was all the world to Sei Shōnagon, and in this she epitomizes the experience of the women and the men who served at the imperial court. Culture and civilization were synonymous with court life, and the closer one was to the Emperor the closer one was to its essence.

Sei Shōnagon was born into what she would have considered the periphery of this world. Her father was a Provincial Governor, a post given to middle-ranking courtiers but far from prestigious in the world of the court, where the requirement to live in the provinces was perceived as a kind of cultural exile. In fact, Governors often contrived to spend a good deal of time in the capital, and there is no record of Sei Shōnagon ever having experienced provincial life. Certainly the only experiences that mattered to her were exclusively to do with life in Heian-kyō.

Verifiable facts about Sei Shōnagon are sparse, and information about her life depends overwhelmingly on her own record in *The Pillow Book*. Even her name is puzzling. 'Sei' is a shorthand reference to her family name of Kiyohara (*sei* being an alternative reading of the character for *kiyo*), while 'Shōnagon' is the name of a bureaucratic post, translated here as 'Junior Counsellor' (See Appendix 5 on ranks and titles). Names were far more changeable and context-dependent than in our modern world, and at court it was traditional to name a gentlewoman by the title of a male relative, though no one has managed to trace definitively the 'Junior Counsellor' from whom Sei Shōnagon derives her name. Tradition has it that her original personal name was Nagiko.*

Balancing a variety of historical evidence, scholars suggest that Sei Shōnagon may have been born around 966, and the last apparently historical reference to her is around 1017. She seems to have been 'married' (although that word only inadequately conveys the fluid nature of marital arrangements at this time)[1] to Tachibana Norimitsu (dates unknown), one of the courtiers who appears in *The Pillow Book*, though in a rather unimpressive role. (See Appendix 2 for a summary of Norimitsu's appearances and that of other major characters.) We can gather that the marriage did not last, and there is certainly no suggestion of husband or children in *The Pillow Book*, although references found in other works of the period indicate that she had at least one child.

Thus Sei Shōnagon's story essentially begins and ends with her relationship with Empress Teishi (977–1000). She seems to have entered Teishi's court as a gentlewoman in either the spring or autumn of 993. She would have been in her late twenties, considerably older than most newly employed gentlewomen, and around ten years older than the Empress. Her service at court presumably came to an end with Teishi's death seven years later.[2] Of Sei Shōnagon's subsequent life nothing is

---

* Japanese name order has the family name (e.g. Sei) first. In *The Pillow Book*, people are generally referred to by their personal name (Shōnagon), although I have used 'Sei' for brevity in the Notes.

known, although tradition states that she degenerated in her final years into a poverty-stricken and unhappy crone. However, tradition may only be serving her what it considered her just desserts.

HISTORICAL BACKGROUND

Although Teishi is here designated as 'Empress', her position was never as secure as that title implies. When Sei Shōnagon entered her service, Teishi was Emperor Ichijō's first Empress (*chūgū*), a position she had held since soon after her powerful father Fujiwara Michitaka had arranged their marriage when she was fourteen and Ichijō eleven years old. Other consorts also lived in the various residences around Ichijō's Seiryōden residence, however, and each of them had powerful family backing, on which their status at court largely depended.

Throughout most of Japanese history, the Emperor himself, for all his prestige, has been effectively powerless. During the Heian period, the real power lay in the hands of the great Fujiwara family. The court was largely composed of Fujiwara men, and members of the family's main branch held the top positions in the court hierarchy. One of their chief aims was to provide from their own immediate family the woman who would become the mother of the future Emperor, and to this end there was perpetual rivalry and jockeying to place their daughters advantageously at court. Thus Teishi's position rested precariously on the continued power of her father Michitaka, for all that Emperor Ichijō seems genuinely to have preferred her above his other consorts.

In *The Pillow Book* we meet Michitaka as the jovial Regent who so delighted Sei Shōnagon with his jokes and banter, a man revelling in his power and the resultant prestige of his family. His beloved daughter Teishi was Empress, her younger sister Genshi had recently become wife of the Crown Prince, his eldest son Korechika was in place to take over the reins of power in his turn, and his other children were likewise in positions of suitable prestige. His brother and rival, Michinaga, was as yet only a peripheral threat. But less than two years later, in 995, Michitaka died after a few months of illness. His brother Michikane became Regent, but when he died in an epidemic a mere seven days later, Michinaga at last attained his goal. His days of power extended until his death in 1027; his glittering career may have played a part in the portrait of the 'Shining Prince' in *The Tale of Genji* (*Genji monogatari*), that most famous of Heian tales, written when he was at the height of his glory.

For Teishi, Michitaka's death was more than a personal sorrow because her position at court was now deeply insecure. It was further undermined when her chief protector, her brother Korechika, was disgraced and effectively exiled with their younger brother Takaie in 996, after a peculiar incident in which they attacked Retired Emperor Kazan, under the (probably mistaken) impression that he was secretly courting a lady who was at the time Korechika's lover. Michinaga's machinations may well have been behind this event, and it certainly played into his hands. Though Korechika was allowed to return from the provinces early in 997, his power had been permanently undermined, and with it Teishi's position at court. In 1000, Michinaga established his ten-year-old daughter Shōshi as the first Empress. Teishi, still at court but her position now threatened on all sides, died at the end of the year, two days after childbirth.

CULTURAL BACKGROUND

Although Sei Shōnagon was profoundly affected by these events, they are almost entirely absent from her *Pillow Book*. Her gaze is determinedly, almost perversely, fixed on the delights to be found in court life; if sorrow momentarily clouds her sky, it is there only to provide the backdrop for some delightful event that relieves it with laughter. Although the history is essential for an understanding of the background to the world she writes about, we will most sympathetically read *The Pillow Book* if we allow ourselves temporarily to forget the grim facts. What Sei Shōnagon wants her reader to experience is the delicious pleasures of life at court, so it is to the details of that life that we should now turn.

Teishi and her gentlewomen inhabited a world that was largely screened from the world around it. Within the building where they spent their days and nights, the Empress herself was ensconced in the large Inner Chamber, and much of the comings and goings of life around her were conducted in the wide aisle area that surrounded this central room on all sides. (See 'The Main House' in Appendix 1.) Although the word 'palace' is often used to describe buildings such as those Teishi and the Emperor inhabited in the inner palace grounds, there was no palatial glitter about these simple wooden buildings. The only walled room was a sort of storeroom-cum-occasional-bedroom that made up one portion of the Inner Chamber; for the rest, 'rooms' were temporary constructions usually made of portable standing screens and standing curtains. Reed blinds and sliding panels were generally all that divided the Inner Chamber from the surrounding aisle, which was a step lower. The gentlewomen had their apartments along the side or back aisle, though the flimsy nature of the partitions meant that privacy was partial at best. Beyond the aisle, divided off by blinds and shutters and another step lower, a narrow veranda surrounded the building. (For definitions of general terminology, see Appendix 4.)

It was to the veranda that a gentleman would come to call on a gentlewoman, or a messenger present himself with a message for the Empress. These visitors from the outer world were received by the gentlewomen, obscured by lowered blinds or standing curtains, behind which they would sit and converse more or less invisibly, or receive the message (written or oral) and deliver it to the Empress within. It was only when they could be sure of being unobserved that the ladies would venture out to sit on the veranda or wander in the garden beyond. Barely a breath of the politics that seethed in the larger world of the palace is apparent in the picture Sei Shōnagon presents. Among the men, advancement in rank and title was the focus of constant rivalry. Sei Shōnagon and her friends were fascinated, though passive, observers of this struggle, and connoisseurs of its finer details, but they would have been surprised at the suggestion that they should want the powers and freedoms allowed to men: their tiny world was for them its own completely adequate centre.

The confined life of the women at court was only relieved by the intense pleasure of occasional expeditions. The highlights were viewing the splendid procession for the annual Kamo Festival (see Appendix 4), and the imperial processions when the Emperor left the palace, but religious events such as the popular Salvation Lotus Discourses could also cause great excitement, as Section 32 so vividly depicts. Even for such excursions, however, high-ranking ladies always remained hidden from view within their carriages, and observed the world through the haze of fine reed blinds.

Far from dulling the senses, however, this dimly lit and circumscribed world in fact vivified the perceptions of its inhabitants. Sei Shōnagon's writing revels in the nuances of sound and scent – the soft tap of a lid placed on a kettle, the faint susurration of fire tongs gently stirring ash in a brazier, or the lingering scent from someone's incense-impregnated clothes resonate with peculiar intensity. Visual awareness is also acute; the glint of firelight on a metal clasp or the glow of a glossed-silk robe receives loving attention.

This is perhaps to be expected, in a dark interior lit largely by an occasional oil lamp or brazier fire, or pale daylight filtered through fine blinds. What is unexpected and astonishing, however, is the vivid and detailed visual awareness of clothes. A figure some distance away, in a poorly illuminated room, will be recalled years later with an enthralled description of the details of clothing, colour and fabric. It is undoubtedly the case that Sei Shōnagon was particularly finely attuned to and observant of such matters, as her fellow-gentlewomen point out, perhaps rather wryly, in Section 78 after hearing a breathless report from her on a courtier's splendid attire, but other writing of the time makes it clear that she was not unusual in her fascination with clothes. The question of what people wore was highly complex and of utmost importance for both men and women at court (see Appendix 6); Sei Shōnagon's fine judgements reveal the degree to which clothing mattered in an estimation of others. Facial features, body type – such merely physical attributes are barely mentioned in describing a person's appearance. A man or a woman is the clothes he or she wears.

This heightened awareness of taste and aesthetic sensibility is everywhere apparent in the court culture that Sei Shōnagon so lovingly documented, and nowhere more so than in relations between women and men. Senior courtiers constantly came calling on gentlewomen, and elegant repartee was the essence of conversations that could apparently continue for hours between the gentleman on his cushion on the veranda and the gentle-woman ensconced behind her blind or curtain close by. The only men who could breach the curtain's boundary were family members, or lovers. Sei Shōnagon seems to have had several lovers during her period at court, a situation probably not uncommon for gentlewomen, but although she recorded her close relationships with these men, there is never a hint of any physicality in her descriptions. As with clothes, so with love – taste and sensibility, rather than the merely physical, are the focus of interest and awareness.

Nothing revealed a person's degree of sensibility more clearly than the art of poetry. It would seem from reading *The Pillow Book* that poetic allusion was woven into every elegant con-versation, and almost any occasion could be turned to the purposes of poetic composition. Anyone who hoped to be admired and accepted had to be deeply knowledgeable about the poetic canon, particularly the poems contained in the classic poetry collections such as *Kokinshū*, and able to weave appo-site allusions to them into her or his own occasional poetry. Wittily nuanced messages, generally containing a poem, flew constantly between members of the court and sometimes beyond; these in turn required a suitable extempore poem in response, written in an elegant hand on paper carefully chosen for appropriateness of colour and quality, in every aspect of which one's sensibility and character would be dis-played for intense scrutiny. Although such exchanges of poetry were common throughout the court, by long tradition it was the romantic relationship that quintessentially embodied the essence of poetic exchange. A man could fall in love with a woman on the evidence of little more than her poems; a woman could decide to sever relations with a man if he demonstrated poetic obtuseness, as Sei Shōnagon several times describes herself doing in *The Pillow Book*.

Sei Shōnagon was a masterful practitioner of the art of witty repartee and poetic exchange, and revelled in recording her finest moments. She also frequently described how nervous poetic composition made her, and with so much at stake this is not surprising. She had the added burden, however, of coming from a family with a high reputation for poetic composition. Her own skills were clearly in the field of clever social verse; it was more serious composition, for poetry contests or in response to an occasion such as the excursion in Section 94 to hear the first call of the *hototogisu* (a small cuckoo whose sweet lilting call was a poetic harbinger of early summer), that she found intimidating.

She was perfectly happy to be the one who intimidated with poetry on other occasions, however, and *The Pillow Book* abounds in tales of various hapless gentlemen's defeat at her hands. She evidently had an astonishingly quick mind, and could cap any allusion that came her way. The situations that caused her most difficulty were those involving allusions from Chinese poetry: not because she was ignorant of it, but rather because it was considered unseemly for a woman to betray any knowledge of it. The Chinese language belonged to the sphere of men: their public and official writing, of both prose and poetry, was conducted in Chinese, and their education was largely devoted to the Chinese classics. Other sources make it clear that it was in fact not unusual for an intelligent woman to gain some surreptitious knowledge of these classics – and indeed the scenes in *The Pillow Book* in which men are heard chanting Chinese poetry show that women were frequently exposed to it – but it was generally frowned on for a woman to flaunt this knowledge. Sei Shōnagon, typically, knew far more than most, and the gentlemen knew she did, and enjoyed seeing her negotiate the difficult challenge of cleverly responding to a Chinese allusion in a suitably roundabout way.

From the above it may seem that Sei Shōnagon's primary social focus was men, and men certainly are the principal players in many of the episodes she related. But the real emotional focus of her life at court was the Empress she served. For all Sei Shōnagon's clear-eyed and acerbic observations on those with whom she came in contact, her vision of Her Majesty was perpetually glazed with something close to adoration. Teishi was by all accounts an enchantingly lively and beautiful young woman, yet even so Sei Shōnagon's worshipful attitude towards her strikes most modern readers as excessive. But we must remember that the Heian court was far from alone in its adulation of emperors and empresses; this kind of adoration, which may appear to us merely sycophantic, was for many centuries and in many lands the norm.

Teishi evidently took pleasure in Sei Shōnagon's company, if we can trust *The Pillow Book* accounts, and certainly enjoyed teasing her, at times a little cruelly, by pretending to test her love. But Sei Shōnagon was in fact a precious asset for Teishi, someone whose fine taste and brilliant wit brought honour to her in a world that placed high value on the reputation of one's salon. When Sei Shōnagon delights everyone with a particularly adroit and ingenious response to a poetic challenge Teishi has posed, a gentlewoman admiringly remarks, 'You epitomize the sort of person who belongs in this court' (Section 279). This was undoubtedly true, and it should be the first thing kept in mind in turning to the question of the origins and purposes of *The Pillow Book*.

WHAT IS *THE PILLOW BOOK*?

The final section [s29] provides its own explanation for how *The Pillow Book* came into being. There Sei Shōnagon gives us this rather cryptic scene:

Palace Minister Korechika one day presented to the Empress a bundle of paper. 'What do you think we could write on this?'

Her Majesty inquired. 'They are copying *Records of the Historian*
over at His Majesty's court.'

'This should be a "pillow", then,' I suggested.

'Very well, it's yours,' declared Her Majesty, and she handed
it over to me.

Unfortunately, precisely what Sei Shōnagon intended by her
reference to a 'pillow' (*makura*)[3] has never been satisfactorily
explained. We can probably dismiss the idea that she meant it
literally. References to '*makura*' in other works of the period
suggest that she may have been requesting to keep the paper by
her pillow for private jottings – she asserts several times that
her writing was never intended for public view, although there
is a strong whiff of false humility in these disclaimers. Still,
paper was a precious commodity, and this was a gift to Her
Majesty, who evidently wished it to be used for some purpose
that might equal or rival the work going on at the Emperor's
court, where they were making a copy of one of the great
Chinese classics. Besides, having read this far, we will know
that it is probable Sei Shōnagon was being witty. Various puns
have been suggested,[4] but a conclusive explanation remains
elusive. The one thing that is clear is that it was as a result of
Sei Shōnagon's suggestion that Teishi gave her the bundle of
paper which became the bound book (*sōshi*) later known to the
world as *Makura no sōshi* (literally 'Pillow Book').[5]

Perhaps we can combine several interpretations and imagine
Sei Shōnagon taking away her pile of paper to keep by her
pillow and write, in the form of private jottings and as if purely
for her own entertainment, a work that would redound to
the credit of Teishi's court – a work conveying the brilliant
wit, exquisite taste and sheer 'delightfulness' for which that
court had become known and which Sei Shōnagon was felt to
epitomize. If this was her aim, she certainly fulfilled it.

The question of when and why the book was written is
rather more complex than this, however. Scholars have used
the reference to Korechika's court title in this scene to date the
gift of paper to between 994 and 996. In the same section, Sei
Shōnagon also describes how her work was disconcertingly

revealed to the world when she put out a mat for the visiting Governor of Ise, Tsunefusa, and discovered too late that her precious 'bound book' was sitting on the mat (though no matter how ill-lit the room, it is rather unlikely that Sei Shōnagon wouldn't have been aware of what was on that mat she apparently guilelessly offered).

Tsunefusa held the post of Governor between 995 and 997, which we might expect to give us a rough guide to when *The Pillow Book* was completed. But whatever Tsunefusa triumphantly made off with and passed around was not the whole work we have today; it contains numerous scenes and references datable to after 997, the latest of them (Sections 6, 222 and 273) belonging to the period immediately before Teishi's death in 1000. Scattered asides elsewhere in the book also reveal that at least in some sections Sei Shōnagon was aware of an audience, one that had begged her 'not to leave anything out', but that was nevertheless likely to be offended by some of what she included. All this suggests that an early version of the work, circulated by Tsunefusa, met with gratifying success, and at the encouragement of her eager readers she continued to add to it for the rest of her time at court and quite possibly beyond.

One of the most striking aspects of *The Pillow Book* as we have it is that it is an extraordinary jumble: some sections are brief while others can be many pages long; there are lists, personal reminiscences and anecdotes, and the author's own thoughts and opinions on all manner of topics, while sections seem to be snatches of scenes for a romantic tale. Sometimes some or all of these flow in and out of each other within a single section. Was there once perhaps more order in the work that subsequently became irrevocably tangled and confused? Since no manuscript of *The Pillow Book* survives from earlier than the thirteenth century, and that version differs from others known from later references to have existed before that date, we cannot know. Scholars still argue over its earliest form, a problem that is further complicated by the existence of four different versions of the work.[6]

One argument suggests that the original impulse for the work can be traced to the lists scattered throughout it. They take various forms, but in the simplest, consisting largely of strings of names or objects belonging to a given category, Sei Shōnagon's interest is almost exclusively to do with their appearance in or association with poetry. Given the importance of poetic allusion in her world, such a compendium would have been of great interest to her readers, in a way it cannot be for us. Perhaps what Sei Shōnagon originally set out to do was create a kind of handbook of poetic references, in the manner of others already in existence?

The famous first section can certainly be read in this way: as a prescriptive list of the times of day that poetically most embody the subjective essence of the various seasons. However, although the second section seems to set out to continue this form, Sei Shōnagon rapidly slips into personal anecdote and extended description, liberally laced with pithy comments, until at the end of this section she seems to have abandoned the projected list altogether. The fact is that Sei Shōnagon's personality is irrepressible, and seldom suffers for long the strict confines of a list; again and again, she cannot resist adding personal comments and asides that sometimes lead off into anecdotes or lengthy opinions in which her list is apparently quite forgotten. It is easy to imagine that her readers would have enjoyed these interjections of direct and personal writing, finding to their delight that their world was being documented for them in intimate and exquisite detail. We cannot tell whether the lists scattered throughout the work constitute its original material or were intended to be a kind of backbone, but in the *Pillow Book* we have today it is Sei Shōnagon's own voice that predominates.

Nevertheless, we should keep in mind that those lists, which could read as a quirky, personal cataloguing of names and things based on highly individual taste, may well have been intended essentially as catalogues of shared taste, responses and knowledge. In the world of the Heian court, as in other conservative societies and periods, the essential role of taste and opinion was to affirm one's identity with others, and individual variation was often looked at askance – a fact to which Sei Shōnagon often reveals herself to be very sensitive. The conflicting claims of individuality and group are always present, of course, and Sei Shōnagon's personality was sufficiently strong to cause her to suffer from them. Yet much that might seem to us simply personal and individual in her writing is really the articulation of her world and its values.

This point is relevant when we consider the key word *okashi*, which is woven throughout her work as a strong motif. Perhaps the best English translation is the earlier meaning of 'amusing': that which entertains, intrigues, delights, pleases and beguiles. Since 'amusing' is now a rather chilly and old-fashioned word, however, I have chosen the more spirited 'delightful' in my translation. English will tolerate far less repetition than classical Japanese, so I have frequently substituted other words with similar meanings, such as 'charming' or 'lovely', and there are of course instances where 'delightful' does not convey the exact nuance intended. But even so, the reader may notice that 'delightful' occurs with great regularity; this is deliberate, since it is important to convey something of the nature of this crucial word's constant, central presence in the work.

There can be no question that when Sei Shōnagon declared an experience or thing to be *okashi* it was a response of genuine feeling, but she did so knowing that her readers would understand precisely what she meant, and smile in agreement. *Okashi* is much more than a matter of merely private and transient responsiveness. It is in essence a kind of aesthetic response, one that can be cultivated and honed, which delights itself by its awareness of the frisson of pleasure that an object or moment produces, and whose pleasure is compounded by the knowledge that it would be shared by others of cultured sensibility. Sei Shōnagon was writing not only for but, in an important sense, *on behalf of* her audience at court as she noted, described and discussed the myriad things that engaged her interest, and the *okashi* sensibility is the unifying theme behind her jumble of apparently random jottings. She does indeed epitomize the sensibility of Teishi's court, and in documenting her own responses to the world she was producing a kind of exposition of that sensibility.

Sei Shōnagon would never have considered her task in these

bald terms, of course, if indeed she considered it at all, and there certainly would have been no talk of 'an *okashi* aesthetic' at the court. Yet she clearly was intent on documenting her world through its lens. Even where the word itself is absent from what she writes, we feel its presence as the constant tenor, as much in her discussion of what fails to delight as in the record of what does. And when we consider the sorrowful and increasingly tragic events that began to overwhelm Teishi and her court a mere two years after Sei Shōnagon arrived, we must be astonished that out of this could have come a work that not only resolutely refuses to acknowledge these sorrows, but that largely refuses to acknowledge sorrow itself, and gives us in its place a world of exquisite delight.

It may well be, as some recent scholars[7] have suggested, that Sei Shōnagon was consciously setting out to present Teishi's court as forever bathed in the rosy glow of *okashi* as an antidote to the historical facts and as a way of salvaging Teishi's sad tale for posterity – and it is certainly true that the wild chronological confusion in the ordering of anecdotes creates a floating portrait of the court detached from time and history (although the author included details that would easily identify the date of some episodes for a reader familiar with her world). As we read, we are always deep inside the moment of experience that comes to us off the page; Sei Shōnagon seems intent on presenting these moments simply for their own sake, not as part of some larger story that we will return to after these present pleasures or irritations have been savoured.

This effect is far stronger for a reader of the work in its original Japanese than for English language readers, for whom an awareness of time as past or present is woven deep into the structure of our language. The language in which Sei Shōnagon wrote was capable of using verb inflections to indicate nuances that make English verb tenses seem clumsy; but a writer did not on the other hand need to specify any time relationship at all, unless she particularly wished to. A narration of a past event could make use of a verb inflection indicating personal reminiscence, for instance, but it could, and often did, dispense with this and simply proceed in a time-neutral verb form. This characteristic of the language is perfect for Sei Shōnagon's purposes. Although there are occasions when a sudden past inflection will ground a scene inside personal reminiscence, by and large the world she gives us is, quite literally, timeless.

This produces some peculiar and intriguing results. In most consecutive writing, context is usually enough to give the reader the necessary information about time, but Sei Shōnagon's writing is anything but consecutive. She will often launch into a new scene without any orienting context except perhaps some thematic or tangential connection with the previous scene, and we find ourselves inside it without any idea of whether it is describing something that she herself once experienced, or that people of sensibility may well experience, or that we are experiencing through the medium of a romanticized scene from a tale. As we read on, we may come across a verb inflection or some other information that answers the question, but often we finish none the wiser, or confused by a description that seems to slip freely between reminiscence and a floating projection of the imagination. This detachment is exacerbated by the fact that the classical Japanese language does not need, and very seldom has, a specified subject to the verb. Is it I, or you, or we, or perhaps she, who is experiencing this? The question will often seem irrelevant, for in many passages, it is enough that the experience exists as we read, and that by reading we too experience it.[8] In *The Pillow Book*, we seem to enter a kind of entranced historical present in which we will often find ourselves experiencing the moment as Sei Shōnagon herself does, but we are more generally the receptive consciousness of an anonymous lady at the Heian court.

LITERARY BACKGROUND

What traditions of writing did Sei Shōnagon draw on when she chose the form her 'pillow' would take? Over at the Emperor's court, they were busy reinforcing the male literary tradition by laboriously copying a Chinese classic. What could a woman, who was barred from this tradition, produce that might in some way match that officially sanctioned endeavour?

Although when men wrote Japanese poetry they used the phonetic script that had evolved for writing the language (*hiragana*), this script, and the spoken native language, were largely the domain of women's reading and writing. In the long, dragging hours when there was nothing much to do, the women would sit together and listen to a reading of one of the many tales written in this script that were then in circulation among the ladies (as well as some rather shame-faced gentlemen) in the better households. Almost all these tales have been lost to us, but they were evidently largely romantic and sentimental, and were inclined to idealized scenes of splendid men, exquisite ladies and affecting circumstances. They were frequently accompanied by illustrations, which the audience would gaze at as the words they heard brought the scene to life.

It seems that these tales, though intended for a female audience, were in fact largely written (anonymously) by men. But there was nothing to prevent a woman creating one – indeed, in the decade following Teishi's death, this tradition would attain magnificent heights in the work of another court gentlewoman, Murasaki Shikibu, in *The Tale of Genji*. We might expect that Sei Shōnagon likewise would have tried her hand at writing a tale; certainly, the influence both of these romantic tales and of their illustrations is pervasive in *The Pillow Book*, and the atmosphere of their world colours her perceptions and responses in fascinating ways. Her prose itself, a form of written Japanese sometimes referred to as 'women's writing' that had evolved relatively recently, and largely through the medium of tales and letters, is necessarily imbued with the language of the tales. There are even a few sections in *The Pillow Book* that seem to be little scenes from a romantic tale, and once she appears to begin one in earnest (Section 294). But Sei Shōnagon was too interested in the real world and its foibles to be able to sustain a romantic sensibility for long. Her forte was close observation and personal comment; if she set out to describe the ideal lover, she ended up providing a hilarious portrait of his mortifying real-life counterpart. The romantic tale was not the genre for her.

The other possibility for 'women's writing' in prose was the 'diary' or private journal that recorded personal experiences and thoughts, ostensibly purely for one's own purposes. Men wrote diaries (*nikki*) too, but they were largely dry notations in Chinese of date and event. Women took the diary form and made it a looser, more subjective and psychologically penetrating record of lived experience. Unlike the tales, these diaries were not read for popular entertainment, but they were an accepted genre of writing that Sei Shōnagon clearly drew on in her descriptions of incidents she had experienced and witnessed. The diaries were the realistic antithesis of the romantic tales. Those that have come down to us, the earliest of which is *Kagerō nikki* (completed *c*. 975), give us a very different world from that of the tales, one in which we read of the sorrows of women condemned to wait and yearn for the visits of a fickle husband or lover, or of the frictions and everyday events that make up so much of life. Their finely nuanced introversion creates a style of writing that Sei Shōnagon's brisk extroversion would have had no truck with. If she was going to write anything resembling a personal journal, she would have to do it in a very different way.

What she came up with was, in fact, so different that it is quite unlike anything known to have come before it. Scholars have pointed to the long tradition of compendiums and catalogues that Sei Shōnagon had to draw on when she conceived her lists, but if this is indeed how she began, she very quickly transformed it into something much more personal and flamboyantly alive. The Heian women's diary form produced masterful examples of the kind of introspection that is perhaps a worldwide characteristic of women's writing; but what Sei Shōnagon produced was an extended, ebullient conversation with somebody else – with her audience. She so engages us because she engages *with* us, we meet her eye across a thousand years. Perhaps it is the letter form that Sei Shōnagon's overall style comes closest to – the random flow of anecdotes and opinions and thoughts, apparently dashed off extempore, veering impulsively from one comment or story to another, each new turn touched off by some random association or tangential connection, or perhaps by nothing at all. The bewildering shifts of tone and content, the rich mix of the elegant and refined with the down-to-earth and acerbic, produce an effect of spontaneity and intimacy that draws the reader into a warm complicity, even when we find ourselves appalled at her frequent snobbery and occasional cruelty.

The literary judgements of posterity, however, generally come down on the side of the serious. The Heian women writers who are still praised are those who evolved and expressed the sombre sensibility later identified as *aware*, a feeling-tone in which responsiveness to the moving nature of the phenomenal world derives from a recognition of its transience. While *The Pillow Book* is always mentioned in any list of the great Heian period classics, attention then often moves on to the *Tale of Genji*, or to the more pensive and melancholy diaries. Sei Shōnagon's apparent frivolity has sometimes tended to condemn her to the margins.

The difficulty for the serious-minded and scholarly who are the arbiters of literary taste is really not just with *The Pillow Book*, its 'shallow' aesthetic and 'erratic' spontaneity. Sei Shōnagon herself seems to irritate. The earliest example is in the diary of the author of *The Tale of Genji*, the somewhat morose and withdrawn Murasaki Shikibu, who was a gentlewoman in the court of the Empress who had supplanted Teishi:

Sei Shōnagon ... was dreadfully conceited. She thought herself so clever and littered her writings with Chinese characters; but if you examined them closely, they left a great deal to be desired. Those who think of themselves as being superior to everyone else in this way will inevitably suffer and come to a bad end, and people who have become so precious that they go out of their way to try and be sensitive in the most unpromising situations, trying to capture every moment of interest, however slight, are bound to look ridiculous and superficial. How can the future turn out well for them?[9]

Sei Shōnagon had long since left the court when these words were written, but this sour judgement shows that she still rankled for Murasaki. Similar opinions have continued to be expressed down the centuries, and modern scholars (men) have often been equally irritated by her. She has been dismissed by some as a mere chatterbox of a woman, and *The Pillow Book* considered to be nothing more than a silly gentlewoman's idle thoughts spilling themselves haphazardly on to the page. It is common in Japan to contrast her with Murasaki Shikibu, and those who side with Sei Shōnagon in this perceived rivalry are often characterized as vacuous and frivolous.

Given this criticism, it is all the more impressive that *The Pillow Book* has always been accorded important status as a classic. Its fascination and odd genius are undeniable, and there have been and are many scholars happy to give it the attention it richly deserves, just as there will surely always be new readers who rediscover its delights.

NOTES

1. Marriage customs were complex. In Sei Shōnagon's world, it was usual for a husband to come and go from his wife's family home where she remained living, at least during the early years of the marriage. Male monogamy often was not strictly practised, and many marriages seem to have been rather tenuous arrangements. See also Section 2, note 4.

2. I follow the custom of giving dates without the fine calculations necessary to adjust to the lunar calendar used in Japan then. Teishi's death occurred in the twelfth month of 1000, which approximates to February 1001 in our Julian calendar. For an explanation of the Japanese calendar, see Appendix 3.

3. The word 'pillow' (*makura*) carries certain overtones in classical Japanese, but they are not to do with the erotic. Rather, the word has a poetic resonance, appearing in literary expressions such as *makurakotoba* ('pillow word', a word that conventionally accompanies a certain word or phrase in early poetry) or *uta-makura* ('poem pillow', a word or image codified for a specific poetic use). Some scholars argue that such connotations are

important in understanding the intentions behind *The Pillow Book*.

4. The most plausible is a pun in which the name of *Records of the Historian* (*Shiki*) is treated as homophonous with the word *shiki* meaning something, such as bedding, that is laid out. Sei Shōnagon would thus be proposing that if the Emperor's court is 'laying out bedding', Teishi's court should cap this by providing the 'pillow'.

5. Sei Shōnagon does not seem to have called it this herself. The work went by a variety of names until the present name became the established one around the mid-sixteenth century. The name apparently derives from the scene in Section [s29] quoted above.

6. Two of these, known as the Sakaibon and the Maedakebon, variously group passages in the same general style (lists, anecdotes and 'essays') separately. These are now considered to be a later ordering of the earlier random order, preserved in different forms and with some differences in content in the other two texts, the Nōinbon and the Sankanbon. (See 'Note on the Translation' for further discussion of these texts.)

7. Mitamura Masako is foremost among these scholars.

8. In an attempt to convey some of this effect, I have frequently chosen to translate passages or whole sections in the present tense, and made that anonymous experiencing subject 'you'. This felicitously both speaks directly to the individual 'you' of the reader and draws the reader into the company of the general 'you' (which would be more formally expressed as 'one'), so has the benefit of creating something close to the kind of complicitness with the reader that Sei Shōnagon's Japanese produces. However, I have given the past tense to the many scenes that clearly mark themselves as narration of specific past events.

9. *The Diary of Lady Murasaki*, trans. Richard Bowring (Penguin Classics, 1996), p. 54.

Further Reading

Very little has been written in English on *The Pillow Book*. The most important studies are:

Fukumori, Naomi, 'Re-visioning History: The Diary-Type Passages in Sei Shōnagon's *Makura no sōshi*', *Journal of the Association of Teachers of Japanese* 31:1 (April 1997), pp. 1–44.

—, 'Sei Shōnagon, the Ese/Essayist: Delineating Differences in *Makura no sōshi*', Ga/Zoku Dynamics in Japanese Literature, *Proceedings from the MAJLS (Midwest Association for Japanese Literary Studies) Fifth Annual Meeting* 3 (Summer 1997), pp. 66–88.

Morris, Mark, 'Sei Shōnagon's Poetic Catalogues', *Harvard Journal of Asiatic Studies* 40:1 (June 1980), pp. 5–54.

For a broader reading in mid-Heian literature, the following translations and their usefully detailed introductions are suggested:

Anonymous, *A Tale of Flowering Fortunes*, trans. W. H. and H. C. McCullough, 2 vols. (Stanford University Press, 1980).

Anonymous, *Tales of Yamato: A Tenth Century Poem Tale*, trans. Mildred M. Tahara (University of Hawaii Press, 1980).

Izumi Shikibu, *The Izumi Shikibu Diary*, trans. E. Cranston (Penguin Classics, 1969).

The Kagerō Diary, trans. Sonja Arntzen (University of Michigan, Center for Japanese Studies, 1997). Earlier translated by E. Seidensticker as *The Gossamer Years: The Diary of a Noblewoman of Heian Japan* (Tuttle, 1964). The author is known only as the mother of Fujiwara Michitsuna.

Murasaki Shikibu, *The Diary of Lady Murasaki*, trans. Richard Bowring (Penguin Classics, 1996).

—, *The Tale of Genji*, trans. Royall Tyler, 2 vols. (Viking, 2001). Earlier translated by E. Seidensticker (Alfred A. Knopf, 1976).

Lady Sarashina, *As I Crossed a Bridge of Dreams*, trans. Ivan Morris (Penguin Classics, 1971).

Other useful background information on the period can be found in:

Dalby, Liza, *Kimono* (Vintage, 2001), Chapter 7 ('The Cultured Nature of Heian Colors').

Morris, Ivan, *The World of the Shining Prince* (Kōdansha International, 1994).

For more academic works that discuss the literature of the period, particularly *The Tale of Genji*:

Bowring, Richard, 'The Female Hand in Heian Japan: A First Reading', in *The Female Autograph: Theory and Practice of Autobiography from the Tenth to the Twentieth Century*, ed. Donna C. Stanton (University of Chicago Press, 1987), pp. 49–56.

Childs, Margaret H., 'The Value of Vulnerability: Sexual Coercion and the Nature of Love in Japanese Court Literature', *Journal of Asian Studies* 58:4 (November 1999), pp. 1059–79.

Field, Norma, *The Splendor of Longing in the 'Tale of Genji'* (Princeton University Press, 1987).

Mostow, Joshua S., *At the House of Gathered Leaves: Shorter Biographical and Autobiographical Narratives from Japanese Court Literature* (University of Hawaii Press, 2004).

Okada, Richard, *Figures of Resistance: Language, Poetry and Narrating in 'The Tale of Genji' and Other Mid-Heian Texts* (Duke University Press, 1991).

Sarra, Edith, *Fictions of Femininity: Literary Inventions of Gender in Japanese Court Women's Memoirs* (Stanford University Press, 1999).

Shirane, Haruo, *The Bridge of Dreams: A Poetics of the 'Tale of Genji'* (Stanford University Press, 1987).

Note on the Translation

A text of this age can be expected to present transcription and manuscript problems, and *The Pillow Book* certainly does so. Four major variant forms of the work exist, and there may well have been more. The version used here is known as Sankanbon, now generally agreed to preserve at least something approximating the work's original form, although it is quite likely that words, sentences, and perhaps even whole sections have been added or removed or otherwise tampered with by subsequent copyists. The Sankanbon text, whose earliest extant copy dates from 1228, traditionally includes a 'supplementary' group of sections that was apparently included in the text proper in a previous version of it, no longer extant. The other main contender is known as Nōinbon,[1] which contains much the same material but frequently in different order, omits some passages found in Sankanbon and adds others. The issue of the relationship of the four variants is complex, and is further confused by the problem of how and in what stages Sei Shōnagon might have composed the work (see Introduction, p. xxii).

My translation is based on the 1997 annotated edition of the Sankanbon text edited by Matsuo Satoshi and Nagai Kazuko and published by Shōgakukan, although I have taken into account the annotations and interpretations provided by other editions as need arose.[2] There are numerous places in the text where scholarly interpretations of meaning differ, and here I choose my way among the various possibilities. Occasionally, the Nōinbon text seems to preserve the more natural meaning, and there I momentarily desert the Sankanbon text for the sake of clarity; these are always acknowledged in the Notes.

The translation of the poetry presents a particular, virtually insurmountable, problem. The traditional Japanese poetic form (*waka*) is syllabic rather than metrical in rhythm, has no rhyme, uses no line division and largely depends for its effect on subtleties of pervasive poetic allusion and other linguistic devices that are untranslatable and require copious notes for a foreign reader (and even for a modern Japanese one). Thus almost no element of a poem can be carried across into English beyond the bare denotative meanings of its words, which generally has the effect of making the poem sound mindlessly simple, stark, or just plain pointless. In order to create at least some semblance of what English readers feel to be poetry, I have followed translation tradition and divided the poem into five lines, corresponding to the syllabic 5–7–5–7–7 demarcations of the original *waka*. Where feasible, I preserve something close to that syllable count, although counting syllables in English is a mental and not an aural exercise; however, where strict syllabic count produces a rhythm that interferes with aural pleasure, I frequently allow a modified iambic to stretch the syllable number into something that sounds more natural to the English reader's ear. Translating the words presents its own problems, particularly as the point of Sei Shōnagon's poetry generally lies in clever punning. Sometimes there is a way to slip the pun directly or indirectly into English, but for the most part I can only follow the imagery while trying to suggest through choice of language where the pun would lie, and hope that at least a little of the poem's interest is thereby preserved. Readers are referred to the Notes for fuller explanations of how the wit works.

The early manuscripts of *The Pillow Book* show that Sei Shōnagon's text was a more or less continuous one, without section divisions. This creates a very different and much more extraordinary reading experience than the subsequent clerical snipping into individual sections allows. With some reluctance, I have followed modern practice by retaining the traditional section divisions, with numbers for ease of reference, and high-lighting the opening words of each section in lieu of a title. (For the supplementary sections, see p. 250.) However, readers are encouraged to ignore these divisions as they read, for by doing so they will often be pleased to discover the subtle, tangential connections that flow backwards and forwards across and among sections that at first appear to be isolated entities.

An asterisk following the section number indicates that general information useful for understanding the section is provided at this point in the Notes. Where a date for the scene described in the section is known or able to be conjectured from internal evidence, it has been given in brackets after the section 'title' in the Notes. The reader is also referred to the appendices for unfamiliar terms not found in the Notes – including general terms, ranks and titles, colours and religious festivals – and to the list of the main characters appearing in the text (Appendix 2).

The Pillow Book is written in a language that became the epitome of classical beauty for subsequent ages, which have always looked back to the glories of Heian culture with reverent nostalgia. However, when Sei Shōnagon was writing it had none of this aura, and seems to have been a written language that had in many ways not yet distinguished itself from everyday spoken Japanese. Sei Shōnagon's *Pillow Book* speaks with a direct and vivid voice, and I attempt to convey this. I will have succeeded if readers can feel, as they read, the pleasure of her company.

NOTES

1. Ivan Morris, in his translation of *The Pillow Book* (1967), chose to base his work largely on the Nōinbon text, and the Penguin Classics edition of his translation (1971) omits many of the list sections as well as other sections deemed too obscure for the general reader.

2. Chief among them are the 1991 edition, ed. Watanabe Minoru,

published as Number 25 of the Shin Nihon Koten Bungaku
Taikei series, and the two-volume 1977 edition, ed. Hagitani
Boku, published as Numbers 11 and 12 in the Shinchō Nihon
Koten Shūsei series.

The Pillow Book

[1]* *In spring, the dawn* – when the slowly paling mountain rim is tinged with red, and wisps of faintly crimson-purple cloud float in the sky.

In summer, the night – moonlit nights, of course, but also at the dark of the moon, it's beautiful when fireflies are dancing everywhere in a mazy flight. And it's delightful too to see just one or two fly through the darkness, glowing softly. Rain falling on a summer night is also lovely.

In autumn, the evening – the blazing sun has sunk very close to the mountain rim, and now even the crows,[1] in threes and fours or twos and threes, hurrying to their roost, are a moving sight. Still more enchanting is the sight of a string of wild geese in the distant sky, very tiny. And oh how inexpressible, when the sun has sunk, to hear in the growing darkness the wind, and the song of autumn insects.

In winter, the early morning – if snow is falling, of course, it's unutterably delightful, but it's perfect too if there's a pure white frost, or even just when it's very cold, and they hasten to build up the fires in the braziers and carry in fresh charcoal. But it's unpleasant, as the day draws on and the air grows warmer, how the brazier fire dies down to white ash.

[2]* *Times of year* – The first month; the third, fourth and fifth months; the seventh, eighth and ninth; the eleventh and twelfth – in fact every month according to its season, the year round, is delightful.

On the first day of the year, the sky is gloriously fresh and spring mists hang in the air. It's quite special and delightful the way people everywhere have taken particular care over their clothing and makeup, and go about exchanging New Year felicitations.

On the seventh day, people pluck the new shoots of herbs[1] that have sprung up in the patches of bare earth amidst the snow – they're wonderfully green and fresh, and it's charming just what a fuss is made over these herbs, which normally aren't to be seen at such close quarters. Those of good family who live outside the palace brighten up their carriages and set off to see the Parading of the Blue Roans. It's fun[2] how, when the carriages are pulled over the big ground beam of the central palace gate, all the ladies' heads are jolted together so that your hair combs tumble out and can easily break if you aren't careful, and everybody laughs. I remember seeing a large group of senior courtiers and others standing about near the Left Gate Watch guardhouse, gaily snatching the attendants' bows and twanging them to startle the horses – also, peeping through the carriage blinds and delightedly glimpsing groundswomen and other serving ladies coming and going near one of the lattice fences further in. Witnessing such a scene, of course you sigh and wonder just what sort of people they must be, to manage to be so at ease in the 'nine-fold palace'. But when I actually saw them at such close quarters at the palace, the attendants' faces were all dark and blotchy where their white powder hadn't covered the skin properly, precisely like black patches of earth showing through where snow has half melted – a truly horrible sight. The horses' rearing and lunging was quite terrifying, so I retreated to the depths of the carriage, where I could no longer really see.

On the eighth day, there's a special thrill in the noise of all the carriages hurtling about as everyone who's received a promotion does the rounds to exchange felicitations.

On the fifteenth day, the day of the full moon, a delightful scene always takes place in the houses of the nobility after the festival food is served. Both the senior and junior gentlewomen of the house go about looking for a chance to strike each other with gruel sticks,[3] constantly glancing behind them to make sure they aren't hit themselves. It's marvellous fun when someone manages somehow to get in a strike, and everyone bursts into delighted peals of laughter – though you can certainly see why the poor victim herself feels upset.

A young man has recently begun to call on his new wife.[4] Now it's time for him to set off for the palace, and lurking in the background peeping out is one of her gentlewomen, gleefully self-important and struggling to contain herself till he leaves. The gentlewomen who are sitting gathered around the girl all smile, realizing perfectly well what's going on, but she secretly motions them to stay quiet. Meanwhile, the girl sits there innocently, seeming to have noticed nothing. Then up comes the gentlewoman, with some excuse such as 'I'll just pick this up', darts over and strikes her and runs off, while everyone collapses in laughter. The young man doesn't take it amiss but smiles amiably, and as for the girl, it's quite charming to see that though she doesn't seem particularly surprised, she is nevertheless blushing slightly.

The gentlewomen strike each other too, and I gather men even get struck sometimes. It's also amusing to witness someone for some reason lose her temper and burst into tears, and roundly abuse whoever has struck her. Even the more exalted people in the palace join in the day's fun.

There's a charming scene in the palace at the time of the Spring Appointments List. It's snowing and everything's icy, and men of the fourth and fifth ranks are walking about holding their letters requesting promotion. The youthful, high-spirited ones inspire you with confidence in them, but there are also old white-haired fellows who go around confiding in people, in hopes that this will improve their chances. They approach some gentlewoman and obliviously set about singing their own praises to her, and they can have no idea that some of the younger gentlewomen are busy imitating them and laughing behind their back. 'Do please mention me favourably to the Emperor or Empress,' they implore us – and it's a fine thing if they actually gain the post they want, but really most pathetic when they fail.

The third day of the third month is full of the soft sunshine of spring. Now is the time when the peach trees begin to bloom, and of course the willows too are particularly lovely at this time. It's charming to see the buds still cocooned in their sheaths like silkworms – but on the other hand, once the leaves have opened they're rather unpleasant.

If you break off a branch of splendidly flowering cherry and arrange it in a large flower vase, the effect is delightful. And it's particularly charming if a gentleman, be it one of Her Majesty's brothers or a normal guest, is seated nearby engaged in conversation, wearing a cloak in the cherry-blossom combination with undersleeves displayed.

And how delightful it all is at the time of the Festival[5] in the fourth month! The court nobles and senior courtiers in the festival procession are only distinguishable by the different degrees of colour of their formal cloaks, and the robes beneath are all of a uniform white, which produces a lovely effect of coolness. The leaves of the trees have not yet reached their full summer abundance but are still a fresh young green, and the sky's clarity, untouched by either the mists of spring or autumn's fogs, fills you with inexplicable pleasure. And when it clouds a little in the evening or at night, how unbearably lovely then to hear from far in the distance the muted call of a *hototogisu*, sounding so faint you almost doubt your ears.

It's delightful, as the day of the Festival approaches, to see the attendants going to and fro carrying tight rolls of dark leaf-green or lavender fabric,[6] wrapped lightly in just a touch of paper. Patterning effects such as graded dye and dapple dye strike you as unusually beautiful at this time.

The little girls who will be in the procession are also enchanting. They've already washed their hair and done it nicely, but they may still be wearing their everyday threadbare and rumpled clothes, and they trot around full of excited anticipation, crying 'Rethread my high clogs for me!' or 'Sew up the soles of my shoes!' But for all their boisterous posturing and prancing, once they're dressed up in their festival finery they suddenly begin parading about with great solemnity, like self-important priests at the head of some dignified procession, no doubt starting to feel thoroughly nervous. It's also touching to see, in the festival procession, a parent or aunt or perhaps an

Cloak

older sister accompanying the little girls and carefully tending their clothing as they walk.

When you see a man who's set his heart on becoming Chamberlain, but who's in no position to achieve his goal just yet, dressed specially in the Chamberlain's green formal cloak[7] for the day of the Festival, you wish for his sake he didn't have to take it off again. It's a pity that it isn't damask like the real one, however.

[3] *Though it's the same it sounds different* – The language of priests. Men's language. Women's language.

Commoners always use too many words when they speak.

[4]* *It breaks my heart to think* of parents sending a beloved son into the priesthood. Poor priests, they're not the unfeeling lumps of wood that people take them for. They're despised for eating that dreadful monastic food, and their sleeping

arrangements are no better. A young priest must naturally be full of curiosity, and how could he resist the forbidden urge to peep into a room, especially if there's a woman in there? But this is criticized as disgraceful too.

Exorcist priests[1] have an even harder life. If they ever nod off, exhausted from their long labours, people complain that they do nothing but sleep. How constrained and miserable this must make them feel!

Well, this is how things used to be, anyway. These days, in fact, priests lead a much easier life.

[5]* *When the Empress moved to the home of Senior Steward Narimasa,* he had his east gate specially upgraded to a four-pillared one, through which her palanquin was carried when she arrived. We gentlewomen were to have our carriages driven in through the north gate, and since we knew there would be no guards in place there yet, and were blithely assuming that the carriages would be drawn right up to the veranda where we could disembark in private, those of us whose hair was a mess didn't really bother to make ourselves look presentable. But the gate turned out to be too small for our palm-leaf carriages to pass through, so they ended up laying down the usual matting from the gate and we had to get down and walk after all. It was all very distressing and infuriating, but it couldn't be helped. And to add to our exasperation, the area round the guardhouse was lined with senior courtiers and lower-ranking men who stood there watching us go by.

When I reported these events to Her Majesty, she smiled and said, 'And do you also imagine no one is going to see you in here? How could you all be so careless?'

'But everyone in here is quite used to seeing us,' I replied, 'and I should think some of them would actually be more surprised if we went out of our way to make ourselves neat and pretty. Anyway,' I went on, turning to the others who were present, 'how on earth can a fine place like this have a gate that carriages can't pass through? I intend to poke some fun at the Senior Steward about it when he comes in.'

No sooner had I spoken than Narimasa indeed arrived.

'Please pass these to Her Majesty,' he said, handing her inkstone and some other objects through to me.

'Well, what a shocking man you are!' I said to him. 'Why should you go and make such a narrow gate for your house?'

He laughed and replied, 'I make my gate to fit my station in life.'

'But think of that man who once made his gate especially grand and tall,'[1] I said.

'Good heavens, how astonishing!' he exclaimed. 'You must be referring to Yu Dingguo. If I weren't a seasoned scholar myself, I would have no hope of understanding this reference. But I happen to have spent some time straying upon these paths, so this much at least I can manage to follow.'

'As to "paths", that path of yours isn't up to much, either,' I replied. 'They laid down straw matting for us, but we kept tumbling into the holes underneath, and it all caused quite a fuss.'

'It must have been due to the recent rain,' he said quickly, and added, 'Well well, you'll come back at me with something else if I'm not careful. I'll take my leave', and off he went.

'What was that about?' Her Majesty inquired. 'Narimasa seemed quite terrified of you.'

'Oh it was nothing, I was only talking about the fact that the carriages couldn't get in,' I replied vaguely, and returned to my room.

I was sharing a room with some younger gentlewomen, and as we were all quite tired we went straight off to sleep without a moment's thought. We were in the eastern wing, and there was no lock on the sliding panel at the northern end of our west aisle apartments, but we'd failed to look into the matter. Being the master of the house, Narimasa was well aware of the way things were set up, and he opened the door. 'May I come in? May I come in?' he repeated over and over, in an oddly husky and penetrating voice. I woke and looked in that direction. The light of the tall lamp was clearly visible behind the standing curtain. He had opened the sliding panel about six inches. How marvellous! I was further fascinated when it dawned on me that this man, who would normally never so

'He had opened the sliding panel about six inches'

much as dream of this sort of lascivious behaviour, was suddenly so recklessly giving way to impulse out of excitement at Her Majesty's presence in his house.

I nudged awake the lady next to me. 'Look over there,' I said. 'Someone unusual has apparently turned up.'

She raised her head to look, and burst out laughing.

'Who is it?' I called. 'You're making yourself quite conspicuous!'

'No no, don't misunderstand, I'm here in my capacity as master of the house,' came his voice. 'I have something to discuss with you.'

'It was the *gate* I was talking about,' I said. 'I wasn't asking you to make the *door* any wider!'

'Yes precisely, that's what I'm here to discuss,' said he. 'May I come in? Please might I come in?'

'How disgusting, of course you can't!' called my companion with a laugh.

'Oh, there's a young lady in there!' he exclaimed, whereupon he closed the sliding panel and retreated. After he'd gone we fell about laughing. If he was going to open the door in the first place, he should have come right on in! Who's going to say 'I don't see why not' when a man asks if he may enter? It was wonderfully funny.

The next morning, I went to Her Majesty and told her the story. 'I've never heard of him doing such a thing,' she said with a laugh. 'He must have been attracted by that conversation last night. Poor fellow, I imagine you made him feel a complete fool.'

Then there was the occasion when Her Majesty was giving instructions for the making of formal wear for the little page girls who attended on the young princess. 'What colour should their "*akomé* gowns"[2] be?' inquired Narimasa, and naturally we all laughed at him yet again.

Then talk turned to the subject of the princess's meals. 'I imagine the usual style of serving would not look very good,' he said. 'It would be best to serve it on a *leetle*[3] serving tray and a *leetle* standing tray.'

'Yes,' said I. 'That would make it all the more suitable for the girls in those "*akomé* gowns" to serve to her, wouldn't it!'

'Now now,' Her Majesty reprimanded me, 'you shouldn't go making fun of him like everyone else does. The poor man is thoroughly in earnest.' I was most touched.

On another occasion, when I was quite preoccupied with other matters, a servant came with the message that the Senior Steward 'had something urgent to impart'.

'I wonder what he'll say this time,' Her Majesty delighted me by remarking, 'to get himself laughed at yet again. Go and hear what he has to tell you,' she continued, so I left what I was doing and went.

'I told the Counsellor[4] about that conversation we had the other night on the matter of the gate,' said Narimasa. 'My brother was most intrigued, and told me he would like to choose an appropriate moment to talk with you at leisure and hear what you had to say.' And that was all. I was on tenterhooks at the thought that he might bring up the events of the other night, but he only said, 'I shall come along to your room presently for a quiet talk', and left.

I went back and reported to Her Majesty. 'So what was it about?' she inquired. When I told the story, one of the gentle-women said with a laugh, 'That's no reason to send word specially and call you out like that. He could have waited till you were in one of the outer rooms[5] or in your own quarters.'

I was most impressed when Her Majesty remarked, 'I imagine he thought you would be as pleased as he was, that someone he puts such store by should praise you.'

[6] *The Emperor's cat* had received the fifth rank, and was given the appropriate title-name 'Myōbu'. It was a charming creature, and the Emperor was quite devoted to it.

One day its carer, Muma no Myōbu,[1] found it lying basking on the veranda. 'How vulgar!' she scolded. 'Back you come inside.' But the cat continued to lie there asleep in the sun, so she decided to give it a fright. 'Okinamaro!' she cried to the dog. 'Here, boy! Come and get Myōbu!' The foolish dog couldn't believe its ears, and came rushing over, whereupon the terrified cat fled inside through the blind.

The Emperor was at that time in the Breakfast Room, and he witnessed this event with astonishment. He tucked the cat into the bosom of his robe, and summoned his men. When the Chamberlains Tadataka and Narinaka appeared, the Emperor ordered them, 'Give Okinamaro a thorough beating and banish him to Dog Island![2] Be quick about it!'

Everyone gathered and a noisy hunt ensued. The Emperor went on to chastise Muma no Myōbu, declaring that he would replace her as Myōbu's carer as she was completely untrustworthy, and thenceforth she no longer appeared in his presence. Meanwhile, they rounded up the dog, and had the guards drive it out.

We all pitied the poor thing. 'Oh dear,' we said, 'and to think how he used to swagger about the place as if he owned it.'

'Remember how on the third of the third month the Secretary Controller decked him out with a garland of willow and a peach-flower comb, and tied a branch of cherry blossom on his back? Who'd have guessed then that he'd meet with such a fate?'

'And the way he always attended Her Majesty at meal times. How we'll miss him!'

Then around noon three or four days later, we heard a dog howling dreadfully. What dog could be howling on and on like this? we wondered, and as we listened dogs gathered from everywhere to see what was afoot. One of the cleaning women came running in. 'Oh, it's dreadful! Two of the Chamberlains are beating the dog! It's bound to die! His Majesty banished it, but apparently it came back, so they're teaching it a lesson.'

Alas, poor creature! It was Okinamaro. 'It's Tadataka and Sanefusa doing it,' someone said.

We sent someone to stop them, but at that point the dog finally ceased its howling. 'It's dead,' came the report, 'so they've thrown it outside the guardhouse.'

That evening as we were sorrowing over poor Okinamaro, up staggered a miserable trembling creature, terribly swollen and looking quite wretched. Can it be Okinamaro? we wondered. What other dog could be wandering around at this hour in such a state?

We called his name, but he didn't respond. 'It's him,' some of us declared, while others maintained that it wasn't, till Her Majesty said, 'Send for Ukon. She would recognize him.' We duly did so, and when she came Her Majesty showed her the dog and asked if it was indeed Okinamaro.

'There's certainly a likeness,' replied Ukon, 'but this dog looks simply revolting. And you only have to say his name and Okinamaro bounds happily up, but this dog doesn't respond at all. It must be a different dog. And they did say they'd killed him and thrown out the corpse, didn't they? How could he have survived after two men had beaten him like that?' This moved Her Majesty to fresh sorrow.

It grew dark. We gave the dog some food, but it didn't eat it, so we decided that it was indeed a different dog and left it at that.

The next morning, Her Majesty had performed her ablutions and had her hair combed, and I was holding the mirror for her to check that all was in order when I spied the dog, still there, crouching at the foot of a pillar. Seeing it I said aloud to myself, 'Oh poor Okinamaro, what a terrible beating he got yesterday! It's so sad to think he must be dead. I wonder what he'll be reborn as next time. How dreadful he must have felt!'

At this the dog began to tremble, and tears simply poured

from its eyes. How extraordinary! I realized it was indeed Okinamaro! It was pitiful to recall how he'd avoided revealing himself the night before, but at the same time the whole thing struck me as quite marvellous. I set down the mirror and said, 'So you're Okinamaro, are you?' and he threw himself on the ground, whimpering and weeping.

Her Majesty laughed with relief, and sent for Ukon and told her the story. There was a great deal of laughter over it all, and the Emperor heard and came in to see what was happening. He laughed too, and observed, 'Isn't it odd to think a dog would have such fine feelings.' His gentlewomen also heard of it and gathered round, and this time when we called the dog he got up and came.

'His poor face is all swollen!' I cried. 'I do wish I could do something for it.'

'Now you're wearing your heart on your sleeve,' everyone teased me.

Tadataka heard from the Table Room, and sent saying, 'Is it really him? I must come and have a look.'

'Oh dear no, how awful!' I declared. 'Tell him it's not Okinamaro at all!'

'He's bound to be found out sooner or later,' came Tadataka's reply. 'You can't go on hiding him forever.'

Well, in due course Okinamaro was pardoned, and everything returned to normal. Now has there ever been such a delightful and moving moment as when Okinamaro began to tremble and weep at those pitying words of mine? Humans may cry when someone speaks to them sympathetically – but a dog?

[7] *The first day of the year and the third day of the third month* should have glorious weather.

The fifth day of the fifth month is best when the weather is overcast all day.

The seventh day of the seventh month should also be cloudy, but the evening sky should be clear, with a brilliant moon and the stars clear and bright.

It's charming when a light rain begins to fall around daybreak on the ninth day of the ninth month, and there should be plenty of dew on the chrysanthemums, so that the cotton wadding that covers them is thoroughly wet, and it brings out the flowers' scent that imbues it. The rain ceases in the early morning, but it should remain overcast, and continue to threaten rain at any moment.

[8]* *The Offering of Official Thanks* after new ranks are conferred is wonderfully entertaining. There they stand, facing the Emperor, with the long trains of their court robes trailing out behind them. Then they perform their thanks and dance, with marvellous flair and vigour.

[9]* *The eastern side of the Temporary Palace* is referred to as 'the northern guardhouse'. There was a towering pear tree there, and we all used to wonder how tall it might be.

On one occasion, Acting Captain Narinobu remarked jokingly, 'Wouldn't it be fun to cut it down and present the entire thing to that giant Bishop Jōchō to use as a branch fan.'[1]

The Bishop was later promoted to Head Abbot at Yamashina Temple,[2] and on the day of the Offering of Official Thanks, the

High clogs

Acting Captain was with the Palace Guards at the head of the procession. Bishop Jōchō was wearing very high clogs for the occasion, and looked quite monstrously tall. After he'd gone, I said to the Acting Captain, 'Why didn't you get him to carry that branch fan of yours for the occasion?'

'You certainly have a long memory, don't you?' he responded with a laugh.

Whoever said, 'A long robe is short on Bishop Jōchō and a short robe is long on Sukuse no Kimi' put it beautifully.

[10]* *Mountains* – Ogura Mountain. Mount Kase. Mount Mikasa. Mount Konokure. Mount Iritachi. Mount Wasurezu. Sue no Matsu Mountain. Mount Katasari – I wonder how it stands aside?[1] Mount Itsuhata. Mount Kaeru. Mount Nochise. Asakura Mountain – I like the line 'now looks askance at me'.[2] Mount Ōhire is special too. It must be because it reminds me of the dancers at the Kamo and Yahata Provisional Festivals.[3]

Mount Miwa has great appeal. So do Tamuke Mountain, Mount Machikane, Tamasaka Mountain and Mount Miminashi.

[11] *Markets* – Tatsu Market in Nara. Sato Market. Tsuba Market in Kashihara – it gives me a special feeling to think that the reason all the pilgrims to Hase Temple stop over here, among all the markets in the region, must be that it has some particular connection to the bodhisattva Kannon. Then there are Ofusa Market, Shikama Market and Asuka Market.

[12] *Peaks* – Yuzuruha Peak, Amida Peak and Iyataka Peak.

[13] *Plains* – Mika Plain, Ashita Plain and Sono Plain.

[14] *River pools* – Kashiko Pool. I wonder what hidden depths someone saw in its heart, to give it such a name.[1] And Nairiso Pool – who told whom not to enter,[2] I wonder? Green Pool is interesting too. You could use it to make the Chamberlain's special green clothes. There is also Kakure Pool and Ina Pool.

[15] *Bodies of water* – Lake Biwa is special. Also Yosa Bay and Kawafuchi Bay.

[16] *Imperial tombs* – Ugurusu Tomb, Kashiwagi Tomb, Ame Tomb.

[17] *Ferry crossings* – Shikasuga Crossing, Korizuma Crossing, Mizuhashi Crossing.

[18]* *Large buildings* – Tamatsukuri.

[19] *Residences* – The Konoe Gate. Nijō and Ichijō are also very fine. Mikai. The Somedono Palace. Segai. The Sugahara Mansion. Renzei-in, Kan-in and Suzaku-in. The Ono Palace. Kōbai. Agata Well. Take Sanjō. Kohachijō. Koichijō.

[20]* *The sliding panels that close off the north-east corner* of the Seiryōden, at the northern end of the aisle, are painted with scenes of rough seas, and terrifying creatures with long arms and legs.[1] We have a fine time complaining about how we hate coming face to face with them whenever we open the door from the Empress's room.

On this particular day, a large green porcelain vase had been placed at the foot of the nearby veranda railing, with a mass of absolutely gorgeous branches of flowering cherry, five feet long or more, arranged in it with the flowers spilling out over the railing. His Excellency Korechika, the Grand Counsellor, arrived around noon. He was wearing a rather soft and supple cloak in the cherry-blossom combination, over deep violet gathered trousers of heavy brocade and white under-robes, and he had arranged the sleeves of his wonderfully glowing deep scarlet-purple damask cloak for display. The Emperor was present, so His Excellency placed himself on the narrow veranda outside the door to converse.

Inside the blinds, we gentlewomen sat with our cherry-blossom combination Chinese jackets worn draped loosely back from the shoulders. Our robes were a fine blend of wisteria and kerria-yellow and other seasonal combinations, the sleeves

Chinese jacket, worn over robes

all spilling out on display below the blinds that hung from the little half-panel shutters.

Suddenly, from the direction of the Imperial Day Chamber came the loud pounding of the attendants' feet as they arrived to deliver His Majesty's meal. The sound of the cry 'Make way!' reverberating through the scene of this gloriously serene spring day was utterly delightful. Then the Chamberlain arrived to report that he had delivered the last tray and the meal was in place, and His Majesty departed by the central door.

Korechika saw His Majesty on his way along the corridor, then returned to seat himself by the vase of blossoms once more. Her Majesty now moved aside her standing curtain and came out to the edge of the threshold near him to talk, and all those present were simply overcome with the sheer splendour of the scene. At this point Korechika languidly intoned the lines from the old poem:

> 'The months and years may pass,
> but let this remain unchanging
> as Mount Mimuro . . .'[2]

– and most enchanting it was, for seeing her splendour we did indeed long for Her Majesty to continue just like this for a thousand years.

No sooner had those in charge of serving the Emperor's meal called the men to remove the trays than His Majesty returned.

Her Majesty now turned to me and asked me to grind some ink, but I was so agog at the scene before me that I could barely manage to keep the inkstick steady in its holder. Then Her Majesty proceeded to fold a piece of white paper, and said to us, 'Now I want each of you to write here the first ancient poem that springs to mind.'

I turned for help to the Grand Counsellor, who was sitting just outside. 'What on earth can I write?' I begged him, but he only pushed the paper back to me, saying, 'Quick, write something down yourself for Her Majesty. It's not a man's place to give advice here.'

Her Majesty provided us with the inkstone. 'Come on, come on,' she scolded, 'don't waste time racking your brains. Just quickly jot down any ancient poem that comes to you on the spur of the moment. Even something hackneyed will do.' I've no idea why we should have felt so daunted by the task, but we all found ourselves blushing deeply, and our minds went quite blank. Despite their protestations, some of the senior gentlewomen managed to produce two or three poems on spring themes such as blossoms and so forth, and then my turn came. I wrote down the poem:

> With the passing years
> My years grow old upon me
> yet when I see
> this lovely flower of spring
> I forget age and time.[3]

but I changed 'flower of spring' to 'your face, my lady'.

Her Majesty ran her eye over the poems, remarking, 'I just wanted to discover what was in your hearts.'

'In the time of Retired Emperor Enyū,'[4] she went on, 'His Majesty ordered the senior courtiers each to write a poem in a bound notebook, but it proved fearfully difficult, and some of them begged to be excused from the task. The Emperor reassured them that it didn't matter whether their calligraphy was skilful or otherwise, nor whether the poem was appropriate to the occasion, and finally after a great deal of trouble they all

managed to produce something. Our present Regent,[5] who was
Captain Third Rank at the time, wrote the following poem:

> "As the tide that swells
> in Izumo's Always Bay
> so always and always
> oh how my heart swells and fills
> deep with love to think of you."[6]

but he changed the last line to read "deep with trust in you, my
lord", and His Majesty was full of praise for him.'

When I heard this, I felt a sudden sweat break out all over
me. I do think, though, that that poem of mine isn't the sort of
thing a young person could have come up with.[7] Even people
who can usually turn out a fine poem found themselves for
some reason at a loss that day, and several made mistakes in
their writing.

There was also the occasion when Her Majesty placed a
bound book of *Kokinshū* poems in front of her, and proceeded
to read out the opening lines of various poems and ask us to
complete them. Why on earth did we keep stumbling over the
answers, even for poems we'd engraved on our memories day
in and day out? Saishō only managed about ten. Others could
produce only five or six, and really, you'd think they could
simply have admitted that they couldn't recall them. But no,
they kept agonizing over the task. 'But we can't be so rude
as to refuse point-blank to answer,' they wailed, 'when Her
Majesty has been so good as to put the question to us', which
I found rather amusing.

Her Majesty then read out the complete poem for each of
those that nobody had been able to answer, marking them with
a bookmark, and everyone groaned, 'Oh of course I knew that
one! Why am I being so stupid today?' Some of us had copied
out the *Kokinshū* many times, and should really have known it
all by heart.

'As I'm sure you are all aware,' Her Majesty began, 'the lady
known as the Senyōden Consort,[8] High Consort in the reign of
Emperor Murakami, was the daughter of the Minister of the

Left, of the Smaller Palace of the First Ward. When she was still a girl, her father gave her the following advice: "First, you must study calligraphy. Next, you must determine to outshine everyone in your skill on the seven-stringed *kin*. And you must also make it your study to commit to memory all the poems in the twenty volumes of the *Kokinshū*."

'Now the Emperor had learned of this, so one day, when he was kept from his usual duties by an abstinence, he took a copy of the *Kokinshū* to the High Consort's quarters, and set up a standing curtain between them. She found this unusual behaviour rather odd, and when he opened a book and began asking her to recite the poem that so-and-so had written on such-and-such a date and occasion, she was intrigued to realize what he was up to – though on the other hand, she would also have been dreadfully nervous that there might be some which she would forget or misquote. He called in two or three of his gentlewomen who were well-versed in poetry, and had them extract the answers from her, and keep count of her mistakes with *go* counters. It must have been a wonderful scene to witness. I do envy them all, even the people who were merely serving on this occasion.

'Well, he pressed her to go on answering, and she went through them making not a single mistake, though she cleverly gave just enough of each poem to show she knew it, and didn't try to complete them. His Majesty decided he would call a halt just as soon as she made a mistake, and as she went on and on he even began to get rather irritated, but they reached the tenth volume and still she hadn't made a single slip. "This has been quite futile," he finally declared, and he put a marker in the book and retired to another room to sleep. All very wonderful it was.

'When he awoke many hours later, he decided that it would never do to leave the matter hanging, and moreover it had better be done that day, since she might refresh her memory with another copy of the work if he left it till tomorrow. So he produced the remaining ten volumes, had the lamps lit and proceeded to work his way through the rest of the poems until long into the night. But she never made a single mistake.

'Meanwhile, word was sent to her father that the Emperor had returned to her quarters and that the test was continuing. The Minister flew into a panic with worry that she might fail the test; he ordered numerous sutras to be said for her,[9] while he placed himself facing the direction of the palace and spent the entire night in heartfelt prayer. Altogether a fascinating and moving story,' Her Majesty remarked in conclusion.

His Majesty too heard the tale with admiration. 'I wouldn't be able to manage more than three or four volumes myself,' he remarked.

'In the old days, even the most inconsequential people were impressive. You don't hear such stories these days, do you,' everyone agreed, and all the Empress's gentlewomen, and those who served the Emperor and were permitted to visit the Empress's quarters, gathered round and began talking. It was indeed a scene to fill the heart with ease and delight.

[21] *Women without prospect*, who lead dull earnest lives and rejoice in their petty little pseudo-pleasures, I find quite depressing and despicable. People of any standing ought to give their daughters a taste of society. They should show them the world and let them become familiar with its ways, by serving as attendants at the palace or other such positions.

I can't bear men who consider women who serve at court to be frivolous and unseemly. Though mind you, one can see why they would. From His Majesty the Emperor, whose name can barely be spoken for reverence, to the court nobles and senior courtiers, not to mention people of the fourth and fifth rank of course, there would be very few men who don't catch sight of us at some point. And have you ever heard tell of a lady who served at court shyly hiding herself from her own servants or others who came from her house, let alone palace maids, latrine cleaners, and general dolts and nobodies? A gentleman wouldn't come across as many people as we gentlewomen do – though probably they do while they're at court, it's true.

I can see why a lady who has served at court could be considered less than suitably refined when she's later installed as someone's wife and is treated with due respect. But surely there's considerable honour in being called Chief Gentle-woman, and sometimes going to the palace and taking part in festival processions.

And she's in a still finer position once she's left court service and settled down at home. If her husband is a Provincial Governor and the family is chosen to provide one of the Gosechi dancers, she won't make a fool of herself with the kind of stupid, boorish questions that country people ask. Now that really is refinement, surely.

[22] *Dispiriting things* – A dog howling in the middle of the day. The sight in spring of a trap for catching winter fish. Robes in the plum-pink combination, when it's now the third or fourth month. An ox keeper whose ox has died. A birthing hut where the baby has died. A square brazier or a hearth with no fire lit in it. A scholar whose wife has a string of daughters.[1]

A household that doesn't treat you hospitably, though you're there because of a directional taboo – this is particularly dispiriting if it happens to be at one of the season changes.

A letter from the provinces that arrives without any accom-panying gift. You might say the same for a letter sent from inside the capital, but this would contain plenty of things you wanted to hear about and interesting news, which makes it a very fine thing to receive in fact.

You've taken special care to send off a beautiful, carefully written letter, and you're eagerly awaiting the reply – time passes, it seems awfully long in coming, and then finally your own elegantly folded or knotted letter is brought back, now horribly soiled and crumpled and with no sign remaining of the brush stroke that sealed it. 'There was no one in', you're told, or 'They couldn't accept it on account of an abstinence.' This is dreadfully dispiriting.

A carriage is sent off to fetch someone you're sure is going to come. You wait, and finally there's the sound of the carriage returning. 'It must be her,' you think, and everyone in the house goes out to see – but the driver is already dragging the carriage back into its shed. He drops the shafts with a noisy clatter. 'What happened?' you ask. 'She's going somewhere else today, so she won't be coming,' he replies offhandedly, then he hauls out the harness and off he goes.

It's also very dispiriting when a man stops coming to visit his wife at her home. It's a great shame if he's gone off with a lady of good family who serves at court, and the wife sits moping at home, feeling ashamed and humiliated.

A little child's nurse has gone out, promising that she won't be long. You do your best to keep the child entertained and comforted, but when you send word saying 'please hurry', back comes a message to the effect that she won't be able to return this evening. This is not just dispiriting, it's downright hateful.

It's even more dispiriting for a man when a woman fails to visit him.[2] And when the night has grown late at his house and suddenly he hears a subdued knock at the gate, and with beating heart he sends to find out who it is, only to have the servant return and announce the name of some other, boring person, well the word 'dispiriting' doesn't begin to cover it.

An exorcist priest comes to quell a spirit that has possessed a member of the household. With a confident air he hands the medium the rosary and the other paraphernalia to induce possession, and sets about his incantations in a high, strained, cicada-like chant. But there's no sign of the spirit shifting, and the medium fails to be possessed by the Guardian Deity.[3] Everyone who's gathered to pray, men and women both, begins to find this rather odd. The exorcist chants on until the change of watch two hours later, when he finally stops, exhausted. 'Get up,' he says to the medium as he retrieves the rosary. 'The spirit just won't budge', and running his hand back from his forehead over his bald head he declares, 'Oh dear, the exorcism was quite futile.' Whereupon he lets out a yawn, leans back against some nearby object and falls asleep. It's truly awful for him when someone not especially important comes over to him, though he's feeling dreadfully sleepy, and prods him awake and forces him into a conversation.

Then there's the house of a man who has failed to receive a post in the recent Appointments List. Word had it that he was certain to get one this year, and all his former retainers, who have scattered far and wide or are now living off in the countryside somewhere, have gathered at his house in anticipation. His courtyard is crammed with the coming and going of their carriages and the tangle of their shafts; if he sets off on an excursion they all jostle to accompany him; and they eat, drink and clamour their way through the days as they wait[4] – but as the last day dawns, there's still no knock at the gate. 'How odd,' they think, and as they sit straining to catch the sound, they hear the cries of the outriders as the court nobles emerge from the palace at the close of the Appointments ceremonies. The underlings who have spent a chilly night shivering outside the palace waiting to hear the news come trudging back dejectedly, and no one can even bring himself to ask them what happened. When some outsider inquires, 'What appointment did your master receive?' they always reply evasively, 'Oh, he's the former Governor of So-and-so.'

All those who really rely on him feel quite devastated. As morning comes, a few among the people who've been packed in together waiting begin to creep stealthily away. Those who've been many years in his service, however, can't bring themselves to leave his side so lightly. It's terribly touching to see them weaving solemnly about as they pace the room, hopefully counting on their fingers the Provincial Governorships due to come to the end of their term the following year.

There are also those times when you send someone a poem you're rather pleased with, and fail to receive one in reply. Of course there's no more to be done about it if it's to a man you care for.[5] Even so, you do lose respect for someone who doesn't produce any response to your tasteful seasonal references. It also dampens the spirit when you're leading a heady life in the swim of things and you receive some boring little old-fashioned poem that reeks of the longueurs of the writer, whose time hangs heavy on her hands.

You have a particularly fine fan intended for some ceremonial event, and you hand this precious thing to a person who you trust will treat it well, but when the day arrives it comes back to you with something quite unforeseen painted on it.[6]

A messenger delivers a congratulatory birth gift or a farewell present, and isn't given any gift in repayment. Messengers should always be given something, such as decorative herbal balls or New Year hare-mallets, even if they're only delivering some object of no permanent use. If he receives something when he's not expecting to, he will feel thoroughly pleased that he made the delivery. However, it's particularly dispiriting when he's come feeling sure he'll receive something for this errand, and his excited hopes are dashed.

A house where four or five years have passed since they brought in a husband but there's still been no joyous birth celebration is most depressing.

A couple has already produced numerous children, all now adult, and indeed of an age at which there could even be grandchildren crawling about, yet the two parents are indulging in a 'daytime nap'.[7] It's dispiriting for the children who witness this, with nowhere to turn while their parents are off behind closed doors.

The purificatory hot bath that you have to get up to take on New Year's Eve is not merely dispiriting, it's downright irritating.

Rain all day on New Year's Eve. Perhaps this is what's meant by the expression 'a single day of purificatory abstinence'.[8]

[23] *Occasions that induce half-heartedness* – The religious services on days of Buddhist fasting. Preparations for something still far in the future. Long periods of seclusion at a temple.

[24] *Things people despise* – A crumbling earth wall.[1] People who have a reputation for being exceptionally good-natured.

[25] *Infuriating things* – A guest who arrives when you have something urgent to do, and stays talking for ages. If it's someone you don't have much respect for, you can simply send them away and tell them to come back later, but if it's a person with whom you feel you must stand on ceremony, it's an infuriating situation.

A hair has got on to your inkstone and you find yourself grinding it in with the inkstick. Also, the grating sound when a bit of stone gets ground in with the ink.

Someone suddenly falls ill, and an exorcist is sent for. They don't find him in the usual place, and a tedious amount of time is spent waiting while they go around in search of him. Finally they manage to locate him, and with great relief you set him to performing the exorcism rites – however, the recent exertions of exorcising some other possessing spirit seem to have worn him out, for no sooner does he sit down and start in on the chanting than his voice grows drowsy. This is utterly infuriating.

A very ordinary person, who beams inanely as she prattles on and on.

People who sit warming themselves at a brazier, stretching their hands out over it and endlessly turning them this way and that. Now have you ever come across a young person acting in this unattractive fashion? But it seems that as they get older, people will even start propping their feet up to warm them on the edge of the brazier, and rubbing them together as they talk. When they come to visit, such people will first fan the area where they intend to sit, to sweep away any dust; then when they do settle down they can't sit still but keep shifting about on their haunches; and they also tuck their hunting costume in under their knees.[1] You might think that such men are all unspeakably lowly types, but I've even heard of people of considerable status who do such things – men such as the Commissioner of Ceremonial, for instance.

It's also quite disgusting to witness men getting noisy and boisterous in their cups, groping round inside their mouth with a finger or wiping their whiskers if they have them, and forcing the *saké* cup on others. 'Go on, have another!' they'll cry, and they wriggle and squirm and wag their heads, and pull down the corners of their mouths in a grimace, and generally perform just like a child singing 'Going to See the Governor'.[2] I've seen even truly great men behave in this way, and I must say I find it most offputting.

I also really hate the way some people go about envying others, bemoaning their own lot in life, demanding to be let in on every trivial little thing, being venomous about someone who won't tell them what they want to know, and passing on

Reed blinds

their own dramatized version of some snippet of rumour they've heard, while making out that they knew it all along.

A baby who cries when you're trying to hear something. A flock of crows clamouring raucously, all flying around chaotically with noisily flapping wings. A dog that discovers a clandestine lover as he comes creeping in, and barks.

A man you've had to conceal in some unsatisfactory hiding place, who then begins to snore. Or, a man comes on a secret visit wearing a particularly tall lacquered cap, and of course as he scuttles in hastily he manages to knock it against something with a loud bump. I also hate it when a rough reed blind catches on the head as someone passes underneath, and makes that scratchy noise. And if someone lowers the weighted bottom of one of the fine reed blinds[3] too roughly, you can clearly hear the knock as it falls – if you raise it carefully as you go through, it won't make a sound. It's also ridiculous the way people will push open a wooden sliding door so roughly. Surely it wouldn't make that clatter if they'd lift it a little as they push. Sliding panel doors will also make a distinct rattling noise if you open them clumsily.

You've just settled sleepily into bed when a mosquito announces itself with that thin little wail, and starts flying round your face. It's horrible how you can feel the soft wind of its tiny wings.

People who go about in a carriage with squeaky wheels are very irritating. It makes you wonder irately if they're deaf. And if you find yourself riding in one you've borrowed from someone, you even begin to loathe its owner.

Someone who butts in when you're talking and smugly provides the ending herself. Indeed anyone who butts in, be they child or adult, is most infuriating.

It's also very annoying when you've made a fuss over some children who have come on a passing visit, and gone out of your way to give them things they'll like, and now they've come to expect this treatment and start constantly turning up and running around knocking things over.

I hate it when, either at home or at the palace, someone comes calling whom you'd rather not see and you pretend to be asleep, but then a well-meaning member of the household comes along and shakes you awake with a look of disapproval at how you've dozed off.

Some newcomer steps in and starts interfering and lecturing the old hands as if she knows it all. This is quite infuriating.

A man you're in a relationship with speaks admiringly of some woman who was once his lover. This rankles even if the affair is now safely in the past, and you can imagine how much more enraging it would be if she were actually a current lover of his. Still, there are also some situations in which it doesn't really bother you.

A person who says something auspicious if they sneeze.[4] In general, anyone other than the master of a household who sneezes loudly is irritating.

Fleas are also infuriating things. They dance about under your clothes so vigorously that you almost expect them to raise your skirts with their leaping.

A chorus of dogs howling on and on is quite hair-raisingly horrible.

And I hate people who don't close a door that they've opened to go in or out.

[26]* *Things that make your heart beat fast* – A sparrow with nestlings. Going past a place where tiny children are playing. Lighting some fine incense and then lying down alone to sleep. Looking into a Chinese mirror that's a little clouded. A fine gentleman pulls up in his carriage and sends in some request.

To wash your hair, apply your makeup and put on clothes that are well-scented with incense. Even if you're somewhere where no one special will see you, you still feel a heady sense of pleasure inside.

On a night when you're waiting for someone to come, there's a sudden gust of rain and something rattles in the wind, making your heart suddenly beat faster.

[27] *Things that make you feel nostalgic* – A dried sprig of *aoi*. Things children use in doll play. Coming across a torn scrap of lavender- or grape-coloured fabric crumpled between the pages of a bound book. On a rainy day when time hangs heavy, searching out an old letter that touched you deeply at the time you received it. Last year's summer fan.

[28] *Things that make you feel cheerful* – A well-executed picture done in the female style,[1] with lots of beautifully written accompanying text around it.

An ox carriage crammed with ladies on their way back from some viewing expedition,[2] sleeves tumbling out in profusion, with a great crowd of carriage boys running with it, skilfully guiding the ox as the carriage hurtles along.

Something written in very delicate strokes with just the tip of an almost impossibly thick brush, on a lovely, clean white sheet of Michinoku paper. Beautiful glossed silk threads tied together in a bundle. A game of dice-matching[3] in which there are lots of matches. A particularly eloquent Yin-Yang master whom you've called in goes down to the dry river-bed and proceeds to rid you of a curse.[4] Water drunk when you've woken in the night.

It's wonderfully cheering and satisfying if a guest, a person you're not particularly intimate with, comes visiting when you're feeling bored – someone in the know about things, well aware of both the public and private sides of life, who sits there chatting and recounting stories of various strange and interesting and unpleasant things that have been happening, but without going on annoyingly.

You go to a shrine or a Buddhist temple to ask for some prayer of yours[5] to be read at the altar, and the shrine priest or temple monk recites it beautifully clearly and fluently, far better than you were expecting.

[29]* *A palm-leaf carriage* should move at a sedate pace. It looks bad if it's hurrying. A basketwork carriage, on the other hand, should move at a smart pace. It's fun when people catch a glimpse of it as it flashes past their gateway, and as they see the outrunners hurry by in its wake they are left wondering who it might have been. It's most unimpressive to see one dawdling along taking its time.

Palm-leaf carriage

[30]* *A priest who gives a sermon should be handsome.* After all, you're most aware of the profundity of his teaching if you're gazing at his face as he speaks. If your eyes drift elsewhere you tend to forget what you've just heard, so an unattractive face has the effect of making you feel quite sinful. But I'll write no further on this subject. I may have written glibly enough about sinful matters of this sort in my younger days, but at my age the idea of sin has become quite frightening.

I must say, however, from my own sinful point of view, it seems quite uncalled-for to go around as some do, vaunting their religious piety and rushing to be the first to be seated wherever a sermon is being preached.

An ex-Chamberlain[1] never used to take up the vanguard of imperial processions, and once he retired from the post you'd no longer see him about the palace. These days things are apparently different. The so-called 'Chamberlain fifth-ranker' is actually kept in reasonably busy service, but privately he must nevertheless miss the prestige of his former post and feel at a loss how to fill his days, so once he tries going to these places and hears a few sermons he'll no doubt develop a taste for it and start to go along on a regular basis.

You'll find him turning up there with his summer under-robe prominently displayed beneath his cloak even in baking summer weather, and the hems of his pale lavender or blue-grey gathered trousers loose and trodden. He has an abstinence tag attached to his lacquered cap, and he no doubt intends to draw attention to the fact that although it's an abstinence day and he shouldn't leave the house, this doesn't apply to him since his outing is of a pious nature. He chats with the officiating priest, even goes so far as to help oversee the positioning of the ladies' carriages, and is generally completely at home in the situation. When some old crony of his whom he hasn't seen recently turns up, he's consumed with curiosity. Over he goes, and they settle down together and proceed to talk and nod and launch into interesting stories, spreading out their fans and putting them to their mouths when they laugh, groping at their ornately decor- ated rosaries and fiddling with them as they talk, craning to look here and there, praising and criticizing the carriages, dis- cussing how other priests did things this way or that in other Lotus Discourses and sutra dedication services they've been to, and so on and so forth – and not listening to a word of the actual sermon they're attending. Indeed they would have heard it all so often before that they'd gain nothing from it anyway.

And then there's another type. The preacher has already seated himself when after a while up rolls a carriage, accom- panied by only a couple of outriders. It draws to a halt, and the passengers step out – three or four slender young men, dressed perhaps in hunting costume or in cloaks more delicately gauzy than a cicada's wing, gathered trousers and gossamer silk shifts, and accompanied by a similar number of attendants. Those already seated move themselves along a little to make way for them when they enter. They seat themselves by a pillar near the preacher's dais and set about softly rubbing their rosaries as they listen to the sermon, and the preacher, who no doubt feels rather honoured to have them there, throws himself with fresh vigour into the task of putting his message across. The young men, however, far from casting themselves extravagantly to the floor as they listen, instead decide to leave after a decent amount of time has passed, and as they go they throw glances in the direction of the women's carriages and comment to each other, and you'd love to know what it was they were saying. It's funny how you find yourself watching them as they depart, interestedly identifying the ones you know, and speculating on the identity of those you don't.

Some people really take things to extremes, though. If someone mentions having been to a Lotus Discourse or other such event, another will say, 'And was so and so there?' and the reply is always, 'Of course. How could he not be?' Mind you, I'm not saying one should never show up at these places. After all, even women of low standing will apparently listen to sermons with great concentration. Actually, when I first started attending sermons, I never saw women going about here and there on foot to them. Occasionally you would find women in travelling attire, elegantly made up, but they were out as part of another excursion to some temple or shrine. You didn't often hear of women attending sermons and the like in this costume, though. If the ladies who went to sermons in those days had lived long enough to see the way things are today, I can just imagine how they would have criticized and condemned.

[31] *While I was visiting Bodai Temple* to hear the Salvation Lotus Discourses,[1] I received a message saying, 'Hurry back. I'm feeling very bored and lonely.' I replied by writing on the back of a lotus leaf:

You long for my return,
but I long only to be drenched
with Lotus dews of Truth –
how should I leave this and go back
to that unhappy other world?[2]

Indeed the sermons were so deeply moving that I felt an urge
to stay on at the temple forever, forgetting, like Sōchū[3] in the
old story, the impatience of those waiting at home.

[32]* *The place known as Koshirakawa* is the home of the
Koichijō Commander,[1] and I remember an occasion when the
court nobles held a set of Salvation Lotus Discourses here under
his auspices. Everyone treated it as a very special event, and we
were warned that late carriages wouldn't be able to find room
to stand, so we rose like the dew at daybreak. The place was
indeed crammed. The carriages were drawn right up on top
of each other as close as possible, shafts overlapping, and the
sermon would probably have been somewhat audible at least
for the first three rows.[2] It was towards the middle of the sixth
month, and the heat was unbelievable. The only way to induce
any sense of delicious coolness was to rest your eyes on the
lotuses in the pond.

Apart from the Ministers of the Left and Right, all the court
nobles were present. The younger ones were dressed in lavender
gathered trousers and cloaks, with light-blue summer under-
robes visible beneath, while those a little older created a wonderfully cool impression in blue-grey gathered trousers and
white skirted trousers. Consultant Sukemasa[3] and the others
were all looking very youthful, and the whole scene was utterly
awe-inspiring and delightful. The blinds around the aisle room
had been raised right up, and the court nobles were seated just
beyond in a long row above the threshold, facing inward. Next
in line[4] behind them were the senior courtiers and younger
court nobles, in marvellous ceremonial hunting costumes and
cloaks. Many of them were wandering about rather than simply
remaining seated, which was great fun to observe. Second of
the Watch Sanekata and Adviser Chōmei,[5] being members of

the household, were coming and going about the place rather more freely. Those who were still very young also looked quite enchanting.

When the sun had risen a little higher, Captain Third Rank Michitaka (as our Regent then was) walked in, dressed in a Chinese-style cloak of lavender silk gauze, with lavender brocade gathered trousers over deep maroon under-trousers, and a shift of brilliant stiff white silk beneath the cloak. Now you'd imagine that in the midst of that assembly of light, cool clothing these clothes would produce a sense of stifling heat, but in fact he looked absolutely splendid. The ribs of people's fans were variously lacquered or of magnolia wood, but the fans themselves were all of red paper, so the combined effect of them was precisely like a field of blooming pinks.

Before the priest had mounted the sermon dais, meal-stands were brought in, and everyone seemed to be served a meal of some kind, though we couldn't make out what. Counsellor Yoshichika[6] was looking even finer than usual, in fact simply marvellous. There he was, in the midst of these gorgeous colours, such dazzling sheens of summer under-robes that there was no choosing among them for beauty, and he was simplicity itself in his single cloak. He kept looking across towards the ladies' carriages, and sending messages over to them. No one who saw him could have failed to find him delightful.

He watched as one of the carriages that arrived late was drawn in near the pond for lack of room, and then he turned to Sanekata and asked him to call someone who could reliably carry a message. Sanekata chose someone and led him over to Yoshichika, who conferred with those around him about what message to send; I didn't hear the words they finally decided on, however.

Yoshichika watched with a smile as the messenger approached the carriage with ostentatious solemnity. From what I could make out, he went to the rear and delivered his message, and he then stood waiting quite a while to receive her reply.

'She'll be composing a poem I should think,' Yoshichika said with a smile, and he turned teasingly to Sanekata and went on, 'you must prepare an answering one for her.' Everyone, including the older men and the court nobles, sat looking in the direction of the carriage, eagerly waiting to hear her reply. It was really very funny the way even the bystanders all had their eyes fixed on it.

Finally, the messenger began to walk back towards the expectant audience, having apparently been given her message, but at this point the lady suddenly thrust her fan out through the carriage blind and waved him back to her again. Judging from the gesture, you could only conclude that she'd realized she'd made some mistake in the poem's wording, but I must say I couldn't help thinking that if it had taken all this time for the poem to emerge in the first place, there should be no reason to be changing it now.

Everyone watched his approach in high anticipation. 'Well, what did she say? What did she say?' people cried. But they had to wait to hear her response while the messenger first presented himself to Yoshichika, since it was he who had employed him on the errand, and there proceeded to relay his message in a most pompous and painstaking manner.

'Oh hurry up and say it!' Michitaka broke in impatiently. 'You'll ruin the reply if you recite it with such a ridiculous amount of poetic feeling', and I heard the man say, 'I wouldn't be ruining it more than it ruins itself.'

The Fujiwara Grand Counsellor[7] was craning in their direction, particularly eager to hear what it was. I think he asked what she'd said, and Michitaka replied, 'Well, our "straight tree" seems to have got rather bent.'[8] The Grand Counsellor burst out laughing, setting off a ripple of laughter throughout the gathering as well, which would certainly have carried to the lady's carriage.

'What did the poem originally say before she called you back?' inquired Yoshichika. 'Can this really be the improved version?'

'I stood there waiting so long that I decided she wasn't going to reply, but then as I was setting off to return she called me back,' the messenger replied.

'Whose carriage is it, does anyone know?' Yoshichika asked curiously, and he was just deciding to try sending a poem this time to see what would happen, when the preacher ascended the dais. With that, everyone fell silent and turned their attention to him, and while no one was looking, the lady's carriage quietly slipped away.

As I recall, the inner blinds of the carriage looked brand new, and the lady's sleeves revealed scarlet unlined gowns, and a figured lavender Chinese jacket worn over an outer gown of maroon silk gauze, while from the back of the carriage hung her expansively displayed indigo-print train. Who can she have been? But good heavens, I do feel that her reply was perfectly fine in fact, much better than some half-baked response.

Seihan, who delivered the morning discourse, was an absolutely glowing presence on the dais, quite wonderful to witness. What with the enervating heat, and the fact that there was work I'd left half done and had to complete that day, I'd decided to stay only a little while to listen and then go home – but when it came to the point, there were such overlapping waves of carriage shafts piled one upon the other that there was no way of extricating myself. Then I decided I must somehow get out as soon as the morning discourse was over, and when I passed on this message to the carriages behind they promptly pulled out to make way for me, presumably delighted at the prospect of thereby getting a bit closer to the dais themselves. Seeing me causing this commotion, many of the men, including some elderly court nobles, sniggered quite loudly in derision, and when I turned a deaf ear and didn't deign to respond but simply squeezed my way out, Counsellor Yoshichika gave a laugh and remarked, 'Well, well, "they do well to depart"', which was wonderfully clever. But I didn't pay this any heed either and merely continued to make my way out, quite flustered with the heat, simply responding with a parting shot that said, 'Surely you too can be counted among that five thousand.'9

There was one carriage that was present from the beginning of the Discourses to the end of the last day. No one ever saw anyone approach it; it just sat there, astonishingly still, for all the world as if it were some carriage in a picture. Yoshichika declared that the lady must be marvellously pious and refined, and wondered what manner of person she was and how he

could manage to meet her, but when the Fujiwara Grand Counsellor heard this he said, 'What's so marvellous about her? She
strikes me as quite creepy and ghastly', which was very funny.

How sad it was when Counsellor Yoshichika suddenly took
the tonsure towards the end of that month. It is the way of the
world that the flowering blossoms should fall and scatter, but
Yoshichika passed from his brief glory even before 'the dew fell
on him'.[10]

[33]* *In the seventh month, when the heat is dreadful*, everything in the building is kept open all through the night, and it's
delightful to wake on moonlit nights and lie there looking out.
Dark nights too are delightful, and as for the sight of the moon
at dawn, words cannot describe the loveliness.

Picture her lying there, on a fresh new mat[1] placed near the
outer edge of the gleaming wooden aisle-room floor, the low
standing curtain pushed to the back of the room in a quite
unseemly way.[2] It should normally be placed at the outer edge,
but perhaps she's concerned about being seen from within.

Her lover must have already left. She is lying asleep, a robe
drawn up over her head[3] – it is pale greyish-violet with deep
violet inner lining, the outer surface a little faded, or perhaps it
is a stiffish robe of rich gleaming damask. Beneath this, she is
wearing a clove-tan or yellow gossamer-silk shift, and the long
strings of her unlined scarlet skirted trousers trailing undone
from below the hem of her clothing tell us that she must have
fallen asleep with trousers still untied after her lover departed.
The soft luxury of hair that lies piled in waves beside her speaks
of its wonderful length.

Nearby is a gentleman,[4] dressed in lavender gathered
trousers, a hunting costume of almost invisibly pale clove-tan,
and a white gosssamer-silk shift, glossy from what could be a
crimson summer under-robe glowing through from beneath.
He has slipped back his mist-drenched cloak from his shoulders,
and his lacquered cap is pulled awkwardly down over sidelocks
that are somewhat bushy and tangled from the night's escapade,
lending him a negligent air. He is on his way home, his mind
distracted as he goes with thoughts of the next-morning letter

he will send before the dew is gone from the morning glory,[5] and wistfully he hums 'the ferns in the flax field'[6] – but as he is passing he has noticed the woman's open lattice shutter and paused to lift a corner of the blind and peep in, intrigued to think of the man who must have recently left her side, surely the night's dew so moving for him too. He stands there at the edge, gazing, and at the head of her pillow he spies a magnolia-wood summer fan, papered in violet, lying open, and glimpses too beside the standing screen a scattering of thinly folded Michinoku paper, perhaps of a subtly glowing azure or crimson.

Sensing his presence, she looks out from beneath her cloak, and sees him sitting there smiling, propped against the threshold. He is not someone she need be particularly ashamed to be seen by, but neither does she feel inclined to be overly familiar with him, and she is vexed that he's seen her like this.

'Someone special must be behind this sleeping late,' he says, and he insinuates himself halfway in through the blind; to which she responds, 'I'm merely sleeping off my irritation at one who leaves before the dew is gone.'

Well, there's no need to write the amusing details of all they say, but still, the picture of these two exchanging their idle banter is surely not without its charm. He stretches out his fan to draw hers towards him from where it lies above her pillow, leaning forward as he does so, but her heart lurches at the thought that he might be about to overstep the bounds and come too close, and she huddles away from him. He picks up the fan and inspects it, flirtatiously exclaiming how stand-offish she is being, and he goes on chiding and teasing her in this vein as the sky grows lighter, the first sounds of people's voices reach them, and at last the sun is on the very verge of rising.

When the dawn mists begin to part, he finally grows concerned at the lateness of that next-morning letter he'd been in such a hurry to compose. Meanwhile, the man who had earlier left her side has already written and sent his letter, attaching it to a branch of bush clover,[7] and the messenger is hovering nearby, unable to deliver it. The paper is heavily perfumed with incense, a delightful scent. This has all become very awkward, and the gentleman finally departs, no doubt entertained to find himself wondering if another man has similarly been visiting the woman whose bed he earlier left himself.

[34] *Flowering trees* – The best among blossoms is the red plum, whether light or dark in colour. As for the cherry, the blossoms should be on slender branches, the petals large and the leaves deeply coloured.

Wisteria blossoms are particularly impressive when they hang long and graceful, with richly coloured flowers.

Around the time of the new moon at the end of the fourth month or early in the fifth, the sight of the orange tree's very white blossoms set amongst the deep green of the leaves, seen in early morning rain, is extraordinarily moving. With its brilliant glowing fruit, like balls of gold nestled among the flowers, it's quite as impressive as a flowering cherry drenched with the dews of dawn. You need only recall its close association with the *hototogisu*[1] and there is really no need to sing its praises further.

The blossoms of the pear tree are generally considered to be horrid things, and they aren't brought into people's proximity, nor even used in some passing way such as attached to letters. The pear is used as a comparison when referring to the sight of an unattractive face, and truly the whole appearance, including the colour of the leaves, lacks beauty and appeal – yet the pear blossom is held in the highest esteem in China, and appears in Chinese poetry, so there must be something to it after all. And indeed, if you take a careful and sympathetic look at it, you may notice that just at the tips of the petals there is the barest hint of a rather lovely lustre. Yes, when you recall that the weeping face of the beauty Yang Guifei, when she met the Emperor's messenger, is compared in the poem to the pear,[2] where it says she is like 'a spray of pear blossom, swathed in the spring rain', you realize that this is after all a rather special flower; in fact it's really quite marvellous and incomparable.

The flowers of the paulownia, being purple,[3] are particularly delightful. The great size of its leaves is most unpleasant – but after all, this tree shouldn't be spoken of in the same breath as

other trees, for it has quite a different air about it by virtue
of being the only tree in which that fabulous bird of Chinese
fame chooses to perch.[4] And how could it be spoken of in
common terms, since its wood is made into stringed instruments
and gives forth all those wonderful sounds? It's an absolutely
marvellous tree, in fact.

The melia is an ugly tree, but its flowers are lovely. They
have an unusual, sere sort of blossom, and I do like the way
they're always in bloom for the fifth day of the fifth month.[5]

[35]* *Ponds* – Katsumata Pond. Iware Pond.

Nieno Pond – it was marvellous to see seemingly endless
flocks of water birds rising noisily from this pond, when we
passed it on our pilgrimage to Hase.

Waterless Pond – this is a strange one. When I asked someone
why it was given such an odd name, they said it was because
all the water dries up in years when unusually heavy rains can
be expected in the fifth month, while it fills with water in spring
when the year promises to be very dry. I wanted to point out
that the name is all very well when you consider how it dries
up, but surely it also fills with water at other times, so it seems
a very one-sided name to give it.

Sarusawa Pond is a very special place, because the Emperor
paid it a formal visit when he heard how one of the Palace
Maidens had drowned herself there.[1] Thinking of Hitomaro's
marvellous words 'her hair tangled as in sleep', there is really
nothing I can add.

One also wonders what was in the mind of the person who
gave the place called 'Divine Presence Pond' that name.

Then there's God Pond. And in the case of Sayama Pond,
one naturally thinks of the interesting association of the water
plant known as burr reed, because of the poem.[2]

There's also Koinuma Pond. And Hara Pond is interesting
because of the song about it which goes 'Oh do not cut the
jewelled weeds'.[3]

[36] *Seasonal palace festivals* – Of the five seasonal palace
festivals, none is better than the fifth month's. I love the way

the scents of sweet flag and wormwood blend on this day, and another striking thing about the day is the way everywhere, from the 'nine-fold palace' to the houses of unmentionably common folk, people compete to spread their roof thick with all the sweet flag and wormwood they can lay hands on. After all, when has this ever been known to happen in any other festival?

The sky is generally heavy with cloud. The Bureau of Clothing sends across to the Empress's palace the little decorative herbal balls that are hung for this festival, with a colourful array of braided threads dangling from them, and we put them up on the pillars to the left and right of Her Majesty's curtained dais in the Inner Chamber. We tie them up in place of the chrysanthemums that have been hanging there, wrapped in plain gossamer-silk cloth, ever since the Chrysanthemum Festival in the ninth month, which we now throw away. I wonder if in fact the herbal balls in turn shouldn't stay up till the next Chrysanthemum Festival, but in reality the coloured threads all get pulled off before long and used for tying things.

Her Majesty is served special festival food, and the younger girls put sweet-flag herbal balls at their waists, and special sweet-flag abstinence charms in their hair, and tie delightful little sprigs of seasonal plants on to long sweet-flag stems with dappled cord and attach them to their Chinese jackets or overrobes. Of course I can't claim there's anything rare and special about all this, still it's most delightful. After all, the cherry blossom blooms every year, but does anyone find it the less lovely for that?

It's also rather fun to watch how all the little lower-class girls who play outside do their best to deck themselves out as smartly as they can, and go about constantly looking at their own clothes and comparing them with others', absolutely bursting with pride in their sweet-flag decorations, till one of the guards' children comes along and playfully tugs them off, and they dissolve in tears. And then there's the delightful custom of finely wrapping a spray of purple melia flowers around purple paper, or a sweet-flag leaf around leaf-green paper, or in the case of white paper a white sweet-flag root. And the sight of a lovely long sweet-flag root enclosed with a letter gives a wonderfully elegant feel. It's also quite charming to see women huddled intimately together sharing the letters they've just received, as they discuss how to respond. Those who are involved in exchanges with a young lady or with someone in high places write particularly careful and elegant letters on this day. Indeed the whole day, down to the way the *hototogisu* gives its signature cry as it flies past in the gathering twilight, is utterly wonderful.

[37]* *Trees that have no flowers* – The maple, the Judas tree, the white pine.

The Chinese hawthorn seems a rather unrefined tree, but it startles with its richly-coloured red leaves showing so unseasonably in the midst of the astonishing green, at a time when all the flowering trees have shed their blossom and everything is a uniform spring green.

Nothing need be said on the subject of the spindle tree.

It's not really worth including here, but the clinging vine is a quite pitiable plant. The *sakaki* is very lovely in the shrine dances of the Provisional Festivals.[1] Many are the trees in this world, but this one is very special for having been born to be offered to the gods.

Even in large stands of camphor trees, no other tree is mixed with them. It's quite creepy to imagine how all that thick dark growth must feel, but when you think of the way its 'thousand branches' are used in poetry to refer to the thousand tangled feelings of a lover's heart, it's rather fascinating, and you wonder who first counted the branches to come up with that expression.

The cypress doesn't grow near human habitation, but the song's words 'this palace with its many roofbeams' make it rather interesting. It's also touching to recall how it supposedly imitates the sound of the rain in the fifth month.[2] The maple has a pretty way of sending out little fresh leaves with reddened tips, all spreading in the same direction, and its frail flowers that look like dried insects are also sweet.

You neither see nor hear of the *asuwa* cypress hereabouts,

but the branches of it apparently brought back by people who have been on the Mitake pilgrimage look terribly coarse, and you wouldn't want to touch them. Still, I do wonder why someone gave it such a foolish promise of a name.[3] It makes me dearly wish to know who this person was trying to convince.

The privet is not a tree that should be considered alongside others, but its tiny delicate leaves are nice.

The melia. The mountain orange. The mountain pear.

The chinquipin is interesting because it's the only one of all the evergreens that is spoken of in poetry as never changing its leaves.

The white oak is the least familiar of all the trees that grow deep in the mountains. It only comes to people's attention when the formal cloaks of the second and third ranks are being dyed, and even then it's only the leaves that are considered, so it can't be treated in any way as an interesting or wonderful tree, but it's deeply moving to be reminded of Hitomaro's poem – about how this tree becomes difficult to distinguish in the heaped snow that falls 'nowhere and everywhere', and the god Susanoo's sojourn in the land of Izumo.[4]

Whether it be plants, trees, birds or insects, I can never be insensible to anything that on some occasion or other I have heard about and remembered because it moved or fascinated me.

The leaves of the *yuzuriha* are glossy and hang in dense clusters, and it has very showy red stems, which make it rather vulgar but interesting. It's quite invisible for most of the year, but it's moving to consider how on the last day of the year it comes into its own, if it's true that its leaves are used for holding the food of the dead. On the other hand, it's apparently also used in serving the 'tooth-hardening' food of New Year, which prolongs life. And then there's the poem from who knows how long ago, 'when autumn reddens the *yuzuriha*',[5] which gives such a feeling of security.

The oak is a wonderful tree, and it's awe-inspiring to know that there's a god in it who protects its leaves. I find it fascinating that the various officers of the Gate Watch are given its name.[6]

It's nothing to look at, but the hemp-palm has a Chinese

feel that makes it look out of place in the gardens of common people.

[38] *Birds* – Although it comes from another land, the parrot is a very touching bird. It apparently mimics things people say. Then there's the *hototogisu*, the water-rail, the snipe, the oystercatcher, the siskin and the flycatcher.

The mountain dove is a very pure-hearted and touching bird – they say it can be comforted by showing it a mirror when it's longing for its mate. It's heart-breaking to imagine how they feel when they sleep separated for the night by a ravine.

The crane is a most ostentatious-looking bird, but there's a magnificence in the way its cry reaches the very heavens.[1]

The red-headed sparrow, the male grosbeak and the wren.

The heron looks quite horrible. The look in its eye is unpleasant, and indeed there's absolutely nothing lovable about it, but on the other hand it's charming to recall how they vie with each other 'and will not sleep alone'.[2]

Among the water birds, the mandarin duck is very touching in the way, for instance, the pair will change places on cold nights to brush the frost from each other's wings.[3] The plover too is a very interesting bird.

The *uguisu* is made out to be a wonderful bird in Chinese poetry, and both its voice and its appearance are really so enchanting that it's very unseemly of it not to sing inside the grounds of our 'nine-fold palace'.[4] People did tell me this was so but I couldn't believe it, yet during my ten years in the palace I did indeed never once hear it. This despite the fact that the palace is near bamboo groves and there are red plums, which would make it a fine place for an *uguisu* to come and go. Yet if you go out, you'll hear one singing fit to burst in a nondescript plum tree in some lowly garden. It doesn't sing at night, so it's obviously rather a sleepyhead, but there's no correcting this fault now, I'm afraid. In summer and right through to the end of autumn it maunders on and on in a wavery old voice,[5] and lower sorts of people change its name to 'flycatcher', which I find quite unfortunate and ludicrous. Though mind you, I probably wouldn't feel so outraged if it was some everyday bird like the sparrow. No doubt I feel this way because the *uguisu* is so well-loved for the fact that it sings in spring – after all, it appears in Japanese and Chinese poetry with the charming association of 'the changing of the year'. How delightful it would be if it only sang in spring. Yet surely, in the world of humans, no one goes out of their way to run down a person who hasn't really made it in the world, or whose reputation is already on the wane. And no one would pause to savour the sight or the sound of some boring bird such as a kite or a crow. So really, it's precisely because the *uguisu* is supposed to be such a marvellous bird that one's perversely more aware of its failings.

You've gone to watch the Return of the High Priestess after the Kamo Festival,[6] and when you draw up your carriage by Urin'in or Chisokuin Temples, you hear a *hototogisu* singing with all the irrepressible feeling of this special occasion – then lo and behold, from deep in the high trees an *uguisu* joins in, in beautifully skilful imitation. It's marvellous to hear them chorusing away together.

No words can suffice to express all the delights of the *hototogisu*. But though it will draw attention to itself by singing very self-importantly, it then has an annoying way of lurking deep among the leaves of a deutzia or orange tree and making itself virtually invisible.

You wake during the brief nights of the rainy season and lie there waiting, determined to be the first to hear the bird – then suddenly your heart is utterly transported with delight, as that dear, exquisite voice comes ringing through the darkness.

Everything that cries in the night is wonderful. With the exception, of course, of babies.

[39] *Refined and elegant things* – A girl's over-robe of white on white over pale violet-grey. The eggs of the spot-billed duck. Shaved ice with a sweet syrup, served in a shiny new metal bowl. A crystal rosary. Wisteria flowers. Snow on plum blossoms. An adorable little child eating strawberries.

[40] *Insects* – The bell cricket. The cicada. Butterflies. Crickets. Grasshoppers. Water-weed shrimps. Mayflies. Fireflies.

The bagworm is a very touching creature. It's a demon's child, and the mother fears it must have the same terrible nature as its parent, so she dresses it in ragged clothes and tells it to wait until she returns for it when the autumn wind blows. The poor little thing doesn't realize that its mother has deserted it, and when it hears the autumn winds begin in the eighth month, it sets up a pitiable little tremulous cry for her.[1]

The snap-beetle is also touching. Though it's a mere insect, it has apparently dedicated itself to the Buddhist Way, for it continually touches its forehead to the ground in prayer as it walks along. It's fascinating the way you find it wandering about in astonishingly dark places, making that clicking sound.

Nothing is more unlovely than a fly, and it properly belongs in the list of infuriating things. Flies aren't big enough to make them worth bothering to hate, but just the way they settle all over everything in autumn, and their damp little feet when they land on your face . . . And I hate the way the word is used in people's names.[2]

Summer insects[3] are quite enchanting things. I love the way they'll fly round above a book when you've drawn the lamp up close to look at some tale. Ants are rather horrible, but they're wonderfully light creatures, and it's intriguing to see one running about over the surface of the water.

[41]* *In the seventh month when the wind blows hard* and the rain is beating down, and your fan lies forgotten because of the sudden coolness in the air, it's delightful to take a midday nap snuggled up under a lightly padded kimono that gives off a faint whiff of perspiration.

[42]* *Unsuitable things* – Snow falling on the houses of the common people. Moonlight shining into such houses is also a great shame. So is meeting with a plain roofless ox cart on a moonlit night, or seeing a cart of this sort being drawn by an auburn-coloured ox.[1]

An ageing woman who is pregnant. It's disgusting when she has a young husband, and even worse when she's in a temper over his going off to another woman.

An old man who's nodding off, or a heavily bearded old fellow popping nuts into his mouth. A toothless crone screwing up her face as she eats sour plums.

A commoner wearing crimson skirted trousers.[2] These days you seem to see them wherever you look.

The sight of the Deputy of the Gate Watch on night patrol. It's also unpleasant to see him dressed in informal hunting costume. That official red cloak that so frightens people is a fearsomely pretentious thing. He's roundly despised, too, if anyone catches sight of him loitering near the ladies' quarters. 'There could be someone suspicious in here,' he blusters, as he steps inside and settles down. And the way he'll sling his skirted trousers over the room's incense-perfumed standing curtain is simply beyond belief.[3]

It looks terrible when a handsome nobleman is a Board of Censors Officer. It was most unfortunate, for example, when Captain Yorisada[4] held the position.

[43] *A lot of us are gathered in the Long Room*,[1] indulging in some rather rowdy chatter, when a fine-looking young fellow or a servant lad to the Palace Guard Captains comes by, carrying a handsome bundle or sack of clothes, with perhaps a trouser cord peeping out, or bow and arrow and lance for some ceremony. 'Who is it for?' we ask, and the nice ones will pause and sit briefly and announce the name before they go on their way, but I do hate it when someone puts on a snooty or embarrassed air and replies gruffly, 'I've no idea', or simply goes off without a word.

[44]* *No menial position could be finer* than that of the palace groundswomen. Of all the various types of maids, they are the most enviable – indeed I'd love to try giving girls of good birth a turn at the position. They're particularly impressive, of course, if they're young and pretty and take care to dress well, but those a little older, who know the ropes and go about their business in a straightforward manner, also look perfect in the role. Wouldn't it be fun to have a sweet-faced one of one's own, and send her out dressed up in finery appropriate to the

various occasions, with the latest in formal trains and Chinese jackets.

[45] *Among the serving men's positions*, the gentleman's escort guard is the finest. Even a thoroughly grand and distinguished-looking nobleman is nothing without his escort guard in tow. The post of Controller is generally considered a wonderful thing, but their formal train-robe is short and they have no escort guard, which greatly undermines the impressive effect.

[46]* *Secretary Controller Yukinari was standing by the lattice fence* in front of the west side of the Office of the Empress's Household, engaged in long conversation with one of the ladies within, so to tease him I butted in and demanded to know who was out there.

'It's only me, the Controller,' said he.

'And what might you be talking about in this intimate fashion?' I said. 'If the Major Controller happens along, she'll turn her attentions to him, you know.'

He had a good laugh at that. 'Now who's been telling you such things?' he said. 'As a matter of fact, I was just begging her to do no such thing.'

Yukinari doesn't put on airs or go out of his way to impress, so people take him simply at face value, but I know the deeper side of him. I've remarked to Her Majesty that he's somebody out of the ordinary, and she too is aware of this. He often quotes that old Chinese saying[1] to me: 'a woman will make her face up for the sake of one who loves her, while a man will die for the sake of one who understands him', which shows how well he knows me too.

He and I speak of each other as 'inseparable as the willow of Tōtōmi'.[2] Because he's plain-spoken, and doesn't mince his words in criticizing things, the younger ladies are very nasty about him. 'He's so horribly difficult to get on with,' they say. 'He doesn't sing songs or take pleasure in things the way other people do. He's such a bore!'

And indeed, Yukinari doesn't flirt with the ladies. 'Even if her eyes slope up and her eyebrows grow up her forehead and her nose spreads sideways, if she has a pretty mouth, and is nice and rounded under the chin and around the neck, and doesn't have a bad voice, I could love her. Though mind you, I do find a really horrible face depressing,' he says – so all the ladies with pointy chins or who are generally unlovely have turned against him quite ridiculously, and even speak ill of him to Her Majesty.

I was the first person he employed to take messages to Her Majesty, and whenever he wants to communicate with her he calls on me even now. If I'm in my room he will summon me, or come and see me, and if I'm back in my own home he'll send a letter, or even come himself.

'If you're returning to the palace late,' he says, 'just send a message relaying what I have to say.'

'You could have someone else at the palace pass it on,' I say to him, but he won't hear of it.

'They say that "in all you do it is wise to use what is to hand, and not revert to habit",' I jokingly admonish him.

He just replies, 'It's the way I am.' Then he adds, ' "The human heart can undergo no change." '

'Well, if that's the case,' say I wonderingly, 'what can it mean when they say "one should never hesitate to correct an error"?'[3]

He laughs heartily at this, and says, 'You know, people have been talking about how well we get on. Why be shy, when we can talk as familiarly as this together? Come on, do show me your face.'[4]

'But I'm terribly ugly,' I say, 'and you did say you couldn't love a really horrible face, so I can't possibly show it to you.'

'Yes, I see your point,' he says solemnly. 'Well, if that's the case, please don't show me.'

And indeed from then on, whenever he could naturally have caught a glimpse of me he would shield his face. So he really meant it, I thought, he wasn't putting it on!

Towards the end of the third month, it had become so warm that the thick winter cloaks were getting uncomfortable to wear, so men had taken to wearing only the formal cloak,[5] and some had pared down their formal wear to the minimal night-service wear. It was around this time that Shikibu and I happened to be sleeping in the little aisle near the Empress's chamber, when towards sunrise the inner door was slid open and out came Their Majesties together. We had no time to get up before they appeared, and scrambled to our knees in disarray, which amused them greatly. We managed to fling over us an odd combination of Chinese jacket over long girl's overrobe. They came across to the jumbled pile of nightclothes where we huddled, and peeped out to watch the comings and goings of the guardhouse outside. The senior courtiers were completely unaware of their presence, and a few came quite close and spoke to us.

'Don't give our presence away,' His Majesty whispered with a smile.

Finally they departed. 'Come along the two of you,' they said, but we declined, declaring that we must first make up our faces.

After they'd left, Shikibu and I were sitting discussing the splendid visit, when I caught a glimpse of a dark shape beside the southern door, in the gap where the edge of the blind was caught over the standing curtain's rail. I concluded it must be Noritaka,[6] and didn't bother to look further but simply went on chatting about this and that. Then a beaming face appeared around the curtain. Still I assumed it was Noritaka, but when I looked at last I saw that the face belonged to a different man. I burst into startled laughter, and he quickly drew the curtain over to hide his face, at which point I realized it was actually Secretary Controller Yukinari – the very man who'd been going out of his way not to see me all this time! I was most chagrined. Shikibu had been facing me with her back to him, so it was only my face he'd seen.

He then emerged from behind the curtain, announcing smugly, 'Now I've gazed to my heart's content.'

'I didn't take any notice because I thought you were Noritaka,' I said. 'Why have you been staring like this, when you said you wouldn't look at me?'

'They say it's rare to catch sight of a woman's face after sleep,' he replied, 'so I decided to peek into a lady's chamber, and then I came along here on the off chance that I'd manage

Standing curtains

to see you too. You didn't realize I'd been here since Their
Majesties were in the room, did you?' And with that he lifted
the blind and, well, it would seem that in he came . . .

[47] *Horses* – In horses, very black ones with just a little white
somewhere are special. Also those with chestnut markings,
speckled greys, strawberry roans with very white manes and
tails – the expression 'wand paper-white'[1] is indeed an appropriate one here.

Black horses with four white feet are also charming.

[48] *Oxen* – An ox should have a tiny splash of white on its
forehead, and the underbelly, legs and tail should all be white.

[49] *Cats* – Cats should be completely black except for the
belly, which should be very white.

[50] *Carriage runners*[1] *and escort guards* should be trim, slightly
on the thin side. This is how serving men in general ought to

be, especially when they're young. Very fat ones look as though they're half-asleep on their feet.

[51] *Page boys* – To be properly impressive and delightful, a page boy should be small, and have very neat hair, with a slight glint to it, and a crisp hairline. He should have a pretty voice, and speak decorously and politely.

[52] *Ox handlers*[1] – An ox handler should be big and well-built and clever-looking, with rather wild hair and a red face.

[53]* *The nightly roll call* of the senior courtiers is a very fine thing. I'm also intrigued by the fact that when the Chamberlain who gives the roll call is in attendance upon His Majesty, he calls the senior courtiers to him and performs it there rather than at the Privy Chamber, as is the normal custom. We ladies place ourselves at the eastern edge of Her Majesty's quarters and strain our ears to listen for the hammering footsteps of the men as they come tumbling out, and a lady will feel that familiar, sudden clutch of the heart as she hears the name of someone particularly dear to her. But imagine what thoughts go through her head when it's the name of a man who no longer bothers even to let her know he exists. It's fun the way we all discuss the men's voices, and pass judgement on how attractive or otherwise each one sounds.

When the senior courtiers' call is finished, the guards twang their bows and emerge with a great clattering of shoes to gather in the palace garden for their roll call. The Chamberlain stamps loudly on the wooden floor, then seats himself in what is called the 'raised-heels position' in the north-east corner by the railing, facing the Emperor with his back to the guards, and proceeds to cry 'Is so-and-so present?' It's wonderfully entertaining. Then they respond in their various voices, some strong and loud, others small. If a certain number aren't present, it's the rule not to perform a roll call. This is announced to the Emperor, and the custom is that the Chamberlain must inquire the reason, and when he's heard their explanation he then departs. But some of the nobles once pointed out to Masahiro[1] that he'd omitted to do this, and as a result he completely lost his temper and gave everyone a great tongue lashing, so that even the guards ended up laughing at him.

Masahiro once left his shoes on the ledge where the Emperor's food is placed.[2] There was a terrible fuss when they were found, and he innocently joined in the general excitement. The serving women and the others all went around exclaiming, 'Whose shoes can they possibly be?' Then Masahiro suddenly realized they were his, and caused a hilarious uproar by impulsively declaring, 'Good gracious, I do believe the filthy things are mine!'

[54] *It's disgusting when a well-bred young man* casually calls out the name of some low-ranking woman he's visiting, in a way that reveals his intimacy with her. It's much more impressive if he pretends not to have it quite right, even though in fact he knows her name perfectly well. If he's visiting the apartments of women in palace service, he should really enlist a groundsman to call her – though of course this is not a good idea at night – and if it's some other place then he should employ one of his retainers. After all, everyone will recognize him if it's his own voice.

However, there can be no objection if it's someone inconsequential, or a young girl.[1]

[55] *Young people and babies* should be plump. Provincial Governors and suchlike people who have some authority should also be on the portly side.

[56] *Little children* waving quaint toy bows or sticks about in play are wonderfully cute. It makes me want to stop the carriage and scoop them up and gaze my fill. And what a delightful whiff of incense from their clothes[1] lingers in the air as the carriage goes on its way again.

[57]* *The central gate of a grand house* lies open, and a new palm-leaf carriage, all fresh and shiny, with lovely, glowing maroon-coloured inner blinds, is parked there resting on its

shafts, creating a wonderful picture. The effect is beautifully enhanced by the sight of fifth- and sixth-ranking men milling about, the ends of their train-robes tucked up into their belts, some carrying their fans resting lightly on their fresh white batons, and escort guards, formally attired and equipped with ceremonial quivers, coming and going in the throng. It's also charming to see a pretty young serving girl emerge from the house and inquire whether Lord So-and-so's men are present.

[58] *Waterfalls* – Otonashi Falls. Furu Falls. It's moving to recall that the Cloistered Emperor once paid a visit there.[1]

Nachi Falls. I gather these are in Kumano.[2] I find the thought of them very moving.

Todoroki Falls. They must indeed thunder[3] quite fearfully.

[59] *Rivers* – Asuka River. It's moving to wonder how its deeps and shallows can shift as the poem says.[1]

Ōi River, Otonashi River, Nanase River. Mimito River – I enjoy wondering just what sound its quick ear caught.[2]

Tamahoshi River, Hosotani River.

Itsunuki River and Sawada River are reminiscent of old *saibara* songs.

Natori River – I'd like to know just what sort of 'name' it had.[3]

Yoshino River. The Plain of Amano River – I love that poem of Narihira's where he 'begs shelter from the Heavenly Weaving Maid'.[4]

[60] *I do wish men*, when they're taking their leave from a lady at dawn, wouldn't insist on adjusting their clothes to a nicety, or fussily tying their lacquered cap securely into place. After all, who would laugh at a man or criticize him if they happened to catch sight of him on his way home from an assignation in fearful disarray, with his cloak or hunting costume all awry?

One does want a lover's dawn departure to be tasteful. There he lies, reluctant to move, so that she has to press him to rise. 'Come on, it's past dawn,' she urges. 'How shocking you are!' and his sighs reassure her that he really hasn't yet had his fill of

'he draws her out to the double doors'

love, and is sunk in gloom at the thought that he must leave. He sits up, but rather than proceeding to put on his gathered trousers he instead snuggles up to her and whispers a few more words from the night's intimacies; then there's a bit more vague activity, and somehow in the process his belt turns out to have been tied. Now he raises the lattice shutter and draws her out with him to the double doors, where he finally slips away, leaving her with assurances that he'll spend the day longing for their next meeting. She sits there watching as his figure disappears, filled with delightful memories.

Then there's the man who suddenly remembers he has someone else to call on, leaps up briskly and starts flapping about getting himself ready to depart. There's a rustle and a swish as he fastens the waist-strings of his trousers, then he rolls up the sleeves of his cloak or hunting costume and thrusts his arms in, tugs the belt good and tight, and next there's the sound of him kneeling down and settling his lacquered cap on his head, with a sharp tug to the strings to tighten the knot firmly. He's left his fan and wad of folded paper by the pillow overnight, and naturally the paper's all got scattered so now he must conduct a search for it – but the darkness prevents him from seeing, so there he is, noisily patting around here and there on the floor, muttering 'Where is it? Where's it got to?' till at last he finds it all. Now he flips open the fan and flaps it boisterously, tucks the paper into the bosom of his clothes, and with a brief 'Well, I'll be off then', out he goes.

[61] *Bridges* – Asamutsu Bridge. Nagara Bridge. Amahiko Bridge. Hamana Bridge. Hitotsu Bridge. Utatane Bridge. The Ship Bridge of Sano. Horie Bridge. Kasasagi Bridge. Yamasuge Bridge. The Floating Bridge of Otsu. The One-Plank Bridge – the idea of it makes the heart shrink, but I like hearing its name.

[62]* *Villages* – Ōsaka. Nagame. Izame. Hitozuma. Tanome. Yūhi. Tsumatori – it's fun to wonder whether he's had his wife stolen or he's stolen someone else's.[1] Fushimi. Asagao.

[63]* *Plants* – Sweet flag. Water oat. The *aoi* is delightful. It's wonderful that it's been used as a sacred hair decoration since the age of the gods, and the appearance of the plant itself is charming too.

The water plantain has an interesting name.[1] I imagine a stuck-up person with her nose in the air.

The water burr and the beach radish. Moss. Herbs that sprout between drifts of snow. The rock ivy. The wood sorrel is lovely because of the woven-cloth patterns that are based on it.

Rootless plants – they are indeed precarious things, when you think how they grow right on the edges of cliffs. The *itsumade* creeper is also a precarious and touching thing, for it grows in places even more likely to crumble than a cliff edge.[2] It's disheartening to think that it probably wouldn't grow on a solid plastered wall.

The *kotonashi* plant is interesting because it suggests someone accomplishing something they decide to do.

The *shinobu* fern is very touching. I also like wayside grasses[3] and blady grass, and I particularly like wormwood. Mountain sedge, creeping fern, mountain indigo, beach mulberry, kudzu vine, bamboo grass, woody vine, shepherd's purse and rice seedlings. The *asaji* reed is also charming.

Lotus leaves are more marvellous than any other plant. The lotus is a symbol of the Buddhist truth – the flowers are used as offerings to the Buddha, and the seeds are strung into rosaries that have the power to help you attain paradise if you pray with them. It's also delightful to see its bright red flowers floating in a green pond at a season when other plants aren't flowering. You also find it described in a Chinese poem.[4]   The rose mallow – the way it bends to follow the sun makes one feel it has more intelligence than a mere plant. The *sashimo* wormwood. The leafy creeper. The dew plant – though I don't care for the way its colour fades so easily.[5]

[64] *Flowering plants* – The carnation pink. The one from China of course, but the native pink is also splendid. The yellow valerian and the balloon flower.

The morning glory. Pampas grass. Chrysanthemums. Wild violets. The gentian – the way it branches is unfortunate, but I love how it appears in its brilliant colour when all the other flowers have withered in the frost. Also the *kamatsuka*, though it doesn't look important enough to be worthy of particular attention, is very sweet. Its name is somehow unpleasant, however. It's written with characters meaning 'wild geese arriving'.[1]

The *kanihi* – the flower isn't very richly coloured, but I like the way it looks a lot like a wisteria flower, and blooms in both spring and autumn.

The bush clover – I love the sight of those graceful stems with their deeply coloured flowers, weighted with the dew, drooping so languidly in ample sprays. It also has a special feel to it because of the idea that the stag seeks it out.[2]

The double kerria.

The moonflower is similar to the morning glory, and when we speak of the two together[3] it suggests that the flower is indeed a charming one – but it's a great pity about the plant's long gourd pods. Why was it born like that, I wonder? If only they were more the size of a lanternflower's pods, at the very least. Still, the name itself is certainly lovely.

The *shimotsuke* rose. The flower of the water reed.

People complain that it's very odd not to include plume grass here.[4] It's plume grass that gives to all the autumn fields their particular loveliness. Can anything be more beautiful than those rusty red grass heads, so richly coloured, trailing low with the weight of the morning dew? But there's nothing worth looking at about them once autumn has ended. After the last of the profusion of colourful flowers has died and scattered, it continues to stand there, flimsily upright till the end of winter, swaying about in the wind, oblivious to the wild disarray of its white hair, for all the world like some aged crone still dreaming of her past glories. One can only feel touched by the sorrow of it, owing to this unfortunate image that it so brings to mind.

[65] *Poetic anthologies* – The *Manyōshū*. The *Kokinshū*.

[66]* *Topics of poetry* – The capital. The kudzu vine. The water burr. Horses. Hail.

[67] *Disturbing things* – The mother of a monk who's embarked on the twelve-year mountain retreat.[1]

The retainers who accompany their master on a visit to some unfamiliar place on a moonless night – to avoid being seen, they don't light a fire but just sit there in a row, waiting uneasily in the darkness for him to reappear.

You give a new servant, whom you don't really know and trust yet, some precious thing to take to someone, and then she's late returning.

A child who's still too young to talk throws his little head back and bursts into tears, and won't let anyone pick him up and comfort him.

[68] *Things that can't be compared* – Summer and winter. Night and day. Rainy days and sunny days. Laughter and anger. Old age and youth. White and black. People you love and those you hate. The man you love and the same man once you've lost all feeling for him seem like two completely different people. Fire and water. Fat people and thin people. People with long hair and those with short hair.

The noisy commotion when crows roosting together are

suddenly disturbed by something during the night. The way
they tumble off their perches, and flap awkwardly about from
branch to branch, squawking sleepily, makes them seem utterly
different from daytime crows.

[69] *Summer provides the most delightful setting* for a secret
assignation. The nights are so very short that dawn breaks
before you've slept. Everything has been left open all night, and
there's a lovely cool feel to the expansive view. The lovers still
have a little more they must say to each other. As they sit there
murmuring endearments, they're startled into a sudden panicky
sensation of exposure by the loud caw of a passing crow – a
delightful moment.

Another delightful moment is in winter, on a fiercely cold
night when you're lying there listening, snuggled far down
under the bedclothes, and the sound of a temple bell comes to
you, with such a deep and distant reverberation that it seems
to be emerging from somewhere buried. And the way a cock
will crow first with its beak still hidden under its wing, in a
muffled cry that sounds deep in the far distance, but with the
growing light its cry will seem to move closer – that's also
lovely.

[70] *A man comes calling*, perhaps for some intimate conversation, or maybe he's simply turned up when there's a large
gathering of ladies talking together behind the screens, so he
settles down and joins them. Time passes, and still he shows no
sign of going home. The man or youth who's accompanied him
peers anxiously in from time to time, muttering glumly, 'I'll be
waiting till the very axe rots[1] at this rate.' He heaves a great
yawn, and says aloud, apparently on the innocent assumption
that no one will overhear, 'Oh me, oh my, the sorrows and
sufferings I go through! Will the night never end?' This is bad
enough under normal circumstances, but of course it's quite
horrible when the gentleman is there to call on the woman he
loves. Not that you care one way or the other about this person
himself, but his words cast a sudden pall over your impression
of the gentleman who's seemed so engaging till now.

Attendants waiting by a lattice fence

Or perhaps, instead of coming out with it so blatantly, he'll merely produce loud sighs and groans, appealing to your sympathies on the 'stays seething deep below'[2] principle.

It's also horrible to overhear someone waiting beyond the lattice fence remark, 'It looks like rain.'

The attendants of the truly top people are not of this sort, and those of nobles and suchlike people are also quite good. But the men who accompany anyone below this level are all like this. People really should be careful to choose someone of good character from among their many retainers to accompany them.

[71] *Rare things* – A son-in-law who's praised by his wife's father. Likewise, a wife who's loved by her mother-in-law.

A pair of silver tweezers that can actually pull out hairs properly.

A retainer who doesn't speak ill of his master.

A person who is without a single quirk. Someone who's superior in both appearance and character, and who's remained utterly blameless throughout his long dealings with the world.

You never find an instance of two people living together who continue to be overawed by each other's excellence and always treat each other with scrupulous care and respect, so such a relationship is obviously a great rarity.

Copying out a tale or a volume of poems without smearing any ink on the book you're copying from. If you're copying it from some beautiful bound book, you try to take immense care, but somehow you always manage to get ink on it.

Two women, let alone a man and a woman, who vow themselves to each other forever, and actually manage to remain on good terms to the end.

[72]* *Our apartments in the Long Room* are a marvellous place. With the upper shutters raised, there's a good breeze, and it's wonderfully cool in summer. It's also delightful in winter when snow or hail comes blowing in. The rooms are small, and it's rather a problem when there are children around, but at least when they're ensconced behind a screen they can't laugh loudly and generally make a noise,[1] as they do in other rooms. I like the way we have to be constantly alert during the daytime, and we certainly can't relax at night either.

Among the continual sounds of people walking past all night, one person's footsteps halt, and as soon as she hears that single finger knocking she knows immediately who it is. He knocks for quite a long time, and there's not a sound from within, but at last it begins to gall her that he may by now be concluding she's gone to sleep, so she shifts slightly to let the rustle of clothes alert him. If it's winter she might give a light tap with the fire tongs, a secretive little sound to prevent drawing anyone else's attention, but when he goes right on knocking she finally says something – and often enough someone else has overheard, and comes slipping quietly over to listen.

It can also happen that, say, a number of voices are intoning Chinese or Japanese poetry. There's no knock, but when you open the door you discover a group of quite unexpected men hovering outside.[2] It's rather delightful if there's no room for them all to come in and sit, and they continue to stand around till dawn breaks. There's a brightly-coloured standing curtain, with the ladies' hems layered there on show beneath it, and there are young noblemen, cloaks gaping at the back,[3] and Chamberlains of the sixth rank in their special green. Unable to come and lean at the sliding door, they stand there with their backs to the wall, sleeves folded politely in front of them. It makes a most charming scene.

Another very lovely picture – seen from outside, a man dressed in richly-coloured gathered trousers and bright cloak, with multi-coloured layers of under-robes beautifully displayed, sits leaning half into the room, pressing in against the dividing blind. He draws towards him a beautiful inkstone and writes something, or borrows a mirror and adjusts his appearance. All of this is delightful to observe. Or again, a three-foot standing curtain has been set up inside the blind, but there's a small gap below the blind's lintel cloth and the top of the curtain, and it's pleasing to see how well their two faces are aligned as they talk to each other from their opposite sides, she sitting inside and he standing without.[4] If one of them were shorter or taller, there would no doubt be problems, but in most cases it seems to work out well.

These apartments are also a marvellous place at the time of the music and dance rehearsals in preparation for the Provisional Festival.[5] The officials from the Office of Grounds lead the way through the garden, chins well tucked in, holding aloft the long pine torches whose leaping flames threaten to brush things as they pass beneath them, while the musicians follow, playing wonderfully on their flutes, and it all strikes you as very special. The young nobles, in full civil dress for the occasion, pause and chat with the ladies, and the sound of their voices, together with the hushed cries as each one's attendant softly cries the way for his master, mingles with the music to produce a strange and most intriguing blend of sound.

We sit there with the shutters open waiting for them to return from their rehearsal, and now we hear the young nobles singing 'Oh let us pluck the rice flowers',[6] in rather finer form than before. Some dour-looking fellows bustle along straight past us. We all laugh, and someone says, 'Not so fast. As they say, "Why do you hasten thus to relinquish this night?"'[7] but they rush grimly on, almost falling over themselves to get away, as if they imagined someone was hot on their tail to seize them.

[73]* *When Her Majesty was in residence* in the Office of the Empress's Household, we all found the view of the garden grove, sunk in its aura of depth and antiquity, and the rather intimidating towering roofs, wonderfully impressive. The Inner Chamber was said to be haunted, so a room was set up on the south side and Her Majesty was ensconced there with her curtained dais, while we ladies waited on her from the secondary aisle room. It was always a great event to hear the senior courtiers and nobles coming past us with their criers, on their way from the Palace Guards gate to the Left Gate Watch Office – the cries for the senior courtiers were much shorter, so we took to referring to them as 'the greater cries and the lesser cries'. Because we heard them so often we got to know the individual voices, and we had fun picking them out. 'That's so-and-so,' we'd say, and then someone else might say, 'No it isn't', so we'd send a servant to check, and if we were right we'd cry, 'I told you so!'

One moonlit dawn of thick mist, some of us ladies went out walking in the garden. Her Majesty heard us and rose too, and then all the ladies came out with her, and the dawn brightened around us as we wandered the garden together. 'Let's go and see the Gate Watch Office!' I suggested, and others enthusiastically joined me, but when we set off we suddenly heard the voices of a large number of senior courtiers chanting that Chinese poem about the voice of autumn[1] – so we rushed back and hurried inside, and conversed with them from there. Several were impressed that we'd been moon-viewing, and set about composing poems for the occasion.

Indeed, visits from senior courtiers never ceased day or night there. Even the young nobles would make a point of dropping by whenever they were at court and had no particular business to attend to.

[74] *Things later regretted* – Someone takes it into her head that she wants to serve at court, then once she's there, does nothing but grumble and mope.

An adopted child who turns out to have an ugly face.

Against his will, the parents bring a reluctant young man in as son-in-law – then they complain because he doesn't live up to expectations.

[75] *Things that look enjoyable* – The 'hare-wand priest'.[1]

The conductor of the sacred *kagura* music.

The person who carries the thing like a banner in the *kagura* procession.[2]

[76]* *The day after the Litany of Buddha Names*, the hell-painting screens are taken to the Empress's quarters, and His Majesty gives her a viewing of them. They are truly the most ghastly things. On this particular occasion, Her Majesty kept urging us to look but I simply couldn't bear to – sheer horror overcame me, and I curled up and hid in a small room nearby.

It was raining hard that day, and time hung heavy on everyone's hands, so His Majesty summoned some of the senior courtiers to the Empress's quarters for a musical entertainment. Junior Counsellor Michitaka was wonderful on the *biwa*. Narimasa on the thirteen-stringed *koto*, Yukiyoshi on the flute and Captain Tsunefusa on the *shō*, played charmingly too.

When they had performed a piece, and the *biwa* had ceased to play, Grand Counsellor Korechika recited,

'The sound of the *biwa* ceased, yet still she would not speak.'[1]

At this, I emerged from my hiding place, and everyone laughed and declared, 'Sin and hellfire may scare her, but she can't resist delights such as these!'

[77]* *When Secretary Captain Tadanobu* heard certain baseless and ridiculous rumours that were circulating concerning me, he set about abusing my name quite horribly. I heard that he'd been saying in the Privy Chamber that he wondered how he could ever have regarded me as a decent person. I was very distressed and ashamed, but I laughed it off, saying, 'It would be a different matter if all this were actually true, but as things

stand he's bound to learn the truth sooner or later and change his mind.'

Not long after this, however, Tadanobu happened to hear my voice as he was passing the Black Door, and he shielded his face with his sleeve and wouldn't so much as glance in my direction. Oh how he hated me. So I in turn chose never to look his way and simply to remain silent, and thus things continued till the end of the second month.

It was pouring with rain, and we were all bored. Tadanobu, who was secluded in the palace as part of an imperial abstinence,[1] apparently declared, 'I must admit it's a shame that things are so frosty between her and me. I think I'll say something to her.'

This was reported to me, but all I replied was, 'I'll believe it when I see it!' I spent the day in my room, and when I went to Her Majesty's apartments that night, she had already retired.

The gentlewomen were gathered in the room beyond the threshold, where they had drawn up a lamp and were playing a writing game.[2] 'Oh good!' they cried when they saw me. 'Come and join us!' – but I just wasn't in the mood, and it seemed a bit pointless to have come. I sat down by the square brazier, but they all gathered round and began chatting.

Then suddenly a maid appeared, and loudly announced the arrival of a messenger for me.

'That's odd. What messenger can this be, arriving out of the blue like this?' I wondered, and sent to inquire. It turned out to be one of the groundsmen, who insisted that he was instructed to give the message to me personally, so out I went. 'The Secretary Captain asks that you be given this,' he said, handing me a letter. 'Please be quick to reply.'

'Considering how he hates me, I wonder what he can have written?' I thought, but it wouldn't do to look right away, so I told the man to be off and that I would send a reply later, and I tucked the letter away and went back inside.

But as I sat listening to the ongoing conversation, back he came. 'The Secretary Captain has said that if there's no reply I'm to bring back his letter. Do be quick,' said he.

This is just like something out of one of the old tales, I thought wryly. I looked at the letter, and found it to be written very beautifully, on thin blue paper. There was nothing in it to justify my nervousness. He had written the line from Bo Juyi,[3] 'You are there in the flowering capital, beneath the Council Chamber's brocade curtains', and added, 'How should it end, tell me?'

'What on earth shall I do?' I wondered. 'If Her Majesty were here I'd most certainly show this to her. It would look bad to parade the fact that I know the next line by writing it in my poor Chinese characters.'

I barely had time to turn the problem over in my mind before the messenger was distracting me again with his urgings to be quick, so I seized a piece of dead charcoal from the brazier and simply wrote at the end of his letter, in Japanese script,

> Who will come visiting this grass-thatched hut?

The messenger duly carried it off, but there was no response.

We all went to bed, and the first thing next morning I went back to my room. Not long after I arrived, the Minamoto Captain[4] was heard crying in grandiose tones, 'Is "Grass-thatched Hut" present?'

'How extraordinary,' I said. 'Why should you think anyone with such a depressing name might be here? Now if you'd asked for "Jewelled Palace",[5] you might have got an answer.'

'Ah good. So you were in your room after all,' he said. 'I was just going to go to ask after you at Her Majesty's quarters', and he proceeded to relay to me the events of the previous evening, becoming increasingly shamefaced as the story progressed. 'A number of smart young fellows, including the sixth-rank Chamberlains, got together in Tadanobu's night-watch room last night, and there was all manner of discussion and reminiscence about various people. In the midst of this, Tadanobu admitted that since he and you had broken off all relations he just hadn't felt right about it. "I've been waiting vainly in hopes that she might send word of some sort," he said, "and I just hate the way she seems to shrug the whole thing off without a thought, and simply ignores me. Why don't we test her once and for all tonight?"

'So everyone put their heads together and sent along that message, and when the messenger came back announcing that you'd gone inside saying you weren't going to read it just yet, Tadanobu sent the man back with a flea in his ear. "Tie her down and don't let her get out of it this time," he ordered, "and if she doesn't produce something then bring back the original letter", and off he had to go again, at the height of the downpour. No sooner had he gone than he was back again. "Here you are," says he, and hands over the message. Tadanobu saw it was his own letter. "So she sent it back!" he said, but as he spoke he looked more closely, and the next instant he cried, "Oh! How extraordinary! Whatever's this?" Everyone gathered round to look, and made a great fuss. "What a clever rogue she is!" we said. "No, you really can't give her up."

'We then set about trying to add the first three lines of your poem, everyone urging me to take on the challenge, and we racked our brains over the task till it grew so late we finally had to give up. We decided it would make a fine tale for future telling, at any rate,' he concluded. 'Your name has now become "Grass-thatched Hut",' he added, and off he hastened.

I was just remarking how awful it was to think of going down in history with such a dreadful name attached to me, when Assistant to Palace Repairs Norimitsu arrived. 'I've just been looking for you at Her Majesty's quarters, to express my heart-felt joy at the wonderful news!' he declared breathlessly.

'What news is this?' I said. 'I haven't heard of any new appointments being announced. What post have you been given?'

'No no, I could barely wait till morning to come and congratulate you on the wonderful thing that happened last night. There couldn't be a greater honour!' Then he proceeded to tell me the same story all over again from the beginning. 'Tadanobu said that he was prepared to dismiss all thought of you from his mind, depending on your response. Everyone got together and came up with something to send you, and actually it was a very good thing that the messenger came back empty-handed the first time. When he did bring the message back, I was in a sweat to know what it was, since it struck me that if your response wasn't up to par that would reflect badly on me as "elder brother" as well. But of course it was anything but, in fact it was excellent, and everyone was full of praise. "Come over here, brother," they urged. "Come and hear this!"

'I was privately thrilled, but I only protested, "I'm in no position to appreciate these poetic refinements,[6] you know."

'"You don't need to tell us what you think, or even make sense of it," they insisted. "It's just so that you can spread the word about it."

'This was rather mortifying for your poor brother, of course, but I finally joined in, and we were at it long into the night, lamenting how impossible it was to find a way to complete the poem. "Actually, there's no particular reason why we should reply in this fashion, you know," some began to claim after a while, and everyone agreed that it would look very bad if we sent something unimpressive, so it all petered out in defeat.

'This is a most wonderful thing for us both, don't you think? Far more cause for celebration than receiving some trifling post in the new Appointments List!'

When I contemplated how innocent I'd been of this full-scale involvement in the plot, it made me nervous all over again to think how easily I could have disgraced myself. And I hadn't realized that this 'sister–brother' relationship was known to even the Emperor, and that the senior courtiers would call him this rather than refer to him by his post!

While we were talking, a message came from Her Majesty summoning me immediately, so I went and presented myself. She too wanted to talk about the incident. It seems His Majesty had laughed about it and told her the story. 'All the gentlemen have written your reply on their fans,' she informed me. I was amazed, and could only wonder what had possessed me to make me produce such a brilliant response.

Anyway, after that Tadanobu no longer raised that shielding sleeve when we met, and seems to have quite changed his mind about me.

[78]* *The following year, towards the end of the second month*, Her Majesty moved to the Office of the Empress's Household. I didn't accompany her on the move, but stayed behind

temporarily in the Mumetsubo.[1] The next day, there was a
letter from Secretary Captain Tadanobu. 'I made a pilgrimage
to Kurama last night,' it read, 'but owing to a directional taboo
this evening,[2] I'm returning by a different route. I should be
back before daybreak, and I have something I must say to you,
so please be ready to let me in and don't make me keep knocking
when I arrive.' However, the Mistress of the Imperial Wardrobe
sent to inquire why I was staying alone in my room like this,
and asked me to come and sleep there, so that is where I spent
the night.[3]

When I returned to my own room, after a lengthy sleep, the
maid told me that there'd been a tremendous knocking the
night before. 'I finally got up and answered it,' she went on, 'and
he said, "So she's with Her Ladyship, is she? Well, please pass on
my message." However, I informed him that there was no point
since you certainly wouldn't get up, and went back to bed.'

I found her stupidity and inconsiderateness most annoying,
but no sooner had she told me her tale than someone from
the Office of Grounds arrived with another message from the
Secretary Captain, saying he had to leave at once, but first he
had something he must tell me. I sent the man off with the
message that I had matters to see to at Her Ladyship's, and I
would meet him there. I was worried that if he came to my
apartment he'd open the door, so I went to a room off the
eastern aisle of the Mumetsubo and raised the half-panel
shutter, instructing him to come there.

Along he duly came, looking magnificent. He wore a
gorgeous damask cloak in the cherry-blossom combination,
with an immaculate lustre to its inner lining, and his gathered
trousers of rich, dark grape colour were woven through with a
dazzling pattern of tangled wisteria vine. The scarlet colour and
glossed silk effect of the inner robe positively shone, and layer
upon layer of very pale violet-grey and other colours were
visible beneath the cloak. The way he seated himself on the
narrow veranda, with one foot hanging from its edge as he
leaned in slightly towards the blind, made him look the absolute
epitome of some splendid figure in a picture, or in the sort of
marvellous scene you find described in a romance.

The plum trees before the Mumetsubo, white on the west side and red on the east, were just beginning to shed their blossoms, but they were still lovely, and what with all this and the glorious soft sunlight that lit the scene, I longed for someone to witness it.

It would have been rather more impressive, however, if the lady inside the screen making her replies to the gentleman beyond had been a young girl, her hair beautifully smooth and flowing luxuriantly down all about her, the way they describe it in the tales. But alas, I was an ageing woman well past her prime, hair not even my own,[4] and frizzled and coming adrift here and there, in mourning clothes that were a far cry from the usual lovely colours, a light grey so pale it was as good as colourless, over various indistinguishable layers, all utterly drab and unflattering. What's more, as Her Majesty was not present I was only in simple court robes, without even a formal train. It all rather ruined the elegance of the scene.

'I'm on my way to the Office of the Empress's Household,' he said. 'Do you have any message? When will you be going there?' and so on; and then he laughingly proceeded to tell me how last night before daybreak he'd come to call on his way back from the west of the city in the bright moonlight, certain I'd be waiting for him whatever the time, since he'd told me he was coming, but when he knocked at my room the maid finally appeared bleary-eyed and gave him a disconcertingly curt response. 'I was thoroughly put off,' he went on. 'Whatever induced you to leave such a person there to deal with me?' I could well imagine his feelings, and I felt both sorry for him and entertained by the story.

After a little time, he left. Anyone looking in and seeing him there would have wondered just who might be the fair maiden inside who was engaging his attention, while if they'd observed the scene from behind me they'd never have imagined from my appearance that the man beyond the blinds could be so splendid.

When it grew dark, I went to attend Her Majesty. There were a great many gentlewomen gathered around her, including some from His Majesty's entourage, and everyone was arguing

over what they did and didn't like about various tales, weighing them up and criticizing their weaknesses. Her Majesty also
joined in, giving her own opinion on the relative merits of the
two heroes Suzushi and Nakatada.

The ladies turned to me when I arrived. 'What do you think?'
they cried. 'Give us a quick answer. Her Majesty is making a
strong case against Nakatada's humble upbringing.'

'Dear me no,' I replied. 'I admit Suzushi played the *kin*
brilliantly enough to bring a heavenly being down to listen, but
he was incredibly dull. And was he the one who gained the
hand of the Emperor's daughter?'[5]

'There you are!' cried the Nakatada supporters, happy to
discover their side was strengthened.

'But no more of this talk of the men in the old tales,' said
Her Majesty. 'If only you'd seen Tadanobu when he came
today, I imagine you would have been beside yourself over how
splendid he looked.'

'Yes, it's quite true,' several ladies chimed in. 'He really did
look even more marvellous than usual.'

'Actually,' I said, 'that is precisely what I came to tell you
about, Your Majesty, but this talk of tales distracted me.' And
I proceeded to describe what had happened.

'Well, we all saw him,' they said, laughing, 'but who else
took in such detail, down to the very threads and stitches?'
Then they all went on chattering about the things he'd said.
'He told us what a marvellously desolate place the west of the
city was, the garden walls all old and moss-covered, and how
he found himself wishing he had a companion to savour it
with him. Then Saishō cleverly inquired, "And were 'the tiles
pine-smothered'?" and he was most impressed, and replied by
intoning, "Though it lies some little distance from the city's
western gate."'[6] It was great fun to hear them so full of talk of
him.

[79] *When one's returned home on a visit* and a senior courtier
or someone of the sort comes to call, it would seem that there's
gossip and criticism. I don't let this annoy me, since after all
I'm not exactly renowned for my modesty and prudence. And

anyway, how am I simply to announce that I'm not at home to people who come calling day or night, and send them away again shamefaced? People will come visiting, even if they really aren't so very intimate with you. Anyway, on this occasion, because of all the fuss I decided not to let it be generally known where I was, and only told a few people such as Captain of the Left Tsunefusa and Narimasa.

Officer of the Left Gate Watch Norimitsu came visiting, and in the course of our talk he told me that the day before, the Captain Consultant[1] had doggedly questioned him about where I was hiding. 'Surely you must know where your own "sister" is. Tell me!' he'd apparently demanded, and when Norimitsu insisted that he had no idea, the Captain Consultant had actively tried to pressure him into confessing. 'I felt terrible having to assert something that wasn't true,' he said to me. 'I could barely suppress a smile. Tsunefusa was sitting there looking all innocence, and I was terrified that I'd burst out laughing if our gaze met even for an instant, so I tried to cover the moment by seizing some seaweed from a nearby table and desperately chewing away at it. People must have found it rather odd to see me suddenly devouring this stuff for no apparent reason. But anyway, thanks to that seaweed I cleverly avoided letting the cat out of the bag. If I'd laughed it would have ruined everything. I did enjoy the way he really seemed to believe I had no idea where you were.'

'Well, do be sure you don't tell him,' I said when I heard this, and so the days passed without his calling.

Very late one night, there was a fierce drumming on the gate. 'What's this?' I thought when I heard it. 'Why beat on the gate so loudly in this inconsiderate fashion, though it's quite close enough to hear a normal knock?' When I sent to inquire, I learned it was one of the guards. He had brought a letter, and said he'd come from Officer Norimitsu.

Everyone was asleep, so I drew up a lamp and read it. 'Tomorrow is the final day of the Great Sutra Readings, so the Captain Consultant is confined to the palace for the imperial abstinence. He is most persistent in begging me to tell him your whereabouts, and I am at my wit's end. I really cannot keep the information from him any longer. Should I tell him? What do you think? I will follow your advice.'

I wrote no reply, but simply wrapped a small piece of seaweed in a sheet of paper and sent it.

Norimitsu came later. 'The Captain Consultant spent the night berating me,' he said, 'and dragging me about to all sorts of impossible places. He really did give me a tongue-lashing. I had a terrible time of it. Look, why on earth didn't you tell me what to do? You only sent some ridiculous piece of seaweed wrapped in paper. What an extraordinary thing to receive! Who would send such a crazy packet to anyone? There must have been some mistake.'

The man is quite clueless! I thought. I was so disgusted I simply couldn't bear the sight of him. I said nothing, and only wrote on the edge of a piece of paper that happened to be by the inkstone:

> The silent seaweed
> said that you must never tell
> the secret dwelling place
> of the diving fisher girl
> concealed in these hidden depths.[2]

and passed this to him.

'Dear me, have you written a poem? I refuse to read it!' he exclaimed, and he flipped it back to me with his fan and fled.

And so it was that this relationship, once so close and mutually supportive, for no real reason began to turn a little sour. Then a letter came from him. 'Though things may have gone wrong between us, still I would wish that you remember the loving vows we made, and when we meet out in the world that you would look on me as one who has been your brother.'

Norimitsu often used to say, 'If a woman chooses to love me, she should never press poems on me. Any woman who does this is no friend of mine. The day you decide you've had enough and you want to break off relations is the day you should send me a poem.'

So in reply to his message, I sent this poem.

> Brother and Sister Hills
> have crumbled, and between them
> Yoshino River flows no more –
> so I can no longer see you
> even as 'he that used to be'.[3]

Whether he read it or not I do not know, but no reply ever came.

Later, Norimitsu was promoted to Deputy Governor of Tōtōmi,[4] and the relationship ended in hostility.

[80] *Things that create the appearance of deep emotion* – The sound of your voice when you're constantly blowing your runny nose as you talk.

Plucking your eyebrows.

[81]* *After our visit to the Guard Office*, I went back to my home, and had spent some time there when a letter came informing me that Her Majesty wished me to come at once. At the edge of the page, the writer[1] had added a personal message from Her Majesty which said, 'I can't get out of my mind the image of you ahead of me when we went to the Guard Office that night. Whatever made you set off so nonchalantly in that old-fashioned get-up? No doubt you thought you looked wonderful.'

I replied with a humble acknowledgement of Her Majesty's summons, and added the private message, 'How could I not think I looked wonderful? Why, it seemed to me that even Her Majesty saw me as "a heavenly maiden hovering".'

No sooner was this sent than back came the reply. 'Her Majesty wonders how you could damage your darling Naka-tada's reputation[2] like that? You must lay everything aside and come at once. If you don't, she will absolutely hate you.'

'Any hatred at all would be bad enough,' I replied, 'but with that word "absolutely" I am prepared to sacrifice life and limb to do as commanded', and I went back to the court.

[82]* *Once when Her Majesty was in residence* in the Office of
the Empress's Household, a Continuous Sutra Reading[1] took
place in the western aisle. A scroll of the Buddha's image was
set up, and of course the monks were seated as usual.

Two days into the ceremony, we heard below the veranda
a queer voice saying, 'Would there be any distribution of
the offerings[2] for me?' and a monk was heard to reply,
'Come come, what can you be thinking? The ceremony's not
over yet.'

Wondering who this person was, I went over to have a look,
and discovered the voice belonged to a nun well past her prime,
dressed in horribly grimy clothes and looking like a little
monkey.

'What is it she wants?' I asked.

At this, she replied herself in a carefully affected tone, 'I am
a disciple of the Buddha, come to ask for the altar offerings,
and these monks are refusing to give them to me.'

Her voice was remarkably bright and elegant for a beggar.
What a pity someone like her should have sunk to this, I
thought, yet at the same time I couldn't help feeling there was
something unpleasantly pretentious and flamboyant about her,
given her circumstances.

'So altar offerings are the only thing you'll eat, are they? This
is wonderfully pious of you,' I remarked.

She was reading me carefully. 'No one's saying I won't eat
other things,' she said slyly. 'It's because there's nothing else
that I'm asking for offerings.'

I put together some snacks and rice cakes and gave the bundle
to her, whereupon she became extremely friendly, and began
to chatter about all manner of things.

Some young gentlewomen then came out, and all set
about questioning the woman about where she lived, and
whether she had a man, and children. She produced such
entertaining replies, elaborating them with jokes and suchlike, that everyone kept drawing her out with endless questions,
such as whether she sang and danced, until she set about
singing,

'Who oh who shall I sleep with tonight?
I think I'll sleep with "Hitachi no Suke"
for I love the silk touch of her skin in bed . . .'

with much more besides. She also sang,

'The peak of Man Mountain stands proud in fame.
Its scarlet tip has quite a name!'²

waving her head about as she sang in a manner that was utterly grotesque. The ladies all laughed in disgust and cried, 'Away with you! Away with you!'

'Poor thing,' I said. 'What shall we give her?'

At this point Her Majesty intervened. 'You've been making the woman act in a way that I've really found very difficult to have to overhear. I simply had to block my ears. Give her this gown⁴ and send her on her way immediately.'

'Here's a generous gift from Her Majesty. Your own gown's filthy, so make yourself nice and clean with this one,' we said, and tossed the gown to her. She abased herself in thanks, and then lo and behold she proceeded to drape the gown over her shoulder and perform a dance!⁵ She really was disgusting, so we all withdrew inside again and left her to it.

This apparently gave her a taste for visiting, because after this she was often to be seen wandering about drawing attention to herself. We took to calling her 'Hitachi no Suke', after her song. Far from wearing the nice clean gown, she still went about in her filthy one, which made us wonder with considerable annoyance what she'd done with the one we gave her.

One day Ukon paid us a visit, and Her Majesty told her about the woman. 'They have tamed her and more or less installed her. She's always coming around now,' she said, and she had Kohyōe take up the tale and give an imitation of Hitachi no Suke.

'I'd love to see her,' said Ukon, laughing. 'Do show her to me. You all seem to be great fans of hers. I promise I won't entice her away from you.'

A little later, another much more refined beggar nun turned

up at the palace. We called her over and questioned her in the same way, and were touched by how shamefaced and piteous she was. Her Majesty gave her a gown, and she abased herself in thanks and retreated, overcome with tears of joy. This was all very well, but Hitachi no Suke happened to come along and catch sight of her as she was leaving. After that, Hitachi no Suke didn't show up again for a long time, and none of us would have given her a second thought I'm sure.

Towards the middle of the twelfth month there was a great fall of snow. The maids collected a large mound of it on the veranda, so then we ladies decided we should have a real snow mountain built out in the garden. We summoned the servants and set them all to work under Her Majesty's orders. The groundsmen who had come in to clean got involved as well, and together they all set about creating an absolutely towering snow mountain. Some of the senior officials from the Empress's Office also gathered to give advice and enjoy the scene. The original three or four groundsmen had soon swelled to around twenty. Her Majesty even sent to ask the servants who were at home to come and help, informing them that everyone involved would receive three days' extra pay, and the same amount would be deducted from all those who didn't come; some who heard this came running hastily to join in, though the message couldn't reach those whose homes were more distant.

When the construction was finally completed, the officials from the Empress's Office were summoned and each was given two large bundles of silk rolls. These they spread out on the veranda, and everyone in turn came and took a roll, bowed and tucked it into his belt, and retired. The senior courtiers, who were dressed in informal hunting costume for the job instead of their usual formal cloaks, remained behind.

'How long do you think it will last?' Her Majesty asked everyone. One guessed ten days, another suggested a little longer. Everyone gave opinions ranging over a week or two.

'What do you think?' Her Majesty then asked me.

'I think it will stay there until beyond the tenth day of the first month,' I replied.

Even Her Majesty thought this highly unlikely, and all the ladies were unanimous in declaring that it couldn't last beyond the end of the year at the very latest.

'Oh dear,' I thought privately, 'I've probably overestimated. I suppose it can't really last as long as that. I should have said something like the first day of the new year instead' – but I decided that even if I turned out to be wrong, I should stand by what I said, and I stubbornly continued to argue my case.

On the twentieth day it rained, but there was no sign of the snow mountain melting away. All that happened was that it lost a little of its height. I was beside myself with fervent prayers to the Kannon of White Mountain[6] to preserve it from melting.

On the day when the snow mountain was made, the Aide of Ceremonial Tadataka came to call. I put out a cushion for him, and during our talk he remarked, 'You know, there's not a place in the palace that hasn't built a snow mountain today. His Majesty has ordered one made in his garden, and they're busy making them in the Crown Prince's residence and in the Kōkiden and Kyōgokudono[7] as well.'

I then had someone nearby convey to him the following poem.

> Our singular snow mountain
> we thought was so uniquely ours
> has multiplied abroad
> and become merely commonplace
> as the common snow that falls.

He sat tilting his head admiringly over it for a while, then he finally said, 'It would be merely flippant of me to attempt to sully this marvellous poem with one in response. I shall simply tell the tale of it to everyone when we're gathered before His Majesty', and he rose and departed. I must say this diffidence struck me as rather odd, in someone with his reputation for being a great poetry-lover.

When I told Her Majesty, she remarked, 'He must certainly have been deeply impressed with it.'

As the month drew to a close, the snow mountain seemed to have shrunk a little, but it still remained very high. One day around midday we'd gone out to sit on the veranda, when Hitachi no Suke suddenly appeared again.

'Why are you back?' we asked. 'We haven't seen you here for ages.'

'Well, the fact is I met with a misfortune,' she replied.

'What was it?' we asked.

'I shall tell you my thoughts at the time in question,' she said, and then she proceeded to recite, in ponderously drawn-out tones,

> 'Alas I am awash
> with envy at the gifts whose burden
> weights her till she limps –
> who is that "deep-sea fisher girl"
> to whom so many things are given?'[8]

and with that she gave a nasty laugh. When no one deigned to look in her direction, she clambered on to the snow mountain and walked about for some time before she finally left.

After she had gone we sent word to Ukon telling her what had happened, and she made us laugh all over again when she replied, 'Why didn't you get someone to accompany her and bring her over here? What a shame! She must have climbed the snow mountain and walked round like that because you were ignoring her.'

The year ended without any change to our snow mountain. On the night of the first day of the new year, there was a great fall of snow.

Excellent! I thought. There'll be a fresh pile of snow for the mountain – but then Her Majesty decided that this wasn't fair. 'We must brush off the new snow and leave the original heap as it was,' she declared.

Next morning when I went to my room very early, the chief retainer of the Office of the Empress's Household arrived, shivering with cold. On the sleeve of his night-watch cloak, which was a deep, almost citron-leaf green, he held something wrapped in green paper, attached to a sprig of pine needles.

'Who is this from?' I inquired, and when he replied that it

came from the Kamo High Priestess, I was filled with sudden delighted awe, and took it and carried it straight back to Her Majesty.

Her Majesty was still asleep when I arrived, and in order to get in I tugged a go-board table over to the lattice shutter facing her curtained dais, and stood on it while I struggled to raise the shutter. It was extremely heavy, and because I was only lifting one end of it, it grated against the next one, which woke Her Majesty.

'Why on earth are you doing that?' she inquired.

'A message from the Kamo High Priestess has arrived,' I replied. 'I simply had to get the shutter open so you would have it as early as possible.'

'Well, this certainly is early,' she said, getting up. She opened the package, and found two hare-mallets, the heads wrapped in imitation of hare-wands, decorated prettily with sprigs of mountain orange, creeping fern and mountain sedge. But there was no letter.

'I can't believe there would be no message,' said Her Majesty, searching, and then she discovered on one of the little pieces of paper that wrapped the mallet heads the following poem.

> When I went searching
> the mountain for the echoing ring
> of the woodsman's axe
> I found the tree he cut was for
> the festive hare-wands of this day.[9]

A delightful poem, and delightful too was the scene of Her Majesty composing her reply. In all her letters and replies to the High Priestess, you could see just how much trouble she took from the number of problems she had with her writing. To the man who had brought the message she gave a white-weave shift, and another of maroon which was I think in the plum combination, and it was lovely to see him making his way back through the snowy landscape with the robes over his shoulder. It's only a pity that I never discovered what Her Majesty wrote in reply.

As for the snow mountain, it showed no sign of melting away but continued to stand there, just as if it really was Koshi's famous snowy mountain.[10] It now looked quite black with dirt, and was not a sight to please the eye, but I nevertheless felt elated at the thought of being proved right, and prayed that it could somehow be made to survive until the middle of the month. Everyone declared that it couldn't last beyond the end of the first week, and we were all waiting anxiously to witness the final outcome, when it was suddenly decided on the third day that Her Majesty would return to the imperial palace. I was terribly disappointed at the thought that I'd have to leave without ever knowing the moment of my mountain's final end, and others also said it was a great shame to have to leave now. Her Majesty agreed, and indeed I'd very much wanted her to witness that my guess had been right. But we had to leave and that was that.

There was great upheaval for the move, with Her Majesty's effects and all the other things being carried out, and in the midst of this I managed to call over to the veranda one of the gardeners who was living under a lean-to roof he had set up against the garden wall, and have a confidential word with him. 'You must take great care of this snow mountain, and make sure no children climb on it and destroy it. Keep a firm watch on it until the fifteenth. If it lasts till then, Her Majesty intends to reward you with a special gift, and you'll get high praise from me personally as well,' I said, and to persuade him further I heaped on him various leftovers, fruit and so on, though this would have enraged the kitchen maids and servants, who disliked him.

All this made him beam with pleasure. 'That's very easily done,' he assured me. 'I'll guard it carefully. The children will be sure to try and climb it.'

'You must forbid it,' I warned him, 'and if there's anyone who won't obey then let me know.'

I accompanied Her Majesty on her move to the palace, and stayed there until the seventh day, when I went home.

I was so anxious about my snow mountain while I was at the palace that I was constantly sending servants of various sorts, from the toilet cleaner to the head housekeeper, to keep the gardener up to the mark. On the seventh day I even sent along some of the leftovers from the Festival of Young Herbs feast, and everyone laughed at the tale of how reverently he'd received them.

Once I was back home the snow mountain continued to obsess me, and the first thing I did every morning was send someone over, just to keep him reminded of how very important it was. On the tenth day I was delighted to hear that enough still remained to last until the fifteenth. Day and night my constant stream of messengers continued, but then on the night of the thirteenth[11] there was a terrific downpour of rain. I was beside myself, convinced that this would finally finish off my mountain. All that night I stayed up, lamenting that it couldn't possibly last another day or two. Those around me laughed and declared that I really had lost my mind. When one of our party left I leapt up and tried to rouse the servants, and flew into a rage when they refused to get up, but finally one emerged and I sent her off to bring a report.

'It's down to the size of a round cushion,' she reported. 'The gardener has looked after it most assiduously, and he hasn't let the children near it. He says it should last till tomorrow morning, and he's looking forward to his reward.' I was absolutely thrilled. I could hardly wait till the next day, when I decided I would compose a suitable poem and send it to Her Majesty with a container full of the snow. The anticipation was becoming quite unbearable.

The next morning I got up while it was still dark. I gave one of the servants a box and sent her off with the order to choose the whitest of the snow to put in it, and be careful to scrape away any that was dirty. But she was no sooner gone than back she came, dangling the empty container, to report that the last of the snow mountain had already disappeared. I was devastated. The clever poem that I had laboured and groaned over, and that I'd looked forward to being on everyone's lips, was to my horror suddenly quite worthless.

'How on earth could this have happened?' I said miserably. 'There was all that snow still there yesterday, and it's disappeared overnight!'

'The gardener was wringing his hands in despair,' replied the maid. 'He said that it was there until late last night, and he'd been so looking forward to getting his reward.'

In the midst of all the fuss, word arrived from Her Majesty, inquiring whether there was any snow left today. Thoroughly mortified, I replied, 'Please tell Her Majesty that I consider it a great victory that it was still there until yesterday evening, despite the fact that everyone predicted it couldn't last beyond the end of the year. But after all, my prediction would have been altogether too impressive if the snow had remained until the very day I guessed. During the night some spiteful person must have destroyed the last of it.'

This was the first subject I raised in Her Majesty's presence when I went back to the palace on the twentieth. I related to her how appalled I'd been to see the maid return with the empty container dangling from her hand – like the wandering performer's act with the empty lid, when he came on announcing 'the Buddha's thrown his body off Snow Mountain and all that's left is his hat'[12] – and I went on to explain how I'd planned to make a miniature snow mountain in the lid and send a poem with it, written exquisitely on white paper. Her Majesty laughed a great deal at my story, as did everyone else present.

'I fear I've committed a grave sin by destroying something you had so set your heart on,' Her Majesty then told me. 'To tell the truth, on the night of the fourteenth I sent some retainers there to remove it. When I read your message, I thought you were wonderfully clever to have guessed something like this had happened.'

The fellow[13] apparently emerged wringing his hands and pleading, but he was told that it was an order from the Empress, and was forbidden to tell anyone from my place about it, on pain of having his house destroyed. They threw all the snow away near the south wall of the Left Palace Guards Office, and I gather they reported that it was packed down very hard, and there was a great deal of it. Her Majesty admitted that it would actually have lasted through even as far as the twentieth, and would no doubt have received some added snow from the first snowfall of the spring, too. Then she went on to relate that His Majesty had also heard about it, and had remarked to the senior courtiers that a great deal of thought had obviously gone into this contest of ours. 'Well then,' she said in conclusion, 'tell us the poem you'd prepared. After all, I've made my confession, and as you can see, you actually won your bet.'

The ladies added their voices to Her Majesty's request, but I replied sulkily, 'I don't see why I should be expected to turn around and tell you my poem, after the depressing things I've just heard' – and in truth I was by this time feeling thoroughly miserable.

At this point His Majesty arrived, and he said to me teasingly, 'I've always believed you were a favourite with Her Majesty, but I must say this has made me wonder.' This only served to depress me even more deeply, and by now I was close to tears.

'Oh dear, oh dear,' I moaned, 'life's so hard! And to think how overjoyed I was, too, about the snow that fell after we'd built the mountain, and then Her Majesty decided it shouldn't count, and ordered it removed.'

Then His Majesty smiled and remarked, 'I suppose she just didn't want to see you win.'

[83] *Splendid things* – Chinese brocade. Ornamental swords. Tinted Buddhist images.[1] Long, richly coloured clusters of wisteria blossom hanging from a pine tree.

A Chamberlain of the sixth rank. He's a quite splendid sight in those special green robes he's allowed to wear, and he can wear damask, which even a high-ranking young nobleman is forbidden. Subordinate officials in the Chamberlain's office, or children from some lower-ranking family who are serving in the house of someone of the fourth or fifth rank, look quite inconsequential at the time, but if they become Chamberlains they undergo an astonishing transformation. When they appear as bearer of an imperial pronouncement, or present the imperial gifts of sweet chestnuts and so forth at one of the great minis-terial banquets,[2] from the magnificent way they're received you'd think they were heavenly beings descended to earth!

If a Chamberlain is delivering a message from the Emperor

to a household whose daughter is Empress, or has been chosen
to become Empress in the future, even the gentlewoman who
puts out his cushion when she receives the letter on her lady's
behalf will take scrupulous care over how she presents her
sleeve as she slips it out from beneath the blind; and from all
the attention that's lavished on him generally, you'd never think
he was a man you'd been used to seeing around every day. He's
even more impressive if he combines his role with that of Gate
Watch Guard, in which case he'll have a long formal train
sweeping along behind him. The head of the household personally offers him a *saké* cup, which you'd imagine must fill him
with a secret delight. And where he would once have been
abasing himself reverently before the young gentlemen of the
household, there he is now taking his place by their side, though
there's still a hint of deference in his dealings with them.

Indeed you feel downright envious of him, to see him in such
close personal contact with the Emperor at night. It's such a
pity if he dresses poorly and wears boring colours during those
precious three or four years when he's in such constant intimate
service on the Emperor. As the time of the Appointments List
approaches and his period as Chamberlain is drawing to an
end, he should already be dreading the loss of his special status
more than death itself, and it really is such a shame that in fact
his only concern is to secure his next posting and take up a
vacant position among the Provincial Governors.[3] In the old
days, Chamberlains would already be lamenting the end of
their service from the spring or summer of the year before it
was due to finish, but these days they just rush to compete for
their next position.

A man of scholarly accomplishment is inexpressibly splendid.
Though he may be of dreadfully lowly rank and no joy to look
at, he fills you with awe and envy at the way he can spend time
in the presence of those at the very highest levels, as their tutor,[4]
and be called on by them for scholarly consultations. It's also
splendid to see him praised for his preparation of a dedicatory
prayer, or a memorial presented to the throne, or some preface
to poetry.

A learned priest is also, needless to say, a splendid thing.

An Empress taking part in an imperial procession during daylight hours.

A formal expedition by the Regent, or his official pilgrimage to Kasuga Shrine.[5]

Grape-coloured figured silk. Violet is a splendid colour wherever it's found – in flowers, in fabric or in paper.

Snow lying thick in a garden.

The Regent.

The water iris is rather less fine than other violet-coloured flowers.

The reason the sight of a sixth-rank Chamberlain on night watch is so delightful is because of the violet in his clothes.[6]

[84] *Things of elegant beauty* – A slim, handsome young gentleman of noble birth wearing court dress.

A pretty girl dressed somewhat casually, without the stiff formal skirted trousers, in a rather loosely stitched girl's over-robe; she's sitting at the veranda railing, shielding her face with her fan, and from her sleeve hangs a herb bag or a hare-mallet, its long coloured strings dangling.

A bound book of fine paper.

A letter on fine green paper, tied to a sprig of willow covered in little leaf buds.

A three-layer fan.[1] A five-layer fan is too thick, and the base looks ugly.

Long stems of sweet flag, laid elegantly on a cypress-bark roof[2] that's neither too new nor too old, are wonderfully fresh and green to the eye. The drapes of a standing curtain in the wood-grain pattern, glimpsed beneath a blind, very glossy, with the curtain cords lifting in the breeze, is a lovely sight. Thin white cord. A brightly-coloured lintel cloth.

A charming cat with a white tag on her red collar walking along by the railing of the veranda beyond the blinds, trailing her long leash behind her, is also a lovely and very elegant sight.

The Sweet Flag Chamberlains who distribute the sweet flag for the Sweet Flag Festival.[3] They wear sweet flag garlands in their hair, and they also wear the special decorative shoulder and waist sashes, rather similar to the red abstinence cords of

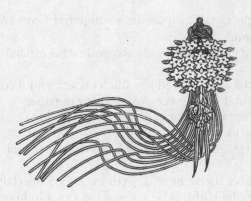

Herbal ball

the First Fruits Festival,[4] though not as brightly coloured. They make a marvellously elegant picture as they move along passing out the herbal balls to the line of waiting princes and nobles. It's also wonderful to watch these men then proceed to attach the herbal ball to their waist and perform a ceremonial dance and obeisance of thanks.

A knotted letter of violet paper, with a long cluster of wisteria blossom attached.

The young gentlemen who take part in the Lesser Abstinence[5] at the time of the First Fruits Festival are also extremely elegant.

[85]* *When Her Majesty provided the Gosechi dancers*, she sent twelve lady attendants. We'd heard that in other places it was considered wrong to provide the attendants from the households of the High Consort or one of the other imperial wives. However, for some reason Her Majesty chose ten gentle-women from her own entourage; the other two were sisters, one from the Empress Dowager's household and one from the Shigeisa's.

On the night of the Day of the Dragon,[1] she had the dancers and their attendants dressed in the special indigo-design Chinese jackets and girls' over-robes, a plan she didn't reveal to her own ladies, let alone to others. The clothes were brought in after dark, when everyone else had already changed into their formal wear. The red cords[2] were very prettily tied with ends trailing, and the figures on the beautifully glossed white robes were hand-drawn rather than stencilled. It was most unusual to be wearing this robe over the figured Chinese jacket, and the little girl attendants in particular looked perhaps the most charming of all. Even the serving ladies[3] appeared in these clothes, and the court nobles and senior courtiers were most intrigued to see them. 'Ladies of the Lesser Abstinence' was the name they gave them, and the young gentlemen of the Lesser Abstinence sat outside the blinds conversing with them.

Her Majesty declared that it was very odd to dismantle the Gosechi retiring rooms before the final day of the festival was over, so that everything inside was visible, and decreed that they should be left pristine and in place until the last night. Therefore, everything was left as it was so that no one was discommoded – the gaps in the standing curtains were drawn together, and the ladies' sleeves were on display as usual.

One of the ladies, Kohyōe, remarked that her red cord had come undone and she wanted help to retie it, whereupon Captain Sanekata came over to where she sat and set it to rights for her, which was rather suggestive. He then proceeded to recite:

> 'A wintry indifference
> freezes the well's blue waters
> to a knot of ice.
> How might I melt that cord
> and loosen its icy knot?'[4]

She didn't respond, perhaps because her youth and the very public situation made it rather difficult for her. The ladies sitting nearby also simply sat there, saying nothing.[5] One of the men from the Empress's Office, who was waiting with interest to catch the reply, could no longer stand it after a while. He made his way over discreetly to where the ladies were seated and apparently asked in a whisper why nothing was forthcoming. I was sitting four people away from Kohyōe, so even if I'd been able to come up with some response it would have been difficult to say it, and besides, how could you offer some merely average poem in reply to one by Sanekata, who was so famous for his poetic skills? Still, I thought, it's no good being bashful and hesitant when it comes to poetic composition. Where does that ever get you? Though your poem might not be so very wonderful, the important thing is that it must be something you come out with on the spur of the moment. And besides, I felt sorry for the fellow from the Empress's Office, who was pacing about snapping his fingers in vexation at the lack of poem.

So I sent the following poem via one of the ladies, Ben no Omoto.

> The cord's knot is loose
> as ice on the water's surface.
> It finds itself undone
> by the warm sunlight of a garland
> of festive fern leaves in the hair.[6]

But Ben no Omoto was quite overwhelmed by it all, and couldn't manage to get the poem out, so the Captain could barely hear it, and had to lean forward and say, 'What was that? What did she say?' She did her best to recite it grandly and make it sound truly impressive, but unfortunately she tended to stammer when nervous, and so the Captain never did manage to hear my poem properly – which was a relief to me really, since it saved me the embarrassment of having my poor poem exposed after all.

Some of those present decided they were feeling a bit indisposed so they wouldn't accompany the dancers to the hall, but on Her Majesty's insistence we all went, which created an unusually great throng of people. One of the dancers was daughter of Chief Equerry Sukemasa; her mother was the fourth daughter of the Somedono Minister of Ceremonial's sister. She was a very charming little girl of twelve. For once, none of the dancers had to be carried out[7] on the last night. Instead, at the end of the dances, there was a rather enchanting procession in which the dancers led the way from the Jijūden, via the east veranda of the Seiryōden, and proceeded to Her Majesty's apartments.

[86] *Another elegant sight* is of a handsome serving man walking past bearing a ceremonial narrow-bladed sword with a flat-weave ceremonial cord attached.[1]

[87]* *At the time of the Gosechi Festival* somehow everything in the palace, even the people you see every day, becomes simply delightful. There's the unusual sight of the bits of coloured fabric that the groundswomen wear in their ceremonial hair combs, rather like abstinence tags. When they seat themselves along the arched bridgeway[1] from the Senyōden, the dapple-dye pattern on the ribbons that bind up their hair stands out beautifully, and the whole effect is somehow quite marvellous. It's perfectly understandable that the serving women and those who attend the dancers should find it all a splendid honour.

Then there's the fine sight of the newly appointed fifth-rank gentlemen, who parade with wicker baskets of wild indigo and climbing fern. To witness the senior courtiers, their cloaks pulled back off one shoulder so that a sleeve trails, walk past the Gosechi apartments beating time with their fans and other objects as they sing 'messengers in waves come swelling our rank',[2] is enough to quicken the heart of even the most seasoned among us. You can also get a terrible fright sometimes, hearing them all suddenly roar with laughter.

Among the special clothing worn for the event, the scarlet glossed-silk train-robe worn by the Chamberlain in charge of proceedings is the most marvellous of all. Cushions are placed for seating, but no one manages to make use of them – instead they're single-mindedly intent on passing judgement on the appearance of the seated ladies who are displaying their sleeves from behind the blinds.

On this occasion, the Chamberlain in charge became dreadfully stern and officious on the first night,[3] and barred the door to everyone except the ladies in charge of the hairdressing and two of the girl attendants. He grew really quite offensive, and when some of the courtiers pleaded with him to make an exception just for one more, he stubbornly refused, on the grounds that it would only make everyone else envy her. The twenty lady attendants from Her Majesty's, however, simply ignored him, pushed open the door and went bustling gaily in, and it was very funny to see him stand there gaping in astonishment, muttering, 'Good gracious me, what's the world coming to!' The rest of the attendants all followed their lead and pressed in, and the expression on the Chamberlain's face was now one of absolute outrage. The Emperor was also present at the time, and he must have found it quite entertaining to witness all this.

The sight of a dancer's face lit by the glow of a nearby lamp as she dozes is also most enchanting.[4]

[88]* *One day His Majesty brought along a biwa* called 'Nameless', which we ladies could examine and try out. I didn't attempt to play it, however, but only stroked the strings. 'What was its name again?' I innocently inquired, and Her Majesty replied, 'Oh, it's not important enough to have a name', which I thought was really a quite wonderful answer. The Shigeisa and others also came to pay a visit, and as they were talking she happened to remark that she had in her possession a very interesting *shō*, which she'd received from their late father.

'Oh, do give it to me!' said her brother Bishop Ryūen. 'I have a very fine *kin* which I'd be happy to exchange for it.' The Shigeisa took no notice of this and simply went on talking about something else, but Ryūen kept repeating his request, pestering her for an answer, until finally Her Majesty turned to him and said, 'She obviously doesn't intend to replace the "Irreplaceable".' This was just the most marvellous thing to say, but unfortunately Ryūen hadn't heard of this *shō* of His Majesty's, and he simply continued to glower and sulk.

I seem to remember that this happened during the time when Her Majesty was in the Office of the Empress's Household. 'Irreplaceable' was the name of one of the *shō* in His Majesty's collection.

In fact the names of all the stringed and wind instruments in His Majesty's collection are fascinating. There's 'Above

Mystery', 'Pastured Horse', 'Water Sluice', 'Wei River Bridge' and 'Nameless'. Then, among the Japanese *koto* there's 'Decayed Wood Knot', 'Salt Kiln' and 'Two Openings'. There's also 'Water Dragon', 'Little Water Dragon', 'Priest Uda', 'Hammer', 'Two Leaves' and so on – I've heard so many names, but have forgotten the others. The Secretary Captain always used to speak of really fine instruments as 'worthy of the Giyōden's top drawer'.[1]

[89] *I remember an occasion before the blinds of Her Majesty's apartment* when the senior courtiers spent the whole day playing the *koto* and the flute. When evening came and the lamps were produced, one was lit near where Her Majesty was seated; as the lattice shutters hadn't yet been lowered, she was clearly visible through the open door, so she raised her *biwa* and held it vertically to shield herself from view. There she sat, in a scarlet robe with quite indescribably lovely gowns and starched robes beneath, in layer upon layer, and it was thrilling too to see how her sleeves fell over the rich glossy black of the *biwa* as she held it, and the sharp contrast of her wonderfully white forehead, clearly visible at the side of the shielding instrument.

I went over to one of the ladies and remarked, 'The maiden who "half hides her face" could not have looked as splendid as this. After all, she was only a commoner, wasn't she?' The lady then made her way through the packed crowd and repeated this to Her Majesty, who laughed and cleverly responded, 'And does she then understand his feelings on "parting"?'[1]

[90] *Infuriating things* – Thinking of one or two changes in the wording after you've sent a message to someone, or written and sent off a reply to someone's message.

Having hurriedly sewn something, you're rather pleased with how nicely you've done it – but then when you come to pull out the needle, you find that you forgot to knot the thread when you began. It's also infuriating to discover you've sewn something inside out.

I remember an occasion while Her Majesty was staying in the Southern Residence,[1] when she announced that some clothes were urgently needed, and ordered us all to set to and sew them then and there. She handed out the pieces of robe, and we all gathered at the front of the building and started work, each on her separate piece. We looked quite crazed, everyone sewing away furiously to see who could do the most, each of us seated on her own and all facing in different directions. Nurse Myōbu raced through her sewing and put down the finished work. However, just as she was in the act of tying off the thread she realized that she'd stitched one of the sleeve pieces together the wrong way round. She flung it down in a panic and rose to her feet, but when her piece was put together with the back section the mistake was discovered. We made great fun of her for this, and told her she had to hurry and re-do it, but she wouldn't hear of it. 'Why should I re-sew it just because I find I've sewed it up wrongly?' she demanded. 'If it's figured cloth or something then you can tell what's back and front, and it would be fair to make anyone who hadn't looked re-sew it in that case, but this is unpatterned cloth, so there was no way of telling. Why should I re-sew this! Get someone who hasn't done any of the sewing to fix it.'

'Well, we can't just leave things at that, can we,' said Gen Shōnagon and Chūnagon, and they drew up the pieces and grimly set about doing the necessary re-sewing. It was most entertaining to observe how Nurse Myōbu sat there staring balefully at them as they worked.

You've just had some lovely bush clover or plume grass planted and are admiring it when some fellows arrive carrying a long box and a couple of spades, set about brazenly digging away at it, and carry it off. This is both depressing and infuriating. They wouldn't dream of doing this if someone of standing were present, but though you do your utmost to stop them, they simply ignore your orders. 'We're just taking a little,' they assure you, and off they go, which infuriates beyond words.

It's also most infuriating for those concerned when a servant from some grand establishment arrives at the residence of someone such as a Provincial Governor and addresses everyone with an offhand rudeness, obviously feeling he can get away with it where such lowly folk are concerned.

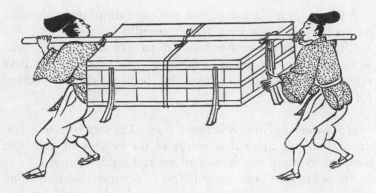

'some fellows arrive carrying a long box'

You've received a letter you're anxious to read, and someone snatches it from you and retreats to the garden, where he stands reading it. Infuriated and miserable, you pursue him as far as the blinds, but there you have to stop.[2] As you stand there watching while he reads, you're almost overwhelmed by the frustrated urge to dash out and retrieve it.[3]

[91] *Things it's frustrating and embarrassing to witness* – A guest has arrived and you're sitting talking when people inside begin a conversation of a confidential nature, and you have to sit there hearing it, powerless to stop them.

Similarly, your lover becomes terribly drunk, and starts coming out with confidential things when he can be overheard.

Someone starts talking about another person, unaware that he's sitting within earshot. This is very embarrassing, even if the person concerned is a mere servant and not someone of consequence.

Witnessing the serving men in the place you're visiting overnight being playful and silly.

Someone insists on telling you about some horrid little child, carried away with her own infatuation with the creature, imitating its voice as she gushes about the cute and winning things it says.

A person of no learning, making ostentatious use of famous names in front of someone truly learned.

It's also painfully embarrassing to have to stand by and hear someone proudly reciting to others a poem of theirs that isn't really much good, or bragging about the praise they've received for it.

[92] *Startling and disconcerting things* – The way you feel when an ornamental comb that you're in the process of polishing happens to bump against something and suddenly snaps.

An ox cart that's overturned. You've assumed that something of such enormous bulk must of course be thoroughly stable, and you're simply stunned to see it lying there, and deeply disconcerted.

Someone bluntly saying things that are embarrassing and unpleasant for the other person.

It's horribly startling and disconcerting to stay up all night waiting, certain that someone will come, then finally begin to give up thought of him as dawn breaks, and drift off to sleep – only to wake with a start when a crow caws suddenly just outside, and discover that it's broad daylight.

Someone with a letter that's to be delivered elsewhere shows it to a person who shouldn't see it.

Someone pins you down and commences laying down the law about something that means absolutely nothing to you, without your being able to get a word in edgeways.

Spilling something is always very startling and disconcerting.

[93] *Regrettable things* – When a dark rain falls instead of snow for the Gosechi Festival or the Litany of Buddha Names.

When an imperial abstinence turns out to coincide with one of the Palace Festivals. You've all been busy preparing for and looking forward to the event, and suddenly this obstruction brings everything to a halt.

It's a great pity when there's a musical gathering, or some other such thing you want someone to see, and you send to have them come, but they don't arrive.

A like-minded company of women or men[1] sets off together

from the palace to visit a temple or some other place. The sleeves spill tastefully out from their carriage, scrupulously, even overscrupulously, arranged – so much so that someone of taste might find the effect if anything a bit repellent – and then, to everyone's deep chagrin, you don't meet with a single horse or carriage bearing anyone who could appreciate the effect. It's quite extraordinary how, from sheer vexation, you find yourself longing for even some passing commoner to have the sensibility to appreciate the scene, and later spread the word.

[94]* *At the time of the Abstinence and Prayer*[1] *of the fifth month*, when Her Majesty was residing at the Office of the Empress's Household, the space between the pillars in front of the Retreat Room was made over for use as a prayer area, which gave it quite a special feel.

It had been overcast and tending to rain since the first day of the month. Some of us were sitting about at a loose end, when I came up with the suggestion that it would be fun to go off on an expedition to hear the *hototogisu*. The others immediately leapt at the idea, so the outing was organized.

Someone said that the *hototogisu* could be heard at that place called Something Point beyond the Kamo Shrine, with a name a bit like the bridge of the Tanabata story but not as pleasant.[2] Someone else, however, maintained that it wasn't *hototogisu* but cicadas.[3]

Anyway, we decided to go there. On the morning of the fifth day we ordered one of the officials to prepare a carriage. Since it was raining, we decided no one would object if we had it brought round to the steps for us via the northern guard gate, and four of us duly got in. The others were filled with envy and demanded that another carriage be ordered for them, but Her Majesty wouldn't hear of it, and off we went, heartlessly ignoring all their pleas.

There was a noisy crowd of people up by the Riding Ground.[4] 'What's going on?' we asked, and were informed that it was the main event of the mounted archery competitions. 'Please be so good as to stay and observe a little,' they urged us, so we halted the carriage to watch.

We were told that everyone was there, from the Captain of
the Left Palace Guards down, but there was no sign of them.
Various low-ranking officials were standing here and there or
wandering about. 'How boring,' we said. 'Quick, let's move
on', and we went smartly on our way.

The scene along the road we travelled was delightfully reminiscent of the Kamo Festival. The house of Lord Akinobu[5] lay
along this way, and we decided to take the opportunity to have
a look at it, so we drew up our carriage and alighted. It was in
the rustic style, bare and simple, and there was a deliberately
old-fashioned air about it, with its standing screens illustrated
with horses, its sliding doors of wicker-weave and its burr-reed
blinds. The building itself, too, had a provisional feel to it. It
was long and narrow, rather like a corridor, quite lacking in
depth though charming for all that. And as for the *hototogisu*,
they were indeed calling back and forth, so loudly in fact that
they made almost too much of a din for comfort. We did feel
sorry then that Her Majesty wasn't there to hear them, nor the
others who'd so wanted to come with us.

Our host declared that since we were in the country we must
see some country things. He produced a bundle of something
called 'rice heads', and called in some girls from nearby houses,
lowly folk but quite neat and presentable, and got five or six of
them to thresh the rice for us. Two of them also demonstrated
some unfamiliar machine that revolved,[6] singing as they worked
it. We laughed with pleasure at how new and strange everything
was, and all these distractions quite dispelled any thought of
composing our *hototogisu* poems.

Food was provided for us on meal-stands such as you see in
Chinese paintings, but none of us was inclined to eat. 'It's rough
country fare, I grant you,' Lord Akinobu said apologetically,
'but I've found that visitors from the capital generally tend to
clamour for dishes of this and that till the host is longing to
escape. It's most uncharacteristic for guests to fail to touch their
food like this', and he coaxed us along by pointing out that he
himself had plucked the little fern shoots we were served.

'But how can we eat lined up here like so many maids before
the table?' I teased him – to which he replied, 'If that's the case,

you should take the dishes down off the stands. Ladies of your station would be used to the face-down pose,[7] no doubt.'

In the midst of all this jollity and hospitality, a servant came in to report that it had begun to rain, and we hastened back to the carriage. 'Now's the time to compose our poems,' someone suggested, but I said, 'Oh, we might as well wait till we're on the road', and we all climbed in.

Noticing masses of white deutzia blossom along the way, we got our men to pick great sprays of it, and threaded all the blinds and sides of the carriage with flowers, and thatched the roof and ridgepole with long stems of it, till the whole carriage looked just like a hedge of flowering deutzia attached to an ox. The men were full of laughter as they helped each other poke more sprays in here and there, with cries of 'There's a gap here!' 'And here's another!'

We were hoping to meet some people along the way, but to our great disappointment all we came across was the odd worthless commoner and a lowly priest or two.

'We really can't end the expedition like this,' I said as we were nearing the palace. 'We must at least make sure the story of this carriage of ours gets told', so we stopped at the Ichijō mansion and sent a messenger to ask if Adviser Kiminobu[8] was there, and to say that we'd just returned from hearing the *hototogisu*.

'I am on my way,' came his reply. 'Please wait, dear ladies.' The messenger added that he'd been lounging informally in the retainers' quarters, but had leapt up and was hastening into his gathered trousers to greet us.

We decided it wasn't really worth waiting, and off we went again – but as we were heading towards the Tsuchi Gate,[9] Kiminobu came dashing up behind us crying 'Wait! Wait!', having somehow scrambled into his court clothes and still fastening his waist sash as he ran down the road. With him came three or four retainers, rushing along in bare feet.

'Quick!' we cried, urging our carriage as fast as it could go, but just as we reached the gate he arrived beside us, gasping heavily.

He roared with laughter at the sight of our carriage. 'This doesn't look like anything you'd find mere mortals riding in!' he exclaimed. 'Please come out and show yourselves.' The others who'd arrived with him were all highly amused too.

'Where are your poems? Come on, let's hear them,' he then demanded.

'Wait till we've told them to Her Majesty,' we replied, and as we spoke it suddenly began to rain in earnest.

'It's times like this,' Kiminobu complained, 'when I particularly resent the fact that for some reason they built this gate without a roof, unlike all the others. But how can I go home now?' he continued. 'My only thought when I came running was whether I could catch you. I didn't pause to wonder about who might see me. Still, I can't go any further looking like this . . .'

'Oh come on,' we cried. 'Come to the palace!'

'But how can I, wearing my lacquered cap?'[10]

'Send someone to fetch your formal wear, then,' we suggested.

It now began to absolutely pour, and our men, who had no rain-hats to shelter under, urged the ox along into the palace grounds as fast as it would go. Resigning himself, Kiminobu opened the umbrella that had been fetched from home for him, and turned and made his slow and dejected way back to the Ichijō mansion, turning constantly to look behind him as he went – a very different sight from when he had arrived. It was charming to watch him trailing mournfully along, in his hand a token spray of deutzia blossom plucked from our carriage.

When we arrived back, Her Majesty asked what we'd seen. Everyone who'd wanted to come with us listened to our tale with expressions of envy and woe, but they all laughed when we got to the story of how Adviser Kiminobu had run along pursuing us down Ichijō Avenue.

'Well then, what of your poems?' Her Majesty inquired, and when we confessed our story, she said, 'This is a great shame. How will it be when the senior courtiers ask to hear what you composed, and you have nothing at all of interest to show them? If only you'd made your poems then and there, when you heard the *hototogisu*. You were obviously too constrained by wanting to create something pedantically correct. Well, you must compose them now. I quite despair of you all!'

This was all perfectly true, and we felt miserable. We were busy discussing what our poems should be, when a poem on the theme of his token spray of deutzia blossom arrived from Adviser Kiminobu, written on thin paper coloured in the deutzia combination – I can't now recall the poem. This required an immediate reply, so we sent someone to fetch an inkstone from our rooms.

'Here, just use this and write your reply quickly,' Her Majesty said, passing us paper and writing implements on the lid of her own writing box.

'Saishō, you must write it,' I said. 'No, it has to be you,' said she, and as we were negotiating back and forth, the sky suddenly grew dark and the rain began to pour down, and then there was a terrific clap of thunder. We were beside ourselves with terror, and rushed about lowering the shutters, and so all thought of composing a reply quite slipped our minds.

The thunder continued for a very long time, and by the time the storm was finally drawing to its end, it was dark. No sooner had we at last sat down to see to the reply to Kiminobu's poem than a number of people, including some court nobles, arrived to ask how we'd fared with the thunderstorm, so we moved out to the western aisle room to talk with them, and the poem was again forgotten. Then finally one of the others declared that it was the person to whom the poem was addressed who should make the reply, and there the matter ended. It was all very depressing – today really did seem a day of bad karma for poetry.

'Well then, let's not even let it be known that we went off like that on the expedition today,' we decided with a laugh.

'Surely all of you who went could manage to create something together,' said Her Majesty, looking charmingly cross. 'Or is it that you're simply not inclined even to try?'

'But the whole thing has become a bore by now,' I replied.

'Good heavens, how can it be a bore!' exclaimed Her Majesty, but the matter was nevertheless left at that.

*

Two days later, we were discussing the excursion when Her Majesty overheard Saishō asking me, 'What did you think of those little fern shoots that he said he'd plucked himself?'

'So that's the sort of thing you recall, is it?' she said with a laugh, and seizing a stray piece of paper that was lying nearby, she wrote,

> It was the little fern shoots
> that I longingly recalled.

'Now make the first part of the poem,' she instructed me. I was delighted, and wrote,

> I went in search
> of the *hototogisu*'s song
> but rather than that voice . . .

'Well, you have a fine nerve I must say!' said Her Majesty with a smile when she saw it. 'Why do you make this a poem on the subject of the *hototogisu*, only to belittle it like this?'

Embarrassed, I threw myself into my self-defence. 'But it was never my intention to write this poem in the first place!' I declared. 'Whenever there's an occasion when people are composing, and Your Majesty instructs me to make a poem, my only impulse is to flee. Not that I don't understand the rules of syllable count, or that I make winter poems in spring, or write about plum blossom or cherry blossom in autumn, or anything of that sort. But after all, I come from a line of people with a name for good poetry, so I'd like it to be said that my poems are a bit better than the average. When I compose something, I want people to say later, "This was a particularly impressive poem composed on that occasion – just what you'd expect, considering her forebears." It's an offence to my late father's name, to fancy myself as a poet and put myself forward to make some plausible-sounding poem, when in fact what I write has nothing special to recommend it at all.'

Her Majesty smiled and replied, 'Well, if that's how you feel, we shall leave it up to you, and not demand that you compose anything.'

'This is a huge relief to me,' I replied gratefully. 'I won't worry myself over composing any more, then.'

This conversation took place at the time of the Three Worms Night.[11] Palace Minister Korechika was engrossed in making elaborate plans for the event. Late that night, a poetry topic was announced, and we ladies were asked to compose on it. Tension was thick in the air as everyone set about the agonizing business of bringing forth a poem, but I meanwhile settled down near Her Majesty and engaged her in conversation on quite different matters. Observing this, His Excellency Korechika said tersely, 'Why aren't you over there with everyone else composing your poem? Here, take the topic and set to work', and he handed it to me.

'The reason I'm not thinking of my poem,' I calmly replied, 'is that Her Majesty has told me that I don't need to, so I have chosen not to compose one.'

'This is very peculiar,' His Excellency said. Turning to Her Majesty he continued, 'Can this be true? Why did you say this to her? It's unheard of!' To me he said firmly, 'Well, I don't know about other occasions, but on this occasion you must compose something.'

For all his scolding, however, I paid him not the slightest notice. Everyone had finished their poems, and they were in the process of being weighed and judged, when Her Majesty jotted down a quick note and tossed it to me. It said,

> And is it then
> the child of Motosuke
> who sits tonight
> choosing to hold herself aloof
> from the poetic gathering?

I was utterly delighted by it, and burst into laughter, which caused His Excellency to exclaim, 'What's this? What's this?'

I replied with:

'It is only because
I am the child of that great man –
If this were not so
I would have been the very first
to provide my poem tonight.'

'Indeed,' I added to Her Majesty, 'if it weren't for the humility I feel, a thousand verses would spring from my lips.'

[95] *It was while we were in the Office of the Empress's Household*, a brilliantly moonlit night close to the full moon of the eighth month. Ukon had been asked to play the *biwa*. Her Majesty was seated near the edge of the aisle. The other ladies were chatting and laughing, but I sat in silence, leaning against an aisle pillar.

'Why so quiet?' inquired Her Majesty. 'Say something. You're looking too forlorn.'

'I'm simply immersing myself in the spirit of the moonlight,'[1] I replied.

'Beautifully put,' remarked Her Majesty.

[96] *There was a large and distinguished gathering* at Her Majesty's, of various family members, nobles and senior courtiers. I was sitting leaning against an aisle pillar talking to some of the ladies, when Her Majesty tossed me a note. Opening it, I read, 'Should I love you, or should I not? How would it be if you were not loved above others?'

This was a reference to something I had said in passing in Her Majesty's hearing. 'I absolutely must be first in someone's heart,' I'd declared. 'If not, I'd prefer to be loathed and treated like dirt. I'd rather die than be second or third in a person's affections. It's first or nothing, for me.' Hearing me, some of the ladies had joked, 'She's Lady *Lotus Sutra* – there can be no other Law.'

I wrote a response to Her Majesty with the writing implements she provided, which said in part, 'Of the nine paths to Paradise, I would happily take even the lowest.'[1]

'This won't do at all,' declared Her Majesty when she

received it. 'You've completely lost your nerve! You should stand by what you say.'

'But it all depends on whom I'm talking about,' I said.

'That is just the problem,' she replied. 'You should wish to be loved first by the one whom you hold first in your own heart.'

It was a delightful thing to say.

[97] *The Counsellor*[1] *paid a visit*, and presented Her Majesty with a fan.

'I've come by some excellent fan ribs,' he said, 'and I was intending to have them papered and give the fan to you, but I couldn't use any old paper for the task, so I'm still searching.'

'What sort of ribs can they be?' Her Majesty inquired.

His voice rose in excitement. 'They're just wonderful! People say they've never seen such ribs, and truly, they're not the sort of thing anyone's ever laid eyes on!'

I was seated nearby during this exchange, and at this point I remarked, 'Well then, they can't be fan ribs, they must be the ribs of a jellyfish.'[2]

'That's very good,' said the Counsellor with a laugh. 'Let's have it that I'm the one who said that.'

Stories of this kind really belong in the 'Things it's frustrating and embarrassing to witness' section. I've only added it here because people have begged me not to leave anything out.

[98] *One wet day during the endless rains*, Her Majesty received a visit from Aide of Ceremonials Nobutsune,[1] who was bearing a message from the Emperor. Noticing how he'd pushed back the cushion that was set out for him as usual, and was sitting oddly far away, I teased him by saying, 'So who else have you brought along?'

He laughed. 'If I sit on the cushion after coming through this rain, I'll leave horrible dirty footprints on it,' he replied.

'Oh well,' I said, 'let's say it's your footman[2] then.'

'Now you can't claim that as your own joke,' he said. 'If I hadn't mentioned leaving footprints, you wouldn't have been able to say it, would you!' and he kept on repeating this, which I found very amusing.

'This reminds me,' I said to him, 'of the famous Enutaki, the servant of the former Empress. When Fujiwara Tokikara, who died while he was Governor of Mino province, was Chamberlain, he went one day to the servants' quarters and said, "So this is the Enutaki they all speak of! Why don't you look like your name?"

'"Sir," she replied, "what I look like depends, as your own name suggests, on when you look."[3] Even the nobles and senior courtiers relayed this tale with great amusement, and everyone declared that one would be hard pressed to come up with such a fine response, even if you could make your choice of names for the exchange. And indeed, the tale is told to this very day.'

'Well, that's another instance of a witticism that "depends on the moment", isn't it,' joked Nobutsune. 'In fact the same thing goes for good poetry in Chinese or Japanese too – its success simply depends on the subject you're presented with.'

'Yes, that's no doubt true,' I said agreeably. 'Well then, I'll propose a subject for you, and let's hear your poem.'

'A fine idea!' he gamely replied.

'And while we're about it, why don't I provide you with lots of subjects,' I went on.

While we were continuing in this vein, Her Majesty's reply to the Emperor's message was brought out, and Nobutsune seized his chance.

'This is beginning to scare me,' he declared. 'It's time I made my escape', and away he went.

'He's run away like this in order to hide the fact that his Chinese and Japanese calligraphy is dreadful, and he's afraid people will make fun of him,' remarked one of the ladies, and we all laughed.

When he was head of the Crafts Workshop, Nobutsune sent someone a draught drawing of something they were making, with a letter saying, 'This is the way it should look.' When I happened upon it, I was astonished at how truly appalling his calligraphy was, and added a note to his letter that said, 'If this is an example of the way it's going to look, it will certainly look very peculiar.' When his letter was duly delivered to the Privy

Chamber, everyone got a great laugh out of it, and Nobutsune was incensed with me.

[99]* *There could be no more splendid celebrations conceivable* than those around the time when the Shigeisa entered the court of the Crown Prince. She moved to his residence on the tenth day of the first month, and though there ensued quite a flurry of letters between her and Her Majesty, they hadn't yet met in person[1] when word came that she would be paying a visit soon after the tenth day of the following month. Her Majesty's quarters were polished and prepared with even more care than usual, and we gentlewomen were all tense with excitement at the prospect.

The Shigeisa arrived in the middle of the night, not long before dawn broke, and His Excellency the Regent and his wife arrived in a single carriage just before daybreak.

A small room in the eastern aisle of the Tōkaden had been carefully prepared to receive her. The shutters were raised very early that morning. On the south side of the room Her Majesty had ordered a four-foot-long screen to be set up, running east–west, and she sat before this. The room was furnished with

Screen

mats and cushions for seating, and a brazier. A great crowd of us gentlewomen was gathered, seated to the south behind the standing screen or in front of the curtained dais.

While I was doing Her Majesty's hair before everyone arrived, she inquired whether I'd caught a glimpse of the Shigeisa yet.

'How might I have done that?' I replied. 'All I've seen is a quick glimpse of her back on the day her carriage arrived at the palace.'

'Well then, you should position yourself by the pillar behind the screen, and sneak a look from behind me. She's very lovely,' said Her Majesty. I was filled with happy anticipation at this, and deeply impatient for the moment to arrive.

Her Majesty wore two plum-pink cloaks, one a heavy brocade and the other with a raised brocade pattern, draped over three scarlet robes of glossed silk. 'Plum-pink is really best when set off with deep purple,' she remarked. 'It's a pity I can't wear it. No doubt at this stage of the season it would be better not to wear plum-pink, but on the other hand I think a colour such as spring-shoot green would be awful.[2] Does this go with the scarlet, do you think?' Despite these concerns, she looked utterly splendid. All the colours she wore were particularly lovely, and beautifully set off her glowing complexion; I was filled with longing to see this other grand lady, who would surely look just as splendid as she.

When the moment arrived for Her Majesty to slide forward on her knees and enter the room, I established myself up against the screen and peeped in. Some of the other gentlewomen muttered in a voice intended to be overheard, 'That's no way to behave! She's bound to get into trouble!' – which I must say amused me. The sliding panels were wide open, so I could see perfectly.

His Excellency's wife wore several layers of white over two robes of stiff glossed scarlet, and a formal train in the style of a gentlewoman[3] over this ensemble, but as she was seated further in, on the inner side of the room, facing east, I couldn't make out much more than this.

The Shigeisa was further to the northern end of the room, facing south towards me. She was dressed in layer upon layer of gowns in lighter and darker shades of plum-pink, with over this a rich damask gown. Her formal over-robe was of a reddish maroon figured silk, and the uppermost layer was a heavy brocade in spring-shoot green, which produced a beautifully youthful impression. I was deeply impressed with the way she sat throughout with her fan shielding her face, and I must say I found her utterly splendid and wonderful.

His Excellency the Regent was seated facing in towards me, his back to an outer pillar. He wore a pale violet-grey cloak and gathered trousers of spring-shoot green figured silk, with layers of scarlet robes beneath, and the neck-cord of his cloak was fastened in the formal manner. He was indulging in his usual joking banter, and beaming at the fineness of the occasion.

While the Shigeisa looked like a glorious picture, sitting there so quietly, Her Majesty was in contrast thoroughly relaxed, her somewhat more mature face set off to glowing perfection by the scarlet she wore, and really there was no one who could compare with her.

Water was brought in for the washing of hands,[4] with two little girls and four servants bringing the water for the Shigeisa via the Senyōden and Jōganden. There were about six of the Shigeisa's gentlewomen seated along the gallery at this end of the Chinese roof section[5] – the rest had returned after accompanying the Shigeisa, as the gallery was too narrow to accommodate them all. It was a truly elegant sight to see the little girls, dressed in wonderful over-robes of cherry blossom over spring-shoot green, plum-pink and so on, long sleeves trailing, receiving the water and passing it on. Nearby sat Shōshō, daughter of Chief Equerry Sukemasa, and Saishō, daughter of the Kitano Consultant, the sleeves of their figured-silk Chinese jackets spilling from beneath the blinds behind which they were seated.

I was drinking all this in with delight, when the turn came for Her Majesty's water to be presented. This too was a charming scene – the serving lady on duty who took the water from the servant wore a green train, the robe shaded deeper at the sleeves, with Chinese jacket, and formal cords at waist and shoulder, and her face was powdered very white. It was all performed most ceremonially, and was delightfully Chinese in its effect.

Then it was time for the meal, and the lady in charge of hairdressing appeared, to put up Her Majesty's hair,[6] followed by the Lady Chamberlains, also with their hair up, who entered carrying the food. At this point, they set about folding back the separating standing screen from behind which I'd been peeping. I felt as if I was being stripped of a magic cloak of invisibility. Bereft, and longing to see more, I hastily moved further round, to a new position between the blind and the standing curtain, and continued to peep from behind a pillar.

However, my sleeves and train were now all left trailing outside the blind, and His Excellency soon caught sight of them. 'Who's that, watching from behind that blind there?' he demanded.

'It must be Shōnagon,' replied Her Majesty, 'wanting to see the proceedings.'

'Dear me, how embarrassing!' he exclaimed. 'She's an old acquaintance of mine, and I hate the idea of her thinking what terrible daughters I have.' He was fairly bursting with pride as he spoke.

Food was now served to the Shigeisa, and meanwhile His Excellency continued to tease. 'I'm filled with envy!' he declared. 'Both you ladies have been given all your food. Hurry and eat what you can, and then pass this old fella and his old lady the scraps please.' He continued this jesting all day, in fact.

After a while, Grand Counsellor Korechika and Captain Third Rank Takaie arrived, leading Korechika's little son Matsugimi, and His Excellency scooped up the charming little boy delightedly, and settled him on to his knee.

The narrow veranda was quite overflowing with the jumble of the men's ceremonial trains. The Grand Counsellor was a most handsome and impressive figure, while the Captain gave the impression of being highly talented and resourceful – indeed both were so splendid that I was struck, as I gazed, by how wonderful must be the karma of Her Ladyship their mother, not to mention of course His Excellency himself.

'Take a straw cushion,' His Excellency urged Korechika, but

he departed quickly, with the explanation that he must be on his way to the Palace Guards Office.

Somewhat later, one of the Aides of Ceremonial arrived bearing a message from His Majesty, and was given a seat on a cushion in the room to the north of the table storage room. Her Majesty composed her reply very swiftly, and he was no sooner gone and his cushion about to be withdrawn than Lieutenant Chikayori arrived with a message from the Crown Prince for the Shigeisa. Since the veranda of the bridgeway was rather narrow, a separate cushion was placed for him on the main veranda further in.

The letter was brought in, and His Excellency, Her Ladyship and Her Majesty perused it in turn. When the Shigeisa couldn't manage to produce a quick reply despite their urging, His Excellency said teasingly, 'I suppose you aren't writing anything because I'm here watching. I gather that on other occasions you can send off streams of letters', and she blushed slightly and gave a quite marvellous, embarrassed little smile.

'Come on, do be quick!' scolded her mother, and at last the Consort turned herself sideways and set about writing something. Her Ladyship went over and helped her to complete it, which seemed to cause her even greater embarrassment.

Her Majesty had a formal over-robe of figured spring-shoot green and skirted trousers put out as a gift for the messenger. Takaie took them and draped them on the Lieutenant's shoulder,[7] and he put a hand on them and departed, looking rather strained beneath their weight.

Everyone listened in enchantment to the charming things little Matsugimi was saying. 'It would be no bad thing if you were to pass him off as your own on occasion,' His Excellency remarked to Her Majesty, which reminded us all uneasily of the fact that she had yet to produce a son.

Around the Hour of the Sheep, there came the announcement that they were rolling out the mat[8] for His Majesty's visit. In no time he arrived, with a fine swish of silks, and Her Majesty withdrew. Since both of them now retired to the curtained dais,[9] all the gentlewomen also withdrew and made their way with a great rustling to the southern aisle. There were a great

'the mat for His Majesty's visit'

many senior courtiers gathered about the gallery there. His Excellency called one of the servants of Her Majesty's household to him and ordered that they should be provided with enough *saké* to get them drunk, along with snacks to accompany it. And indeed they all did get drunk, and there was apparently great fun on both sides as they proceeded to bandy words with the gentlewomen.

Their Majesties rose around sunset. Grand Counsellor Yamanoi was called in to assist with His Majesty's robe change, and he departed. He made a splendid figure, in cherry-blossom cloak and scarlet robes, all aglow in the evening light – but here awe halts my hand. Although the Grand Counsellor was not a full brother, he was on very good terms with Her Majesty's family. He was even more refined and handsome than Grand Counsellor Korechika, his half brother, and I must say it was a great shame that people spoke so ill of him. The two Grand Counsellors, together with the Captain and the Director of the Court Repository,[10] accompanied His Majesty back to his residence.

Muma no Naishi later arrived bearing a message from the Emperor to say that Her Majesty's presence was required there that evening.

'Oh dear, I really can't tonight,' Her Majesty grumbled, but her father heard this and berated her roundly. 'How shocking of you!' he declared. 'You must go at once.' What with constant messages now coming from the Crown Prince to summon the Shigeisa as well, there was quite a hubbub of activity. More gentlewomen from the Emperor's court arrived to urge her to make haste and come, and the Crown Prince had meanwhile sent Jijū on a similar mission.

There was now a wonderful scene where everyone conferred. 'Surely the Shigeisa should be the first to depart,' Her Majesty said to her father.

'But why should I be the first to go?' the Shigeisa demurred, which Her Majesty countered by offering to see her off personally.

Finally it was decided that the one with farther to go should leave first, and the Shigeisa departed. When His Excellency and the others had returned from bearing her company, Her Majesty in turn departed for the Emperor's palace. We were recalling His Excellency's jokes as we made our way back from accompanying her, and we all fell about laughing so much that we were in danger of tumbling off the temporary bridgeway.[11]

[100] *A branch of plum from which the blossoms had fallen* arrived one day from the Privy Chamber, with the message: 'What do you make of this?'

My response was simply, 'The flowers have already scattered.'[1]

When they learned of my reply, a large group of senior courtiers who were seated in the Black Door room set about chanting this poem. His Majesty happened to overhear, and remarked, 'This is a better response than merely writing a good poem. She's made a fine answer.'

[101] *Around the end of the second month* a terrific wind blew up, the sky grew quite black, and a little snow had begun to

swirl down, when one of the groundsmen appeared at the Black Door and called me over. When I approached, he produced a letter, saying, 'This is from Consultant Kintō.'[1]

On a piece of notepaper he had written:

> There is about this day
> some tiny touch of spring.[2]

It did indeed well express the feel of the day, and I set about racking my brains over how to add the earlier lines to complete the poem.

'Who is there to hear it?'[3] I inquired, and he told me the names. They were all poets fit to shame me, and I was in agony for fear of sending something inferior, particularly since the recipient was the great Kintō himself. I longed to be able to show it to Her Majesty for advice, but His Majesty was present and they were secluded together.

Meanwhile, the messenger was urging me to make a swift reply. And indeed it would make a bad poem even worse to take too long in sending it, so I threw caution to the winds and wrote in a trembling hand:

> The tumbling snow
> so like spring's tumbling petals
> falls from a chilly sky.

As I handed him the poem, I wondered miserably what they'd make of it. While I did long to hear their opinion, on the other hand I felt I'd rather not know if they were rude about my response. But later, the Captain of the Left Gate Watch[4] (who at that time held the post of Captain of the Palace Guards) told me the only reaction was that Consultant Toshikata had suggested I should be promoted to High Gentlewoman, so I was greatly relieved.

[102] *Things with far to go* – The work of twisting up the long cord of a hanpi jacket.[1]

Someone crossing the Ōsaka Barrier just beyond the capital, setting out for distant Michinoku.

A newborn child, at the start of the long journey to adulthood.

[103] *Masahiro is a great laughing-stock.* I wonder how his parents must feel when they hear all the hilarity at their son's expense. People will call over some long-standing attendant of his and tease him. 'Why on earth are you in such a fellow's service?' they'll say. 'How does it feel?' He comes from a household where they prepare their clothes beautifully, and seeing him wearing those wonderfully coloured train-robes and elegant cloaks, so much finer than everyone else's, people sigh and say, 'If only they were on someone else instead of Masahiro!'

What's more, he can say the most peculiar things.

There was the occasion when he ordered two men to go to his home to fetch the clothes for his night watch. 'I can do that by myself,' one of the men replied.

'Don't be crazy,' said Masahiro. 'How is one person going to carry the load of two? Can you put two measures into a one-measure pot?'

No one had any idea what he was talking about, and we were all in fits of laughter.

Then there was the time when a messenger was demanding a quick reply to his message. Masahiro got quite upset. 'The man's driving me mad with his fretting,' he declared. 'What's he up to, tossing his beans in the oven like this?[1] Now who's stolen the brush and ink from the Privy Chamber, just when I need them? You could understand someone making off with them if they were food and drink . . .' – and everyone laughed at him again.

When the Empress Dowager was ill, Masahiro was sent to inquire after her, and on his return people asked him who'd been present at the time. He gave the names of four or five people, and when someone asked if there had been anyone else, he said, 'Well, there were a few sleepers as well.' This was odd

Standing lamp

enough, but the fact that people actually laughed at it was also rather odd.

Once when no one was about, he came along and said to me, 'Excuse me, I'd like to say something. People have been saying you're the person I should tell.'

'What is it?' I asked, and went over to the standing curtain to converse. 'Well, there's this person who was trying to say "bring your body closer", and instead of "body" he said "your bodily appendages"!'[2] Of course he got laughed at again then.

Another time, on the second night of the Conferring of Ranks, Masahiro was in charge of the lamp-lighting, and he was filling a standing lamp with oil. He put his foot on the oilcloth it stood on, which was covered in fresh sticky oil, so that his sock stuck firmly, and when he set off to walk away, the lamp came down with a crash. Dragging the cloth along like that, it was as though terra firma literally trembled at his tread.[3]

Nobody sits down to table in the Privy Chamber until the Chamberlains have seated themselves. However, on one famous occasion Masahiro had sneaked a handful of beans, and when someone pulled aside the low standing screen nearby, there he was crouching behind it, busily eating them. Everyone laughed uproariously.

[104] *Things that are distressing to see* – Someone wearing a robe with the back seam hitched over to one side, or with the collar falling back to reveal the nape of the neck.

A woman who emerges with a child slung on her back to greet a special visitor.

A priest acting as Yin-Yang master, who conducts his purification ceremony with that little white paper cap stuck on his forehead.[1]

I do hate the sight of some swarthy, slovenly-looking woman with a hairpiece, lying about in broad daylight with a scrawny man with hair sprouting from his face.[2] What kind of a picture do they think they make, lounging there for all to see? Of course this is not to say they should stay sitting upright all night for fear people will find them disgusting – no one can see them when it's dark, and besides, everyone else indulges in the same thing at night. The decent thing to do is to get up early once it's morning. No doubt it doesn't look quite as bad for people of high station to take daytime naps in summer, but anyone less than attractive will emerge from a nap with a face all greasy and bloated with sleep, and sometimes even a squashed cheek. How dreary for two such people to have to look each other in the face when they get up!

It's most distressing to see someone thin and swarthy dressed in a see-through gossamer-silk shift.

[105] *Things that are hard to say* – It's very difficult to give someone's message from beginning to end without slipping up, when it includes long stretches of some high-ranking person's words.[1]

The reply to a rather overawing person who's sent you a gift.

Some young person who's only just reached adulthood asks

you an unnerving question about something you find it difficult
to talk about in front of her.

[106]* *Barrier gates* – Ōsaka Barrier. The barrier at Suma. The
barrier at Suzuka. Kikuta, Shirakawa and Koromo Barriers.

It seems to me that the barriers of Tadakoe and Habakari
are completely different from each other.

Yokohashiri Barrier. The barriers at Kiyomi and Mirume.

Yomoyomo Barrier – one longs to know just what the person
thought better of.[1] Perhaps the idea was that they thought
'don't come', as in the name of Nakoso Barrier. It would be a
miserable thing if this was applied to the lovers' meeting of
Ōsaka Barrier.

[107] *Forests* – Ukita Forest. Ueki Forest. Iwase Forest. Tachikiki[1] Forest.

[108] *Plains* – Ashita Plain. Awazu Plain. Shino Plain. Sono
Plain.

[109] *Around the end of the fourth month*, we went on a
pilgrimage to the temple at Hase. Our carriage was loaded on
to a ferry at the famous Yodo Crossing en route, and as we
crossed the river we noticed what looked like quite short stems
of sweet flag and reeds growing in the water nearby, but when
we had them picked they turned out to be extremely long. It
was fascinating to see boats loaded with reeds ferrying to and
fro across the river. It looked precisely like the scene of that
line from the song, 'cut from Takase Pool'.[1]

On our return when we arrived back here on the third day,
we saw a most delightful scene, such as one finds painted on
screens – a light rain was falling, and there were men and
children out in the water gathering sweet flag,[2] the men wearing
very small sedge rain-hats, their clothes tucked up high above
their long shanks.

[110] *Common things that suddenly sound special* – An ox cart
on the first day of the year.[1] Also the cock's crow on that day.

Someone clearing his throat at dawn – and of course the sound of music at dawn too.

[111] *Things that lose by being painted* – Pinks. Sweet flag. Cherry blossom. Men and women described in tales as looking splendid.

[112] *Things that gain by being painted* – Pine trees. Autumn fields. Mountain villages. Mountain paths.

[113] *Winter is best when it's fearfully cold*, while summer is most summer-like when it's impossibly hot.

[114] *Moving things* – A child dressed in mourning for a parent.

A young man of good birth, engaged in rigorous preparations for undergoing the Mitake austerities.[1] It's terribly moving to think of him secreting himself away in a room alone and performing the dawn devotions, his forehead pressed to the floor. One imagines someone close to him, waking in a nearby room and hearing him at his prayers. While he's away on the rigorous austerities she waits quietly, fearful for his safety, and how wonderful when he returns to her safe and sound. It rather lowers the tone of things if he wears his lacquered cap, however. I've heard that even very exalted people dress in extremely shabby clothing when they perform the Mitake austerities.

It seems that Deputy of the Right Gate Watch, one Nobutaka,[2] once declared that he found this ridiculous. 'What's wrong with wearing nice clean clothes for the austerities?' he demanded. 'I really can't imagine that the deity has stipulated one must go dressed in rags.' And so he set off, at the end of the third month, dressed in deep violet gathered trousers, white overcloak and extremely gaudy kerria-yellow robes. He took with him his son Takamitsu, Deputy Officer of Grounds, who wore a green overcloak over scarlet robes, and short hunting trousers in an elaborate print pattern. The men who came back from Mitake at the time, as well as those who were there with him, were all astonished at the sight, and averred that no one dressed like this had ever been seen on the mountain before.

He returned on the first day of the fourth month, and on the tenth day of the sixth month he was promoted to Governor of Chikuzen Province – which just goes to show, everyone said, that he'd been perfectly right in what he said. This story isn't related to the topic of 'moving things', I've just added it because of the connection with the Mitake austerities.

It's very moving to see a good-looking young man or woman dressed in deep black.[3]

The voice of the autumn cricket, around the end of the ninth month or the beginning of the tenth, so frail and tentative that you scarcely know whether you hear it or not. A mother hen crouched low over her chicks. Dew glinting like multi-coloured jewels on the grasses in the garden in late autumn. Waking at dusk or dawn and hearing the wind rustling the bamboo. Anything you hear when you wake at night.

A mountain village in snow.

A young couple who love each other but who can't be together as they long to be because someone is preventing it.[4]

[115]* *It's delightful to be on retreat* at a temple over the New Year when it's terribly cold and there's a feeling of snow in the freezing air. On the other hand, it ruins the mood of the occasion if the skies are instead heavy with the threat of rain.

You've come on pilgrimage to the temple at Kiyomizu, say, intending to seclude yourself in one of the private seclusion rooms; the carriage is drawn up to the foot of the long stairs leading up to the temple, and while the room is being prepared, you observe the young monks, dressed only in little waist-robes[1] and wearing those high clogs they wear, trotting perfectly non-chalantly up and down the steep stairway, murmuring scraps of sutra or chanting the four-word verses of the *Kusha Sutra*[2] as they go. It's a scene that goes perfectly with the place. Though the climb up the stairway feels most precarious, and when you have to do it yourself you keep to the side and cling to the railing, it's intriguing to see how these young monks seem to treat it just as if it were a flat, boarded path.

A monk goes over to a carriage and announces, 'The rooms are ready. Please come along'; shoes are fetched, and the ladies are helped to descend. Some have their long hems tucked up, while others appear all decked out in train and Chinese jacket. It's delightfully reminiscent of the palace, to see people shuffling along in lacquered leather shoes or short boots as they enter the hall.

The women are accompanied by children and by a group of young men who have the run of the temple inside and out, who are instructing the women on where to take care as they go – 'There's a step down here', 'It goes up a bit there', and so on. Some rude folk, heaven knows who, press up close to the ladies or try to push in front of them. 'Hold back there!' they're told. 'That's no way to behave. There are ladies of quality present!' But while the more sensitive will take the point and retreat, there are others who pay no notice and simply push in to be the first to reach the sacred image[3] and worship there.

It's most unpleasant to have to pass in front of the rows of kneeling pilgrims as you make your way to your room, but that glimpse of the inner sanctum beyond the lattice screen has filled you with a feeling of reverence, and with your freshly kindled faith you wonder how you could have let such a long time pass before your pilgrimage here.

The lamps that burn in front of the sacred image are not the usual ones, but those that people offer as dedicatory lamps for the inner sanctum. They burn quite terrifyingly fiercely, and the sight of the sacred image glittering in their light overwhelms you with reverence. The priests gathered on the dedication platform before the altar keep raising aloft the dedicatory petitions of the pilgrims, swaying slightly as they intone the accompanying vows and prayers. Such an incessant drone of voices fills the hall that it's impossible to distinguish any individual prayer, yet the straining voices of the priests still manage to carry clearly above all the surrounding noise, and you'll suddenly catch an occasional phrase – 'one thousand lamps offered with the humble prayers of So-and-so', or the like. As you perform your obeisance before the image, the worshipper's sash draped over your shoulder, a monk approaches with a few words and presents a sprig of star anise leaves,[4] and the scent of it fills you with reverence and delight.

A priest comes over to you from the other side of the dividing lattice screen and engages you in conversation. He tells you that he's presented your petitions to Kannon most satisfactorily, and asks how many days you're staying, mentioning the names of some others who are also in retreat here. Then he disappears, and you're brought a brazier, snacks, a water scoop into which hand-washing water is poured, and a little handleless bucket to hold the water. Finally, monks appear and announce which rooms your attendants are to lodge in, and as they're called they rise in turn and go off.

It's a comforting feeling to think, as you hear the bell rung for the sutra recitation to begin, that it's also ringing on your behalf. Next door you can hear a man, someone of quite high birth it seems, chanting and praying, and to judge from the way he sounds as he discreetly prostrates himself and rises, you have the impression that he's someone of considerable sensibility. He continues this throughout the night without pause for sleep, and you find it most moving to think of him there, so ardently engaged in his austerities. When he does break off from his prayers it's to chant sutras, at a decently moderate volume, and this too you find touching and inspiring. You rather long to be able to speak to him, and the way he tearfully blows his nose from time to time, though not at all loudly or unpleasantly, sets you to wondering just what it is that's weighing on his mind, and wishing you could somehow help his prayers to be answered.

Back then, if you were staying at the temple for some days you had a certain amount of leisure during the day. The male attendants, the serving girls and the little girls would go off to the priests' quarters, and we remained idling away the hours in our rooms, from time to time startled by the sudden loud blowing of a conch horn[5] close by.

Some gentleman, accompanied by an attendant holding his beautifully folded dedicatory prayer for him, lays down his sutra offerings and calls out for a temple attendant, his voice echoing about the surrounding mountains quite dazzlingly.

The sutra bell now sounds with an increased urgency, and as you're wondering who this dedication might be for, you hear the priest speak the name of some exalted person and continue, in an impressively potent voice, 'For the safe delivery of her child' – and you find yourself impulsively drawn to worry and pray on her behalf.

This is the sort of thing that happens when you're there on any normal occasion. If it's at New Year, though, the place is simply an uproar of noisy activity. You have no hope of pursuing your own practice, you're too busy watching the endless melee of people coming to the temple to offer up prayers for this and that.

Those who arrive as it's growing dark will be here to spend time in seclusion at the temple. The young monks move smartly to and fro, managing to carry in impossibly large standing screens, and laying down mats, till before you know it they've set up little temporary rooms, swishing blinds up into place over the lattice of the inner sanctum,[6] all with impressive aplomb. It looks so simple, watching them do it. With a rustle of silk a number of ladies now arrive, and hearing the refined voice of a rather elderly lady speaking in lowered tones, you guess that some of the women will be returning home, having seen their mistress here, for she's apparently instructing them to be careful about certain matters there, to make sure no fires occur and so forth. You're also enchanted to hear the sweet voice of a boy of seven or eight, speaking to the servants in an authoritative tone, and then there's the most endearing sound of a small child of about three, who's just woken and gives a timid little cough. He calls the name of his nurse, then he says 'Mama', and you long to know who the mother might be.

The priests keep up a great clamour of sutra chanting throughout the night, so that you get no sleep. After the pre-dawn service you manage to doze off, when suddenly you're jolted awake again by the sound of fierce and awe-inspiring chanting. The voice, which is reciting the special sutra of the temple, belongs to a man who seems to be a mountain ascetic, and not a particularly impressive-looking one, who's spread his straw coat out to sit on as he chants. It's most moving to hear him.

Then there's the interesting scene of one of the day visitors, evidently quite a personage, who's dressed in cotton-padded blue-grey gathered trousers and multiple layers of white robes, with a couple of young men who are apparently his sons, wearing most charming ceremonial outfits. Some youths are accompanying them, and they're quite hemmed in by numerous retainers. They have set up a temporary enclosure of standing screens, and seem to be performing a few perfunctory obeisances to the altar.

You always wonder who it is if you don't recognize them, and it's fun to try to identify the ones you think you do recognize. The young men will tend to hang about near the ladies' quarters, and not so much as glance in the direction of the sacred image. They'll call the temple superintendent out and discuss something with him in lowered voices, and you can surmise that they're people of considerable standing.

It's also fun to undertake a temple seclusion around the end of the second month and the beginning of the third, at the time when the blossoms are at their height. Along comes a group of two or three fine-looking young men, who have the air of being heads of their respective households. Their overcloaks in the cherry-blossom or willow combinations are most attractive, and the way they've tied the furl of their gathered trousers up high above the ankle is most distinguished. They're accompanied by attendants carrying beautifully decorated lunch boxes, who set the scene off to perfection, and the young retainers are dressed in plum-pink or spring-shoot green hunting costumes, variously coloured robes and skirted trousers in a printed pattern. It's delightful to witness them beating the prayer gong,[7] with slender youths evidently of good retainer families in tow holding branches of cherry blossom. One of them is someone you recognize, but he has no means of guessing your presence there. It's amusing to overhear another lady murmur longingly, 'Oh, I do wish there was some way to give him a sign', from the sheer frustration of watching someone pass by and go on his way without being aware of her.

It really feels rather pointless to stay at temples like this, or indeed to go anywhere unusual, if the only people with you are your own attendants. You do need to ask along one or two others, or if possible more – people of the same standing as yourself, with whom you get on well and with whom you can discuss all the things that take your fancy or that you find unpleasant. There may well be some among your own attendants who don't disappoint in conversation, but the problem is that they're people you see every day. Men must feel the same way, since they make a point of inviting others along when they go off on expeditions.

[116] *Deeply irritating things* – A man who sets off alone in his carriage to see an event such as the Kamo Festival or the purification ceremony that precedes it, something that the men all love to go to. What sort of crassness is this? Surely he should invite along some other young men who'd love the chance to go, even if they aren't of particularly high birth. There he sits, oblivious, a vague, solitary figure dimly seen behind the blinds of his carriage, gazing intently at the proceedings. How boorishly mean-spirited and horrid, you think at the sight of him.

Rain on the day when you're to go out for some special event or a temple pilgrimage.

Happening to hear one of the people in your service complaining that you don't like her, and someone else is your favourite of the moment.

Someone you don't particularly care for, who jumps to ridiculous conclusions and gets upset about nothing, and generally behaves with irritating self-importance.

[117] *Miserable-looking things* – Someone travelling along the road at a listless pace, in a dowdy carriage hitched to a wretched-looking ox, at the height of a hot late summer afternoon in the sixth or seventh month.

A carriage with its rain cover[1] in place, on a fine day.

A poorly dressed woman of the lower classes with a baby strapped to her back, on a very cold or very hot day.

An aged beggar.

A dingy-looking wooden shack, weathered dark with age, standing in the rain. Also, an outrider riding a little pony in pouring rain. It's not quite so bad in winter, but in summer his gown and train-robe stick together miserably.

[118] *Things that look stiflingly hot* – The hunting costume of a chief escort guard.[1] A heavy patchwork surplice. A Lieutenant of the Guards on duty to oversee the imperial games.[2]

An extremely fat person with a great deal of hair.

A high priest performing prayers and incantations through the midday hours in the sixth or seventh month.

[119]* *Embarrassing things* – The heart of a man.[1]

A night-priest[2] who's a light sleeper.

Who knows when there might not be a thief hiding in some secret place nearby and watching? Oblivious to him, someone chooses a moment under cover of darkness to steal something lying about. The thief would find it most amusing to witness another with the same urge as himself.

The night-priest is a rather embarrassing person in general, for he eagerly takes in all the things that the younger gentle-women tend to say about other people when they get together – the gossip and the funny stories, the maligning and the carping. 'Come come, that's quite enough!' the older ladies near Her Majesty will scold them, but they take no notice of this, and on and on they chatter, until at last they settle down to sleep in an unmannerly way. This is very embarrassing, when you consider the night-priest who overhears it all.

I must say I'm ashamed for any woman who's taken in by some man who is privately thinking, 'How depressing! She's not at all what I hoped she'd be. She's full of irritating faults', but when he's with her will fawn and flatter and convince her to trust him. This is particularly true of someone who has a reputation for the dashing nature of his love affairs – such a lover will certainly never act in a way that would suggest to the woman that he's lacking in feelings for her. And then there's the man who doesn't keep his criticisms to himself, but will speak his mind about one woman's faults to another woman, and do the same about her when he's with the first, while she never suspects that he slanders her in the same way to the other, and assumes that his confiding these criticisms to her can only mean that she's the one he really loves. I must say, if ever I do come across a man who seems to feel for me at all, I immediately assume he's actually quite shallow-hearted, so I have no need to expose myself to potential embarrassment.

I really do find it astonishing the way a man will fail to be in the slightest bit affected by the moving nature of a woman's deep unhappiness, when he considers abandoning her. Yet how glibly he'll criticize the actions of others! And then there's the man who takes advantage of a lady at court who has no one to protect her interests, wins her over, and when she falls pregnant, repudiates the affair completely.

[120] *Awkward and pointless things* – A large ship left beached by the tide. A great tree that's blown over in the wind, and lies there on its side with its roots in the air.

An inconsequential little man strutting about scolding a retainer.

In the grip of foolish jealousy, a wife takes herself off and goes into hiding from her husband, certain that he'll come looking for her – but he's in no mind to do so, and goes about his business with brazen indifference, so she must face the fact that she can't stay away from home indefinitely, and finally decides to return of her own accord.

[121] *Prayers and incantations* – The Nara style is best. Their performance of the protection mantras[1] is wonderfully elegant and awe-inspiring.

[122] *Awkward and embarrassing things* – Going confidently out to greet a visitor on the assumption that it's for you, when he's in fact called to see a different person. It's even worse when he's brought along a gift as well.

You happen to say something rude about someone, and a child who overhears it repeats your words in front of the person concerned.

Someone tells you an affecting story, tears streaming as she speaks – but though you can well understand how moving it is as you listen, not a tear emerges from your eyes. This is terribly awkward. You make a tearful face and do your best to look sad and moved, but quite without success. On the other hand, if you see or hear something wonderful, you can find yourself overwhelmed with tears.

On the way back[1] from the imperial procession to the Hachiman Shrine, His Majesty's palanquin was drawn up at a point beyond the viewing stand[2] erected for Her Imperial Highness the Empress Dowager, and his greetings were presented to her. This was so moving and marvellous to witness that tears absolutely poured down my face, washing off all my make-up and making me look quite dreadful. It was delightful to see Consultant Captain Tadanobu approaching the viewing stand bearing His Majesty's message. He was accompanied only by four retainers, dressed in splendid ceremonial costume, together with some slender attendants to hold his horse, whose faces were made up white. It was thrilling to see the Captain come thundering down the beautiful wide expanse of Nijō Avenue on his magnificent horse, then dismount at a little distance and proceed to the viewing stand on foot to present the message through one of the nearby blinds. And I can't even begin to describe just how impressive it was to witness him receive her reply, return with it and present it to His Majesty. I could barely contain the urge to jump with delight, imagining with just what feelings Her Imperial Highness must be watching her son go by. This is the sort of occasion when I can't stop crying, to everyone's great amusement. Even for us lesser people, it's a wonderful thing to witness one's own child doing well in the world, so I was filled with awe to imagine Her Imperial Highness's exalted emotions.

[123]* *The Regent was to emerge* from the Black Door, and we ladies were all gathered in a tight crush to welcome him. 'Well, well,' he declared as he made his way through, 'what a fine collection of beauties we have here! How you all must be laughing, to see this old fellow.' The ladies by the door raised the doorway blind, displaying their multi-coloured layers of

sleeve as they did so, and Acting Grand Counsellor Korechika
fetched his father's shoes and helped him on with them. He did
look marvellous, so weighty and dignified and finely dressed,
and with his train flowing out behind him, his presence bulked
impressively large. 'Ah, what a fine moment,' I thought, 'for
the Regent to have his shoes presented to him by the Grand
Counsellor, his own son!'

Grand Counsellor Yamanoi and others of lesser rank who
were not closely related lined the courtyard from the Fujitsubo
wall all the way to the front of the Tōkaden,[1] their black trains
spilling out behind them. The Regent, looking wonderfully
slender and elegant, paused to adjust his ceremonial sword. By
the door stood Commissioner Michinaga, and it seemed to me
that he would be unlikely to bow before his brother, but as the
Regent came forward he did in fact abruptly sink to his knees.
What a scene it was! What past action, I wondered with awe,
might have led to the good fortune of attaining such present
glory.

That day happened to be a day of abstinence for Chūnagon,
and she was pursuing her devotions most piously. 'Here,' I
said, 'lend us that rosary of yours, so we can win our way to
glory too with some prayers', and everyone gathered round her
laughing. But for all our joking, the Regent really was most
glorious. When Her Majesty heard of my remark, she said with
a smile, 'It seems to me that one would do far better to become
a buddha than a regent', which was a wonderful response, I
thought.

When I kept mentioning to Her Majesty how Commissioner Michinaga had bowed before the Regent, she smilingly
teased me by referring to him as 'that perennial favourite of
yours'. If she could have lived to witness the greatness he later
attained, she would have realized how right I was to find him
so impressive.

[124] *It's beautiful the way the water drops* hang so thick and
dripping on the garden plants after a night of rain in the ninth
month, when the morning sun shines fresh and dazzling on
them. Where the rain clings in the spider webs that hang in the

open weave of a screening fence or draped on the eaves, it forms the most moving and beautiful strings of white pearly drops.

I also love the way, when the sun has risen higher, the bush clover, all bowed down beneath the weight of the drops, will shed its dew, and a branch will suddenly spring up though no hand has touched it. And I also find it fascinating that things like this can utterly fail to delight others.

[125] *When we gathered the herbs* on the sixth day of the first month, the day before the Festival of Young Herbs, there was a happy bustle as everyone spread them out. The children had brought in some plants I'd never seen before.

'What do you call that one?' I asked.

At first they were stumped for a reply. They looked at each other in silent bewilderment, hoping for inspiration, then finally one of them said, 'It's called the No-ears plant.'[1]

'Oh yes,' said I laughing, 'it would be, wouldn't it. No ears for hearing questions, just like you.'

Someone had also picked a dear little freshly-opened wild chrysanthemum flower, and I longed to recite this poem to them:

> Though you pinch and pluck
> these little earless ones, alas
> the poor things cannot hear.
> Among them the only 'ear' belongs
> to the bright chrysanthemum.[2]

But I knew this would go right past their little ears too.

[126]* *In the second month, an event called The Selection* is held in the Office of State, but I don't know quite what it is. It's probably the event where they display the pictures of Confucius. Odd-shaped rice cakes called *sōmé*[1] are offered on earthenware plates to Their Majesties.

Well, one day a groundskeeper brought me a gift of what looked like a picture of some sort, wrapped in white paper and

attached to a sprig of beautifully flowering plum. It came from
Secretary Controller Yukinari. I opened it eagerly, expecting a
picture, and there instead I discovered two *heitan* cakes,[2] side
by side and neatly wrapped. With this was an official straight-
folded letter, some kind of formal communication, which said
in stiff language:

For Presentation:
One packet heitan cakes
hereby presented in accordance with precedent.
From: The Master of the Household   To: The Junior Counsellor

with the date appended, and signed 'Mimana Nariyuki'.[3] At
the end of the letter, in the most delightful handwriting, was
added: 'The above-signed humble servant would like to make
an appearance in person, but it would appear that he refrains
from doing so in daylight hours owing to his ugly appearance.'[4]

I took it along and showed it to Her Majesty. 'What splendid
writing!' she exclaimed, and taking it in her hand she went on
to praise the witty way he'd composed it.

'How should I respond?' I wondered aloud. 'Should I give
the messenger who brought it some gift? I do wish there was
someone who knew about this kind of protocol.'[5]

Overhearing me, Her Majesty remarked, 'I just heard Korenaka's voice.[6] Why not call him over and ask him', so I went
to the edge of the room and told one of the servants that I
wished to speak with the Minister of the Left.

He arrived looking terribly smart and proper.[7] 'Oh no, I'm
afraid this is a merely personal matter,' I told him, and I proceeded to ask what if anything should be given to the messenger
in a case where a certain Controller has sent this particular
thing to a Junior Counsellor.

'Nothing is given,' he replied. 'He simply takes it and eats it.
Why do you ask? Might you perhaps have received something
from someone in the Office of State?'

'Good gracious no, how could you imagine that!' I replied.

In response I wrote on beautiful red thin paper, 'Such handsome cakes they look, but it looks most "unhandsome" of that

servant not to present them himself',[8] and I sent it to him attached to a lovely spray of red plum blossom.

He appeared in no time, announcing, 'The humble servant is at your service!' When I went out to meet him, he said admiringly, 'I would have expected the person who received that to respond with some half-baked poem, but your reply was brilliant. A woman who fancies herself as a poet generally leaps at the chance to compose, but I much prefer someone who doesn't behave like that. For the likes of me, a person who loves to reply with a poem comes across as actually having a much poorer sensibility than someone who doesn't.'

We ended the conversation by my saying with a laugh that he must be talking about Norimitsu. I later heard from someone that Yukinari had repeated this story when a lot of people were gathered in His Majesty's presence, and His Majesty had said that I had spoken very cleverly.

It's very unseemly of me to boast like this, I know, but on the other hand I do think it's an entertaining story.

[127]* *One day someone idly said*, 'I wonder why the baton held by a man who's just begun to serve in the sixth rank is made from a piece of wood from the south-east corner of the wall surrounding the Office of the Empress's Household? You'd think something from the east or the west wall would serve just as well.' Then we began to come up with various other idle questions.

'It's most peculiar how some clothes have such weird names,' someone else said. 'Take the case of the name "thin-long", for instance. Or why is a "sweat-garment"[1] called that?'

Others came up with other examples. 'And what about "long-bottom",[2] those things young boys wear?' 'And why "Chinese jacket"? It should be called a "short-jacket", surely.'

'But that's because it's worn by people in China,' someone else pointed out.

'It's reasonable to call an overgown and overtrousers by those names,' said another. '"Underlayer" is a good name too.'

'And "wide-mouth",[3] there's another reasonable one. The hem openings are wider than the trousers are long, aren't they?'

'But "hakama" is a very boring name.'

'And why do we have the name "sew-and-pull"?[4] It would be better to call them "leg clothes", or even "sacks", surely.'

And on they all went, criticizing everything they could think of, till I finally said, 'Now come on, that's enough noise. I don't intend to say any more on the subject. Do go to sleep.'

In response to this, the voice of the night-priest nearby suddenly broke in, rather angrily, 'No no, that's a very bad idea. Do keep talking all night, ladies.'

This was not only very entertaining, but also gave us a terrible start.

[128] *After the late Regent's death*, Her Majesty had religious services for his soul performed on the tenth day of each month, and in the ninth month these took place at the Office of the Empress's Household. A great crowd of court nobles and senior courtiers attended. Seihan was the preacher, and his sermon was so sad and affecting that all the young people were apparently weeping, though one wouldn't have expected them yet to have a very deep sense of the sorrows of worldly transience.

After the service the *saké* went round, and the men proceeded to recite Chinese verses. Secretary Captain Tadanobu's strong-voiced recitation of the poem:

> Once more the moon comes round to autumn
> but where is he gone who loved it then?[1]

was wonderfully appropriate. How did he manage to come up with such a perfect poem for the occasion, I wonder?

I left the proceedings, and made my way through to where Her Majesty was sitting. I met her as she was coming out. 'That was marvellous,' she declared. 'He must surely have prepared that poem especially for today's proceedings.'

'I left off watching to come and say that very thing to Your Majesty myself,' I said. 'I do think it was quite wonderful.'

'Yes, I'm not surprised that you think so,' was her teasing reply.[2]

Tadanobu often made a point of calling me out to meet

him, and whenever we met he would start on his complaints. 'Why can we never really get close?' he would say. 'I know you don't dislike me, so I find it very strange. Such a long-standing acquaintance as ours surely can't simply end without intimacy. Come the time when I'm no longer at the palace night and day, what will I take away with me as a memory of our relationship?'

'Yes, you're right,' I replied. 'There'd be no difficulty in our getting together. But if we did, I wouldn't be able any longer to sing your praises to others, and that would be a great shame. How can we afford to become too close, when it's my role to praise you to Her Majesty? So please just love me from a distance. I'd be too embarrassed and conscience-stricken to say anything good about you if we were lovers.'

'But why is that? I know people who praise their lovers more than they seem to deserve.'

'Well, that's all very well, but I happen to hate that sort of thing. I can't stand people, men or women, who adore their lovers, and are always taking their side and praising them, and get upset when anyone refers to some little fault of theirs,' I replied.

'Oh, you're hopeless!' said he, which amused me greatly.

[129] *One evening, Secretary Controller Yukinari* visited the Office of the Empress's Household, and stayed talking far into the night. He finally left as dawn was approaching, remarking that he must return by the Hour of the Ox,[1] since he was obliged to stay at the palace all that day owing to an imperial abstinence.

The next day he sent a wonderful and very lengthy message on several pieces of official paper from the Chamberlain's Office, saying, 'My heart is still full of regrets for yesterday. I thought to stay till dawn speaking with you of things past, but the cock's crow hastened me early on my way.'

In reply I wrote, 'That cock you say you heard so late last night, could it have been the false cock of Lord Mengchang?'[2]

'They say,' wrote Yukinari in return, 'that Lord Mengchang's cock opened the Kanko barrier gate and thus allowed his three thousand followers finally to escape – but the barrier gate in my case was the lover's barrier gate of Ōsaka.'[3]

So I sent back the following:

> That innocent guard
> hearing the night's deceptive call
> opened and let them through –
> but, my friend, this lover's gate
> will fall for no such ruse.

'There's a vigilant guard at this gate,' I added.

And again came a reply:

> The gate of Ōsaka
> can be all too easily crossed
> by those who aspire –
> surely it lies open waiting
> whether the cock's crow sounds or not.

The first of his letters came into the hands of Bishop Ryūen, who was quite overawed by it,[4] and the others I gave to Her Majesty. Anyway, Yukinari's Ōsaka poem was too much for me, and I couldn't manage a reply, though this was very bad form.

Yukinari later told me that all the senior courtiers had seen my poem. 'Well,' said I sarcastically, 'this is a clear sign of how much you really care for me. After all, there's no point in having something wonderful if you don't share it, for others to pass around and talk about, is there – while I, on the other hand, hid your letters firmly away and didn't breathe a word of them to anyone, for fear of such ugly things getting spread abroad. This shows a consideration for you that's quite on a par with yours for me.'

'I must say, I find that it's this deep perceptiveness of yours that sets you off from others,' Yukinari replied with a laugh. 'And there I was, assuming you'd respond like most women would, and simply say something like "That was very shallow and frivolous of you."'

'Whatever do you mean? I was intending to compliment you,' I said.

'But I'm deeply touched and thrilled that you should want to hide my letters,' he replied. 'I would have been mortified if you hadn't. Do please continue to do so, I beg you.'

Some time later, when Captain Tsunefusa visited, he said, 'Are you aware that the Secretary Controller has been praising you to the skies? He's been telling us all about your exchanges the other day. I must say I was delighted to hear another person praising someone I'm so fond of myself.' He was most amusingly earnest about it.

'Well, this is wonderful news on two counts,' I said. 'One is that he's been praising me, and the other is that I'm numbered among those you care for.'

'Good heavens, you seem as delighted as if this was some fresh and unusual piece of news!' said he.

[130] *One dark, moonless night in the fifth month*, there was a sudden loud commotion of voices outside crying, 'Is someone in attendance there?'

'Go out and see who can be making this extraordinary fuss,' Her Majesty instructed me.

So out I went. 'Who is it, clamouring and carrying on in this fashion?' I inquired.

There was no reply, but the blind was silently raised and with a rustle there emerged from beneath it – a branch of bamboo.

'Well, well,' I said. 'So it's "this gentleman",[1] is it?'

Hearing me, the senior courtiers beyond the blind – His Highness the Minister of Ceremonial's son Captain Yorisada, a sixth-rank Chamberlain and a few others – declared in astonishment that they must take the story straight back to the Privy Chamber, and off they went.

Only Secretary Controller Yukinari stayed behind. 'Now what can have got into them?' he said. 'What happened was that we took a branch of bamboo from the garden of the Seiryōden, with the idea of composing poems on the subject. Then someone suggested we'd do just as well to go to the Office of the Empress's Household and call out the ladies to take part, so that's what we did. And now the poor things have rushed off, because you were so ready with that name! How is it that you can say things like that, the sort of thing most people wouldn't know? Who taught you?'

'But I had no idea that was the name of the bamboo,' I protested. 'They must have thought me terribly rude.'

'No, of course, how could you know?' said he with a touch of sarcasm.

We stayed there talking about other more serious matters, and after a little time the senior courtiers reappeared and joined us, chanting the line 'He planted it and called it "this gentleman".'

'I was very puzzled at the way you went off like that, when we hadn't managed to achieve what we'd planned to come here for,' the Secretary Controller said to them.

'Well, we couldn't possibly have come up with an answer to her,' they replied. 'A bad response would have made us look even worse', and they went on to tell how this story had had a fine reception in the Privy Chamber, and His Majesty had heard of it and enjoyed it as well. The Secretary Controller then fell in with them in chanting the poem over and over. A great deal of fun was had, and everyone stayed till dawn, engaged in various conversations. Even after they'd left, they could still be heard chanting the poem, till they entered the Left Gate Watch guardhouse.

Next morning, Shōnagon no Myōbu came hastening over bearing a letter to Her Majesty from the Emperor, and while she was about it she told Her Majesty the story of my response. I was summoned from my apartment, and asked if this had indeed happened.

'I know nothing about it,' I replied. 'I was quite unaware of such a thing. This must have been some story that Lord Yukinari made up.'

'Well, whether he made it up or not . . .' said Her Majesty with a smile.

It's quite delightful the way Her Majesty takes such pleasure on behalf of whomever it is that the senior courtiers are reported to have praised.

[131]* *When the year of mourning* for Retired Emperor Enyū's death was over, everyone left off wearing their mourning clothes. It was a most moving time, and everybody both in the palace and beyond was filled with sad memories of the Retired Emperor. One day when it was raining heavily, a hefty lad bundled up in a straw raincoat that made him look like a basket-worm appeared at the apartments of Her Ladyship Tōsanmi. He proffered a straight-folded letter on a presentation stick[1] of white wood, and asked that it be given to her.

'Who is it from?' her gentlewomen inquired. 'Her Ladyship is observing an abstinence today and tomorrow, and her shutters are down', and they received the letter over the top of the lower shutter.[2] They informed Her Ladyship about it, but she firmly declined to read it that day on account of the abstinence, so it was left as it was, attached to the top of the lower shutter.

Next morning, Her Ladyship washed her hands and inquired, 'Now what became of that Record of the Readings that came yesterday?' and she asked someone to fetch it. Bowing reverently, she proceeded to open it, and was bemused to discover that it was written on a thick page of white-backed walnut-brown paper.[3] Opening further, she found written in a priest's quirky handwriting the following:

> These deep-dyed clothes
> coloured with the unchanging oak
> I wear in memory –
> there in the city, have you changed
> and your fresh leaves forgot him?[4]

She was terribly shocked and disturbed. Whoever could have done this? Could it be the Abbot of Ninnaji? But no, surely he'd never do such a thing. It must be the Fujiwara Grand Counsellor,[5] since he was Master of the late Emperor's household. She felt deeply anxious and perturbed, and longed to get word of this to the Emperor and Empress as soon as possible, but she was obliged to contain her impatience and remain cloistered for another day under strict abstinence orders.

The morning after, she sent a poem in reply to the Grand Counsellor, who courteously responded in turn. Taking the two messages she'd received, Her Ladyship then hastened to the palace and, in His Majesty's presence, told Her Majesty the story. Her Majesty innocently ran her eye over the poems, and remarked, 'This doesn't look like the Grand Counsellor's writing to me. I should say it's a priest's hand,' adding very seriously, 'one can only imagine it's the doing of some demon from the past.'[6]

Well then, who could it be? Was there someone among the court nobles or priests who would enjoy this sort of trick? Her Ladyship suspiciously began to go through possible names.

At this point His Majesty broke in, saying with a playful smile, 'That paper looks very like paper I've seen around here', and he produced another sheet of it from the small cabinet nearby and held it out for her to see.

'Oh, how dreadful!' cried Her Ladyship. 'Tell me how this has happened. Oh, my poor head! I must hear the explanation right this minute!' Her face was wreathed in smiles as she set about bewailing and reproaching him.

His Majesty proceeded to confess the details, telling her that the 'demon' lad who had gone there as messenger was in the service of one of the maids from the Table Room, and he thought it was Kohyōe who had organized it by talking him into carrying the letter. Her Majesty was laughing too, and now Her Ladyship shook her, crying with an exasperated laugh, 'Why did you set me up like this? And there I was believing it was a Record of Readings, washing my hands carefully and prostrating myself in front of it!' Her look of happy pride[7] as she berated them was utterly charming.

The story was also told in His Majesty's Table Room to much laughter. Her Ladyship returned to her apartments, and asked for the lad who'd delivered the letter to be found. When he arrived he was shown to the gentlewoman who'd taken it in, who vouched that he did indeed appear to be the messenger, and Her Ladyship then set about questioning him over who had written it and who had given it to him. However, he simply grinned foolishly and scampered away, without saying a word.

As for the Grand Counsellor, he got a thorough laugh out of the story when he heard it later.

[132] *Occasions when the time drags by* – An abstinence that you must observe away from home. A game of *sugoroku* when you can't manage to get your pieces off the board. The house of someone who's failed to get a promotion in the Appointments List. And of course the worst of all is simply a day of heavy rain.

[133] *Things that relieve such occasions* – A game of *go* or *sugoroku*. Tales. A child of three or four chattering entertainingly, or a very young child talking. Snacks of fruit and nuts.

When a man turns up who has a talent for being amusing and clever, you'll always ask him in even though you're under abstinence restrictions.

[134] *Worthless things* – Someone who's both ugly and unpleasant. Clothing starch that's gone bad[1] – I know an awful lot of people hate this, but that's no reason why I shouldn't note it here.

And why should I avoid mentioning here the fire tongs that are burned in the post-funeral fire?[2] After all, these are things that exist in the world. I never intended this book to be seen by others, so I've written whatever came into my mind, without worrying about whether people would find it strange or unpleasant.[3]

[135]* *Things that are truly splendid* – For things that are truly splendid, nothing excels the two Provisional Festivals. The Rehearsal of Performance is also wonderfully entertaining.

It's spring, a glorious day of soft warm skies. Members of the Housekeeping Office have spread mats in the Seiryōden courtyard, and here the imperial envoys sit, facing north, while the dancers sit facing towards the Emperor[1] (though my memory may be mistaken here).

It's impressive to watch the men from the Chamberlain's Office bring the high trays for the banquet and place them before all the seats. It's only at this courtyard performance that the dancers' musicians can come and go in the presence of the Emperor. The court nobles and senior courtiers all take turns with the celebratory *saké* cup, and finish by drinking a round from a spiral-shell cup before they stand, at which point the leftover-gatherers emerge – these are offputting enough to witness when they're men, but in the case of this imperial event even women appear. They suddenly come scampering out from the guard's fire hut, which you've assumed till that moment to be empty, and start scrabbling for the food, but the ones who try to grab all they can get keep spilling it, and they lose out to those who make a swift grab and then turn and run. It's most entertaining to watch them making clever use of the handy fire hut as a store for their booty.

No sooner have the Chamberlains' Office men removed the mats than officials from the Office of Grounds emerge, each with a broom, and proceed to sweep the sand smooth. Then from in front of the Shōkyōden there comes the sound of flutes and rhythmic clappers. You wait with bated breath for the musicians to appear – and now here they come, stepping out from beside the fence round the stand of bamboo, to the strains of 'Udohyō',[2] and as you hear the *koto* plucking the accompaniment you feel you'll simply burst with delight. Two dancers step up for the first dance, matching sleeve with sleeve most beautifully, and stand to the west facing the imperial presence. They're followed by the other dancers, who come forward one after another, stepping in time to the music. Their hands move ceaselessly, adjusting the ties of their *banpi* jackets, their headgear, the neckbands of their cloaks, etc., and they dance and sing 'Mount Koma'[3] and other songs. It's all absolutely splendid. When they form the great circle at the end of that dance cycle you feel you could keep watching the dances all day and never tire of them. You're filled with regret that the cycle is ending, and eager for the next dancers to begin. And now the strings of the *koto* are raked, and in no time at all the dancers come stepping out from behind the bamboo. What a truly wonderful moment. The glossy sheen of their softened-silk robes, the way their long formal trains weave and twine about each other as they dance this way and that – but no, if I say any more it will only destroy the magic.

This is the final dance, and no doubt that's why you feel particularly bereft when it draws to a close. As the nobles and others all get up and file out after the dancers, you're filled with a frustrated longing for more, but this is assuaged in the case of the Provisional Kamo Festival by the Returning Dance.[4] There's a most moving and marvellous atmosphere then, with the slender ribbons of smoke rising from the courtyard watch-fires and the wonderful wavering pure notes of the *kagura* flute lifting high, and the voices of the singers. It's piercingly cold, the glossed silk of your robes is icy against the skin and your hand as it clutches the fan is chilled, but you notice none of this. I like the way the head dancer takes a terrific pleasure in performing the long-drawn-out call that summons the comic entertainers for the interlude.

If I'm back at home, I can only see the dancers as the procession passes by, but often this isn't enough for me, and I go to the shrine to watch as well.

The carriage has been drawn up under the great cedars. The smoke from the torches trails among the trees, and in the flickering firelight the cords of the dancers' *hanpi* jackets and the glossy silk of their robes glow far more impressively even than during the day. What with the thrilling way the dancers make the bridge thunder with their stamps and sing in chorus as they dance, and the murmur of the stream blending with the sound of the flutes, the gods too must surely find it all quite wonderful. There's a story about a man called the Secretary Captain,[5] who took such pride in being one of the dancers each year that after he died his ghost began to haunt the area under the shrine bridge. This story filled me with terror, and made me determined not to follow his example and become too attached to anything – but I'm afraid I simply can't give up my attachment to these splendid events.

On one occasion, His Majesty heard how we complained at feeling so let down at the end of the Yahata Provisional Festival because there's no Returning Dance. 'Why is it they don't come back and dance again?' we said to each other. 'That would be great fun. It's awful to watch it all end with the dancers receiving their gifts and leaving one by one from the back of the line.'

'Then I shall have them dance,' declared His Majesty.

'Oh, truly?' we cried. 'That would be just marvellous!' Over-joyed, we then gathered round Her Majesty, reporting his words to her and begging her to make sure he kept his promise.

And indeed they did come back and dance that year, and we were absolutely thrilled. The unfortunate dancers were thrown into a terrible state by the unexpected imperial summons to return, and became quite beside themselves in the mad flurry to prepare. And what a scene it was to see the ladies who were down in their rooms come rushing back to the Seiryōden in a great fluster for the performance. We had a fine laugh as we watched them come hurrying in, some with their trains caught up on their heads,[6] without any thought of the retainers and courtiers who were observing them.

[136]* *After the Regent had departed this life*, certain events were set in train in the world. There was considerable upheaval and commotion, and Her Majesty left the palace and moved to the Konijō mansion. Things felt rather difficult for me at this time, so I retired to my home for a lengthy period. But I remained deeply uneasy over how matters stood with Her Majesty, and in fact I wouldn't have been able to sustain the estrangement for very long.

One day Captain of the Right Tsunefusa came to call, and he reported to me as follows. 'I paid a visit to Her Majesty today, and I must say I was deeply moved by it. The gentle-women were all still carefully maintaining formal court dress, with trains and Chinese jackets to match the season. I peeped in past the edge of a blind, and there I saw eight or nine ladies sitting in a row, wearing fallen-leaf ochre Chinese jackets, pale violet-grey trains and robes in aster or bush-clover combin-ations, all very lovely. The garden was deep in grass, but when I asked why it hadn't been cleared, Her Majesty replied through Saishō that she expressly wished to see the dew on it,[1] which I found most touching. The ladies all said how miserable they were that you'd retired to your home. "No matter what's

occurred," they said, "Her Majesty feels that she must surely
be here with her now that she's living in such a place – but she
won't listen." I had the impression that they intended I should
pass this on to you. Why not try returning? It's a very moving
place. And there are lovely peonies[2] by the balcony,' he added.

'Well, I don't know,' I replied. 'I wasn't liked, and I didn't
like it . . .'

'Plainly spoken,' he said with a laugh.

In fact, Her Majesty had never given me real cause to be
concerned over how she felt about me. It was the others around
her who were getting together and saying I was in league with
the Minister of the Left. Whenever they saw me come from
my room they'd suddenly stop talking. I'd never been spurned
like that before, and I hated it. That's why I chose to ignore
Her Majesty's repeated summons to return. Besides, everyone
around her would be saying I was on the other side, and there'd
be all sorts of baseless rumours about me.

Then Her Majesty's summons ceased. As the days passed I
sank deeper into dejection, till at last one day one of the serving
ladies brought a letter for me. 'Her Majesty gave this to me
secretly via Saishō,' she whispered, ridiculously conspiratorial
about it even here.

This must mean Her Majesty herself had written the message
rather than simply relayed it through another, I thought
excitedly, and I opened it with pounding heart. The page was
empty – all I found enclosed was a single kerria petal, on which
was inscribed the following: 'and never rises into words'.[3]

All my long unhappiness at the break between us was swept
away by this wonderful message. Observing my joy, the serving
lady said, 'I hear that Her Majesty is constantly recalling you
in the course of conversation, and all her ladies are also mystified at how long you're staying away. Why don't you go back?'
Then she rose, saying she was just going to make another visit
nearby, and would return again before long.

After she'd left, I settled down to compose my reply, but I
simply couldn't recall the beginning of the poem Her Majesty
had used. 'How extraordinary!' I muttered to myself. 'There
can't be anyone who doesn't know an old poem like that! I've

almost got it, but it just won't come. What on earth can I do?'

Hearing me, a young serving girl sitting nearby prompted me by saying, 'It's "Greater the feeling / that in the waters of the heart . . ."' Now how could I have forgotten that? It was most amusing to find myself instructed by my own serving girl.

Not long after I'd sent my reply, I returned. Still feeling quite unsure of my reception, I was much more tentative than usual, and when I first went before Her Majesty I could only peep timidly out from behind the standing curtain, but she laughed and said teasingly, 'Is that someone new to service I see there?'

'I don't care for that poem I used,' she said to me, 'but I do think it was perfect for my purposes at the time. I simply couldn't rest easy until I'd run you to ground.' She really didn't seem at all changed towards me.

She laughed greatly when I told her how the serving girl had quoted to me the lines I needed. 'Yes, that does happen,' she said. 'It's all too easy to forget an over-familiar old poem we've ceased to have any respect for.' Then she proceeded to tell the following story.

'This reminds me,' she said, 'of a famous game of Riddles.[4] One of the people involved, a man of considerable skill and experience in these matters and who was in a position to be impartial, offered to be the first to pose a riddle for the Left team. "Leave this one to me," he said, and they happily did so, firm in the faith that he would come up with something good. Well, they all set about making their riddles, and when it came time to select the best for the contest he firmly instructed them to ask no questions but simply to leave matters to him. "See how confident I am?" he said. "You can be sure you won't regret it", and they did indeed see his point. And so the day drew to a close. They asked him to reveal his riddle, just in case someone else had come up with the same thing, but this only upset him. "If that's how you feel, I'll have no more to do with it. You can count me out," he replied huffily, so when the day arrived they were still none the wiser, and feeling rather anxious.

'Well, the men and women all gathered to sit on their two sides, and there were rows upon rows of witnesses for the event.

The man in the First Left place was looking so smug and well-prepared that those on both sides found themselves waiting with bated breath to hear the riddle he'd produce. "What am I?" he began, in a provokingly confident voice, and then he continued, "A bow drawn in the heavens."[5]

'Those on the opposing team were absolutely delighted at this, while the Left side were quite enraged, and the thought flashed through their minds that the loathsome fellow was actually working for the other team and had set out purposely to make them lose.

'The speaker from the Right burst out laughing. "Oh, dear me," he chuckled, "this is ridiculous!" and then he went on sarcastically, with a comical smirk, "Hmm, I just can't guess . . ."

'No sooner had the words left his mouth, than the man from the Left promptly claimed a score for his side. The opposing contestant tried to argue the case. "But this is absurd!" he cried. "Everyone knows the answer to this riddle! It's quite out of order to claim a score!"

' "How can you assert you didn't lose," responded the man from the Left, "when you clearly said you had no idea of the answer?" – and he went on to argue his way through each ensuing riddle to claim a win for his team as well.

'Well, it's all very well to admit you don't know when you really can't recall something everyone knows perfectly well, but you can imagine how everyone on the Right berated him later for saying such a thing in this case.'

'They certainly would have been angry,' I agreed, laughing. 'What an unfortunate way to answer! And how awful it must have felt for everyone on the Left, when they heard that riddle!'

Though it was a rather different situation from my own, Her Majesty no doubt intended this story as another example of saying you don't know something that everyone knows perfectly well but has forgotten.

[137] *It's towards the middle of the first month*. Heavy black clouds are darkening the sky, but through them the sunlight flashes intensely. The barren field beside the house of some

lowly folk is a tumble of untended earth, and in it stands a healthy young peach tree, thick with little branchlets. One side still holds its green leaves, while the other is covered in rich, glossy, rust-red leaves that shine in the sunlight, and in the tree is clambering a beautifully slender youth, hunting costume rather torn but hair well-kempt. A little boy, his hems hitched high and shins bare above his short boots, stands beneath the tree. 'Cut me one for a bat!' he begs the lad.

Now three or four little girls with pretty hair come along, in ragged *akomé* gowns and limp skirted trousers but with nice robes beneath. 'Cut us some sticks for good hare-mallets!' they cry. 'Our mistress wants them.' The boy cuts some sticks and throws them down, and the children under the tree all scramble for them, some pausing to look up and cry, 'Lots for me!'

And now a man in black skirted trousers comes running up and asks the boy for sticks, and when he refuses the man shakes the tree dangerously, and the boy clings there like a monkey, protesting loudly. A charming scene!

You can see similar scenes when the plums ripen.

[138] *A good-looking man has spent the day* engrossed in playing *sugoroku*, and now as night draws in he seems still intent on playing, for he lights a low standing lamp and turns up the wick to shine brightly. His antagonist is earnestly praying

Playing sugoroku

over the dice instead of slipping them promptly into the dicing cup, and our man stands the dicing cup on the board as he waits. The neck-band of his hunting costume has ridden up till it rubs his face, and his other hand goes up to push it back into place. He tosses his head irritably to reposition the flap of his limp lacquered cap while he continues to gaze impatiently at his opponent, and you can see he's thinking, 'Whatever curse you try to put on my dice, I'm still going to beat you, my friend.' How delightfully arrogant he looks!

[139] *It's also amusing to see* someone of high standing playing *go* against a social inferior. He lounges there relaxed, the ties of his robe loosened, casually scooping up the pieces and putting them on the board, while the man of lesser rank sits a little back from the board, maintaining a carefully respectful posture, and when he leans forward to play he'll politely raise his other hand to draw back the hanging flap of his sleeve.

[140] *Alarming-looking things* – Thorny acorn husks. A hairy yam that's been baked. The prickly water lily. Water chestnuts.[1] The sight of a man with a lot of hair, drying it after washing.

[141] *Things that look fresh and pure* – Earthenware cups.[1] Shiny new metal bowls. Rushes to be used for making mats. The transparent light in water as you pour it into something.

[142] *Distasteful-looking things* – The baton of an Aide of Ceremonial. A bad hairline in black hair. A new screen lined with simple cloth.[1] One that's already old and discoloured is so beneath notice that it doesn't bother you any more. I'm speaking here of some new one with, say, a colourful picture of flowering cherries painted on it with white and red pigments.

A cabinet with sliding doors. A fat priest. Real Izumo matting.[2]

[143] *Things that make the heart lurch with anxiety* – Watching a horse-race. Twisting up a paper hair-binding cord.[1] When a parent looks out of sorts, and remarks that they're

not feeling well. This particularly worries you to distraction when you've been hearing panicky tales of plague sweeping the land. Also, a little child who can't yet talk, who simply cries and cries, refusing to drink from the breast or even to be comforted when the nurse picks it up and holds it.

Your heart naturally lurches when you hear the voice of your secret lover in an unexpected place, but the same thing happens even when you hear someone else talking about him. It also lurches when someone you really detest arrives for a visit.

Indeed the heart is a creature amazingly prone to lurching. It even lurches in sympathy with another woman when the next-morning letter from a man who stayed with her for the first time the night before is late in arriving.

[144] *Endearingly lovely things* – A baby's face painted on a gourd. A sparrow coming fluttering down to the nest when her babies are cheeping for her.

A little child of two or three is crawling rapidly along when his keen eye suddenly notices some tiny worthless thing lying nearby. He picks it up in his pretty little fingers, and shows it to the adults. This is very endearing to see. It's also endearing when a child with a shoulder-length 'nun's cut' hairstyle[1] that's falling into her eyes doesn't brush it away but instead tilts her head to tip it aside as she examines something.

A very young son of a noble family walking about dressed up in ceremonial costume. An enchanting little child who falls asleep in your arms while you're holding and playing with it is terribly endearing.

Things children use in doll play. A tiny lotus leaf that's been picked from a pond. A tiny *aoi* leaf. In fact, absolutely anything that's tiny is endearing.

A very white, plump child of around two, who comes crawling out wearing a lavender silk-gauze robe with the sleeves hitched back, or a child walking about in a short robe that looks more long sleeves than robe. All these are endearing. And it's very endearing when a boy of eight or ten reads something aloud in his childish voice.

It's also enchanting to see a pretty little white chick, its lanky legs looking like legs poking out from under a short robe, cheeping loudly as it runs and pauses here and there around someone's feet. Likewise, all scenes of chicks running about with the mother hen. The eggs of a spot-billed duck. A green-glass pot.

[145] *Times when someone's presence produces foolish excitement* – A mother who's pampering and praising her spoilt child, who is actually nothing out of the ordinary.

The little introductory cough you give when you're about to address someone who overawes you.

A child of four or five from a neighbouring place is playing up and annoying people, throwing things about and damaging them. You seize him to prevent him from behaving so wilfully, but then his mother arrives and the boy, emboldened by her presence, starts tugging at her sleeve and whining, 'Show me that, mama! Let me see it!' His mother is deep in conversation with the adults and doesn't pay him any attention, so the child then goes and pulls the thing out himself for a look, and starts creating havoc. This is quite infuriating. However, the mother doesn't take it from him and put it out of his reach and scold him, but only smiles and says mildly, 'Don't do that, dear' or 'Don't you break it now' – at which point you begin to loathe her as well. It's unbearably frustrating to have to sit there biting your tongue.

[146] *Things with terrifying names* – River deeps. Mountain caves. 'Scale-board' walls. Iron. Clods. Thunder – not just the name, but the thing itself is extremely terrifying. Gales. Ominous clouds. Comets. 'Arm-umbrella' rain.[1] The wilds.

Robbery is terrifying in every way. Violent monks are very terrifying indeed. So are *kanamochi*. Living spirit possession. The snake berry. Devil fern. Devil vine. Thorn bushes. Chinese bamboo. Roasted charcoal. A bull-demon.[2] Anchors – the sight of one is more terrifying than the name.

[147]* *Things that look ordinary but become extraordinary when written* – Strawberries. The dew plant. The prickly water

lily. Spiders. Chestnuts.[1] Doctors of literature. Postgraduate students. Acting Master of the Empress Dowager's Palace. The arbutus tree.

People write the name 'knotweed' with characters meaning 'tiger's staff'. A tiger doesn't look as though it would need a staff!

[148] *Repulsive things* – The back of a piece of sewing. Hairless baby mice tumbled out of their nest. The seams of a leather robe before the lining's been added.[1] The inside of a cat's ear. A rather dirty place in darkness.

A very ordinary woman looking after lots of children. The way a man must feel when his wife, who he's not really very fond of, is ill for a long time.

[149]* *Occasions when something inconsequential has its day* – Daikon radishes at New Year. The Imperial Attendant ladies during an imperial procession. The ladies from the Palace Gates Office, at the time of the imperial accession. Lady Chamberlains in the Bamboo Breaking ceremonies[1] at the end of the sixth and twelfth months.

The Master of Solemnities at the Great Sutra Readings of the second and eighth months. How splendid he is in his red ecclesiastical robes, solemnly intoning the names of all the monks!

The people who decorate the hall for the imperial Litany of Buddha Names or the Great Sutra Readings. Escorts from the Palace Guards at the time of the Kasuga Festival. The foodtaster on the third day of the new year.[2] The priests who present the hare-mallets to the Emperor. The ladies who do up the dancers' hair for the Gosechi dances rehearsal night. The Palace Maidens who serve at the imperial table during the five Palace Festivals.

[150] *People who look as though things are difficult for them* – The nurse of an infant who cries during the night. A man with two lovers, both of whom are jealous. An exorcist who's struggling to defeat a stubborn spirit. His incantations ought to begin taking effect very promptly, but in this instance things

are going differently, and he looks quite agonized as he prays frantically on, desperate not to become a laughing-stock.

A woman who's adored by a man who's prone to groundless suspicions.

Someone who wields power and influence in the household of one of the great men can't have an easy life, but it must be nice nevertheless.

Someone who's constantly irritable.

[151] *People who seem enviable* – You set about learning to recite a sutra, stumbling along, going endlessly over the same places and constantly forgetting bits. When you hear the same words tripping smoothly off the tongue of others – not only the priests, but other men and women – you wonder enviously if you'll ever be able to perform it like that.

You're feeling ill and miserable, and you witness people going by laughing and joking together, apparently without a care in the world. How you envy them!

You have an urge to go on a pilgrimage to Inari Shrine,[1] and as you're laboriously gasping your way up the steep mountainside to the middle shrine, you're filled with admiration to see others who've obviously started behind you go climbing straight up without the least effort; when you arrive, there they stand, already at their worship.

Once, on the day of the shrine festival in the second month, I set off for the pilgrimage at sunrise, but hurry though I might it was already mid-morning by the time I'd reached the halfway point along the mountain path. It grew really quite hot as the morning drew on, and feeling by then thoroughly wretched, I paused for a while, tearfully wondering why on earth I had to choose such a hot day to come, when another day would have made it all so much easier. As I sat there, I overheard a woman of forty or more, not even dressed in travelling wear but simply with her robes tucked up, remarking to someone she'd met on the path as she descended, 'I'm performing seven pilgrimage circuits. I've already completed three, and it'll be no trouble to do the remaining four. I should be off the mountain again by early afternoon.' It wouldn't have struck me as anything worth noticing in another situation, but at the time how I longed to be her!

I thoroughly envy anyone – man, woman or priest – who has fine children. Also people with lovely long, smooth hair with beautiful ends. And I very much envy great people when I see how everyone reveres them and attends to their every need. And people who write in a beautiful hand and are good at poetry, who are called on for every occasion.

You'd think that when some fine lady who's surrounded by a bevy of gentlewomen plans to send a message to someone of particular distinction, she could safely assume that none of her ladies would write it in some dreadful chicken scrawl.[2] But no, she sends especially for one among them who happens to be back in her room at the time, and offers her own inkstone for the task. How I envy that lady! Once a gentlewoman has been in service for a long time, even if her writing is little better than a beginner's copybook level, in normal situations she'll be able to produce something appropriate enough – but now the occasion is a special one, a letter to a court noble, for instance, or in response to a request that someone's daughter be permitted to enter service there. Her mistress prepares things for the task with scrupulous care, beginning with a painstaking selection of the paper to be used, and meanwhile the other ladies gather round and jokingly declare how they envy her the task.

If you're learning one of the woodwind or stringed instruments, just as with calligraphy, while you're still in the beginning stages you wonder when you'll ever become as good as others.

The nurse of the Emperor or the Crown Prince. Also, gentlewomen in the Emperor's household, who have the freedom to come and go in the households of the various imperial wives.[3]

[152] *Things whose outcome you long to know* – When one of the various forms of tie-dyeing, such as roll dye or dapple-dye, is in process.[1]

When someone's just had a child, you long to know whether it's a boy or a girl. This is particularly the case when the parents are of high birth, but you still long to know even when it's some ordinary person or someone of low birth.

The morning following the announcements of the Appointments List. Even if no one you know is likely to be given a new appointment, you're still dying to hear who got what.

[153] *Occasions for anxious waiting* – You've sent some fabric to someone for urgent sewing, and now you sit impatiently expecting it back at any moment, gazing anxiously in the direction you sent it.

Someone's expecting a child, but the due date has come and gone and there's still no sign of the birth beginning.

When you receive a letter from a distant man you care for, how nervously you struggle to open the tight seal on it!

You set off late to see a festival, and alas the procession has already begun. You glimpse the white batons of the policemen who are clearing the way ahead of the procession, and while your carriage is being manoeuvred into a closer position in the crowd, you're filled with despair at the thought of what you'll be missing, and long to be able simply to get out and walk.

A person has called whom you would prefer didn't know you were there, and you've told one of the ladies what she should say to him, while you wait anxiously in the background, hoping the strategy will work.

It's the fiftieth or hundredth day since the birth of an anxiously awaited child, and now you find yourself feeling apprehensive over what will become of him in life.

Trying to thread a needle to do an urgent bit of sewing, when it's already beginning to grow dark. It's bad enough when you're attempting to do it yourself; it's still worse if you've asked someone else to do it for you while you hold the needle for her, to indicate where you think the eye is, and she's too flustered to be able to get the thread through. 'Oh, never mind,' you say, 'you needn't bother', but she appears mystified that she can't do it, and simply refuses to give up. By this point, you're not only anxious, you're downright angry as well.

You're in a hurry to set off for somewhere, and someone

says, 'I just have to go to such-and-such a place first, I'll send the carriage back for you before long', and you wait for it with mounting irritation. How disappointed you are when you've heard a carriage coming down the main street and think with joy, 'There it is!', only to have it disappear in a different direction. And you quite despair if you're waiting to go off to see a festival, and overhear someone remarking, 'The procession will have begun by now.'

A baby has been born, and time passes but still no afterbirth appears.

You're setting off to see a festival, or on a temple pilgrimage, and the carriage has called in at the home of someone who's to join the expedition. It's drawn up waiting at the house, but she's taking her time to appear, and you feel so exasperated as you wait that you long simply to leave her behind and be on your way immediately.

It takes an awfully long time to get roasted charcoal to light, which is very irritating when you need it in a hurry.

You become very anxious when you have to make a quick response to someone's poem, and you can't come up with anything. If it's a lover there's no particular need to hurry to send a reply, but there are times when circumstances make it necessary. And if it's some exchange with a lady, nothing special, and you feel you can just dash something off, that's precisely when you're inclined to make an unfortunate blunder.

When you're not feeling well, or when you're afraid of something, how anxiously you wait for the night to end!

[154]* *When Her Majesty was in mourning for the previous Regent*, she was required to leave the palace at the time of the Great Purification at the end of the sixth month. However, the Office of the Empress's Household happened to be in a forbidden direction at the time, so she moved instead to the Aitadokoro, which belonged to the Council of State.

Our first night there was hot and extraordinarily dark, and we spent it feeling cramped and rather anxious as we waited for the dawn. The following morning we took a look at the building. It was in the Chinese style, very flat, with a low tiled roof, and altogether quite unusual-looking. Instead of the customary lattice shutters, it was enclosed only by blinds. It was such a strange and charming place that we ladies went out into the garden to entertain ourselves in the unusual surroundings. There we found a massed planting of day lilies, with a rough woven fence. It was most effective to have such a vivid array of nodding flower clusters in the garden of a formal place such as this.

The Timekeeping Office was just across the way, and we were intrigued at the unusually close sound of the watch-drum.[1] About twenty of the younger ladies went across and climbed up a staircase into the high watchtower to investigate. Watching them from our building, their climbing figures all in light-grey trains and Chinese jackets, with unlined summer gowns of the same light-grey and scarlet skirted trousers, they looked, if not exactly like heavenly beings, at least like creatures that had descended from the sky. It was amusing to see the one who'd helped the others climb by supporting them from below and so couldn't join them up there herself, standing below gazing enviously up at them, though she too was young enough to be able to climb.

They also went across to the guard office of the Left Gate Watch, and apparently some of them were misbehaving there, tumbling about and creating a great racket. People sternly castigated them, telling them it was most inappropriate to go climbing on to the chairs that the court nobles sit on and damaging the officials' benches, but they paid no heed to this.

The Aitadokoro was incredibly hot, perhaps owing to the extreme age of the building and the fact that the roof was tiled, and at night we slept out on the veranda, beyond the blinds. What's more, because it was so old, the place was plagued by creatures known as centipedes[2] which kept dropping from the ceiling all day long, and also great wasps' nests where the wasps gathered and clung, which was all quite terrifying.

Senior courtiers would call by every day, and when someone overheard one of them who'd remained there talking till dawn, he amused us greatly by intoning in mock recitation:

> Who ever would have thought
> to see these Council Chambers now
> the haunt of nightly trysts?[3]

Even when autumn came, the place wasn't of the kind to be cooled by so much as the 'one-side breeze'[4] of the old poem, yet sure enough the autumn insects still sang there in season. Her Majesty was to return to her own quarters on the eighth day, so the Tanabata festival of the seventh was spent here in the Aitadokoro, and we seemed to have an unusually close view of the proceedings, probably because the place was relatively less spacious.[5]

One day, Consultant Captain Tadanobu came visiting, along with others including Captain Nobukata and Junior Counsellor Michikata. A number of us went out to talk to them, and in the midst of conversation I casually asked, 'What do you plan for tomorrow?' Without a moment's hesitation for thought, Tadanobu replied, 'This time it will be the fourth month and the world of humans.'[6] This was wonderfully amusing. It's impressive enough when somebody can recall something from some time ago and cleverly refer to it later, but men generally forget more than women do in this regard. People tend to have a poor memory even for their own past poems, let alone others', so Tadanobu's reply was particularly delightful. Naturally enough, neither the ladies inside the blinds nor the men outside had any idea what he was referring to.

This is the story – on the first day of the fourth month that year, a great many senior courtiers were standing about by the fourth north-west door of the Long Room in the Palace. Gradually they began to slip away, until the only men left were Secretary Captain Tadanobu, Captain Nobukata and one of the Chamberlains. They were talking of this and that, and entertaining themselves by reciting sutras and poetry, till one of them remarked, 'It's past dawn. Let's go back.' Thereupon Tadanobu intoned, 'Dew is the tears of lovers who part at dawn',[7] and Nobukata happily joined him in the song.

'You're very beforehand with your Tanabata, aren't you!' I remarked.

This displeased them thoroughly. 'Oh dear, oh dear, I was simply saying what came into my mind on the spur of the moment about a dawn parting,' Tadanobu complained. 'You have to constantly watch what you say around here, or you land in terrible trouble', and they went on in the same vein, with many a chuckle over it. 'Don't tell anyone about this, will you,' Tadanobu finished by admonishing me. 'I'd be bound to be laughed at.'

It had by now grown quite light, and finally off he went, his parting words being, 'It's time the ugly old Kazuraki god gave up and left.'

Well, ever since then I'd been dying to bring this up again when Tanabata came round. However, Tadanobu had since been promoted to Consultant, so I was worried that I couldn't be sure of seeing him at that particular time; I was planning to send him a letter through one of the groundskeepers, but then to my delight he turned up right at Tanabata. Pondering how best to make my move, I decided that if I directly mentioned that night he'd be sure to realize what I was up to, whereas if I suddenly slipped in a glancing reference he'd probably be left scratching his head in puzzlement. That would be the moment for me to introduce the subject. I was truly delighted when he picked up on my reference[8] without an instant's hesitation.

I'd spent these months so eager for the day to arrive that it even struck me that, whimsical connoisseur though I know I am in these matters, this was carrying whimsy rather far – so how did Tadanobu come to be apparently as prepared as I was? Nobukata, on the other hand, who had been quite as put out as Tadanobu at the time, heard our little exchange without comprehending a thing. It was only when Tadanobu reminded him by saying, 'Don't you remember how we were scolded that morning?' that he laughed and said, 'Oh yes, of course, of course!' – which was hardly very impressive, I thought.

Another example of this is the conversations I had with Tadanobu where we'd use the terms of a game of *go* to talk about courtship – if a man and a woman were becoming intimate we'd refer to it as 'he's played a leading stone on her', or 'it's into the final stones', or 'he'll be rallying his stones' and so on, which of course other people couldn't be expected to understand. Tadanobu and I would talk in this mutually understood code, and Nobukata would hang around trying to follow, saying, 'Eh, what does that mean?' He got quite upset when I wouldn't tell him, and demanded that Tadanobu explain, so in the end, because they were good friends, he obligingly did so.

'They've got to the point where they're breaking up the board'[9] meant that the lovers had finally become one. Anyway, Nobukata was now dying to let me know that he was in on our secret language. One day he said to me, 'Do you have a *go* board here? I'd like a round of *go* with you. How about those stones of yours, eh? Will you lay them down for me? My game's as strong as Tadanobu's, you know. Don't make any distinctions between us in this.'

'But if I did this sort of thing, surely I'd be "playing a round",'[10] I replied. He reported this to Tadanobu, who told me he was delighted with what I'd said. I do enjoy people who remember things that have happened.

When Tadanobu became Secretary Captain, I remarked in His Majesty's presence how wonderfully well he recited Chinese poetry. 'Who else can recite "Magistrate Hsaio of K'uai-chi passed by the ancient shrine"?'[11] I went on. 'I wish he could continue to visit us a little longer before he's promoted. It's a great shame.'

His Majesty laughed greatly at this, and delighted me by replying, 'Well, I shall tell him you said so and I won't promote him after all, then.'

But he was promoted nevertheless, and I was very lonely. Nobukata, meanwhile, had decided that he was quite as good as Tadanobu, and went about preening himself on his elegant accomplishments. One day I was talking about Tadanobu, and happened to say, 'No one recites the poem "He had not yet reached the time of his thirties"[12] like he does.'

'Why shouldn't I be as good as him?' responded Nobukata. 'I'll show you I'm even better,' and he proceeded to intone it.

'Well, yes, that's not too bad I suppose,' said I.

'Oh dear!' he exclaimed. 'I really must learn to recite like him.'

'There's just something so enchanting about the way he does the bit that goes "the time of his thirties",' I went on, and at this he walked off laughing bitterly.

Well, it seems that he proceeded to call Tadanobu over from the Gate Watch Office, told him what I'd said and asked him to show him how to recite the piece, which he did with an obliging laugh. I was quite unaware of this. Nobukata then turned up outside my apartment and gave an extremely good imitation of Tadanobu's recitation. Intrigued, I inquired, 'Who's that?' You could hear that he was beaming from ear to ear as he replied, 'Let me tell you something marvellous', and proceeded to relate to me how he'd called Tadanobu from the Watch Office the day before and got him to teach him how to do it. 'And now it really does seem I sound like him,' he finished, 'since you asked in such a sweet voice just now who was reciting.'

I was amused that he'd gone to all the trouble of learning Tadanobu's style, and from then on he had only to recite this poem and I'd go out and talk to him. 'I'm deeply obliged to the Secretary Captain for this,' he'd say. 'I should bow and pray in his direction.' If I was in my apartment and decided to put him off by sending a message saying I was attending on Her Majesty, he only needed to start on the poem and I'd confess I was actually there. Her Majesty laughed when I told her all this.

One day, when there was an imperial abstinence, I received a letter delivered by Mitsu-somebody, one of the clerks in the Right Gate Watch Guards, written on folded paper. 'I was intending to visit,' it said, 'but owing to the imperial abstinence ... May I "He had not yet reached the time of his thirties" later?'

In reply I wrote, 'I believe that time has already passed for you, even if you haven't yet reached the time at which Zhu Maichen admonished his wife.'[13]

This upset Nobukata all over again. He told the story to His Majesty, who later said to me when he called on Her Majesty,

'However do you come to know such things? Nobukata was lamenting that you really managed to hit home there, since it's perfectly true, he was thirty-nine when he admonished his wife.'

When I learned that Nobukata had told all this to His Majesty, I decided that he really must be a bit mad.

[155] *The name 'Kōkiden'* referred to the High Consort, daughter of the Kan'in Commander of the Left.[1] In her service was a lady called Sakyō, the daughter of the lady commonly known as 'Lie-down',[2] and people were joking that Captain Nobukata was courting her.

Well, Nobukata had called round one day when Her Majesty was at the Office of the Empress's Household, and was sitting there complaining to us. 'It falls to me to attend on Her Majesty for the night watch from time to time,' he said, 'but I must say I've been remiss in my duties because you ladies don't treat me in the appropriate fashion. I'd give very loyal service if only I were provided with a night-watch room.'

'Yes indeed, we can see that,' said everyone soothingly, but I broke in and remarked, 'Yes, people do like to have somewhere they can relax and lie down, don't they. You apparently avail yourself of just such a thing quite often.'

'I'm not speaking to you any more!' he declared, in a terrific huff. 'I've taken you for a friend, but you're obviously just accepting all those old rumours people have spread about me.'

'Good heavens, how odd you are!' I exclaimed innocently. 'Whatever can I have said? I can't see that there was anything for you to take offence at.'

I tugged at the lady next to me to support my case. 'She's said nothing offensive about you,' she chimed in, 'so why are you so hot under the collar? It just shows there must be something going on here after all', and she gave a loud laugh.

'She's put you up to that!' declared Nobukata, deeply outraged.

'Truly, I'm not saying any such thing,' I repeated. 'Why, even hearing it from others would make me angry', and I withdrew.

But in a later conversation he began again. 'You've made

false and shameful insinuations about me,' he said bitterly. 'You must have picked this up and repeated it because all the senior courtiers are laughing about it.'

'Well, if that's the case,' said I briskly, 'it makes no sense that it's only me you're blaming.'

And that was the end of relations between us.

[156] *Things now useless that recall a glorious past* – A fine embroidery-edged mat[1] that's become threadbare.

A screen painted in the Chinese style, that's now turned dark and discoloured and developed a scarred surface.

A painter with poor eyesight.

A switch of false hair seven or eight feet long, that's now fading and taking on a reddish tinge.

Grape-coloured fabric when the ash dye has turned.[2]

A man who was a great lover in his day but is now old and decrepit.

A tasteful house whose garden trees have been destroyed by fire. The pond is still there, but it's now uncared for and thick with pond weed.

[157] *Situations you have a feeling will turn out badly* – A son-in-law who has a fickle nature and tends to neglect his wife, and who now hasn't visited her for some time.

Someone given to lying nevertheless makes himself out to be capable and dependable, and is given an important task to undertake.

A boat with sails raised high in a strong wind.

Someone in their seventies or eighties who's been ill for some days now.

[158] *Sutra readings* – Continuous Sutra Readings[1] are particularly moving.

[159] *Things that are near yet far* – The Miyanobe Festival.

Relationships between siblings or relatives who don't like each other.

The winding path up to Kurama Temple.[1]

The first day of the new year, seen from the last day of the old.

[160] *Things that are far yet near* – Paradise.
The course of a boat.[1]
Relations between men and women.

[161] *Wells* – Horikane Well. Tama Well.
It's interesting that Hashiri Well is at Ōsaka.
I wonder why the mountain well[1] came to be used as an example of shallowness.
I like the way Asuka Well[2] is praised as being 'chill of water'.
Chinuki Well. Shōshō Well.[3] Sakura Well. Kisakimachi Well.

[162]* *Plains* – Saga, of course. Also the plains of Inami, Kata, Tobihi, Shimeshi and Kasuga. Sōke Plain is somehow interesting too. One wonders why they gave it such a name.
The plains of Miyagi, Awazu, Ono and Murasaki.

[163] *Court nobles* – Commanders of the Left and Right. Master of the Household of the Crown Prince. Acting Counsellor and Acting Grand Counsellor. Consultant Captain. Captain Third Rank.

[164]* *Nobles* – Secretary Captain. Secretary Controller. Acting Captain. Junior Lieutenant Fourth Rank. Chamberlain Controller. Adviser Fourth Rank. Chamberlain Junior Counsellor. Chamberlain Second of the Watch.

[165] *Acting Provincial Governors* – Acting Governors of Kai, Echigo, Chikugo and Awa provinces.[1]

[166]* *Commissioners* – Ceremonials Commissioner. Left and Right Gate Watch Commissioners.

[167] *Priests* – Fifth-ranking priests. Palace priests.

[168] *Ladies* – High Gentlewoman. Chief Gentlewoman.

[169] *Sixth-rank Chamberlains* – The post of Sixth-rank Chamberlain is not one that anyone should aspire to.[1]

Once he's promoted to Acting Provincial Governor or some other fifth-ranking title, he gets himself a cramped wooden-roofed house; adds a nice little, new, board fence; puts a carriage in the carriage house; plants a few foot-high bushes near the front of the house; and ties his ox there to feed on the grass. It's all thoroughly contemptible.

There's something so depressingly staid and unambitious about the way he keeps his courtyard meticulously swept, puts up flashy Iyo blinds hung on purple leather thongs all round the house and cloth-lined sliding doors, and gives strict instructions each night to bar his precious gate against intruders.

What he should do is make use of someone else's house – his parents' or father-in-law's is the obvious choice, but it could be an uncle's or brother's house if the owner happens to be away, or the empty house of some Provincial Governor he's got to know well and who happens to be away on his provincial duties, or, failing that, one of the many imperial or princely houses. He should borrow such a place and bide his time there until he's promoted to a better position, when he can go looking for some fine place to make his own.

[170]* *A place where a lady lives alone*, in a badly dilapidated dwelling surrounded by a crumbling earth wall, the garden pond full of water weed, and the courtyard, if not literally overrun with wormwood, at any rate with patches of green weeds showing here and there through the gravel, is a truly forlorn and moving sight. There's nothing more boringly un-romantic than a place where the lady has got down to business and had everything repaired and smartened up, meticulously locks her gate each evening and generally keeps the place run in punctilious fashion.

[171] *The home of a lady in court service* should ideally have both parents living there. Visitors constantly come and go, from the inner rooms comes a babble of voices, and outside can be

heard a busy sound of horses, but there's no harm in all this noise and commotion.

But picture a different kind of household. A particular guest of yours drops in for a passing visit, either privately or publicly, saying 'I hadn't realized that you were back home', or 'When will you be returning to the palace?' – after all, how could a man who cared for you not come along to pay you a call? But how very annoying it is to be aware that the members of the household who have the gate opened for him are thinking, 'What a racket! And such cheek, to stay on into the night like this!'

'Is the main gate closed?' comes a voice, and the rather disgruntled voice of a servant responds, 'No, there's still a guest here.'

'Well, close it up as soon as he's gone then,' comes the reply. 'There are a lot of thieves about lately. And be careful about fire.' This is most dispiriting to have to hear, and what's worse the guest is overhearing it too.

The man's retainers, not at all inconvenienced by his lengthy visit, will no doubt be laughing at the servant who keeps poking his head out to see whether the guest is leaving yet. How he berates them when he catches the retainers mimicking him!

Even if the man doesn't come right out with his feelings, still the very fact that he's paying a visit must mean that he cares for you. Nevertheless, if he's an earnest sort of fellow he might say with a smile at this point, 'It's late. They seem to be anxious to close the gate', and make his departure. If he really feels strongly about you, though, a man will stay on till the dawn, ignoring all your urgings that he should go. The night watchman makes frequent appearances to check if he's still there, and when dawn is about to break he declares in horrified tones so that the guest will overhear, 'How dreadful, the gate has been left open all night!' and he proceeds to lock it, though by now it's dawn and the action is quite pointless. This really is infuriating behaviour.

Things are difficult enough if it's your own parents' house, but if they're not your own parents then you worry terribly about what they think of his visit, and the same can no doubt be said of a situation in which it's the house of a brother you don't get on with particularly well.

On the other hand, it's charming when, be it night time or dawn, undue care hasn't been taken over the gate, and various ladies in service in the household of one of the princes, or from the palace or one of the great houses, appear together to greet the visitor.[1] The lattice shutters are left raised, everyone sits talking right through the winter night till first light, and after the guest has left they linger there to watch his departing figure. It's even finer if there's a moon in the dawn sky. After he's left, playing on his flute as he goes, the ladies don't go off to sleep straight away but savour the experience together. It's lovely if everyone finally drifts off to sleep amid desultory talk of this person and that, and the poems people have composed.

[172]* *One day in the ninth month*, at a certain place, a gentleman who, though not exactly a court noble, was renowned at that time as a man of marvellous charm, taste and sensibility, pays a visit to Lady Someone. Dawn is breaking, thick mists diffuse the light of a glorious moon, and he bends all his powers to the task of producing words that will leave her heart aglow with memories of their night together. Ah, now he departs – she sits on and on, gazing into the distance after him. A scene of inexpressibly resonant beauty.

He makes as if to go on his way, but surreptitiously turns and retraces his steps to secrete himself by the lattice fence. Seeing her deep reluctance to rise and leave, he bethinks himself to say something further to her of what is in his heart, but now he hears her murmur softly to herself the lines:

> 'though there in the dawn sky
> the moon hangs bright'.[1]

The woman he gazes at in secret is bending forward, so that her hair falls away from her head and hangs perhaps six inches before her face. It glows there like a candle, borrowing added light from the moonlight, and in astonishment at the sight the man chooses this moment to slip quietly away.[2]

This was a tale that someone told.

[173] *It's quite delightful when the snow is falling*, not thick on the ground, but softly, to lie as a thin cover.

It's also delightful on an evening when the snow lies piled high, and two or three congenial friends settle down together around a brazier near the veranda to talk of this and that. Darkness descends as their conversation continues, but no lamp is lit nearby, and the light from the high-heaped snow beyond shines wonderfully white, while they sit idly stirring the ash in the brazier with the fire tongs as they talk on together, of moving and entertaining matters.

Just as they're beginning to feel that the night must be growing late, they hear shod footsteps approaching. Startled, they peer out, and find that it's a man who sometimes arrives like this, unannounced, at just such times.

'I've been imagining how you'd be enjoying the snow today,' he says, 'but I was held up with one thing and another, and ended by spending the day elsewhere.' No doubt he's alluding to the poem 'The man who comes to call today'.[1]

They talk of the day's happenings, and move from there to speak of all manner of other things.

They've put out a straw cushion for him, and he sits there on the veranda with one foot dangling over the edge, while they all talk on together, neither the man nor the ladies within showing any signs of tiring of the conversation, until the temple bell sounds for dawn. Just as the light is about to break he prepares to leave, and as he does so he most charmingly recites 'snow lay thick upon certain mountains'.[2]

If they'd been by themselves, the ladies wouldn't really have been able to stay up like this talking till dawn, and after he's gone they speak together of how much more delightful it was to have him there with them, and how charming and elegant he is.

[174] *Once, during the reign of the former Emperor Murakami,* there was a great fall of snow. The moon was bright. His Majesty heaped snow in a bowl, stood a spray of flowering plum in it and gave it to the Lady Chamberlain, Hyōe, saying, 'See what poem you can compose on this.' Her response was to recite the words of the Chinese poem, 'At times of snow, moonlight and blossom',[1] for which he praised her very highly. 'There's nothing unusual in producing a poem,' he said, 'but it's far more difficult to say something that is so precisely apt for the occasion.'

There's also the interesting story about the occasion when His Majesty was keeping company with this same Hyōe, and happened to pause at the empty Privy Chamber, where he noticed smoke rising from one of the wooden braziers. He asked her to go and investigate, and when she returned she recited to him:

> 'When I went to look
> I saw the fishermen who row
> upon the ocean depths
> had snared themselves a frog and now
> were scorching home with it.'[2]

It was a frog that had leapt into the brazier and been scorched.

[175]* *The lady known as Miare no Seji* once made for the Emperor a delightful little five-inch doll representing a child of a noble family, with hair bound in the boys' *mizura* style,[1] and dressed beautifully in formal court robes. Under the clothes she wrote the name 'Prince Tomoakira', and the Emperor was utterly delighted when she had it presented to him.

[176] *When I first went into court service*, everything seemed to overwhelm me with confusion and embarrassment, and there were times when I could barely hold back my tears. I attended Her Majesty each night, behind her low standing curtain, and she would bring out pictures and so on to show me, but I was so hopelessly nervous that I could scarcely even stretch out a

hand to take them. She described what was in each picture, asked what I thought was happening and generally tried to set me at ease with her talk. I had to bend to see them by the light of the oil lamp that stood on a standing tray,[1] and I was painfully aware of how the details of my hair would show up even more clearly than in the daylight hours. It was a fearfully cold time of year, and the glimpse of her hands emerging from the wonderful, glowing pale plum-pink sleeves filled me with deep awe. I remember gazing at them in astonishment, still fresh from home and new to all I saw, and thinking, 'I never knew someone so marvellous could exist!'

When dawn arrived that first day, I hastily prepared to return to my room, and Her Majesty gently teased me by remarking, 'Even the god of Kazuraki wouldn't be in quite such a hurry to hide himself away!' I kept my head low, fearful of exposing myself to her in profile, and didn't dare raise the lattice shutters. The servants who'd entered gave the order that the shutters be opened, but Her Majesty forbade it, and they smiled knowingly and went out again. Her Majesty then detained me with questions and talk for quite a while longer, till finally she said, 'You must be wanting to go back to your room. Off you go then, and be sure to return as soon as evening comes.'

No sooner had I slid away on my knees and hidden myself from view than they threw open the shutters, and there beyond, snow was falling. There's a lattice fence close to the front of the Tōkaden, which makes the garden rather small. It's quite delightful in snow. During the course of the day Her Majesty sent several messages urging me to come to her again before evening. 'You needn't fear being too visible,' she added. 'The snowy weather will see to that.'

The head of my room[2] also scolded me for my shyness. 'This is most unseemly,' she said. 'Do you intend to go on cowering in your room like this? Her Majesty is showing how she feels about you by choosing to allow you into her company so astonishingly easily, you know.' Thus urged along on every side, I miserably did as required and presented myself, though I was feeling quite beside myself with shyness and unhappiness.

Snow lay piled high on the roofs of the little fire huts, a

strange and lovely sight. Near Her Majesty, there was a good
fire alight in the usual square brazier, but no one was bothering
to sit there. A senior gentlewoman was in attendance to see to
Her Majesty's needs, seated close by her, and she herself was
seated before a round incense-wood brazier decorated with an
inlay design of pears. Beyond the pillars, a crowd of ladies was
sitting packed close together round a long brazier, their Chinese
jackets informally slipped back from the shoulders, and I was
filled with envy to witness their easy nonchalance. I watched as
they carried messages to and fro, stood or sat, came and went,
without a trace of diffidence, chatting and smiling and laughing
together, and was overcome just to imagine that I might ever
one day be able to mingle with them like that. There seemed to
be a group of three or four further back, gathered together
looking at pictures.

Before long, there came the high cry of a retainer clearing
the way. 'It sounds as if His Excellency[3] is on his way here,'
people said, and they began to tidy up the various things left
lying about. I was longing to return to my room, but I couldn't
get myself out of the way at such short notice, so I simply
withdrew somewhat deeper into the room – yet some curiosity
must have made me still peep out from an opening in the
standing curtain.

But it was Grand Counsellor Korechika who arrived, his
cloak and violet gathered trousers glowing most beautifully in
the light from the snow. He settled himself at the foot of a
pillar. 'I've been kept away by an abstinence these last two
days,' he said, 'but with this heavy snowfall I decided to call
and see how you were.'

'I feared that "the path is gone", with all this snow,' came
Her Majesty's reply. 'How did you get here?'

He smiled. 'Are you "truly moved"[4] to see me, then?' he
inquired. Could there be anything more splendid? I wondered.
As I listened in awe to their elegant exchange, I marvelled that
there must surely be nothing more wonderful. It seemed to me
precisely like a scene from those tales where the storyteller
gives her imagination free rein and describes it all in the most
extravagant terms.

Her Majesty was dressed in layers of white with a scarlet Chinese damask over-robe, and the vision of her there, her flowing hair black against the scarlet, felt utterly dream-like, the kind of sight I'd seen depicted in paintings but never before in reality.

The Grand Counsellor now set about chatting and joking with the ladies. Listening to them responding to his banter without the least sign of embarrassment, and contradicting and arguing with him when he asserted something false, I couldn't believe my ears, and I felt an astonished blush creeping irrepressibly over my face. He proceeded to take some nuts, and hospitably offered some to Her Majesty as well.

Then he must have asked who was behind the curtain, and the ladies' replies seemed to have whetted his interest, for he stood, and when I expected him to move in another direction he instead came over to where I was hiding, seated himself very close and proceeded to talk to me. He asked me about various things he'd heard concerning the time before I came to court, and whether they were true or not, and it all felt quite unreal to me to find myself so astonishingly close to him, when even from a distance the sight of him had filled me with awe and confusion. How could I possibly answer, sitting there wracked with embarrassment as I was, soaked in a nervous sweat at my shameful impudence and folly in daring to presume I could serve at court? – I, who had always hastened to draw the inner blinds and spread my fan as a shield in case my form was somehow discernible from outside, if his glance had so much as strayed in the direction of my carriage as he rode with His Majesty in some procession I'd gone to watch.

The Grand Counsellor now went so far as to take away the prudent fan with which I was shielding myself from his gaze. In my desperation, I longed to shake my side-locks forward in an attempt to cover my face, knowing full well how unseemly this would appear to him. I cowered there, agonizingly aware that my consternation was quite exposed to his gaze. Surely he would now rise and leave me alone! But instead he sat turning the fan over in his hands and talking a while longer, asking me who had commissioned the painting on it, while I pressed the sleeve of my Chinese jacket against my bowed face so hard that I must surely have rubbed off great patches of powder, leaving me with a humiliatingly mottled complexion.

Her Majesty apparently understood what agony the Grand Counsellor was subjecting me to by so cruelly lingering on talking like this, for she interrupted him. 'Here,' she said to him, 'look at this and tell me who you think wrote it.'

'Let me see it over here,' he replied, but she insisted that he come to her.

'But this lady has seized me and won't let me go,' he joked. This was wonderfully modish of him, but I writhed at how inappropriate it seemed in relation to someone as unworthy as I.

Her Majesty now drew out a bound notebook with samples of people's free calligraphic style,[5] and they looked at it together.

'Yes, whose can it be?' said the Grand Counsellor. 'We must show it to this lady here. I'm sure she can recognize the hand of all our present-day writers', and he carried on saying extraordinary things of this nature, doing his best to induce me to respond.

As if matters weren't distressing enough already with only the Grand Counsellor present, there now came a voice announcing the arrival of another visitor, and a second similarly dressed figure appeared. This man was rather more glamorous and ebullient than the Grand Counsellor, and he made everyone laugh with his joking and buffoonery. The ladies responded with tales of the doings of this or that senior courtier, and hearing all this I felt as if I was witnessing angels or creatures descended to earth from some higher plane – though later when I'd grown used to court service I realized how little this was the case in fact! All those gentlewomen you witness with such awe will have felt much as you do when they first arrived, and once you begin to really understand such things, you naturally come to take court life much more for granted.

On another occasion, while talking to me of this and that, Her Majesty suddenly said, 'Are you very fond of me?'

'How could I not be?' I answered, but just as I spoke there

came a loud sneeze from the Table Room, and Her Majesty immediately said, 'Oh alas, I see you've lied to me!⁶ Ah well, so be it', and she withdrew.

Mortified, I thought to myself, 'But how could I be lying? Surely my feelings for Her Majesty are anything but average, in fact. This is absurd! It's the sneeze that lied, not me', and I went on to wonder who could have done this horrible thing to me. 'After all,' I thought, 'no one welcomes a sneeze, and people generally do their best to suppress it when they feel one coming on. How infuriating of her to have sneezed at precisely this moment!' But I was still new to court life, and the night drew to a close without my finding a way to answer Her Majesty's accusation. Dawn came, and I returned to my room, but no sooner had I arrived there than there came a message, written in an elegant hand on pale-green thin paper. Opening it, I read:

> How could I have known,
> how might I have discovered that
> you did not speak the truth,
> were it not for heaven's Tadasu
> who judges between true and false?

'This is how Her Majesty feels',⁷ the lady who scripted it had added at the end.

I was caught between delight and dismay, and filled again with a fierce resentment at whoever had sneezed the night before.

> We may judge a flower
> by the strength or weakness of its hue –
> but that red nose bloomed false.
> And so my flowering heart withers alone
> to find itself in misjudged misery.⁸

'Please take this to Her Majesty to lift her spirits,' I said, and added, 'The god of divination knows all. I stand in great awe of him . . .'⁹

After she'd left with my message, a fresh wave of unhappiness descended on me, and I continued to wonder miserably why the woman had to sneeze at that of all moments.

[177] *People who feel smug* – The first person to sneeze at new year. People of quality don't follow this superstition, it's only the lower classes.

The look on someone's face when he's succeeded in getting his son appointed Chamberlain at a time when there's fierce competition for the post. Also, someone who's been given the governorship of the year's top province in the Appointments List. When people congratulate him and say, 'What a splendid posting to receive!' how smug he is as he replies, 'No no, far from it. I gather it's an extraordinarily run-down place.'

A man who's been chosen as son-in-law from among a large and fiercely competitive group of suitors will no doubt feel very pleased with himself.

A Provincial Governor who's been promoted to Consultant seems much more inclined to consider himself important and splendid than someone equivalent who's from a noble family.[1]

[178]* *Nothing is more splendid than rank.* How different a man is when he's called Commissioner or Adviser and can be snubbed with impunity, from the same man once he's become Counsellor, Grand Counsellor or Minister, when he's held in awe and can throw his weight around! The same thing seems to hold further down the ranks too, with Provincial Governors and suchlike. Those who've done duty in a number of provinces, and become Deputy, or fourth or third rank, are apparently treated with considerable respect by the court nobles.

Women, on the other hand, are much less impressive. Certainly an imperial nurse who attains third rank or the title High Gentlewoman is of considerable importance, but she's already past her best, and what's so good about it after all? And most women never even get so far. It seems that a lady who goes into the provinces as a Governor's wife is envied as having achieved the epitome of prestige by normal standards. But surely much more impressive is someone from an average family who becomes the wife of a court noble, or a court noble's daughter who becomes an Empress.

However, it's a most impressive thing to watch a young man's rise.

As for priests, what's so wonderful in going about bearing this or that priestly title? Even a handsome priest who performs the sutras magnificently isn't really taken seriously by the ladies who make a fuss over him. Still, nothing can compare to the extraordinary awe and reverence given to someone who's become Bishop or Archbishop – it's as though the Buddha himself had appeared on earth!

[179] *Awe-inspiring things* – No one fills you with more awe than the husband of a nurse. This goes without saying if she's the nurse of an Emperor or prince, of course, but even if she's attached to one of the lesser households of the high-ranking, or that of a Provincial Governor, her husband is treated by those around him with the respect accorded to the household in question, so he begins to put on fine airs and consider himself to have the backing of the master of the house. He acts for all the world as if the child were his very own, which is all very well if it's a girl, but when it's a boy he'll attach himself to the child like a limpet and serve his every need, and if anyone dares to cross the boy he'll leap to the attack, and go about slandering the man to others. Villain though he is, no one will dare to gainsay him or come right out and complain, so he continues to have his way, and bosses everyone around in an incredibly high-handed fashion.

But he doesn't come out of it quite so well if the child is still an infant. As the nurse will be sleeping next to the mother, her husband has to sleep alone in his own room – and if he goes off to see another woman, there'll be a tremendous fuss about his infidelity. He may demand that his wife comes and sleeps with him rather than beside the mother, in which case the unfortunate woman will find herself on a cold winter's night hastily having to reach for her clothes and rush to the child when the mother calls her urgently. This is so in the finer houses as well, and indeed there are a great many more problems besides.

[180]* *Illnesses* – Internal illnesses. Illnesses caused by spirits.[1]
Beriberi. Also, the feeling that you somehow just can't face any
food.

It's engaging to witness some very attractive young lady of
eighteen or nineteen, with a beautiful sleek head of hair hanging
the length of her back, wonderfully thick at the ends, a lovely
plump figure and very pale face, who is suffering from a terrible
toothache. She sits there, hand pressed to her bright red cheek,
quite unaware that her side-locks are all sodden from weeping.

Or another picture – it's some time in the eighth month, and
we see a lady dressed in a flowing white shift and handsome
skirted trousers with an exquisite robe in the aster combination
draped over her, lying languishing with some internal illness. A
large number of gentlewomen who are friends of hers have
come to visit, and beyond the blinds there's also quite a gathering of young nobles. 'Oh dear, poor thing,' someone says in a
carefully casual tone. 'Does it often get bad like this?' Meanwhile (the perfect touch) the man who loves her feels his heart
breaking with pity. How affecting she is as she sits up to vomit,
sleek long hair tied back from her face.

His Majesty hears of her illness and is kind enough to send
a priest to chant for her, someone with a fine voice, who settles
down nearby behind a screen that's drawn across for him. It's
a rather cramped space, and the ladies crowded in to visit are
clearly visible to the priest as they sit listening to the sutras.
One can only think that he's surely courting karmic retribution,
to let his eyes keep drifting their way as he chants.

[181] *It's delightful to see someone who's a great ladies' man*,
and is pursuing numerous love affairs, arriving home at dawn
from who knows what night-time tryst. Sleepy though you can
see he feels, he nevertheless sits down and draws the inkstone
up to write his next-morning letter to her. See how carefully he
grinds the ink to a fine consistency, and how tenderly he bends
to the task of writing, not merely dashing off whatever springs
to mind but putting himself heart and soul into what he writes.

He's wearing kerria-yellow or scarlet over layers of white
gown, and as he finishes the letter his gaze lingers on the

'to write his next-morning letter to her'

crumpled sleeve of his white shift.[1] He doesn't just give his
letter to the serving woman nearby, but takes the trouble to
stand up and go over to call a young member of the guards or
one of his retainers who's suited to the task, and hands it to
him with whispered instructions. After the man has left he sits
on there, lost in thought, softly murmuring to himself some
appropriate bit of the sutras until he's ushered inside to avail
himself of the washbasin and morning gruel that's been prepared. But even as he walks in, he pauses to lean at his desk
and read a little. It's enchanting to witness him come across a
particularly good passage, and raise his voice to recite it aloud.

He washes his hands, slips into a cloak and sets about reciting by heart the sixth volume of the *Lotus Sutra*.[2] This is all
most impressive – but then the messenger reappears (no doubt
the lady lives somewhere nearby) and signals his arrival, and
our gentleman abruptly ceases chanting and turns his eager
thoughts to the contents of her reply . . . an amusing scene, for
surely he's actually courting karmic retribution by this lapse!

[182] *It's the middle of a fiercely hot day,* and you're finding it
impossible to stay cool – your fan only moves the warm air
about, and you keep dipping your hands in ice water and
moaning about the heat. And then someone brings you a message written on brilliant red thin paper, attached to a flowering
Chinese pink, also bright crimson – and you sense how hot he

must have felt as he wrote it, and how much you must mean to him, and find yourself unconsciously laying down the fan (that was anyway proving so useless even when plied while the other hand soaked in ice water), your complaints suddenly forgotten.

[183] *The floorboards of the southern or perhaps the eastern aisle* are polished to a reflective shine, and a lovely fresh new mat has been placed on them. When the three-foot standing curtain, with its marvellously cool-looking drapes, is pushed aside, it glides surprisingly far along the shiny floor – and there, near where it comes to rest, a lady is reclining. She wears a white gossamer-silk shift with scarlet skirted trousers, and a purple robe, still fairly well starched, is draped over her as sleep-wear.

A light burns in the lamp that hangs from the eave. Farther off, at about two pillars' distance, the blind has been raised high, and two gentlewomen and several little girls are seated leaning against the threshold, or lying stretched out beside a lowered blind. A coal burns deep in the ash of the incense burner, and the faint scent of incense that wafts from it deepens the feeling of tranquility and refinement.

The night is already well advanced when there comes a stealthy tap at the gate, and a knowing gentlewoman slips over and solemnly and stealthily ushers him in to where the lady waits, keeping a keen eye out to make sure he isn't discovered as she does so – a scene made to delight.

Another charming scene: he and the lady are sitting talking together. A particularly fine-sounding and elegant *biwa* lies there beside them, and in the occasional pauses of their conversation he plucks at it very softly with the tips of his fingers.

[184] *It's enchanting to overhear*, from a house that lies close to a main thoroughfare, someone go past in a carriage, blinds raised to enjoy the dawn moon, reciting in a fine voice as he goes the line: 'The wanderer sojourns on beneath a waning moon.'[1] It's also lovely to hear a passerby do this if he's on horseback.

Staying in such a place, you may also hear the sound of a

saddle's mudguards flapping as a horse passes. Intrigued to know who it might be, you lay down whatever you're doing and go to look – only to discover some perfectly boring person going by. This is most annoying.

[185] *Things that prove disillusioning* – Nothing in all the world could be worse than a man or a woman who turns out to use words vulgarly. I wonder what the strange quality is in a single word that can make it vulgar or tasteful – though of course the person making this judgement isn't necessarily so very splendid herself! And if that's the case, how can one judge what's good and what's not? Well, I don't know about others, I simply go by my own feelings in the matter.

It's actually not a bad thing to use vulgar or unseemly words intentionally, knowing them for what they are. What's astonishing is when someone produces a word from their private store without pausing to consider its nature. I also hate it when someone who should know better, an older person or a man, affects a rustic way of speaking. It's only natural that any young person should want to simply sink through the floor with embarrassment, when they witness an adult unashamedly using wrong or bad language.

You instantly sound dreadful if, instead of saying 'I'm going to do it' or 'I'm going to say it' or 'I'm going to do this or that', you drop the 'to' and instead say 'I'm gonna say it' or 'I'm gonna go home'.[1] And of course this is even more the case if you write it. If the author of a tale uses poor language it makes you quite despair, and you find yourself squirming with embarrassment for the writer as well. Then there are the people I've heard say 'a single cawidge' instead of 'a single carriage', and everyone seems to pronounce 'look for' as 'lek for' these days.[2]

[186] *It's very unseemly for a man* who's visiting a gentlewoman to eat while with her. Any lady who provides him with food is also despicable. Naturally, if the lady who loves him comes sweetly offering him food, he's going to eat it – after all, he can hardly clamp his mouth shut and turn his face away as if he loathed the very thought!

Personally, even if a man is terribly drunk and ends up having to spend the night, I won't feed him so much as a dish of warmed-over rice. It wouldn't matter to me if he decided I was heartless and unfeeling, and never called again. Of course you can't do much about it if you're at home and food is produced for him from the northern quarters[1] – though even this is far from desirable.

[187] *Winds* – Storm winds. The soft wind of the third month that carries in gentle gusts of rain at evening.

The wind mixed with rain that blows in the eighth and ninth months is a very moving thing. When the wind is howling and blowing the rain gusts sideways, it's delightful to take down summer's padded robe from the stand where it's been airing, and lay over it a gossamer-silk shift to sleep under[1] – delightful, too, to find yourself wondering at the fact that it's suddenly so cool, when it had earlier been so stiflingly hot that you longed to throw off even this gossamer shift.

And I love it when you open the lattice shutters or double doors at daybreak, and a sudden gust of stormy wind stings your face.

Around the end of the ninth month or in the tenth month, the sky darkens and a howling wind blows up, which spills the yellow leaves from the trees in flurries – a forlorn and touching sight. The leaves of cherry trees and elms are particularly quick to blow off.

Places that have a garden full of trees are marvellous around the tenth month.

[188] *The day after a typhoon* is extremely moving, and full of interest. The lattice and open-weave fences around the garden have been left in a shambles, and the various garden plants are in a miserable state. Great trees have been blown over, and branches ripped off; it gives you quite a shock to discover them lying there across the bush clover and valerian. Leaves are carefully lodged in all the little spaces of the lattice weave, such a delicate effect that you can't imagine it was the doing of that wild wind.

And now a splendid sight – a most elegant and beautiful lady, wearing a dark purple robe with a sheen muted by wear, and a brocaded formal over-robe of autumn-leaf ochre, or a thin weave, now appears, having only just risen after a night made sleepless by the clamour of the wind. She emerges a little distance from the Inner Chamber on her knees, the hair hanging about her shoulders somewhat puffed and disarrayed by the wind. She gazes with evident emotion at the garden, and reveals her fine sensibility by reciting the poem, 'I see why the word "storm".'[1] Meanwhile another, a girl of seventeen or eighteen, no longer little but not yet truly adult, stands pressed against the blind, watching enviously as a group of girls and young women works here and there in the garden to gather up the plants that have been uprooted by the wind, and prop up others. We see her from behind, an enchanting figure in badly-worn gossamer-silk shift and re-dyed, faded azure robe with over it a pale violet-grey night-robe, her gleaming hair, in beautiful array, hidden beneath her robe, down the length of her back, with its prettily fluffed ends like plume grass peeping out below the robe, between the full folds of her skirted trousers.

[189]* *Elegantly intriguing things* – It's delightful to hear, through a wall or partition of some sort, the sound of someone, no mere gentlewoman, softly and elegantly clap her hands for service. Then, still separated from view behind, perhaps, a sliding door, you hear a youthful voice respond, and the swish of silk as someone arrives. It must be time for a meal to be served, for now come the jumbled sounds of chopsticks and spoons, and then the ear is arrested by the sudden metallic clink of a pouring-pot's handle falling sideways and knocking against the pot.

Hair tossed back, but not roughly, over a robe that's been beaten to a fine gloss, so that you can only guess at its splendid length.[1]

It's marvellous to see a beautifully appointed room, where no lamp has been lit and the place is illuminated instead by the light of a brightly burning fire in the square brazier – you can just make out the cords of the curtains around the curtained dais glimmering softly. The metal clasps that hold the raised blinds in place at the lintel cloth and trefoil cords[2] also gleam brightly. A beautifully arranged brazier with fire burning, its rim swept clean of ash, the firelight revealing the painting on its inner surface, is a most delightful sight. As also is a brightly gleaming pair of fire tongs, propped at an angle in the brazier.

Another scene of fascinating elegance – it's very late at night, Her Majesty has retired to her chamber, everyone is asleep and outside a lady is sitting talking with a senior courtier. From within comes the frequent sound of *go* stones dropping into the box. Delightful too to hear the soft sound of fire tongs being gently pushed into the ash of the brazier, and sense from this the presence of someone who isn't yet asleep.

A person who stays up late is always elegantly intriguing. You wake in the night to lie there listening through the partition, and realize from the sounds that someone is still up. You can't hear what is said, but you catch the sound of a man's soft laugh, and you long to know what they're saying together.

Another scene – Her Majesty has not yet retired. Her ladies are attending her, and the High Gentlewoman or perhaps some other senior gentlewoman from the Emperor's residence, someone who adds formality to the occasion, is also present. People are seated near Her Majesty, engaged in conversation. The lamp is extinguished, but fine details of the scene are illuminated by the light of the fire that burns in the long brazier.

A lady new to the court, someone not of particularly impressive background but who the young gentlemen would naturally consider an object of elegant interest, is attending Her Majesty rather late at night. There's something attractively intimate in the sound of her silk robes as she enters and approaches Her Majesty on her knees. Her Majesty speaks quietly to her, and she shrinks like a child and responds in a barely audible voice. The whole feel of the scene is very quiet. It's also very elegant the way, when the gentlewomen are gathered seated here and there in the room talking, you hear the silk rustle of people as they leave or enter and, though it's only a soft sound, you can guess who each one would be.

Some gentleman of intimidating rank has come visiting the

rooms one evening. Your own lamp is extinguished, but light from nearby penetrates from above the intervening screen, faintly illuminating the objects in the room. Since he's someone she would never sit so close to in daylight hours, she bashfully draws over a low standing curtain and lies close beside it, head bent over, though even so he would surely be able to judge her hair. His cloak and gathered trousers are draped over the standing curtain – something of suitably high rank, of course, although the special olive-green of a Chamberlain of the sixth rank would be just about acceptable. However, if it's one of those deep green cloaks of a normal sixth-ranker, you'd feel inclined to take it and roll it into a ball and consign it to the far reaches of the room, so that when it comes time for him to leave at dawn he'll be dismayed to discover he can't lay hands on it.

It's also quite delightful, in summer or winter, to take a quick peep from the corridor, where you guess someone's sleeping behind a standing curtain from the clothes draped over one end of it.

The scent of incense is a most elegantly intriguing thing. I well remember the truly wonderful scent that wafted from Captain Tadanobu as he sat leaning by the blind of the Little Door[3] of Her Majesty's room one day during the long rains of the fifth month. The blend was so subtle there was no distinguishing its ingredients. Of course it's natural that scent is enhanced by the moisture of a rainy day, but one couldn't help remarking on it even so. It was no wonder that the younger ladies were so deeply impressed at the way it lingered until the following day in the blind he'd been leaning against.

Rather than stringing along a large crowd of retainers of varying heights, none of whom looks particularly smart or impressive, it's far more refined for a gentleman to go about in a beautifully gleaming carriage that he's had for only a little while, with ox drivers dressed with appropriate smartness, who can barely keep up with the spirited ox as it rushes along ahead of them.

What really does catch the attention with its elegant suggestiveness is the sight of a slender retainer dressed in graded-dye

skirted trousers in lavender or some such colour, with upper
robes of something appropriate – glossed silk, kerria-yellow –
and shiny shoes, running along close to the axle as the carriage
travels.

[190]* *Islands* – Yaso and Uki Islands.[1] Taware[2] Island. E
Island. Matsugaura and Toyora Islands. Magaki Island.

[191] *Beaches* – Udo Beach. Naga Beach. Fukiage Beach. Uchiide Beach. Moroyose Beach. Chisato[1] Beach – one imagines it
as very large.

[192] *Bays* – Ou Bay. Shiogama Bay. Korizuma Bay.[1] Nadaka
Bay.

[193]* *Woods* – Ueki Wood. Ihata Wood. Kogarashi Wood.
Utatane Wood. Iwase Wood. Ōaraki Wood. Tareso Wood.
Kurubeki Wood. Tachigiki[1] Wood.
   Yokotate Wood is very odd to the ear. Why should it be
called a wood, when there's only one tree?[2]

[194]* *Temples* – The temples of Tsubosaka and Kasagi. Hōrin
Temple. It's moving to think that Ryōzen is the dwelling place
of the Buddha.[1] The temples of Ishiyama, Kohata and Shiga.

[195] *Sutras* – The *Lotus Sutra*, of course. Also the *Fugen
Jugan*, the *Senju*, the *Zuigu*, the *Kongō Hanya* and the *Yakushi
Sutras*, and the second volume of the *Nin'ō Sutra*.

[196]* *Buddhas* – Nyoirin. Senju. All six Kannons.[1] Yakushi.
Shaka. Miroku. Jizō. Monju. Fudō Myōō. Fugen.[2]

[197]* *Chinese writings* – *Monju. Monzen. Shinbu. Shiki* and
Goteihongi.[1] Prayers and petitions to the Buddha. Memorials
to the Emperor. The promotion requests that Doctors of
Literature write for people.

[198]* *Tales* – *Sumiyoshi*.[1] *The Tale of the Hollow Tree*.[2]

Changing Residence. Yielding Up the Country is an unpleasant tale.

The Sunken Log. The Lady Who Waited for the Moon. The Mumetsubo Captain. Encouragement in Faith. The Pine Branch. In *The Tale of Komano*, the part where the hero finds the old fan and sets off with it is interesting.

The Envious Captain. I don't like the part where he gets Lady Saishō with child and asks for a robe as keepsake. Also *The Katano Minor Captain*.

[199] *Darani incantations* are best when performed at day-break. Sutras are best at twilight.

[200] *Musical performances* are best at night, when you can't see people's faces.

[201] *Games* – The smallbow. *Go*. Court kickball[1] is enjoyable, though you couldn't call it elegant.

[202]* *Dances* – The Suruga Dance. 'Motomego' is delightful. The swords used in 'Taiheiraku' are horrible, but it's a wonderful dance. It's also fascinating to hear that in China opponents used to face off in this dance.

The Bird Dance.[1]

In the *Batō* Dance, the dancer tosses his hair about. The

'Motomego'

expression of his eyes and face is terrifying, but the music is wonderful. In the Crouch Dance the two performers dance with knees low to the ground.[2]

The Lion Dance.[3]

[203] *Plucked instruments* – The *biwa*. The best pieces are 'Fukō', 'Ōshiki' and the fast section of 'Sogō'. Also the piece called 'The Song of the *Uguisu*'.

The thirteen-string *koto* is very splendid. Its best piece is 'Sōfuren'.

[204] *Wind Instruments* – The transverse flute is utterly delightful. It's lovely when you hear it played from a distance and the sound gradually approaches. Also when the sound begins nearby and then moves into the far distance, becoming very very faint.

Whether he's in a carriage, or on foot, or on horseback, a man can always have his flute tucked away in the breast of his robe, quite hidden from view. There really is nothing more marvellous. Hearing a tune that's familiar to you is wonderful as well. And it's delightful to discover beside your pillow at daybreak the handsome flute that your lover has inadvertently left behind him. When you wrap it up to be returned with the man who's been sent to fetch it, it looks just like one of those official straight-folded letters.

It's delightful to catch the sound of a *shō* as you sit in your carriage on a night of bright moonlight. It's a cumbersome-looking instrument, and looks very awkward to play – and as for the face of the player![1] Though mind you, the transverse flute player can also look rather odd, depending on who the player is.

The little *hichiriki* is very hard on the ear. The autumn insect its sound most resembles is the shrill giant cricket, and you certainly don't want to hear it from close by. It's even worse when it's played badly. At that point during the Provisional Festivals when the musicians are still hidden, waiting to appear before the Emperor, when someone is playing beautifully on the flute and you're lost in delight at the sound, and suddenly the *hichiriki* breaks in to accompany it, such a feeling runs through everyone that you imagine even the most elegant heads of hair must be standing on end. It's wonderful when the musicians then begin to step out into the open, in time to the flute and the *koto*.

[205] *Spectacles* – The Provisional Festivals. Imperial progresses. The procession for the Return of the Kamo High Priestess on the day after the Kamo Festival. The procession of the heads of state to the Kamo Shrine the day before the Festival.

It's quite inexpressibly delightful on the day of the Provisional Kamo Festival when the sky is overcast and chilly, and a light snow is drifting down on to the indigo-printed cloaks and artificial flowers in the hair of the people in the procession. The black scabbards and broad spotted sheaths[1] of the dancers' swords stand out starkly, and the cords of their *hanpi* jackets that dangle there so beautifully rubbed and glossy, and the glimpse of gleaming glossed cloth that emerges almost like a flash of ice from among the folds of their blue-and-white-printed skirted trousers, all are simply marvellous. You wish there were a few more people in the procession, but after all, the imperial envoys actually aren't always very distinguished, and there's no pleasure to be had from looking at boring old Provincial Governors and so forth – although it's a pretty sight when people's faces are hidden by the wisteria sprays in their hair.

When the procession has passed by and you turn to watch it moving on, the impression is rather spoiled when you see the dancers' musicians in their vulgar willow-combination robes and kerria-flower hair decorations, but it's delightful the way they beat loudly on the horses' mudguards and sing 'As the shrine priests will bind their robes'.[2]

And what can compare with an imperial progress? When you see the Emperor travelling past in his palanquin, you lose all sense of the fact that you spend your everyday life in close service in his palace; you're overcome with awe and veneration, and the various ladies in the procession, whom you normally wouldn't look twice at, and even the Imperial Attendant ladies, all seem extraordinarily exalted and marvellous. The Captains and Lieutenants who are the Rope Escorts[3] are also delightful.

The Commanders of the Palace Guards are particularly wonderful. Indeed the Palace Guards Office in general is a delightful thing.

Most incomparably splendid of all must have been the imperial progress of the fifth month. It's a great pity that it no longer occurs. You hear people's tales of it, and try to imagine the scene, but just what can it really have been like? Sweet flag is spread everywhere on that day, and even the usual places look especially wonderful, so imagine how the Butokuden[4] and the temporary grandstands for the procession must have looked, all spread with the leaves; everyone wore sweet flag in their hair, and the most beautiful of the Lady Chamberlains who distribute the sweet flag was chosen to help His Majesty bestow herbal balls on the assembled people, which they ceremonially received and attached to their waists. How wonderful it must all have been! The Ebisu Residence Move and the shooting of the wormwood arrows[5] would also have been farcical and fun. As the imperial palanquin returned, dancers pranced before it performing lion and dog dances,[6] and just imagine what a moment it would have been, when a *hototogisu*'s call chimed in incomparably to add the perfect seasonal touch!

Imperial progresses are certainly a wonderful thing, but still, it's a shame that there are no carriages crammed with handsome nobles driving gaily up and down the road[7] on these occasions. It's always so thrilling when such a carriage works its way through the crowd and finds a place near yours at other events.

The procession for the Return of the Kamo High Priestess is a most delightful thing. Everything has been cleaned and prepared the day before, and the First Avenue lies wide and gleaming, ready for the procession. The sun's rays are hot, and dazzling when they penetrate the carriage, so you shield your face with your fan and adjust your position to avoid them as you sit there uncomfortably waiting on and on, the perspiration oozing and dripping. Everyone has hurried out to get here early, and on the carriages parked near Urin'in and Chisokuin, sprays of *aoi* and laurel flutter in the breeze. The sun is out, but the sky is nevertheless quite overcast, and you're moved and thrilled to hear the *hototogisu* – you've been waking up each morning and waiting, yearning to hear this song, and now here they are, calling to and fro all around as if they're everywhere. Then an *uguisu* cheekily sets off singing its wavery old song in brave imitation, which is annoying but rather delightful too.

You see a group of men in red hunting costume coming from the direction of the Upper Shrine. 'Has the procession begun yet?' you ask, and they reply, 'No, and who knows when it will', and on they go, carrying the empty palanquin back.[8] You're impressed and awestruck to think that this is what the priestess herself rides in, and appalled that such lowly people could serve in such close proximity to her.

Despite what they've said, in fact it's no time before her return. Everything about the attendant ladies, from their fans to their dark leaf-green robes, looks delightful, and the way the men from the Chamberlain's Office are clothed, in green formal cloak over layers of white gowns with just a touch of white hem tucked into the belt, produces such an illusion of being near a hedge of white deutzia flowers that you almost expect a *hototogisu* to be hidden there.[9] All those crazy young nobles who yesterday were crammed into a single carriage, with their matching lavender formal cloaks and gathered trousers or hunting costumes all in disarray and the blinds off their carriage, are now decorously dressed in formal attire, each in his own lonely carriage, on their way to the public banquet as accompanying guests, with charming young page boys seated behind them.

No sooner has the procession passed than a sort of hysteria takes over, with everyone pushing to get out ahead of the others in a most dangerous and frightening fashion. You thrust out your fan and order your men not to be in such a hurry, but they take no notice, so you resign yourself to getting the carriage out to somewhere with a bit of space where you finally insist it be drawn to a halt; the men are of course most resentful of this, but the way they now turn to watch the carriages coming behind is rather entertaining. It's particularly delightful if the next carriage to emerge is one bearing some unknown man, and when your two carriages finally go their separate ways he quotes the poem about clouds 'parted by the mountain peak'.[10] Sometimes, you're still so fascinated by the procession that you follow along to watch it right up to the gates of the High Priestess's shrine.

To avoid the great melee caused by the carriages of the High Priestess's attendants and the rest all setting off for home, you decide to return by a different route, and find yourself in an area that's movingly reminiscent of some mountain village – there sure enough is a deutzia hedge, in reality a very wild and unkempt thing with lots of nasty branches poking out into the road. You have the men break off some sprays where the flowers are still more or less in bud rather than fully opened, and attach them here and there to the carriage, a charming replacement for yesterday's now sadly wilting laurel branches. And it's fun too to wonder how you'll ever get through the narrow lane ahead, only to find as you approach it that it's possible after all.

[206] *Around the fifth month* it's great fun to make an excursion to a mountain village.

In swampy ground, the grass and water together form a single wide swathe of green to the eye, with the surface a beguiling luxuriance of grasses, but if you take your time and travel its length, it's delightful how the unexpected water beneath, though not deep, will burst forth under the weight of a human tread.[1]

As you go on your way, the various hedges to left and right will thrust an occasional branch into the carriage, and you quickly try to snap one off as you pass, lamenting the way it's gone again before you can seize it. And then there's the lovely moment when some wormwood gets caught and crushed by the carriage wheel, whose turning then carries it round and up, right to where you're sitting.

[207] *When it's fearfully hot*, it's a deliciously cooling sight to witness, just at that point in the cool of the evening when the dusk has begun to blur the shapes of things, a passing carriage,

perhaps that of some gentleman with outriders ahead, or even just some everyday carriage going by with the blinds up at the rear and one or two men inside. You particularly regret watching it disappear if it's accompanied by the sound of a *biwa* or a flute being played. It's really very odd how the sudden unfamiliar smell of the ox's leather crupper can nevertheless strike you as rather pleasant.

It's also lovely, on a dark moonless night, to catch the smell of smoke from the pine torch being carried up ahead, that penetrates the whole carriage.

[208] *On the evening of the fourth day of the fifth month,*[1] it's delightful to see the men in their red robes walking along carrying over both shoulders great sheafs of beautifully cut green sweet-flag leaves.

[209] *On the way to the Kamo Shrine,* women are out planting the rice fields – a large group of them are standing there singing as they work, wearing hats that look just like newly-made serving trays. They walk backwards doubled over, doing something invisible with their hands. You watch them, fascinated to learn what they're up to, and then you're distressed to catch the words of the song and realize that they're actually singing something very rude about the dear *hototogisu*:

> 'Yah! You there!
> *Hototogisu*!
> It's your chanting
> sets us planting!'[1]

they sing, and hearing it reminds you to wonder just who could have said '*Hototogisu*, / oh please do not sing so loud.'[2] I really do hate those awful people who claim the *uguisu* is better than the *hototogisu*, just like those who say horrible things about Nakatada's childhood.[3]

[210]* *At the end of the eighth month,* I went on a pilgrimage to Uzumasa. On the way, I came upon a noisy crowd of people

gathered by a paddy field looking at the ripe rice heads, and realized it must be the harvest.

> How recently it was
> that they took up the young rice plants[1]

says the poem, and truly time had passed all too swiftly, and look what had now become of those seedlings of the visit to the Kamo Shrine. Now instead of women it was men working in the fields, gripping the green stems with their rich red ears of grain and cutting them. It looked so easy, the way they sliced the base with some sort of tool, that I felt I'd like to try it myself. I was intrigued at how for some reason they spread the ears on the ground and squatted over them in a row, and also by the little huts in the fields.[2]

[211] *Soon after the twentieth day of the ninth month*, on a pilgrimage to Hase,[1] I stayed along the way in a very rough and simple lodging house. I was quite exhausted, and fell into a deep sleep.

Late that night, I woke and was deeply moved at the sight of the moonlight shining in through a window and casting its white light over the bedclothes of the sleeping forms around me. This is precisely the sort of moment when people compose poems.

[212] *Setting off to climb the slope* up to Kiyomizu and suchlike temples, it's delightful to find oneself deeply moved by the scent of burning firewood.[1]

[213] *The sweet flag leaves from the fifth month* remain through autumn and winter.[1] They're all white and withered and scruffy-looking, but if you pull one down and snap it, it gives off the most delightful lingering scent.

[214] *A well-scented robe* that's been left on the scenting frame[1] for two or three days before you remember and open it up, will release a wave of incense scent much more wonderful than that of incense that's presently burning.

[215] *On a bright moonlit night*, when your carriage is crossing a stream, it's lovely the way the water will spray up in shining drops at the ox's tread, like shattered crystal.

[216] *Things that should be big* – Houses. Provisions bags.[1] Priests. Fruit and nuts. Oxen. Pine trees. Inksticks.

If a man in someone's service has small eyes, he looks too feminine. On the other hand, great glaring eyes[2] are terrifying.

Braziers. Winter cherries.[3] The flowers of the kerria. Cherry blossom petals.

[217] *Things that should be small*[1] – Thread for sewing something in a hurry. The hair of women of the lower classes. The voice of someone's daughter. Lampstands.

[218] *Things that a house should have* – An elbow-shaped corridor.[1] Spiral-weave straw cushions. Low standing curtains. Large serving girls. Good-quality lady attendants. Retainers' quarters. Serving trays. Small and medium-sized meal-stands. Legged screens. *Oharaki* and *kakiban*.[2] Nicely decorated provisions bags. Chinese-style umbrellas. A cabinet with drawers. *Saké* kettles and pots.

[219] *On your way somewhere*, if you come across a slender, fine-looking fellow hurrying along the road with an official straight-folded letter, you do wonder where he can be off to.

Or you come across a good-looking young girl, her *akomé* gown subdued in colour and hanging rather limply, lacquered high clogs nice and shiny but their base all smeared with mud, carrying some large parcel wrapped in white paper, or volumes of bound books piled in a lid,[1] and you long to call her over and see what she has there.

As for the servant you see and call over as she's passing near the gate, who rudely refuses to answer and simply goes on her way, well, you may easily judge the quality of the person who's employed her.

[220] *It irritates me more than anything* to see some poorly-decked-out person, off on an excursion in a miserable carriage. Mind you, it's perfectly suitable if it's a sermon she's gone to hear, since she's there to rid herself of her sins – though even then it's hard to bear the sight of someone who takes this to extremes. As for the Kamo Festival and such occasions, you can only wish she hadn't come along to watch. There she is, no inner blinds on her carriage, and a mere sleeve of a white shift draped out. You, meanwhile, have gone to endless trouble over your inner blinds in anticipation of this event, and are there in something you dare to hope will pass muster with the others, and if you notice another carriage that's finer than your own, you despairingly wonder why you ever bothered coming – so one can only wonder how on earth this woman must be feeling, at the sight of everyone else in their finery.

You've turned up early, having chivvied the men along in order to get a good place, and you're waiting in the carriage, now sitting, now standing, to try to cope with the stifling heat. At last seven or eight carriages appear one after the other from the direction of the High Priestess's shrine, bearing senior courtiers, gentlemen from the Chamberlain's Office, Controllers, Junior Counsellors and so forth, on their way to the High Priestess's Banquet, and you realize with joy that the procession is ready to set off.

It's also great fun to park your carriage in front of the viewing stands to watch. Some of the senior courtiers will send messages over to you. Outriders from the Chamberlain's Office draw their horses up to the foot of the stand to be treated to a dish of rice gruel, and it's fun to watch how a senior courtier who's recognized the son of someone he knows will send a servant down from the stands to hold the mount's bridle while the rider eats. On the other hand, you feel rather sorry for the others in the procession who don't receive so much as a glance.

I also love it when the High Priestess's palanquin passes and all the carriages lower their shafts to the ground in homage, and then as soon as it's gone by the men rush to lift them back on to their stands again.

Someone has parked their carriage in front of another. There are strong demands that they move it, but the men stand their ground rebelliously, claiming there's no reason why they shouldn't park there, so, since communication has broken down, the lady resorts to dealing directly with the carriage's occupant through messages. This is great fun to watch. Then there's the marvellous occasion when some high-ranking carriage arrives with numerous attendant carriages in tow, though the place is already crammed full. You wonder where on earth they can be put, but the outriders are already leaping off their horses and wading in, thrusting other carriages out of the way and managing to squeeze even the attendant carriages into place. How disconsolate the poor displaced carriages look, as they're hitched to their oxen and go swaying off in search of a new space to park. The more splendid-looking carriages aren't pushed aside in the same way, however. There are also people whose carriage may look magnificent, but in fact they're always calling over some low-ranking nobody and inviting him up for a better view of the procession.

[221] *I heard people saying there'd been a man in the Long Room* who had no business being there. He'd been seen emerging at first light and going off with his umbrella up. As I listened, it dawned on me that the rumours were actually about me. Well, he may not be a senior courtier, I thought to myself, but he's not someone who should be so simply dismissed after all. I was musing on how odd the whole rumour was, when someone came with a message from Her Majesty, requesting an immediate reply. I wondered what it could be, and when I opened it there was a picture of a large umbrella with a hand holding it, but no figure of a person, and below this the words:

> Dawn had lit the mountain's edge
> and morning had arrived . . .[1]

How marvellous she is, I thought, even in foolish little matters such as this; yet I was also appalled that this unpleasant and embarrassing rumour should have reached Her Majesty's ears, as I'd so hoped it wouldn't. Nevertheless, the situation was an entertaining one, so on another piece of paper I drew pouring rain, and underneath wrote:

> . . . did not fall, and yet
> my name has turned to mud.

'That umbrella has left me "in wet clothes",' I added.

Her Majesty proceeded to relay this story, with much laughter, to Ukon.

[222]* *When Her Majesty was in the Sanjō Palace*, a palanquin full of sweet flags arrived on the fifth day,[1] and festive herbal balls were presented. The Mistress of the Imperial Wardrobe, together with the younger gentlewomen, made herbal balls and tied them on to the clothes of the little Prince and Princess.[2] More delightful herbal balls arrived from elsewhere as well, together with some green-wheat cakes. I laid these on thin green paper in the lid of an elegant inkstone box and presented them to Her Majesty with the words, 'These came from across the fence.'[3]

Her Majesty tore a strip from the edge of my letter and wrote in reply the following splendid poem:

> While all about me
> is filled with busy fluttering –
> flowers and butterflies –
> the only one who truly knows
> my heart today is you, my friend.

[223] *When Nurse Taifu* went off to Hyōga, among the fans that Her Majesty gave her[1] was one which depicted on one side a large group of country villas on a glorious sunny day, and on the other, a palace in the capital with the rain pouring down around it. She had added in her own hand:

> Face to the bright sun
> as you will be when you have gone
> to sunny Hyōga,
> turn and remember how our tears will fall
> as ceaseless rain here in the capital.[2]

It was wonderfully moving. She must have found it terribly hard to leave the service of such a splendid person.

[224] *Once when I was in retreat at Kiyomizu Temple,* Her Majesty specially sent a messenger to me with a letter written in flowing script on red-tinted Chinese paper:[1]

> Dusk's temple bell
> tolls one by one its long slow notes
> under the mountain –
> surely each stroke counts for you
> the loving thoughts that fill my heart.

'Yet still you stay away!' she added.

I'd forgotten to bring with me any paper that would be suitable for a reply, so I wrote my response on a violet lotus petal.[2]

[225]* *Posting Stations* – Nashihara, and the posting station at Mochizuki.

I find it very moving to make a list of mountain posting stations, since I've heard such affecting things about them, and had such moving experiences at them myself.

[226] *Shrines* – Furu Shrine. Ikuta Shrine. Sacred resting shrines.[1] Hanafuchi Shrine It's interesting to wonder whether there really is a sacred power in the cedar at the Cedar Shrine, as the poem says.[2] The god of Kotonomama sounds as though it would indeed answer prayers. You have to feel sorry for a god who is said to 'answer each and every prayer'.[3]

Aritōshi Shrine is fascinating because this is the god to whom

Tsurayuki composed his poem when the god had caused his horse to fall ill.[4] I don't know whether the following story is true or not, but they say this is the reason for the shrine's name.

Once upon a time there lived an Emperor who cared only for young people, and killed everyone once they turned forty. People fled and went into hiding in distant lands, and no one over forty was left in the capital. There was at that time a Captain, a brilliant and popular man, whose parents were both nearing seventy years of age. The parents were in terror for their lives, seeing that even people as young as forty were forbidden in the capital. But the Captain was a man of great filial piety. He declared that he couldn't bear not to see them at least once a day, so rather than send them to live in a distant land he instead secretly dug a hole in the earth under his house, where he built a room. There he settled them, calling in constantly to see that all was well, and he gave out to the court and to the people at large that they had disappeared.

Why should it have mattered to the Emperor as long as they stayed shut up in the house, I wonder? What a horrible age it must have been. The parents can't have been from the upper echelons, with a Captain as a son.[5] He was a very wise man, this Captain, a man of great knowledge, and though he was young he had a fine reputation and a most penetrating mind, so it seems the Emperor held him in the highest regard.

Now the Emperor of China was trying to get the better of this Emperor and seize his country, and he kept menacing him by engaging him in disputes and tests of knowledge. One day, he sent him a piece of planed wood about two feet long, beautifully sleek and shiny and rounded at the edges, with the question, 'Which is the base and which is the head?' There was no way of telling the answer to this, and the Emperor was greatly perplexed, but the Captain, feeling sorry for him in his quandary, secretly took the problem to his old father. 'All His Majesty needs to do is go to a swift-flowing river, stand on the bank and throw the wood in sideways. The end that turns and heads downstream will be the top,' his father instructed. The Captain then went to the Emperor and, pretending that the idea was his own, offered to carry out the plan. So he and his companions went and threw the wood into the river as instructed; they indicated the end that had turned downstream as the top, and sent it back to China, and apparently it was indeed correct.

On another occasion the Chinese Emperor sent two snakes of exactly the same length, roughly two feet long, with the question, 'Which is male and which is female?' This too was impossible to judge. Our Captain then went again to his father and asked what to do. 'Line them up,' said his father, 'and put a straight stick against their tails. The one that doesn't move its tail will be the female.' The Captain went back to the palace and did just this, and sure enough one moved its tail and one didn't, so they were marked accordingly and sent back.

A long time passed, and then the Chinese Emperor sent a tiny twisted jewel which had seven curves and a central hole running through it, and an opening at the two ends. 'Thread this and return it to me,' was the instruction. 'We can all do this here.' All the court nobles and senior courtiers, and everybody else as well, declared that even the cleverest crafts-man would be defeated by this task. So the Captain went again to his father and told him the problem. 'Catch two large ants,' the old man said, 'tie a thin thread round their abdomens, then attach a slightly thicker thread to this. Then smear the other end of the jewel with honey.' The Captain passed this advice on to the Emperor, then followed the instructions, and when the ants were put into the hole they smelt the honey, and emerged from the other end in no time. When the threaded jewel was sent back to the Chinese Emperor, he acknowledged that Japan was indeed a clever country, and never did such things again.

The Emperor was deeply impressed with the Captain's sagacity, and inquired what he could do for him or what rank he wished to receive as a reward. The Captain replied, 'I wish for no rank or title. I only beg that my old parents who have hidden themselves away be discovered and allowed to live in the capital again.'

'Nothing could be simpler,' the Emperor replied, and he forthwith decreed that they could return. When all the other aged parents learned of this, they too were overjoyed. The

Emperor elevated the Captain to court noble and made him
Minister.

The father seems to have become the god of Aritōshi, for
I've heard tell that once when someone was worshipping at
that shrine, the god appeared at night and spoke the following
poem:

> Is there any man
> who does not understand that I,
> Aritōshi's god,
> sent the two ants into the hole
> and the thread through the twisted jewel?

[227] *The Ichijō Palace went by the name of 'The Tempor-*
ary Palace'. The Emperor resided in the Seiryōden,[1] and Her
Majesty was in the building to the north of this. To east and
west were connecting covered bridgeways which were used by
the Emperor and Empress in crossing between buildings, and
in front was a charming garden, with plants and a woven
bamboo fence.

Around the twentieth day of the second month, on a balmy
spring day of brilliant sunshine, His Majesty was playing his
flute in the western aisle of the bridgeway. With him was
the Minister of War, Takatō, who was His Majesty's flute
tutor, and they were playing together over and over the tune
known as 'Takasago'.[2] The expression 'absolutely splendid' is
altogether too commonplace and inadequate to convey the
scene. It truly was marvellous to hear Takatō playing his flute
to demonstrate various musical matters. We ladies had gathered
to watch the scene from behind the blinds, and we felt not a
trace of 'Plucking Wild Parsley' sorrows as we gazed.[3]

On another occasion, His Majesty played the tune of the
Suketada song. This man Suketada was Secretary in the Office
of Carpentry and became a Chamberlain, a very uncouth and
unpleasant man, and the senior courtiers and gentlewomen
nicknamed him 'Mr Rough-and-Ready', and made a song about
him, which went:

He doesn't beat about the bush.
The reason's plain to see,
for he hails from the backwoods
of provincial Owari.

This was because his mother was the daughter of Kanetoki of
Owari Province. I happened to be in attendance when His
Majesty began to play this tune, and I urged him to play it
louder. 'Suketada won't be able to hear it,' I pointed out.

'Well, I don't know about that,' replied His Majesty. 'Would
he realize what it was if he did hear it?' and though he usually
played only quietly, on this occasion he came across to Her
Majesty's rooms and played it at full volume, with the remark,
'He's not here, after all, so I can play to my heart's content.' It
was all very splendid.

[228] *Among the people who show you* what it must be like to
be reborn as a heavenly being, there's the gentlewoman in
ordinary service who becomes an imperial wet-nurse. She no
longer wears the usual Chinese jacket, or for that matter a
formal train; she sleeps beside Her Majesty, and is at home in
the imperial bedchamber; she calls on the other ladies to send
messages down to her own rooms, or deliver letters for her –
in fact there's no end to the list of special privileges she enjoys.

It's also a splendid thing for a lowly official in the Chamberlains' Office to become a Chamberlain. In last year's Provisional
Festival in the eleventh month he was merely a bearer of the
koto, and seemed completely inconsequential, but now here he
is, going about in the company of the young nobles, and he fills
you with admiration. Other people who become Chamberlain
don't at all give the same impression.

[229] *It's lovely to see, on a day when the snow lies thick* on
the ground and still it keeps snowing, a group of fresh-faced
and youthful men of the fourth or fifth rank, coming along
through the snowy landscape. Their beautifully coloured formal cloaks bear the mark of the leather from their stone belts,
and are tucked up at the waist in the style of a night-guard.

They wear violet gathered trousers whose colour glows all the more vibrantly against the snow, and the *akomé* gowns beneath their cloaks, scarlet or brilliant kerria-yellow, show at the sleeves. They carry Chinese umbrellas, held at a slight angle against the strong wind and slanting snow, and on their feet they wear deep leather shoes or short boots, covered to the leggings in pure white snow.

[230] *It's also charming to witness*, very early in the morning when you open the sliding door of the Long Room, a senior courtier who's just emerged from the long side passage by the Imperial Bathroom, at the end of his night duty. His crumpled cloak and gathered trousers are dreadfully old and worn, and as he makes his way towards the northern guardhouse he's busily tucking in trailing bits of various-coloured clothing. Realizing that he's about to pass in front of your open door, he pulls the long tail of his lacquered cap round to hide his face as he goes.

Sliding door

[231] *Hills* – Funa Hill.[1] Kata Hill. It's delightful that the song's bamboo grass grows on Tomo Hill.[2] Katahira Hill. Hitomi Hill.

[232] *Things that fall* – Snow. Hail. Sleet is unpleasant, but it's lovely when it falls mingled with white snowflakes.

Snow is splendid on a cypress bark roof, particularly when it's just on the point of melting. It's also delightful when just a little has fallen, and it lies nestled in all the joins between the roof tiles, emphasizing their lovely black curves.

For autumn showers and hail, a shingle roof is best. Frost is also good on shingles, and in gardens.

[233] *Kinds of sun* – The setting sun. Just after it's set, it's very moving to see how a reddish light lingers along the rim of the mountains, with pale yellow clouds trailing in the sky above.

[234] *Kinds of moon* – The dawn moon, rising thin over the rim of the eastern mountains, is very moving.

[235] *Stars* – The Pleiades. Altair. The evening star. Shooting stars have a certain interest.[1] They'd be even finer if it weren't for their tail.

[236] *Clouds* – White, violet and black clouds are lovely. Also rain clouds on windy days. It's also delightful to see the way at dawn the dark night clouds will gradually disappear as the sky whitens. There's a Chinese poem that describes something like 'the colours that depart with morning'.[1]

A wispy cloud lying across the face of a very bright moon is moving.

[237] *Things that create a disturbance* – A sudden shower of sparks. Crows on the rooftop eating the offering portion of a monk's morning meal.[1]

The crowd that goes to Kiyomizu Temple on the eighteenth day of the month for the retreat.[2]

A number of people have gathered at a house as darkness

comes on but before the lamps are lit. There's even more disturbance when the master returns from some distant place such
as the provinces.

News arrives that a fire has broken out nearby. In the instance
I'm thinking of, however, the fire didn't take hold.

[238] *Slovenly-looking things* – Serving women with their hair
tied up for work. The rear view of a man wearing a stone belt
in Chinese paintings. The behaviour of holy men.[1]

[239] *People of rough speech* – The man who recites the prayers
in the Miyanobe festival.

Boatmen.

The thunder guards.

Wrestlers.

[240] *People who are smug and cocky* – Present-day three-
year-olds.

The woman who's brought in to pray for a child's health or
to massage someone's painful belly.[1] She asks for the materials
she needs for her invocations, then proceeds to make the necessary articles, setting up a great stack of folded paper, then
attempting to cut through it with a knife so blunt that it would
have trouble cutting even a single sheet. But no, she maintains
this is the one she must use, and she shoves and hacks away
with her mouth twisted with effort. Then she splits open a
length of bamboo with some toothed object,[2] attaches the paper
strips to it with a deeply reverent air and proceeds to wave this
about and pray – altogether a fine show of being knowing and
smug. Throughout all this, she keeps up her chatter: 'The son
of Prince So-and-so,' says she, or 'The little master of the So-
and-so residence, was taken fearfully ill, but I managed to root
it out and rid him of the problem completely, and they gave me
a fine reward for the job. They'd called in this person and that
person, but they'd had no success. They still call on me to this
day. A wonderful support, they are ...' and so forth, with such
an unpleasant expression on her face, too.

The female head of some lowly house.

Fools – the cocky ones who presume to instruct those who really do know.

[241] *Things that just keep passing by* – A boat with its sail up. People's age.
Spring. Summer. Autumn. Winter.

[242] *Things that no one notices* – All the inauspicious days. The ageing of people's mothers.

[243]* *I particularly despise people who express themselves poorly in writing*. How horrible it is to read language that rides roughshod over manners and social conventions. It's also very poor to be over-polite with people who should rightly be treated less formally. It's bad enough to receive poorly written letters oneself, and just as disgraceful when they're sent to others.

Generally speaking, even when you hear someone use language in this sort of slovenly way when talking face to face, you wince and wonder to yourself how they can say such things, and it's even more appalling when it's directed to someone eminent. Though when it's some country bumpkin who's speaking like this, it's actually funny, and therefore quite appropriate to them.

It's very bad to speak poorly to the master of the household. It's also wrong for a retainer to refer to his master in front of a guest with expressions such as 'he is gracious enough to' or 'he kindly said'. As a general rule, when you hear this kind of over-respectful expression you wish you could change it to something neutrally polite.[1] In such a situation, if I say to someone whom I'm able to rebuke, 'Dear me, how unpleasant you sound! Why is your language so crude?', both the person spoken to and those who hear will laugh. I suppose it's because I react like this that some people criticize me for making too much of an issue of such things – no doubt it does look rather ill-mannered of me, in fact.

It's awful to hear people referring to senior courtiers, Consultants and so forth by simply using their name, quite without any respect, but on the other hand in the case of, say, a woman who serves a gentlewoman, if somebody chooses not to call her straightforwardly by name but refers to her as 'madam' and so forth, she'll be thrilled at this rare courtesy, and praise the speaker extravagantly.

You should refer to senior courtiers and court nobles simply by the title of their post, unless speaking in front of someone exalted. And how can people use informal language to refer to themselves, when speaking among themselves but within earshot of the Emperor or Empress? Surely you should have the respect to avoid such language in front of Their Majesties, and there can be no reason why you shouldn't.

[244] *Horrid filthy things* – Slugs. The tip of a broom used to sweep some shabby wooden floor. The bowls in the Privy Chamber.[1]

[245] *Terrifying things* – Thunder at night. A thief breaking into a nearby house. If it's your own place he's broken into, you're too beside yourself to know what's happening.

A fire nearby is also terrifying.

[246] *Things that give you confidence* – Healing incantations performed with a large number of accompanying priests, when you're ill.

To be comforted when you're feeling low, by someone you truly love.

[247] *A son-in-law is brought in*[1] after elaborate preparations, but in no time he's ceased to base himself at home with his new wife. He must surely feel a pang of guilt whenever he comes across his father-in-law.

One young man, who married into the household of a man at the height of his fame and fortune, was never very diligent in calling on his new wife, and ceased coming altogether after a mere month. He was roundly condemned on every front, and some people such as the girl's nurse went so far as to curse him outright. Then in the New Year he was made a Chamberlain. I'm sure he was aware that people were discussing him, and saying how astonished everyone was at how he could have managed this, 'considering how matters stand with the family'.

In the sixth month of that year, everyone gathered to attend the Lotus Discourses that a certain person was dedicating, and there was this son-in-law the Chamberlain, dazzlingly attired in damask skirted trousers, black *hanpi* jacket and so forth, seated so close to the carriage of his neglected wife that his jacket cord might well have snagged on the tailpiece of her carriage.[2] All the people in the other carriages who knew the details of the situation were thinking, 'Poor thing, how must she be feeling to see him there?', and others who weren't present at the time also later declared themselves astonished at his nerve in blithely sitting so close to her like that.

It does seem that men don't have much sympathy for others, or understanding of how they're feeling.

[248] *Being disliked by others* is really a most distressing thing. How crazy would you have to be, to accept calmly the fact that you're probably the sort of person nobody likes? But it's a terribly sad fact that, both in the palace and among parents and siblings, there are those who are loved and those who aren't.

Not only among the upper crust but even in lowly families, when a child is the apple of his parents' eye then everyone will pay him particular attention and be particularly devoted to his needs. Of course if he's actually someone who's worthy of this kind of attention it seems quite natural, and no one pauses to question it. But it's very moving to see a parent's love for a child, even if he's actually nothing out of the ordinary, and consider that it's precisely because they're a parent that they feel like this.

Yes, there's nothing more wonderful than to be well-loved, not only by parents but by the one you serve and by all those you have close dealings with in life.

[249] *Men have most peculiar and unlikely feelings.* How extraordinary it is to see a man abandon a truly lovely woman in favour of some unpleasant one. A man who's constantly in and out of the palace, or the son of a fine household, can surely

take his pick, and select a charming girl. And if he loves someone, even if she's someone too exalted to be within his reach, a
man must put his life absolutely on the line and devote himself
heart and soul to her.

A man will apparently fix his sights on someone's daughter
or a girl he's not yet caught a glimpse of, if he hears good things
said of her. Still, I wonder why men will fall for a woman who
from a woman's point of view seems quite unattractive?

It's simply astonishing and outrageous when a beautiful,
charming and sensitive girl sends a chiding letter, elegantly
penned and with a most touching poem – yet though the man
responds with suitable gallantry, he keeps his distance and
won't go near her. To think that he can turn his back on this
girl who's obviously grieving so piteously, and abandon her for
another! Everyone who witnesses this can only be distressed by
it, yet the man himself is not in the least perturbed.

[250] *Nothing is more wonderful than sympathy* – in a man of
course, but also in a woman. It may be only some passing
remark, it may not be anything particularly deeply felt, but to
hear that someone has said of a sad situation, 'How sad for
her', or of some touching circumstance, 'I do wonder how she
must be feeling', makes you much gladder than hearing it said
directly face to face. I always long to find a way to let such a
person know that I've learned of their sympathetic response.

You don't feel particularly surprised and moved, of course,
in the case of someone whom you can rely on to feel for you or
visit you at such times. But if someone unexpected responds to
the tale of your sorrows with reassuring words, it fills you with
pleasure. It's such a simple thing to do, yet so rare.

It's unusual to find someone, either man or woman, who's
overall both tender-hearted and truly talented – though actually
there must be many such people around.

[251] *I really can't understand people who get angry* when
they hear gossip about others. How can you not discuss other
people? Apart from your own concerns, what can be more
beguiling to talk about and criticize than other people? But,

sadly, it seems it's wrong to discuss others, not to mention the fact that the person who's talked about can get to hear of it and be outraged.

Of course if it's someone you have a close bond with, you pause and consider the pain you might cause, and choose to keep your criticism to yourself – though if it weren't someone close to you you'd no doubt go ahead and say it, and have a laugh at their expense.

[252] *The thing about someone's face* that's particularly fine always makes you think, 'Ah, how delightful! How special!' no matter how many times you see it. Pictures, on the other hand, cease to attract the eye if you see them a number of times. The painting on a screen that stands close by, for example, may be absolutely marvellous, but you never pay it any attention. But people's appearance really is endlessly attractive. How your eye is drawn to the one good point in a face whose 'furnishing' is otherwise unattractive! It's a great pity to find yourself feeling much the same way about some feature that's ugly.

[253] *Old-fashioned people put on their gathered trousers* in a very time-consuming and awkward way. They pull the front panel up against their stomach and proceed first of all to tuck all the layers of robe in under it, leaving the back strings dangling till they've got the front completely straight and tidy, then they bend forward to reach for the back panel, groping behind them with both hands. They look like monkeys with their arms tied behind their backs, standing there fumbling about with the strings like that. You can't imagine how they could ever get dressed and out the door in time for any urgent appointment.

[254] *Once, towards the middle of the tenth month* when the moon was very bright, fifteen or sixteen of us decided to go for a walk to enjoy the moonlight. We wore deep purple robes over our gowns for the occasion, with the hems folded back, but Chūnagon had put on a stiff scarlet robe, and her hair was drawn round in front, under her chin. She looked just like some

newly created stupa. 'Dolly',[1] the young ladies called her. She had no idea they were laughing at her behind her back.

[255] *Captain Narinobu was wonderful at distinguishing people's voices*. It's impossible for most people to identify the voice of another person in the same establishment unless you're used to hearing her, and men are even worse at identifying voices or handwriting. But Captain Narinobu could very cleverly pick out any voice, from even the softest murmur.

[256] *No one had sharper ears* than the Minister of the Treasury.[1] He truly could have heard the fall of a mosquito's eyelash. When we gentlewomen were living in the western aisle of the Office of the Empress's Household, I was speaking in his presence to Minister of the Left Michinaga's adopted son Narinobu, the newly appointed Captain, when one of the ladies beside me whispered, 'Say something to him about that matter of the fan painting.'

'Wait till the gentleman yonder leaves,' I murmured to her very quietly, so quietly that she herself couldn't catch what I said, and bent closer saying, 'What was that?'

But though he was sitting quite far from us, the Minister of the Treasury exclaimed, 'That's terrible! If you say that, I'll stay put here for the day!' I was astonished at how on earth he'd managed to hear me.

[257] *Things that give you pleasure* – You've read the first volume of a tale you hadn't come across before, and are longing to go on with it – then you find the other volume. The rest of it can sometimes turn out to be disappointing, however.

Piecing back together a letter that someone has torn up and thrown away, and finding that you can read line after line of it.

It's extremely pleasing when you've had a puzzling dream which fills you with fear at what it may portend, and then you have it interpreted and it turns out to be quite harmless.[1]

It's also wonderfully pleasing when you're in a large company of people in the presence of someone great, and she's talking, either about something in the past or on a matter she's only just heard about, some topic of the moment, and as she speaks it's you she singles out to look at.

Then there's the pleasing moment when you've heard that someone who matters a lot to you and who's far from you – perhaps in some distant place, or even simply elsewhere in the capital – has been taken ill, and you're worrying and wringing your hands over the uncertainty, when news arrives that the illness has taken a turn for the better.

Someone you love is praised by others, and some high-ranking person comments that his talents are 'not inconsiderable'.

When a poem that you've composed for some event, or in an exchange of poems, is talked of by everyone and noted down when they hear it. This hasn't yet happened to me personally, but I can imagine how it would feel.

It's very pleasing when someone you don't know well mentions an old poem or story that you haven't heard of, and then it comes up again in conversation with someone else. If you come across it later in something you're reading, there's the delightful moment when you cry, 'Oh is *that* where it comes from!', and you enjoy recalling the person's mention of it.

Managing to lay hands on some Michinoku or any good quality paper.

You feel very pleased with yourself when a person who rather overawes you asks you to supply the beginning or end of some bit of poem they quote, and you suddenly recall it. It so often happens that as soon as anyone asks you, even something you know perfectly well goes clean out of your head.

Finding something you need in a hurry.

How could you fail to feel pleased when you win at a matching game,[2] or some other kind of competition?

Managing to get the better of someone who's full of themselves and overconfident. This is even more pleasing if it's a man, rather than one of your own circle of gentlewomen. It's fun to be constantly on your guard because you're expecting him to try to get even with you, and it's also fun to have been fooled into relaxing your guard over time, as he continues to act quite unconcerned and pretend nothing's happened.

When someone you don't like meets with some misfortune, you're pleased even though you know this is wicked of you.

You've sent out your robes to be freshly glossed for some event, and are holding your breath to see how they come out, when they're delivered looking absolutely beautiful. A comb that's come up delightfully with polishing is also pleasing. There are a lot of other things of this sort too.

It's very pleasing when you've finally recovered from a nasty illness that's plagued you day in, day out for months. This is even more the case when it's not your own illness but that of someone you love.

And it's wonderfully pleasing when a crowd of people are packed into the room in Her Majesty's presence, and she suddenly spies someone who's only just arrived at court, sitting rather withdrawn by a distant pillar, and beckons her over, whereupon everyone makes way and the girl is brought up and ensconced very close to Her Majesty.

[258] *I was talking with some people in Her Majesty's presence* – or it may have been something I said as a result of her own words – and I remarked, 'At times when I'm beside myself with exasperation at everything, and temporarily inclined to feel I'd simply be better off dead, or am longing to just go away somewhere, anywhere, then if I happen to come by some lovely white paper for everyday use and a good writing brush, or white decorated paper or Michinoku paper, I'm immensely cheered, and find myself thinking I might perhaps be able to go on living for a while longer after all. And when I unroll a section of fresh green Kōrai matting, thick and finely woven and with the edging design in vivid black and white, I'm overcome with the feeling that life itself is just too wonderful, and I really couldn't bear to relinquish it[1] just yet.'

'The simplest trifles console you, don't they,' remarked Her Majesty with a smile. 'It must have been a very different sort of person who gazed at "the moon above sad Obasute Mountain".'[2]

The others who were present also teased me with such comments as, 'You've certainly come up with an incredibly easy version of a magical formula for averting trouble!'[3]

Not long after this, when I'd gone back home and was in great distress, Her Majesty sent me a wrapped gift of twenty bundles of magnificent paper. With it came a message, relayed through one of the gentlewomen, asking me to make haste and return, and saying, 'Her Majesty asks me to tell you that this is because of what you said that day. She doubts if it's fine enough for copying out the Sutra of Longevity[4] . . .' I was absolutely thrilled. It would have been wonderful enough even if it hadn't been Her Majesty but some ordinary person who'd recalled a conversation I'd long forgotten myself, but in this case the words were particularly special for me. I was thrown into delighted confusion by them, and could find no way of responding, so I simply gave the messenger by way of reply:

> Most inexpressible
> my gratitude to one on high
> whose god-like paper gift
> has granted me new lease of life –
> the crane's renowned longevity,[5]

'though please say to Her Majesty that I fear this is overstating it,' I added. I gave the messenger, one of the serving women from the Table Room, a gift of a green damask shift.

Yes indeed, I thought to myself with pleasure, it will be fun to be distracted from my worries by throwing myself into the business of creating a bound book[6] from this paper.

Two days later, a man dressed in red appeared, bearing a mat. 'Here you are,' he unceremoniously announced.

'And who are you, to be standing there with the room in full view like that?' cried the maid, rather harshly, whereupon he put the mat down and made himself scarce.

I had someone inquire where he'd come from, but the reply came that he'd already left, so they brought the mat in, and it turned out to be a rather special one such as is used by important people, with a very beautiful Kōrai edging. I had a private hunch that this must surely have come from Her Majesty, but as I felt somewhat uncertain, I sent someone off to investigate. However, the man had indeed disappeared by then. It was mystifying, but there was no point in going on wondering since he was not to be found, and I had to assume that if he'd misdelivered it he'd surely come back of his own accord and say so. I would have liked to send to the palace and inquire, but if in fact it wasn't Her Majesty who sent the mat this would make things awkward, so I was left wondering who on earth could have sent this unsolicited gift, and most intrigued at the thought that it had probably come under instructions from Her Majesty.

Nothing further was heard on the matter, so after two days, more than ever convinced that the sender was Her Majesty, I sent a message to Ukyō telling her the story. 'Have you noticed anything of this?' I asked. 'Please tell me secretly what's been going on. If you haven't seen any evidence of it, don't breathe a word about this request of mine.'

'Her Majesty took great pains to hide it,' came the reply. 'You must absolutely on no account reveal that I've told you.'

So it was just as I suspected! I thought delightedly. I then proceeded to write a letter[7] to Her Majesty, and sent it off with instructions to place it unobtrusively on the veranda railing of the palace, but the messenger apparently fumbled and dropped it, and the letter ended up falling to the foot of the stairs.

[259]* *On the twenty-first day of the second month*, the Regent held a Dedication of the Complete Sutras ceremony in the hall of Sakuzen Temple in the Hōkō Palace. The Empress Dowager was to be present as well as Her Majesty, and around the beginning of the second month Her Majesty moved to the Nijō Palace[1] for the occasion.

I was so sleepy at the time of the move that I didn't take in anything of the surroundings. The following morning, I woke to brilliant sunlight streaming in, and discovered an enchanting building all white with newness,[2] with blinds and indeed everything seeming just freshly put in place the day before. The place

was beautifully appointed, and I found myself wondering when
the Chinese lions and the Korean dogs[3] could have arrived and
settled in so comfortably. A tall cherry tree, over three metres
high, was blooming magnificently at the foot of the stairs. 'How
early it's flowered!' I thought. 'The plum is still only just at its
peak' – but when I looked more closely, I realized it was an
artificial one. Everything about it, even the lovely gloss of the
flowers, was just as wonderful as a real cherry. What astonishing trouble someone had gone to! It was very sad to think that
it would all wilt with the first shower of rain. The place had
just recently been built on a piece of land where a number of
small houses had previously stood, so the garden lacked any
stand of trees and established plants that would have lent it
interest, but the building itself was delightfully warm and
attractive.

The Regent came over to pay a visit. He was dressed in
gathered trousers of blue-grey heavy brocade, and a cherry
blossom cloak worn directly over[4] three scarlet gowns. Everyone from Her Majesty down was wearing robes of lighter or
darker plum-pink figured silk, and heavy or unfigured brocade,
and the whole gathering seemed to glow with light. The Chinese
jackets were of spring-shoot green, willow or plum pink.

His Excellency seated himself before Her Majesty and engaged her in conversation, and as I watched I found myself
wishing that everyone back home could have even just a glimpse
of the scene, and witness how perfectly Her Majesty replied to
his questions.

His Excellency surveyed the assembled gentlewomen and
declared, 'Well, what could Her Majesty possibly have to say
about all of you? I only wish I had her luck, to be able to cast
my eyes over such a line-up of lovely ladies. Not one of you
that isn't pretty, and all from such fine families what's more.
Ah dear me! Just take good care you look after her well, won't
you now. Still, I wonder what you all really make of Her
Majesty, to have come along like this to serve her in such a fine
crowd. She's actually incredibly stingy, you know. Why, I've
served her hand and foot ever since the day she was born, and
never yet have I received so much as a robe from her in return!

See, I make no bones about saying it right in front of her . . .'
And on he went, hilariously. 'No no, I'm perfectly serious!' he
cried, when we burst out laughing. 'You're making fun of me,
laughing like that. Now you've made me embarrassed!'

He continued in this vein, till an Aide of Ceremonial arrived
from the palace with a letter from His Majesty. Grand Counsellor Korechika took it and passed it on to His Excellency, who
set about unwrapping it, remarking jovially, 'Now this I would
like to see! Might I have Your Majesty's permission to open it?
But no, I see you're looking nervous,' he went on, 'and besides,
I hesitate to interfere with a missive from His Majesty', and he
handed the letter to her. She took it, but made no move to open
it – a marvellous act of courtesy, I thought.

One of the ladies pushed out a cushion for the Aide of
Ceremonial from behind the blind, and three or four ladies
went and sat themselves by the standing curtain to wait on him.
'I'll go back home⁵ and provide a gift for the messenger,' said
His Excellency, rising to leave, and it was only when he had
gone that Her Majesty read her letter. She then wrote her
reply on thin paper of plum pink; witnessing the scene, I was
overcome with regret that no one would ever be able to imagine
just how marvellous she looked at that moment, with the colour
of the paper so perfectly echoing the colour she wore.

His Excellency provided the messenger's gift, a set of
women's ceremonial clothes together with a long divided robe
of plum pink, remarking that this was after all a special
occasion.⁶ Food and *saké* were also provided and the messenger
was encouraged to drink his fill, but he declined the offer. 'I
fear I'm in charge of an important function today, so do please
excuse me, Your Excellency,' he said apologetically, and he rose
and departed.

His Excellency's daughters were beautifully made up, and in
clothes of plum pink that were quite as fine as the rest of the
company. His third daughter was larger than her sisters, the
Mistress of the Imperial Wardrobe and the middle sister, Nakahime, and rather than address her as a daughter it seemed more
fitting to give her her wifely title of 'Your Highness'.⁷

His Excellency's wife was also present, but a standing curtain was drawn across to hide her from the view of us newly arrived gentlewomen, to our great frustration.

Some of the gentlewomen got together in a huddle to discuss what clothes and fans to choose for the coming ceremony, but others were more inclined to be prickly and secretive about it. 'Why should I bother?' they said nonchalantly. 'I'll just make do with whatever's to hand', to which the others spitefully replied, 'There you go again, that's just typical of you!' Many of the gentlewomen went back home when night fell, and because of the special circumstances[8] Her Majesty didn't feel she could require them to stay.

His Excellency's wife came every day, and was there in the evenings as well. Her daughters were also present, so Her Majesty was always surrounded by people, which was a very fine thing. Messengers arrived daily from the palace.

The beauty of the artificial cherry in the garden was not improved by the dew-fall, and in the sunlight its petals dried and shrivelled – and then its dismal state was further compounded by a night of rain, which left it absolutely ruined the next morning. I rose very early to see it. 'This blossom is a far cry from the tear-wet face of the girl the poet "parted from at dawn",'[9] I remarked. Her Majesty had meanwhile awoken, and hearing this she said, 'Yes, I did notice it raining last night. I must see how it looks' – but His Excellency had by then sent over a great bevy of servants and underlings, who crowded in around the tree and set about dragging it down with the intention of quietly removing it.

I was entertained to hear one of the servants scolding while the men tugged and hauled, saying, 'Our instructions were to have this done while it was still dark, but here it is, already dawn. This won't do. Come on, hurry up!' If he'd been a person of quality, I'd have asked whether he had in mind that poem of Kanezumi's, 'Let him scold if he will.'[10] But instead I simply cried, 'Who's that stealing the cherry blossoms? How dare you!' at which they fled, hauling the tree off with them as they went. I must say His Excellency showed delightful refinement in removing the tree so promptly. I imagine if it had been left standing the branches would have made a most unpleasant sight with the wet petals all stuck to them. I went back inside, without saying anything more.

Her Majesty rose after someone from the Housekeeping Office had come to raise her lattice shutters, and the place had been thoroughly cleaned by one of the groundskeepers. When she discovered that the tree had disappeared, she exclaimed, 'Good gracious! Where have the blossoms gone?' Then she continued, 'I did hear you say at dawn that someone was stealing the flowers, but I assumed they were just taking a spray or two. Who has done this? Did you see them?'

'No, not exactly,' I replied. 'I wasn't really able to see because it was still dark. I could make out some pale shapes out there, and I was worried that they might be taking some blossoms, which is why I spoke like that.'

'But how could they remove all of it like this?' said Her Majesty, and she added with a smile, 'It must be that His Excellency has simply had it hidden.'

'Oh, surely he wouldn't do a thing like that,' I replied. 'It must have been the doing of the spring wind.'

'You're saying that to hide the truth, aren't you,' said Her Majesty. 'No one was stealing it, it's simply disappeared thanks to "the rain of passing time".'[11] There was nothing particularly remarkable in what she said, yet it seemed to me absolutely wonderful.

His Excellency arrived at that point, and I withdrew into the background, not wishing him to see the untimely 'morning glory' of my sleepy face.[12] No sooner had he appeared than he cried, feigning surprise, 'Why, your cherry has disappeared! How could someone have stolen it from under your very nose like this? It must have been the fault of those slovenly gentlewomen of yours, sleeping in late and not noticing what was going on.'

'But,' said I in a soft voice, 'I had the impression that there was someone who'd come there "still earlier than I myself".'[13]

His Excellency instantly caught my words, and burst into laughter. 'I thought as much!' he said. 'Who else would have "come to it" and seen those blossoms? I guessed that you and Saishō would be about the only ones likely to do such a thing.'

'Despite that,' said Her Majesty with a most delightful smile, 'Shōnagon "blamed the spring winds".'[14]

'So it's the lie she's blamed on the winds, not "the blame that lies" on them,' said His Excellency, picking up the theme, 'though "even in the mountain fields the rice must be planting" by now', and he proceeded to chant the poem, in most elegant fashion. 'But how infuriating,' he continued, 'that they should have been caught at it, though I gave them such firm instructions about this. It's a great shame that there's such a vigilant guard here. Still,' he went on, 'that was clever of her to cast her lie on the sky's spring winds',[15] and he chanted the poem all over again.

But Her Majesty demurred. 'I fear it was an annoyingly pretentious way to treat a mere everyday statement,' she said apologetically,[16] and then went on, 'But speaking of this, I wonder how the blossoms would have looked this morning if the tree were still standing', and she added a light laugh.

At this point one of the ladies, Kowakagimi, said, 'But Sei Shōnagon pointed out very early this morning how their heads were hung in shame at looking worse than the girl's "tear-wet face"'', at which His Excellency made a delightful show of being deeply put out.

On the eighth or ninth day I returned home, though Her Majesty pleaded with me to stay until a little closer to the day of the Ceremonies. One day, when the spring sunshine was particularly bright and warm, Her Majesty sent a note asking, 'Have the blossoms "opened their hearts" yet? I do wonder how things stand with you', to which I responded, 'Although autumn is not yet upon us, my heart longs to "go to your presence nine times a night".'[17]

On the night of Her Majesty's move to the Nijō Palace,[18] there was no particular order to the carriages, and everyone was scrambling to get in first, which I found very distasteful.

'What pandemonium!' my friend and I said to each other. 'They're virtually falling all over themselves – it's as bad as the rush to get away after the Festival procession. How disgusting!

Let's wait till we can board with a bit of dignity. If there turns out to be no carriage left for us, Her Majesty is bound to notice and send one.'

The others all pushed past us and scrambled in, and when everyone had managed to grab a place someone said, 'Is that everyone now?' and apparently another answered, 'No, there are still people waiting here.' Thereupon a palace officer came over and exclaimed in great surprise, 'Who's still here? This is extremely odd. I thought everyone had boarded just now. Why are you so late? We were about to put the servants in. Really, how extraordinary!' and he ordered the men to draw up a carriage for us.

'Well then, do go ahead and board the servants as you'd planned,' I said. 'We'll board after them.'

When he heard me say this, the officer lost his temper. 'What impertinence!' he cried. 'You've been sitting here waiting in the background out of sheer perversity, haven't you!' Since he was railing at us like this, we meekly boarded the carriage, but found that we were indeed in one intended for the servants. Chuckling together at how ill-lit it was, we finally proceeded to the Nijō Palace.

By the time we got there, Her Majesty's palanquin had long since arrived, her room was prepared, and she was already ensconced. She'd been asking for us, and the younger gentle-women Ukyō and Kosakon had been watching for us as each carriage of ladies arrived, but without success. With each fresh carriage, the four newly arrived ladies went to Her Majesty to pay their respects and announce their arrival, and unbeknownst to us Her Majesty had been bewailing our continued absence, saying, 'How very odd! Still not here? What can have happened to them?' – so when the two finally discovered us after all the others had made their appearance, they hastily pulled us along, relaying her words and scolding us for our lateness. When we finally entered, we were intrigued to see how at home Her Majesty already was in her new surroundings.

'Now why is it,' inquired Her Majesty, 'that you couldn't be found for so long, when we were searching and wondering like this?'

I made no reply, so the lady who had come with me spoke up. 'There was no way round it, Your Majesty,' she declared miserably. 'How can the people in the last carriage arrive early? As it is, we were only given our carriage because the servants took pity and let us in. And it was horribly dark and nasty . . .'

She made such a heart-rending tale of it that Her Majesty declared, 'The people in charge have behaved reprehensibly! And they aren't the only ones at fault. Someone who's not familiar with things can't be expected to speak up for herself, but you, Uemon, why didn't you complain?'

'But,' protested Uemon, 'we couldn't very well hurry over and push our way in ahead, surely.' No doubt the others were far from pleased to hear this.

'There's certainly nothing praiseworthy about ignoring protocol and taking a place among one's betters,' said Her Majesty crossly. 'The most seemly thing to do is wait your proper turn.'

I stepped in here and pointed out that their unseemly haste had no doubt been caused by their anxiety and eagerness to arrive in Her Majesty's presence.

I returned from my home the evening before Her Majesty was to go to the temple in preparation for the Sutra Ceremonies. When I looked in at the northern side of the South Hall,[19] lamps were burning on standing trays, and by their light I could see intimate little groups of two or three or four ladies gathered here and there, separated from each other by a screen or in some cases a standing curtain. Then there were other larger groups, sitting together sewing their gowns into order or adding decorative touches to their formal trains,[20] or applying their makeup, all quite meticulously of course; but even more impressive was the care they were putting into binding their hair, so extravagantly artful indeed that you felt its like would be hard to find again once this event was over.

'Her Majesty is to proceed to the temple at around three in the morning,' someone said to me when I arrived. 'Why have you taken so long to come? A messenger was given your fan[21] and sent off in search of you.'

Well, we dressed ourselves in our formal attire and were

ready and waiting as instructed, believing that it was indeed to be the pre-dawn hours when Her Majesty must depart, but the dawn came, the sun rose, and still we didn't leave. Finally, word came that our carriages were being drawn up to the veranda of the western wing, under the Chinese eaves, so we all set off along the bridgeway in a body, the more recently arrived among us feeling very self-conscious. Her Majesty was already there in the north wing, which was His Excellency's residence, and His Excellency compounded my discomfort by declaring that he and his assembled company would first watch as we boarded our carriages, which they proceeded to do – Her Majesty, the Shigeisa and His Excellency's third and fourth daughters, together with his wife and her three younger children, all seated or standing behind the blinds.

Grand Counsellor Korechika and Captain Third Rank Takaie stood at either side of our carriages to help us board, raising the carriages' outer and inner blinds for us. If we could all have stayed in a crowd there would have been some way to keep at least a little hidden from view among the others, but we were called over four at a time, our names read in order from a written list, and I felt quite excruciatingly exposed when I was forced to step out to board at the sound of my name. What's more, I was miserably aware of Her Majesty's gaze among those of everyone watching from behind the blinds, convinced that she must be wincing to see what a sorry figure I cut, and the mortification made me perspire so that I was sure my carefully arranged hair would be all frizzled from the sweat. And then, safely past all the watchers beyond the blinds at last, I was confronted with the sight of the Grand Counsellor and the Captain Third Rank, looking quite dismayingly handsome, standing there watching me with beaming faces as I approached. It all felt more dream than reality. I nevertheless boarded without a stumble, though I was at a loss to decide whether it was thanks to courage or to sheer brazenness that I'd managed to achieve this feat.

Once the others had boarded, our carriage set off, and when we arrived at Nijō Avenue our carriage shafts were settled on to their stand and we were intrigued to find ourselves in among

quite an assembly of carriages, parked there as if awaiting some
festival procession. It made my heart flutter with pleasure to
imagine how the sight of us would impress bystanders in just
the same way. Men from the fourth, fifth and sixth ranks were
constantly milling about, and pausing by the carriages to adjust
them and to talk with the ladies. Lord Akinobu in particular
was thoroughly elated, and swaggering about.[22]

His Excellency, with the senior courtiers and lesser gentlemen
in train, now appeared to greet the Empress Dowager. We were
waiting in high anticipation, knowing that Her Majesty was
due to arrive after the Empress Dowager, and then, when the
sun was already well risen, the Empress Dowager's procession
finally made its appearance. There were fifteen carriages including her own, four of which were for the accompanying nuns.[23]
Her own carriage was in the Chinese style. The four nuns'
carriages that followed had lowered blinds, with inner blinds
of pale violet-grey, slightly darker at the bottom edge, and they

Chinese-style carriage

revealed from beneath the blinds at their rear a marvellous display of crystal rosaries, dark grey trains, surplices and robes. After them came the ten carriages of her gentlewomen, with wonderfully elegant displays of cherry-blossom Chinese jackets, pale violet-grey trains, deep purple robes, and clove-tan and pale violet-grey outer gowns. Though the sun shone brightly, the sky was a misty blue, which went beautifully with the ladies' formal robes, creating an effect even more elegant than the marvellous figured silks and variously coloured Chinese jackets, and the whole was utterly delightful.

The Regent and his younger brothers all greeted the Empress Dowager with great ceremony and accompanied her in, and we who were witnessing this for the first time exclaimed together in admiration at the sight of it all. No doubt our own line-up of twenty carriages was similarly impressive to other onlookers.

Now we all waited eagerly for Her Majesty to arrive, but time passed and there was still no sign of her. We were beginning to feel anxious when at last her entourage emerged, with eight escorting Palace Maidens on horseback. It was delightful to see how their formal trains of green shaded darker at the edges, and their decorative sashes trailing from shoulder and waist, fluttered out on the breeze. The Palace Maiden by the name of Buzé was the lover of Director of the Office of Medicine Shigemasa. She was wearing figured grape-coloured gathered trousers, which led Grand Counsellor Yamanoi to remark with a laugh, 'Shigemasa's been granted access to the "special colours"!'[24]

When the ladies had all come riding out, Her Majesty's palanquin emerged. Oh, there could be simply nothing to compare with how marvellous it looked! The sun was shining brilliantly by this time; it lit the golden onion-flower finial on the palanquin's roof magnificently, and everything down to the very drapes glowed quite stunningly. The attendants steadied the palanquin with tightened ropes as it moved forward, and as I watched those drapes swaying gently to and fro, I felt the literal meaning of the expression 'it raises the hairs on the back of your neck'. Having witnessed this sight, any among us whose

Palanquin with onion-flower finial

hair was disarrayed could later blame it on this experience! Her Majesty really created such an astonishingly magnificent spectacle that I was quite overawed and impressed with myself at being actually in her service.

Then, as the palanquin was carried past, there was the indescribably glorious moment when our lowered carriage shafts were hastily hitched up to the oxen again, and we fell into place in the procession behind the palanquin.

When Her Majesty's palanquin arrived at the gate of the temple, there was such an outburst of welcoming entertainment that I felt quite faint – Korean and Chinese music, and lion and Korean dog dances, with wild flute music and drums beating. Can I have arrived in the Buddha's heavenly realms? I thought, hearing the music all around me reverberating to the skies. There was also something quite unearthly about the whole marvellous sight that greeted us once we'd entered the temple grounds, where various brocade-draped pavilions had been set up, hung about with lovely fresh green blinds and dividing curtains.

Our carriages were drawn up to Her Majesty's stand, and now the same two accompanying gentlemen[25] came over and urged us to alight without delay. It had been embarrassing enough when we boarded, but now the day was brighter and we were even more exposed to view, and I was so sure that the carefully placed hairpiece in my hair that I had tucked inside my Chinese jacket was by now quite frizzled and hideous, and even the contrast between the hairpiece's reddish tinge and my own black hair would be clearly visible, that it took some time for me to summon the courage to emerge. 'Do go first please,' I urged the lady seated behind me, but she appeared to be feeling much as I did about the prospect, for she said to the gentlemen, 'Would you be so good as to step back a little? We don't deserve such solicitous attention.'

'You seem embarrassed!' they said with a laugh, as they retreated.

Once we had at last managed to alight, the Grand Counsellor came over and said, 'That wasn't very sensible of you, you know. We were only standing there like that because Her Majesty had expressly asked us to shield you from the sight of Munetaka and the others', and he hastily led us into Her Majesty's presence. I was terribly touched to realize how thoughtful Her Majesty had been on our behalf.

When we appeared before Her Majesty, eight ladies who had arrived ahead of us were already seated right at the edge of the stand, where they could get a good view of proceedings, while Her Majesty sat on the upper level, somewhere about two feet above them.

'We have led the ladies here out of sight, as instructed,' the Grand Counsellor announced, at which Her Majesty emerged from behind her standing curtain to inquire after us. She looked quite magnificent, still dressed in the formal train and Chinese robes she'd worn earlier. How could those wonderful scarlet gowns look merely commonplace? Particularly outstanding were a Chinese damask gown in the willow combination, five layers of grape-coloured gowns, red-purple figured Chinese jacket, and gauzy train of indigo on white, picked out in gold, all of quite incomparable colours.

'How do I look?' she inquired.

'Quite splendid, Your Majesty,' I replied, aware as I spoke just how trite my words were.

'You must have thought I was taking forever,' she continued. 'The reason I was held up was that my father suddenly declared that people would look askance if he was seen wearing the same formal train-robe he'd worn when he accompanied the Empress Dowager, so he had a new one sewn on the spot. What a dandy he is!' and she laughed.

Her Majesty's beauty was still more plain to see, owing to the unusually brightly-lit surroundings. I was simply entranced by the way the pins which supported her hair at the front clearly created a slight imbalance in the way her hair was parted.

Two three-foot standing curtains stood together separating Her Majesty and the gentlewomen. Behind this, a mat had been placed lengthways, with its edge meeting the edge of the threshold, and two ladies – Chūnagon, daughter of His Excellency's uncle Captain of the Right Gate Watch Tadakimi, and Saishō, granddaughter of the Tominokōji Minister of the Right – were seated there to watch the event. Her Majesty surveyed the arrangement and said, 'Saishō, would you go over and watch from where the other ladies are sitting?'

Saishō saw what she had in mind. 'Three people can easily see from here, Your Majesty,' she replied.

'Very well then, come on in,' Her Majesty said to me, drawing me over to join them.

The ladies seated below smiled at this, and joked rather snidely, 'She's just like a Constable specially allowed in to the Privy Chamber.'

'You see me as some upstart then?' I inquired, to which another lady responded, 'More on the level of a stable boy.' Nevertheless, it was a glorious moment, to have the honour of being permitted to watch from above. No doubt it's unseemly for me to be boasting like this, and it may well redound unforgivably on Her Majesty's reputation, by giving an opportunity to those who would set themselves up as shallow judges of worldly matters to wag their heads sagely and declare, 'To think that Her Majesty should favour such a creature!' – yet I can only write the facts as they stand, after all. I freely admit that I was of a quite unworthy station to be the recipient of Her Majesty's special attentions in this manner.

It was marvellous to be able to view the Empress Dowager's stand and the various other stands that stood about in the temple grounds. His Excellency passed Her Majesty's stand and spent some time at the Empress Dowager's, before coming to ours. The two Grand Counsellors, Korechika and Michiyori,[26] accompanied him, and Captain Takaie, still in his guise as Palace Guard, was looking most fitting and splendid with his bow and quiver slung over his shoulder. Rows of accompanying senior courtiers and other men from the fourth and fifth ranks also sat behind His Excellency.

When His Excellency entered, he saw before him the fine spectacle of Her Majesty and her sisters, even the Mistress of the Imperial Wardrobe, all dressed in their formal trains and Chinese jackets. Her Excellency, his wife, wore instead a formal over-robe.

'What a perfect picture you all make!' he declared. 'And you, Madam,' he continued jokingly, turning to his wife, 'are certainly dressed like a lady today, aren't you? But Madam, you should remove Her Majesty's formal train, you know. She's the one who's mistress in this particular gathering.[27] After all, it's no everyday matter to have Palace Guards specially stationed in front of your stand like this' – and the thought of it brought sudden tears to his eyes.

Everyone grew rather tearful at the truth of this, whereupon His Excellency neatly turned the conversation by observing my red-purple weave jacket and cherry-blossom five-layered gowns, and crying, 'Aha – there was a nasty moment earlier when we discovered we were short one priest's cloak, but we should have borrowed yours.[28] Or are you perhaps monopolizing red cloaks?'

Grand Counsellor Korechika, who was seated a little behind and overheard this, kindly broke in at this point and joked, 'No, surely what you see there is the cloak of Bishop Sei.'

Every word of all this was quite marvellous, I thought.

His Excellency's son, Bishop Ryūen, delighted us by coming and walking about among the gentlewomen. He wore a red-purple silk-gauze formal cloak with violet surplice, and very pale violet-grey gowns over gathered trousers, and with his charming bluish shaven head he looked like an image of the Bodhisattva Jizō.[29] 'He should be off being suitably dignified with the other top clergy,' we laughed. 'It doesn't look good to be seen among the ladies like this!'

Grand Counsellor Korechika brought his little boy Matsugimi across from the Grand Counsellors' stand. The boy was dressed in a figured grape-coloured cloak, deep-purple glossed damask robe and plum-pink figured jacket, and was accompanied by a crowd of fourth- and fifth-ranking courtiers as usual. When he arrived in our stand, he was carried in among the gentlewomen, but something upset him and he burst into tears. Even this only added to the fine spirit of the occasion, however.

The ceremonies began with the truly awe-inspiring pageantry of a great procession, starting with the priests and proceeding on through the court nobles, the senior courtiers, lower-ranking gentlemen and sixth-ranking men, not to mention numerous others, bearing the Complete Sutras scroll by scroll, each on a pink lotus flower. Then the officiating priest entered, and the sermon began. This was followed by dancing.[30] After watching this all day long, my eyes were quite exhausted and aching.

One of the fifth-ranking Chamberlains arrived with a message from the palace, and it was most impressive to see him seated on a special folding chair before Her Majesty's stand to wait once he had delivered it.

As night was falling, we were visited by Aide of Ceremonial Norimasa.[31] 'His Majesty states that he requires Her Majesty to present herself at the palace directly this evening. I am to accompany her,' he announced, and he remained there to fulfil his mission.

'I shall return to my quarters first,' said Her Majesty, but then the Controller Chamberlain arrived to report that a message to the same effect had also been sent to the Regent, so Her Majesty bowed to the Emperor's command and decided to proceed directly to the palace.

Meanwhile, messages were coming and going between Her Majesty's stand and the Empress Dowager's, from which a poem referring to 'the close salt kilns of Chika'[32] arrived. A wonderful exchange of charming gifts flew back and forth between them.

When the Ceremonies were finally over, the Empress Dowager returned to her residence. This time, the escorts were divided, with half the retinue from her household assigned to Her Majesty, and the other half, along with the court nobles, accompanying the Empress Dowager. The servants had no idea that Her Majesty was proceeding directly to the palace that night, so they returned to the Nijō Palace and waited on and on there, expecting her to arrive at any moment, but the night grew late and still there was no sign of her entourage. Meanwhile, we who had accompanied Her Majesty to the palace were vainly waiting for them to arrive with our nightclothes, but there was not a sign of them. There we were, still got up in our special finery, feeling uncomfortable and by now quite cold, and we were furious with them, but to absolutely no avail. When they appeared the next morning we demanded to know how they could have been so dim-witted, but they had their answers to that of course.

The following day it rained. 'I take this contrast with yesterday's glorious weather as a sure sign of my excellent karma,' His Excellency said to Her Majesty jubilantly. 'What do you say?' And indeed one could well see why he should be feeling so pleased with himself.

But these events, which seemed to us so splendid and auspicious at the time, all look very different when compared with the present,[33] and this is why I've set it all down in detail, with heavy heart.

[260] *Venerable things* – The 'Nine-Section Staff'.[1] The prayer for salvation of all sentient beings that's recited at the end of the Amida invocations.

[261] *Songs* – Folk songs, in particular 'The Cedars Standing by the Gate'.

The *kagura* songs that accompany god dances are also delightful.

Imayō songs are long and have unusual melodies.

[262] *Gathered trousers* – Dark violet. Spring-shoot green.

In summer, lavender. On very hot days, trousers in the lapis lazuli blue of summer insects give a sense of coolness.

[263] *Hunting costumes* – Clove-tan. Soft white silk. Red-purple weave. Pine-leaf green. Leaf green. Cherry blossom. Willow. Also, green wisteria.[1]
Men wear all manner of colours.

[264] *Shifts* – White. For daytime formal wear, one should wear a more relaxed, scarlet unlined version of the *akomé* gown. Still, white is always particularly good.
I cannot bear people who wear a white shift that's slightly yellowed. Some people wear gloss-yellow robes,[1] but I nevertheless much prefer white.

[265] *Formal train-robes*[1] – In winter, azalea. Cherry blossom. Softened silk. In summer, lavender. Also, white on white.

[266] *Fan ribs* – Those made from the wood of the *hō* tree. The colour[1] should be red, violet or green.

[267] *Cypress fans*[1] – Undecorated, or painted in the Chinese style.

[268]* *Deities* – The deity of Matsuo. The deity of Yahata is particularly wonderful because it was once the Emperor of this land,[1] and it's also awe-inspiring to see the onion-flower finial on the imperial palanquin for the procession to this shrine.
Ōharano. Kasuga Shrine has a very wonderful deity. Hirano. I once asked someone what an empty building there was used for, and was overawed to learn that it was where the deity's festival palanquin was kept. I paused long there beside its vine-smothered fence, thrown into a reverie by the vine's occasional red leaves, recalling the Tsurayuki poem that speaks of such unseasonal leaves as unable to 'hold back the season's change'.[2]
The deity of Mikomori is also delightful. Also the deities of Kamo, and of Inari.

[269] *Promontories* – Karasaki. Miho.

[270] *Huts* – The 'thatched hut' and the 'eastern hut' of poetry.[1]

[271]* *The calling of the night watch is a wonderful thing.* Deep on a freezing night, I love to hear the clatter of the night watchman dragging his shoes along as he approaches, and the sound of the bow twanging and his distant voice crying his name and the hour – 'Third quarter, Hour of the Ox' or 'Fourth quarter, Hour of the Rat'. Then comes the sound of the peg going into the time-board. Countrified people will say 'Rat nine strikes' or 'Ox eight strikes';[1] but with us, whatever the hour, the strike only comes at 'four', since it's always only on the fourth quarter that the peg is struck in.

[272] *At noon on a beautiful sunny day,* or very late, around the midnight hour, when you believe His Majesty must be asleep, it startles and awes you to hear him suddenly calling for his Chamberlains. Also, it's very splendid to hear the sound of his flute at night.

[273]* *Captain Narinobu* is the son of His Reverend Highness, Minister of War.[1] Not only is he extremely handsome, he also has a delightful personality. I felt very sorry for him when the Governor of Iyo, Kanesuke, took his daughter back to Iyo with him, leaving poor Narinobu unable to forget her. How touching to imagine his lonely cloaked figure making its way home beneath the moon at daybreak, after bidding her farewell before her dawn departure.

He was always calling round to talk to us, and in his judgements of people he never hesitated to criticize where criticism was due.

This reminds me of a lady, someone meticulous in observing the abstinences and such things, who had a very odd family name.[2] She took the name 'Taira' when she was adopted by a branch of that family, but the younger ladies enjoyed making fun of her by using her original name. She was not particularly pleasing in appearance, and she didn't have a very interesting personality, but naturally enough she wanted to mix with the others and not be singled out like this. Her Majesty remarked that it was quite unseemly to tease her in this way, but everyone was too mean-spirited to pass this on to the people concerned.

When rooms for the gentlewomen were set up in the Ichijō Palace, Shikibu and I stayed day and night in our delightful room in the little aisle, that looked straight out on to the East Gate of the palace, and would only allow visitors we liked. His Majesty himself would often come to call on us there.

One night, we decided to sleep inside instead of in our little room, so we settled down in the south aisle. Suddenly, we heard someone insistently calling my name. 'Let's ignore this noise,' we agreed, and we lay there pretending to sleep, but he only called more loudly, until even Her Majesty said, 'Do get her up. I'm sure they're not really asleep.' Then this Hyōbu[3] I'm speaking of came along to wake us, but we made out we were sound asleep, so off she went again to report to the visitor that we couldn't be roused. She then appeared to settle down there and start talking with him herself.

Time passed, and the hour grew very late, but still the conversation continued. 'It sounds as if that's Captain Narinobu,' we said to each other. 'What can they be talking about for so long?' and we began secretly to giggle at the thought, which of course she couldn't have known. He stayed talking with her till dawn, when he finally returned home. I was still chuckling about it, and saying to my friend, 'What a dreadful man. I'll never speak to him again! What can they have been talking about, for him to stay till dawn like that?' when the nearby door slid open and in came the lady in question.

Next morning, when I was back in my little room as usual, I was puzzled to overhear one of the ladies say in the course of conversation, 'I do feel sorry for someone who comes calling in a heavy downpour. Even if I happened to be feeling somehow low, or was unhappy over him for some reason, if he came along soaked to the skin I'd forget all my reservations and sorrows.' Now why should she say such a thing? Of course if he's been turning up constantly, night after night, and now in the pouring rain he refuses to be put off but still insists on calling, I can imagine she'd feel very touched to see that he didn't want to be parted from her for even a single night. But if he doesn't come around much, and she's been spending days and nights in miserable uncertainty over him, surely the fact that he's turned up on a night like this should hardly be enough to reassure her of his intentions. Well, I can only conclude that everyone's different. I should say that if he's courting a lady of experience, discernment and evident sensibility, but is also visiting a number of other ladies, and has a wife in the background as well, and now, after constantly neglecting her, he chooses to show up on an awful night like this, it can be put down to a calculated desire to have people speak admiringly of his noble, self-sacrificing gesture. Yet if he really has no feelings at all for her, then what can he be up to in going out of his way to make it seem otherwise like this? Mind you, I always feel very out of sorts when it's raining – all that lovely fine weather of the previous days suddenly feels quite unreal, and I dislike everything, and am even resistant to the charm of the splendid Long Room, for once. And if I'm in some ordinary, unattractive house of course I long even more for the rain to stop. No, there's certainly nothing either delightful or moving about a rainy day.

However – on a bright moonlit night, how the imagination will call up before your eyes scenes from the past and even scenes yet to be, in complete and vivid detail, till you're quite overcome with the incomparably splendid and moving experience of it! And if a man came calling on such a night, a man who has thought to call on you again after a lapse of ten or twenty days, or a month, or a year, or even perhaps seven or eight years, you'd be thoroughly delighted to see him. Even if it was some highly inappropriate place for such a meeting, and you had to be careful not to be seen with him, you'd certainly want to exchange some furtive conversation before sending him on his way, even if you had to stay standing as you talked, and if it was a situation where he could spend the night, you'd surely urge him to do so.

Is there any occasion to match a moonlit night for sending your thoughts winging to distant places, and recalling past moments, their sorrows and joys and pleasures, as if it were today? *The Tale of Komano* hasn't anything much of interest in it, its language is old-fashioned and there are few noteworthy scenes, but I do find it touching when the hero is recalling the past as he gazes at the moon, and takes out the moth-eaten summer fan and sets off to visit her house, murmuring the line 'knowing he knows the way of old'[4] as he goes.

Well, it's probably because I find rain so unpoetic that I hate it when there's the least shower. If there's some splendid event at court, something that should be filled with pleasure, or a solemn and impressive sacred ceremony of some sort, the mere fact that it's a rainy day fills me with unspeakable despair – so I really can't imagine how anyone could feel thrilled to have some sodden fellow turn up feeling sorry for himself on a rainy night. I like the hero in *The Tale of Ochikubo*, who criticizes Lieutenant Katano, but that rainy night-visit scene is delightful for the special reason that he's come visiting her for the last two nights.[5] I don't care for the part where he washes his muddy feet, though. They must have been awfully dirty!

On the other hand, it's a delightful and reassuring thing for a man to come calling on a wild, windy night. And a snowy night visit is most splendid of all. He arrives humming to himself the line 'How could I forget her?'[6] or something of the sort, and of course the scene is particularly charming if he's a secret lover, but even if there's nothing secret about it, there would be something utterly delightful in the sight of his cloak, say the special green formal cloak of a Chamberlain, all chilled and damp with snow. Even if it's just the sixth-ranker's normal cloak, I wouldn't mind as long as it was snow that had wet it. I gather that in the old days a Chamberlain would always come along in his special green cloak when visiting a lover at night, and simply wring it out if it had got soaked in the rain. Nowadays they seem not to bother to wear it even during the day, but turn up with just the sixth-rank cloak draped over them. And it used to make an even more delightful impression if a Chamberlain wore his Palace Guard costume instead.[7]

Well, I don't imagine hearing these opinions of mine is going to stop any man from setting forth on foot on a rainy night. But I remember one delightful moment on a brilliantly moonlit

night, catching sight of a lady pondering a sheet of bright red
paper on which were written only the words 'even if you do
not share',[8] by the light of a moonbeam that slanted into the
aisle room. That's not a scene you could have if it was raining,
now is it?

[274]* *You have a lover who always sends a next-morning*
poem, who one morning leaves in high dudgeon, proclaiming
that he doesn't know why he bothers with you. 'It's pointless
to try and talk about it,' he declares. 'This is it!' There's not a
peep out of him the next day, and when the following dawn
breaks no servant appears with the usual letter. You spend the
day feeling quite out of sorts, and marvelling at the way he
could so simply turn his back and call it quits.

The day after, it rains heavily. There's still no word from him
all day. He really has given me up, you think.

You're seated at the edge of the veranda that evening when
a messenger with an umbrella appears with a letter for you.
With more haste than usual, you open it, to find there only the
words 'the rising floods of rain'[1] – this gives you much more
delight than would whole pages full of poems.

Though the morning has given no hint of this, the sky suddenly grows black with heavy clouds, and swirling snow
darkens the air. You gaze out at it, deeply disconsolate. Before
your eyes the piles of white snow grow deeper, and still the
snow pours down. Then you're delighted to see a slender man
with umbrella raised, dressed rather like an escort guard, enter
through the door in the side wall and proffer a formal letter on
very white paper, Michinoku or perhaps decorated paper; the
ink of the brush stroke that seals it at the knot has frozen as it
dried, so that it trails off into a blur at the edges. You watch
with pleasure as the lady opens and reads it. It's tightly rolled
and knotted, which has made little hollows in the paper at the
rolls. The ink varies from rich black to pale, the lines are closely
spaced and the writing sprawls over two sides of the page. She
sits there for some time, poring over it repeatedly, and you're
intrigued to imagine what it might contain, and particularly
long to know the words that cause a momentary smile – but

since she's seated at some distance from you, all you can do is guess at the meaning of the parts where the ink is blackest.

Another charming scene is of a lovely lady, with fine features and hair falling long over her forehead, who receives a letter in a dark room and is so anxious to open it that she doesn't take the time to light a lamp, but instead picks up a glowing coal from the brazier with the fire tongs and sits straining to make out the words by its light.

[275] *Things of splendour and spectacle* – The sight of the Commanders as outriders in an imperial progress. Imperial rites and sutra readings for the *Peacock King Sutra*,[1] and those for the Five Great Kings. The Great Purification.[2] The Chamberlain Aide of Ceremonial parading through the South Garden during the Blue Roans Festival. The Gate Watch Deputies will tear up any items of forbidden printed clothing they find being worn on this day. The Rite of the Holy Star King.[3] The Seasonal Sutra Readings. The Rite of the Golden-Wheel Buddha.[4]

[276] *When there are great thunderclaps*, special thunder guards are placed outside, and I find the whole thing quite terrifying. I feel very sorry for the Commanders, Captains and Lieutenants who must stand at the ready by His Majesty's shutters.[1] Once the thunder has ceased, the Commander dismisses the guards with the cry 'Go down!'

[277] *The Kongenroku screen is a fascinating thing.* I hear the *Kanjo* screen depicts glorious deeds. And the Screen of the Months[1] is delightful too.

[278] *A seasonal directional taboo* or the like has sent you on a roundabout route, and you've made your way back late on a bitterly cold night, teeth chattering so hard your jaw aches. Finally you arrive, and draw up the brazier – and how absolutely wonderful it is to discover, when you unearth the charcoal from beneath the fine ash, that the fire is still as alive as ever, with no burnt-out blackened bits.

On the other hand, I hate it when you're sitting so deep in

conversation with someone that neither of you bothers to notice the fire has burnt down to nothing, and then someone else comes along and makes it their business to fuss about putting in fresh charcoal and relighting it. Mind you, it's nice when the pieces of charcoal are placed in a circle with the flame enclosed in their centre. What really annoys me is when someone pushes aside all the pieces that are still glowing, makes a fresh mound of charcoal and relights it at the top of the mound.

[279] *The snow was piled high*, and Her Majesty's shutters were for once left down. We were all gathered in her presence chatting, with the square brazier alight, when Her Majesty said to me, 'Shōnagon, what do you make of the snow of Kōro Peak?'[1] Thereupon I ordered that the shutters be lifted, and raised the outer blind high. Her Majesty laughed. One of the ladies also remarked appreciatively, 'I know the poem, and even use it in my own poems, but I wouldn't have thought of that. You epitomize the sort of person who belongs in this court.'

[280] *The little boy employed by the Yin-Yang masters* is terribly clever. When the master has arrived to perform a purification, and settles down to chant the prayers, no one bothers to listen very closely, but the boy will leap up alertly at certain points and run over to perform the necessary tasks, without the master having to say, 'The *saké*', or 'Now pour the water.' It fills me with envy to see how perfectly he understands the proceedings, and never needs to be told what to do. It would be wonderful to have someone as bright as that in my own service.

[281] *In the third month, I left the court* to perform an abstinence, and spent a little time in someone's home. None of the garden trees was particularly special, and there was a willow there that had none of the willow's usual elegance. Its leaves were unpleasantly broad, and I remarked that it couldn't really be a willow, but my host insisted that there were different varieties and this was one of them.

Yin-Yang master

> What a house this is,
> where the eyebrow's willow curves
> sprout so rudely thick
> spring's beauty is quite smothered
> and she has lost all 'face'![1]

is how it seemed to me.

Around the same time, I stayed in a similar place on another
abstinence. By the middle of the second day, I was feeling
overwhelmed with boredom and longing to go back to court
that very minute, when a message from Her Majesty arrived. I
opened it with joy. Saishō had written in a charming hand on
light green paper:

> How ever did I pass
> the time before I knew you?
> I think of that past time
> as now I pass each passing day
> in lonely sorrow, lacking you.

'So says Her Majesty. As for me, I feel as if this one day were a thousand years to wait. Do hasten back with tomorrow's dawn.'

Saishō's message was delightful enough, but I could only feel deeply grateful for Her Majesty's words, and I wrote:

> So you too, Your Majesty,
> found this spring day unbearable
> in your exalted world?
> And here I thought my misery
> sprang from this mournful place.

'For my part, I feel I could well turn into that Lieutenant[2] during the course of the night.'

When I returned to court at daybreak the following day, Her Majesty said, 'The word "unbearable" in your reply was very unfortunate.[3] Everyone criticized it roundly.' I was mortified. She was perfectly right.

[282]* *On the twenty-fourth day of the twelfth month*, the service of the Litany of Buddha Names was held at Her Majesty's palace. It must have been some time past midnight when everyone emerged from hearing the priest perform the second service . . .[1]

The snow that has been falling for some time has finally lifted, and a fierce wind blows. Long icicles hang from everything, heaps of glittering snow lie here and there on the ground, and all the roofs are white with it, so that even the mean houses of the poor are hidden from view beneath its blanket. The landscape is brightly lit by a pre-dawn moon, and the whole scene is utterly delightful. The houses seem roofed in sheets of silver, while the icicles hanging everywhere along the eaves, some long, some short, as if specially arranged there for display, put one in mind of waterfalls of crystal. In the midst of this unspeakably marvellous scene, the moon shines deep into the carriage as it travels along, since it lacks outer blinds and the inner blinds have been raised right up. The moonlight glows beautifully on the rich sheen of the lady's deep-purple over-robe, worn over seven or eight layers of gowns of pale violet-grey, white and plum pink. Beside her, the man wears grape-coloured heavy brocade gathered trousers, over which are numerous layers of white gowns, with kerria-yellow and scarlet. His sleeves spill from the carriage, and the pure white silk cords that fasten his cloak are untied so that it lies open and the tumble of spilled sleeves is marvellously exposed to view. One of his legs, swathed in the brocade of his trousers, is resting on the carriage step, and anyone who meets the carriage along the road must surely be delighted by the sight all this makes. It's charming the way the lady keeps shrinking shyly away from the bright moonlight, deeper into the carriage, while he embarrasses her by continually drawing her back to his side and exposing her to view again.

How splendid it is, with him chanting over and over the line 'The cold spreads crystal clear'![2] You wish you could ride about in that carriage all night long, and you're very sorry when it draws close to its destination.

[283]* *When gentlewomen in the palace leave* their own particular courts and gather somewhere, they'll each sing the praises of the master or mistress they serve, and gossip together about various gentlemen and palace household matters, which is fascinating for the head of the household to overhear.

Ideally, the house for this kind of gathering should be large and beautiful, with separate rooms not only for the relatives but for the intimate friends and court ladies who gather there. At the appropriate times, everyone would gather in one place to talk. There'd be considered discussions of the poems people have written, and when a letter for someone was delivered everyone would read it and help to compose the reply; if a gentleman called to pay court to one of the ladies he'd be welcomed into a beautifully presented room, and if rain prevented him from leaving he'd be kept entertained. And when someone was required back at the palace, everyone would help prepare her just as she wished, and see her on her way.

I wonder if it's wrong to feel a fascination with the way those in high places live.

[284] *Things that imitate* – Yawns. Children.[1]

[285] *Things one must be wary of* – Low types. Still, at least you know better where you stand with them than with people who have a good reputation.

Boat crossings. It's marvellous weather, the water is splendidly smooth and calm, as if swathed in glossy pale-blue silk, and there's not the slightest hint of danger in the scene. The young lady is in *akomé* gown and skirted trousers; her youthful retainer is singing splendidly as he pulls at what I believe is called the 'oar',[1] and it's altogether the sort of charming picture that begs for an exalted audience to appreciate it. But as they ply their way, a fierce wind suddenly blows up, and the sea surface turns wildly choppy. Now as they hurry towards their destination, faint with terror, the waves flooding over the boat make it impossible to believe that only a moment earlier the sea could have been so calm and smooth.

Now that I come to think of it, there's no one so impressive and downright awe-inspiring as men who go about in boats. Even if the water's not particularly deep, how can they go rowing off so nonchalantly in such a frail and unreliable thing? Let alone when there are unfathomable depths of water below! Then there's the boat at the loading wharf – it's already stacked so high that the water is lapping a mere foot or less below the rim, yet the lads are fearlessly dashing about on it, though you'd imagine that the slightest wrong move would send it to the bottom, and it's downright terrifying to watch them blithely tossing up to half-a-dozen great pine logs, each quite two or three feet thick, on to this overloaded boat.

The boats are rowed from the roofed end.[2] The person on the inside looks far more secure. It's the sight of the man who stands on the edge that makes you feel faint with terror for him. The loop of rope that holds the oar in place looks so precarious! What would happen if it snapped? He'd be certain to tumble straight into the water. Yet even such a vital bit of rope is far from thick.

The boats I've travelled in are beautifully made, and when you open up the double doors and raise the lattice shutters, you don't feel you're right down on the level of the water, so it's rather like being in a tiny house.

The thing that really fills you with unease is looking out at the little boats round about. The ones in the distance look exactly like bamboo leaves fashioned into tiny boats and scattered here and there over the water. It's also charming to see the boats in the port at night, each with its individual light burning.

The sight of a tiny two-man craft moving over the water in the early morning is very moving. The 'white retreating waves'[3] of the poem really do disappear behind it in no time. One certainly feels that a boat is no way for people of quality to travel. Of course travelling on foot is also rather frightening, but at least it's far, far more reassuring to be on firm ground.

A stretch of water may seem terrifying, but your spirits sink still further at the thought of the fisher girls who dive for shells. If that thin rope tied to their waist ever snapped, whatever would they do? It would be all very well if it were men doing the diving, but it must feel miserable for women. The men are on board, singing away lustily, moving the boat along with the women's waist ropes dangling into the water. You'd imagine they'd be feeling full of anxiety and trepidation. Apparently, when the woman wants to come up to the surface she tugs on the rope, and you can quite see why the men should scramble to pull her up as fast as possible. Even an onlooker must weep salt tears to witness the gasp of the woman as she breaks surface and lays her hand on the edge of the boat – really, I find it utterly astonishing to see those men sending the poor women overboard while they float lazily about on the surface!

[286] *A certain Officer of the Right Gate Watch* had a far from respectable father, and was racked with shame at the thought of others laying eyes on him, so while his father was travelling up from Iyo Province on his way to the capital, he pushed him overboard. Everyone was horrified, and exclaimed to each other that there was no plumbing the depths to which the human heart could sink. When the seventh month's Festival of the Dead came round, the Officer set about preparing his offering,

and seeing this, the Holy Adept Dōmei composed the following delightful poem:

> Touching indeed to see
> this man who thrust his father down
> into the ocean deeps
> now hastening to draw him up
> with ritual offerings for his soul.[1]

[287] *The mother of the Ohara gentleman*[1] went to hear the Lotus Discourses at Fumon Temple; the following day, there was a large gathering at the Ono Villa, where music was played and Chinese poems were composed. She composed the following splendid poem:

> We 'carried firewood'
> for the eight Lotus Discourses
> that ended yesterday.
> Today we'll lose ourselves in play
> and let that axe rot here at Ono.[2]

Such stories have come down to us apparently as a result of being noted down at the time they occurred.

[288] *The letter Narihira's mother the Princess sent him,* which goes 'my longing grows the more intense',[1] is terribly touching and fine. I can just imagine Narihira's feelings as he opened and read it.

[289] *It's terribly depressing to discover* some quite worthless person blithely reciting a poem that you yourself had particularly liked and carefully copied down in a notebook.

[290] *If a mere common woman* praises some man of good birth, saying how very attractive and engaging he is, people will immediately lose respect for him. On the other hand, if he's spoken ill of by such people, this is a point greatly in his favour. Even ladies should not be praised by lowly people. Besides,

such people are inclined to express themselves so clumsily that praise from them can make you sound quite absurd.

[291]* *The Officers of the Left and Right Gate Watch* are also known as 'Vice-Superintendents of Police', and how deeply feared and revered they are! It's quite disgusting the way they slip into the ladies' quarters while on night patrol and sleep with them.

They'll sling their white cotton skirted trousers casually over the standing curtain, and bundle up that long, ostentatious cloak of theirs and toss it on top, in a way that's thoroughly improper. But I admit it's a fine sight to see them wandering about with the hem hitched up on the hilt of their sword. Just think how elegant they'd look if only they made a habit of wearing the Chamberlain's special green.[1] Who was it who spoke of 'the dawn that once I saw'?[2]

[292] *Grand Counsellor Korechika presented himself one day* to the Emperor and delivered a talk on Chinese poetry. As always happens, the night grew late while he spoke on, and those present unobtrusively slipped away in ones and twos to sleep behind a standing screen or curtain. Only I sat on, fighting off my drowsiness, until the hour of the Ox fourth quarter[1] was announced.

'It must already be dawn,' I murmured as if to myself.

But the Grand Counsellor evidently wasn't inclined to allow sleep. 'It is pointless to retire at this stage, madam,' he said.

Oh dear, I thought, whatever made me say that? If only other people had been present, I would have been able to sneak off and sleep unobserved. His Majesty was leaning against a pillar and dozing, so the Grand Counsellor turned to Her Majesty and said, 'Look at that, Your Majesty. Should His Majesty be asleep like this, when here it is gone dawn already?'

'Quite so,' responded Her Majesty with a smile. But the Emperor dozed on, oblivious.

At this point, one of the serving girls came along with a hen she'd caught, and hid it nearby with the intention of taking it home with her next morning – but the dog somehow managed to find it and gave chase, and it fled to a shelf in the corridor, setting up a terrible squawking which roused everyone from their slumbers.

His Majesty too was startled awake, and demanded to know how a hen came to be there.

Thereupon the Grand Counsellor absolutely delighted me by reciting in a resounding voice the line, 'That sound awakens the wise king from sleep.'[2] Indeed it made the eyes even of lesser people snap wide awake!

Both Their Majesties were very taken with how wonderfully appropriate the Grand Counsellor's words were to the occasion. This sort of moment is really quite splendid.

The following night, Her Majesty went to the Emperor's room. Having accompanied her, I came out into the corridor in the middle of the night and called for a servant to come for me. 'Are you going back?' inquired the Grand Counsellor. 'Let me see you home.' I hung my train and Chinese jacket[3] on the standing screen, and we set off.

His cloak glowed wonderfully white in the bright moonlight, and he trod the loosened hems of his gathered trousers as he walked. 'Don't fall,' he said, taking hold of my sleeve, and then he delighted me by reciting 'The wanderer sojourns on beneath the late moon.'[4]

'You do get pleasure out of that sort of thing, don't you!' he remarked with a smile – but really, how could you not find it enchanting?

[293] *I was sitting one day with Bishop Ryūen's nurse Mama*[1] in the apartments of the Mistress of the Imperial Wardrobe, when a man approached the veranda close to where we sat.

'A terrible thing has happened to me, Madam!' he declared. 'To whom might I address my tale of woe?'[2] and he looked ready to burst into tears on the spot.

'What is it?' I inquired.

'One day when I had departed my house on a passing errand, the place conflagrated to the ground. Like the hermit crab, I have backed myself for precarious shelter into another's

abode. The fire proceeded from a building containing the hay
for the Imperial Stables, which was just over the fence from my
own, and my wretched spouse, who was asleep in her boudoir,
barely escaped with life and limb intact. Nothing could be
saved!'

Her Ladyship burst into laughter when she heard him.

I then wrote the following:

> On that spring day
> when grasses for the stable
> burst forth in glowing hue
> why should Yodono's grassy bed
> also be kindled in like kind?[3]

and tossed it over to where the gentlewomen were sitting, saying
'Here, give him this.'

Giggling, they handed it over to him, saying, 'One of the
ladies here has taken pity on you for having your house burn
down, and wants to give you this.'

He opened it and took a look. 'What is this promissory
note?[4] he asked. 'How much am I getting?'

'Just read it,' they urged.

'But how can I,' he said, 'when these eyes of mine are quite
unlettered?'

'Show it to someone, then. Her Majesty has just summoned
us, so we must hurry and present ourselves. What are you
thinking, fellow! Just look at the wonderful thing you're receiving!' they cried, and everyone went merrily off to attend Her
Majesty, laughing fit to burst.

We told her the tale, and Mama added, 'I wonder if he's
shown the poem to anyone yet? How furious he'll be when he
gets home!' and we fell about laughing all over again. Her
Majesty joined in, saying as she laughed, 'Why on earth are
you all so silly today?'

[294]* *There was a man whose mother died.* His father was
deeply fond of him, but then he took a second wife who made

things difficult, and the son felt obliged to respect her wishes. He was no longer allowed into their quarters, and the father was forced to delegate the son's clothing requirements and so forth to his old nurse, or to the women who had served his first wife.

The son now lived in one of the wings of the building, and he set it up beautifully, giving it all the attractiveness of a guest's quarters, with fine paintings on the screens and sliding panels. The general opinion was that he acquitted himself well in his conduct as senior courtier, and the Emperor too looked kindly on him, calling on him constantly and engaging him to play together in musical gatherings. Yet the young man's heart remained somehow heavy, he felt at odds with the ways of the world, and he threw himself immoderately into affairs of the heart.

Now this man had a sister, the most esteemed and beloved wife of a court noble, to whom he spoke all that was on his mind, and who was a great source of comfort to him . . .

[295] *A certain gentlewoman was courted by the Governor of Tōtōmi's son.* However, she learned that he was secretly making love to another gentlewoman in the same court.

'What shall I say to him?' she lamented to me. 'He declares upon his father's honour that this is a dreadful slander and he hasn't so much as dreamt of meeting her.'

My response was the following:

> Swear then if you will
> not only on the Governor
> but on the very gods
> that you have truly never known
> the lovely bridge of Hamana.[1]

[296] *Stealing an illicit conversation with someone* in an awkward place, my heart was racing. 'Why are you so agitated?' he asked.

I replied:

> At Ōsaka Pass
> the racing waters of the heart
> surge up continually
> fearing that those who pass may find
> us meeting by Hashiri Well.[1]

[297] 'Can it be true that you're leaving the capital before long?' someone asked.

I replied:

> Who set the fire
> of that wild rumour running
> through the moxa grass
> that grows upon Mount Ibuki?
> I never lit on such a plan![1]

Extant versions of the Sankanbon text include the following sections as 'supplementary'. A copyist's note at this point in the text states that they are found after Section 141 'Things that look fresh and pure' in another version, which is no longer extant, but may have preserved an earlier form of the Sankanbon text.

[s1] *Things that are better at night* – The glow of deep purple softened silk. Flossed silk.

A large-browed woman with beautiful hair. The sound of the seven-stringed *kin*. Someone whose appearance is rather unattractive but who has a pleasant personality. The *hototogisu*. The sound of a waterfall.

[s2] *Things that look worse by firelight* – Violet figured silk. Wisteria flowers. Everything of this colour looks worse by firelight. Scarlet looks bad in moonlight.

[s3] *Things that are hard on the ear* – The sound of someone with an unpleasant voice talking or laughing uninhibitedly. A drowsy priest droning mantras. The voice of someone talking while they apply tooth-black.[1] This is also true of the sort of

person who has nothing particular to recommend her, talking
with her mouth full. The sound of someone learning to play
the piercing *hichiriki*.

[s4] *Things whose Chinese characters make no sense*, though
there must be some reason to them[1] – Table salt. *Akomé* gown.
Summer under-robe.[2] High clogs. Rice paste. Tub. Trough.

[s5] *Things that look lovely but are horrible inside* – Screens
decorated with Chinese paintings. A limed wall.[1] A heaped plate
of food. The top of a cypress-bark roof. The prostitutes of
Kōjiri.[2]

[s6]* *Women's outer gowns* – Pale violet-grey. Grape. Spring-
shoot green. Cherry blossom. Plum pink. All pale colours.

[s7] *Chinese jackets* – Red-purple weave. Wisteria, and in summer, lavender. In autumn, 'dried grass'.

[s8] *Trains* – The wave-and-sea-motif indigo-dyed pattern.

[s9] *Girls' over-robes* – In spring, azalea and cherry blossom.
In summer, dark leaf-green and fallen-leaf ochre.

[s10] *Figured silks* – Violet. White. Plum pink is good, but the
eye wearies of it terribly quickly.

[s11] *Damask patterns* – *Aoi*. Wood sorrel. Hail pattern.

[s12] *Thin paper and decorated paper* – White. Violet. Red.
Hay-dye yellow. Green is also good.

[s13] *Writing boxes* – A two-tiered box with a lacquer design
of clouds and birds.

[s14] *Writing brushes* – Winter animals' hair is both good to
use and attractive to the eye.
    Rabbit's fur brushes.

[s15] *Inksticks* – Rounded ones.

[s16] *Shells* – Empty shells. Clam shells. The tiny little seashells that look like plum blossom petals.

[s17] *Comb boxes* – Designs featuring foreign creatures[1] are good on comb boxes.

[s18] *Mirrors* – Large ten-inch ones.

[s19] *Lacquer designs* – Foliage in arabesques.

[s20] *Braziers* – Red. Green. White with a tinted ink-painting design is also good.

[s21] *Tatami mats* – Those with Kōrai edging. Also, those whose edges are of designs on a yellow ground.

[s22] *Palm-leaf carriages*[1] – A palm-leaf carriage should move at a sedate pace. A basketwork carriage should move at a smart pace.

[s23]* *A grove of tall pines shades the mansion*, and all the eastern and southern lattice shutters are raised, providing a wonderful coolness to the unobstructed view through to the Inner Chamber. There we see an enclosure of large standing curtains, and before it on a straw cushion sits a most handsome priest of around forty, beautifully attired in ink-black priestly robe and silk-gauze surplice, clove-tan fan in hand, intently chanting mantras.

The mistress of the house lies racked with suffering, in the grip of spirit possession. A hefty young girl has been chosen as the medium, and she now shuffles out on her knees, wearing a gossamer silk shift and long brightly-coloured skirted trousers, and seats herself alongside the curtained enclosure. The priest twists sideways to hand her the splendid gleaming single-pointed *vajra*, and continues his awe-inspiring flow of supplications and mantras.

single-pointed vajra

A large number of gentlewomen are seated nearby as witnesses, watching the proceedings with riveted attention. It isn't
long before the medium begins to tremble and falls into a
trance, and the awesome power of the Buddha then reveals
itself in response to the priest's invocations.

The brothers and relatives of the possessed lady meanwhile
are free to come and go from the room. Were she in her right
mind, how appalled and ashamed the medium would be to
realize just what is taking place before the reverent crowd of
people gathered there watching her. While well aware that this
suffering is the spirit's and not the girl's own, nevertheless
those who know her are filled with pity to witness her fearful
lamenting and wailing, and they sit beside her and attempt to
keep her clothing straight as she writhes there.

In due course the patient improves, and the priest orders that
medicinal tea be given to her. Some of the younger ladies retire
to the kitchen area to bring it, and they hurry anxiously back
with it to see how she is. They're attired in beautiful shifts, and
their pale violet-grey trains are quite pristine and undishevelled.

The spirit is forced to grovel and beg for forgiveness, then is
finally dismissed. Returned suddenly to her senses, the medium
is now aghast. How extraordinary, she thinks. Here I am,
exposed to public view, and I was sure I was behind the curtains!

Whatever can have happened? and she hastily shakes her hair forward to shield her face as she moves to slip back in behind the curtain.

'Wait a moment,' commands the priest, and he pronounces a short incantation over her. 'There now,' he says with a smile when it's over. 'How's that? Are you feeling better now?' However, this seems only to add to her embarrassed confusion.

'I would like to linger,' he says, 'but I'm afraid it's time to go off and conduct the service.' He takes his leave and, despite encouragement on all sides to stay a little longer, hastily begins to make his way out.

At this moment, a lady who is evidently of the highest rank slides out and addresses him from behind the blinds. 'We are filled with the deepest gratitude,' she says, 'that you have come like this, and overjoyed that, thanks to you, the poor suffering patient has so wonderfully improved.'

He replies briefly, 'The spirit seemed a very tenacious one. I advise continued vigilance. I'm delighted that the patient has improved.' With this, he makes his departure, leaving everyone deeply impressed by his wonderful powers, and with the awed sense that the Buddha himself has been among them.

Ideally, a priest should have a great reputation and be in constant demand hither and yon, and he should be accompanied by numerous assistants – handsome young boys with beautiful hair, or larger lads with surprisingly lovely hair despite their sprouting beards, or else powerfully built boys whose hair is almost disgustingly thick.

[S24] *The best places for palace service* – The imperial court. The Empress's court. The courts of those such as her daughter the First Princess. The court of the Kamo High Priestess, though an offence to Buddhism,[1] is very entertaining, and the other imperial family courts are even more so. Also, the court of the High Consort, mother of the Crown Prince.

[S25]* *A dilapidated house* with a garden overgrown with trailing weeds and knee-deep in wormwood, flooded with moonlight from a brilliant rising moon. Also, the moonlight that seeps in through cracks in the decaying boards of such a house.

The sound of the wind, as long as it isn't fierce.

[s26] *A place with a pond*, in the fifth month when the rains are falling, is a very moving thing. It's deeply affecting to sit for hours on end staring out at the garden, a sea of monochrome soft green with the pond's water as deep green as the sweet flag and reeds that crowd it, and the heavy rain clouds hanging above. Indeed all places with ponds are at all times moving and delightful, and of course this is so too on winter mornings when the water is frozen over. Rather than a carefully tended pond, I find delightful the sort that have been left neglected to the rampant water weed, where patches of reflected moonlight gleam whitely on the water here and there between the swathes of green.

All moonlight is moving, wherever it may be.

[s27]* *I found it most offensive*, when we were in our rooms during our pilgrimage to Hase, to be confronted with a seated row of rough commoners, trouser hems trailing.

We'd embarked on the pilgrimage full of pious resolution, but the sound of the river was terrifying, and we were utterly exhausted by the long climb up the covered stairway to the temple. We longed for the moment when we would at last arrive before the Kannon. When we got there, I was immensely irritated by the throngs of white-robed priests and scruffy commoners, looking like ragged bagworms, who crowded into the worship hall, standing or sitting, some prostrating themselves, and no one paying us the slightest attention. I wanted to simply shove them over! It's always the same at temples.

They do clear everyone away from around the rooms of the most exalted people there on pilgrimage, but in the case of us lesser ones it's apparently impossible to control the mob. I was well aware of this, yet when it came to the point it still infuriated me to witness it all with my own eyes.

It's also annoying to drop a nicely cleaned comb in the dirt.

[s28] *When gentlewomen come and go from the palace*, we sometimes have to borrow a carriage from someone for the purpose. The owner will speak most politely when he lends it to you, but the drivers can be a different matter – they'll sometimes shout quite fiercely at the ox instead of their usual shooing, and beat it into a swift trot, which is most alarming for the ladies in the carriage. If the carriage attendant is grumpy, and orders the drivers to 'get a move on or we won't be there before nightfall', well, you can judge the real nature of the owner from this, and you dismiss all thought of asking him for his carriage again.

Lord Naritō's[1] carriage was the only exception to this – this sort of thing never occurred when anyone borrowed his carriage, be it midnight or dawn. He maintained a fine discipline. Once his carriage came upon a lady's carriage which had got stuck in a deep hole in the road. The drivers were trying unsuccessfully to haul it out, and were in a great fury, so he sent over his own men to help beat the ox, which goes to show how he always made sure his men behaved correctly.

[s29]* *I have written in this book* things I have seen and thought, in the long idle hours spent at home, without ever dreaming that others would see it. Fearing that some of my foolish remarks could well strike others as excessive and objectionable, I did my best to keep it secret, but despite all my intentions I'm afraid it has come to light.

Palace Minister Korechika one day presented to the Empress a bundle of paper. 'What do you think we could write on this?' Her Majesty inquired. 'They are copying *Records of the Historian* over at His Majesty's court.'

'This should be a "pillow",[1] then,' I suggested.

'Very well, it's yours,' declared Her Majesty, and she handed it over to me.

I set to work with this boundless pile of paper to fill it to the last sheet with all manner of odd things, so no doubt there's much in these pages that makes no sense.

Overall, I have chosen to write about the things that delight, or that people find impressive, including poems as well as things such as trees, plants, birds, insects and so forth, and for this reason people may criticize it for not living up to expectations and only going to prove the limits of my own sensibility. But after all, I merely wrote for my personal amusement things that I myself have thought and felt, and I never intended that it should be placed alongside other books and judged on a par with them. I'm utterly perplexed to hear that people who've read my work have said it makes them feel humble in the face of it. Well, there you are, you can judge just how unimpressive someone is if they dislike things that most people like, and praise things that others condemn. Anyway, it does upset me that people have seen these pages.

When Captain of the Left Tsunefusa was still Governor of Ise, he came to visit me while I was back at home, and my book disconcertingly happened to be on the mat from the nearby corner that was put out for him. I scrambled to try and retrieve it, but he carried it off with him, and kept it for a very long time before returning it.

That seems to have been the moment when this book first became known – or so it is written.[2]

Appendix 1
Places

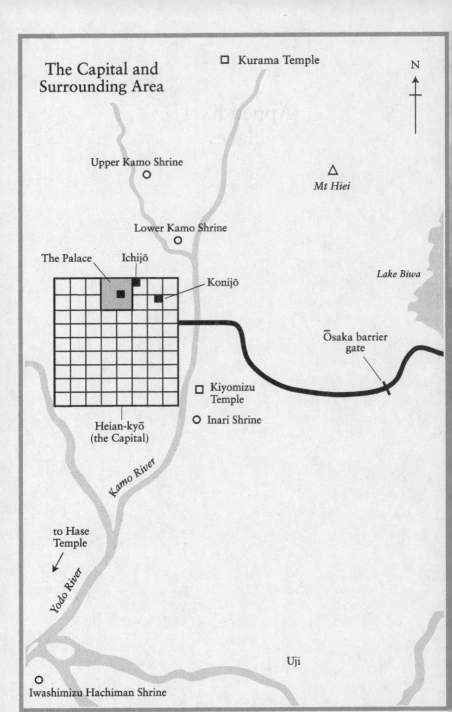

The Capital and
Surrounding Area

Kurama Temple

N

Upper Kamo Shrine

Mt Hiei

Lower Kamo Shrine

The Palace   Ichijō

Konijō

Lake Biwa

Ōsaka barrier
gate

Kiyomizu
Temple

Inari Shrine

Heian-kyō
(the Capital)

Kamo River

to Hase
Temple

Yodo River

Uji

Iwashimizu Hachiman Shrine

The Inner Palace

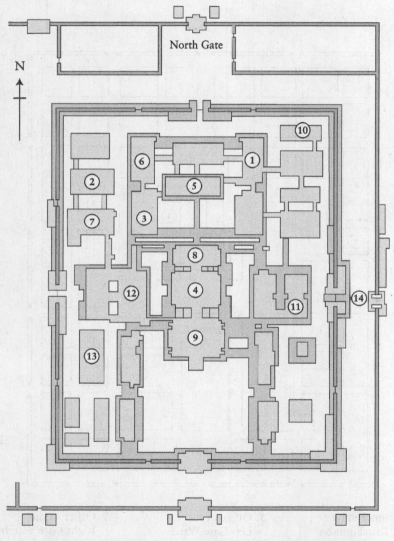

North Gate

N

1. Senyōden
2. Mumetsubo
3. Kokiden
4. Jijūden
5. Jōneiden
6. Tōkaden
7. Fujitsubo
8. Jōkyōden
9. Shishinden
10. Shigeisha
11. Unmeiden
12. Seiryōden
13. Chamberlains' Office
14. Kenshunmon

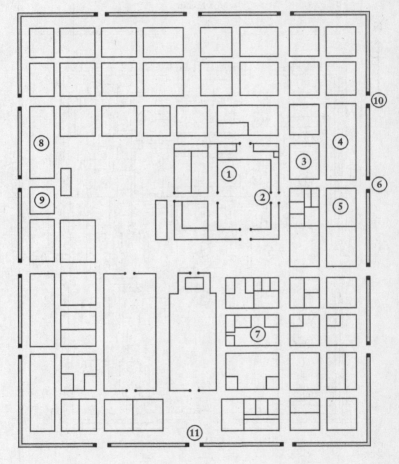

The Outer Palace

N

1. Inner Palace
2. Kenshunmon
3. Office of the
   Empress's Houshold
4. Office of the
   Left Palace Guards
5. Office of the
   Left Gate Watch
6. Yōmeimon
7. Aitadokoro (see p. 155)
8. Office of the
   Right Palace Guards
9. Office of the
   Right Gate Watch
10. Jōtōmon
    (Tsuchi Gate)
11. Suzakumon

Typical Palace Architecture

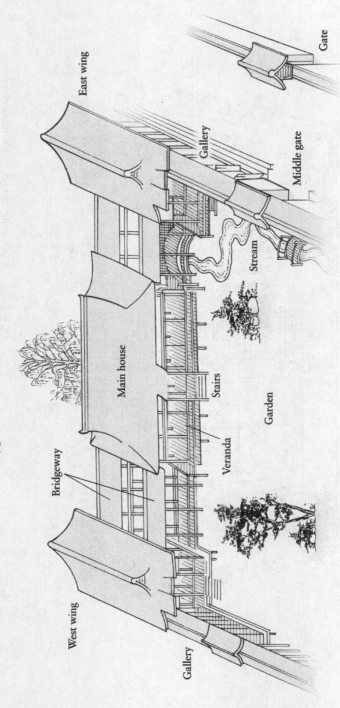

Gate

East wing

Gallery

Middle gate

Stream

Main house

Garden

Bridgeway

Stairs

Veranda

West wing

Gallery

The Main House

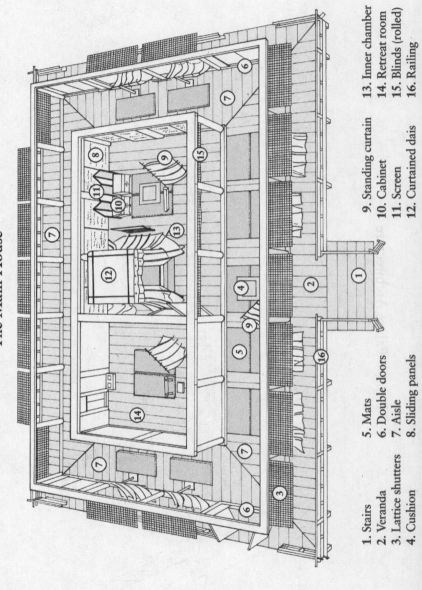

1. Stairs
2. Veranda
3. Lattice shutters
4. Cushion

5. Mats
6. Double doors
7. Aisle
8. Sliding panels

9. Standing curtain
10. Cabinet
11. Screen
12. Curtained dais

13. Inner chamber
14. Retreat room
15. Blinds (rolled)
16. Railing

Appendix 2
People and Where They Appear

This is a list of important people and those who appear more than once in *The Pillow Book*, with a brief summary of those appearances. Where the title ('Lord', etc.) is consistently used as part of the name, the name is given as such. Court nobles and senior courtiers frequently changed title through promotion, and these are omitted. Dates are given when known.

Numbers are section numbers.

Akinobu, Lord *Akinobu no Ason*. Takashina Akinobu, Teishi's maternal uncle.
  94: Sei Shōnagon and her friends visit his country house. 259: Proud of his family connections.

Chūnagon *Chūnagon no kimi*. A gentlewoman in Teishi's court.
  123: Seen busy at her devotions. 254: Nicknamed 'Dolly'. 259: Teases Sei Shōnagon about her special treatment.

Emperor. See Ichijō.

Empress Dowager. See Senshi.

Genshi *Fujiwara Genshi* (981?–1002). Usually referred to as the Shigeisa (or Shigeisha), from the name of the palace building she occupied. Younger sister of Teishi. Became Consort of the Crown Prince Harunomiya (later Emperor Sanjō) in 995.
  85: Provides a Gosechi dancer.
  88: Visits Teishi and they discuss musical instruments. 99: Pays a formal visit to Teishi and her family. 259: Present with her family.

Ichijō (980–1011). Son of Emperor Enyū (see Section 20, note 4). Reigning Emperor 986–1011, including the period covered by *The Pillow Book*. Teishi, his first Empress, was later supplanted by Michinaga's daughter Shōshi. Atsuhira (1008–1036), his son by Shōshi, became emperor Goichijō (reigned 1016–1036).
  Appears throughout *The Pillow Book*.

Kamo High Priestess. See Senshi, Princess.

Kishi *Takashina Kishi* (d. 996). Michitaka's wife; mother of Teishi, Korechika, etc.

99: Is present at the grand family gathering. 259: Calls in frequently while Teishi is living nearby.

Kohyōe. A gentlewoman in Teishi's court.

82: Gives an imitation of the beggar nun. 85: Is too young and embarrassed to respond to Sanekata's poem. 131: Organizes a trick played on the Emperor's nurse.

Korechika *Fujiwara Korechika* (974–1010). Son of Michitaka, Teishi's brother. In 996 he and his brother Takaie attacked Retired Emperor Kazan; they were sent to the provinces, and returned 997.

20: Visits Teishi. 76: Takes part in a musical recital. 94: Scolds Sei Shōnagon at a poetry competition. 99: Visits with his son Matsugimi. 123: Presents his father's shoes. 176: Embarrasses Sei Shōnagon with flirtatious questioning when she is new to the court. 259: Takes part in the Dedication of the Complete Sutras preparations, and is kind to Sei Shōnagon. 292: Scolds Sei Shōnagon for sleepiness, then pleases her with poetry. [s29]: Presents Teishi with the paper that will be used for *The Pillow Book*.

Masahiro *Minamoto Masahiro* (975–1015). Chamberlain, 996–9.

53: Makes a fool of himself in the Chamberlain's roll call. 103: Is depicted as a laughing-stock.

Michinaga *Fujiwara Michinaga* (966–1027). Brother and rival of Michitaka. He seized power after Michitaka's death.

123: Grudgingly bows before Michitaka. 136: Sei Shōnagon is suspected of favouring him after he's seized power and ousted Teishi and her family from the court.

Michitaka *Fujiwara Michitaka* (953–995). Regent to Ichijō. Father of Teishi, Genshi, Yamanoi, Korechika, Takaie, Chikayori and Ryūen. His death brought about the eclipse of his family at court.

20: Writes a clever poem in his younger days. 32: As a younger man, is present at the Salvation Lotus Discourses. 99: Plays genial host at the grand family gathering. 123: Emerges impressively from the Black Door. 176: Visits Teishi's quarters and jokes with the ladies. 259: Sets up an artificial cherry tree in new residence for Teishi and visits her.

Mistress of the Imperial Wardrobe *Mikushigedono* (d. 1002). Younger sister of Teishi. Known also as *Jōganden*, from the building where she normally resided. Commonly referred to by the title of her post. See also Appendix 6.

78: Invites Sei Shōnagon to join her for the night. 222: Makes herbal balls. 259: Visits Teishi with her father. 293: Sei Shōnagon visits her apartments.

Murakami (926–967). Reigned 946–67. Emperor Ichijō's grand-father.

20: Submits his High Consort to a test of *Kokinshū* poems, in Teishi's story. 174: Praises the Lady Chamberlain for her apt poetic response.

Narimasa *Minamoto Narimasa* (975–1041). A senior courtier.

76: Among the musicians. 79: One of Sei Shōnagon's confidantes when she hides at home.

Narimasa *Taira Narimasa*. Senior Steward in the Empress's Office. His home was used for the birth of Teishi's three children, and was where she died.

5: Causes hilarity and is teased by Sei Shōnagon when they move to his house.

Narinobu *Minamoto Narinobu* (b. 979?). Adopted son of Michinaga. Took the tonsure at the age of 23.

9: Makes fun of Bishop Jōchō's height. 255, 256: Can distinguish people's voices remarkably well. 273: Sei Shōnagon spurns him on a rainy night and is chided for it.

Nobukata *Minamoto Nobukata* (d. 998). A senior courtier.

77: Reports to Sei Shōnagon on the reception of her poem. 154: Is envious of the jokes that Sei Shōnagon and Tadanobu share. 155: Loses his temper when Sei Shōnagon teases him.

Norimitsu *Tachibana Norimitsu*. Apparently Sei Shōnagon's husband before she came to court; they subsequently retained a friendly semi-familial relationship.

77: Delighted in his unofficial position as 'elder brother' when Sei Shōnagon's wit is praised. 79: Fails to understand her wit and poem, and is spurned by her. 126: Sei Shōnagon jokes about his lack of poetic understanding.

Ryūen, Bishop (980–1015). Son of Michitaka, younger brother of Teishi. Became Bishop at the age of 15.

88: Wants to exchange instruments with the Shigeisa. 129: Is impressed by Yukinari's poem. 259: Resembles a bodhisattva. 293: His nurse.

Saishō *Saishō no kimi*. A gentlewoman in Teishi's court. Known like Sei Shōnagon for her wit.

20: Performs poorly in a test of poetic memory. 78: Impresses Tadanobu with a poetic reference. 94: Is rebuked by Teishi after the visit to Lord Akinobu's house. 136: Sends a secret message to Sei

Shōnagon from Teishi. 259: Teases Sei Shōnagon about her special treatment. 281: Sends a message from Teishi.

Sanekata *Fujiwara Sanekata* (d. 998). Considered the finest poet of his day.

32: Takes part in the teasing during the Salvation Lotus Discourses. 85: Flirts with Kohyōe and sends her a poem.

Seihan (962–999). A priest renowned for his moving sermons.

32: Gives the Salvation Lotus Discourses to the assembled company. 128: Gives the memorial service for Michitaka.

Senshi *Fujiwara Senshi* (962–1001). Empress Dowager. Mother of Emperor Ichijō, widow of Emperor Enyū, younger sister of Michitaka.

85: Provides a Gosechi dancer. 103: Is ill. 122: Views her son's imperial procession. 259: She and her retinue are present at the Dedication of the Complete Sutras ceremony.

Senshi, Princess (964–1035). Referred to by the title Kamo High Priestess (*saiin*), which she held 975–1031. Daughter of Emperor Murakami. A talented and highly respected woman with a renowned salon of gentlewomen.

82: Sends a gift of a hare-wand and poem to Teishi.

Shigeisa. See **Genshi.**

Shikibu *Shikibu no omoto.* A gentlewoman in Teishi's court.

46: She and Sei Shōnagon are surprised by the Emperor and Empress when they share a room. 273: They share a room.

Tadanobu *Fujiwara Tadanobu* (967–1035). A senior courtier known for his erudition and poetic skill.

77: Sei Shōnagon's witty response wins him back when they have a falling out. 78: Visits looking splendid. 79: Attempts to learn her whereabouts. 122: An impressive imperial message-bearer. 128: Sei Shōnagon teasingly resists his advances. 154: He and Sei Shōnagon share private jokes. 189: Wears a wonderful incense.

Tadataka *Minamoto Tadataka.*

6: One of the Chamberlains who deal with the dog Okinamaro. 82: Disappoints Sei Shōnagon by declining to respond to her poem about the snow mountain.

Takaie *Fujiwara Takaie* (979–1044). Son of Michitaka, younger brother of Korechika, Teishi's brother. In 996 he and Korechika attacked Retired Emperor Kazan; they were sent to the provinces, and returned 997.

97: Reports excitedly on fan ribs. 99: Is present at the family gathering. 259: Accompanies Sei Shōnagon at the Dedication of the Complete Sutras.

Teishi *Fujiwara Teishi* (977–1000). Eldest daughter of Michitaka and Kishi. Entered the court as a consort of Emperor Ichijō at the age of 13, was subsequently elevated to Empress, and bore him 3 children. Owing to the sudden decline in family fortunes, she took the tonsure in 997.
Appears throughout *The Pillow Book*.

Tsunefusa *Minamoto Tsunefusa* (969–1023). Senior courtier.
76: Among the musicians. 79: Is let in on Sei Shōnagon's whereabouts. 129: Reports Yukinari's praise to Sei Shōnagon. 136: Visits her in voluntary exile. [S29]: Is inadvertently given an early version of *The Pillow Book*.

Ukon *Ukon no Naishi*. A gentlewoman in Emperor Ichijō's court, known for her wit.
6: Is called in to identify the dog Okinamaro. 82: Is intrigued at the tale of Hitachi no Suke. 95: Plays the *biwa*. 221: Teishi tells her of a witty exchange with Sei Shōnagon.

Yamanoi *Fujiwara Michiyori* (971–995). Michitaka's eldest son; half brother of Teishi, Korechika, etc.
99: Escorts the Emperor from the family gathering. 123: Is among those present to welcome the Regent. 259: Makes a racy remark.

Yorisada *Minamoto Yorisada* (977–1020). Grandson of Emperor Murakami.
42: Sei Shōnagon laments his appearance as Board of Censors Officer. 130: Among the men who flee when Sei Shōnagon responds too wittily to their challenge.

Yukinari *Fujiwara Yukinari* (972–1027). A senior courtier.
46: He and Sei Shōnagon have a special relationship. 126: Sends her *heitan* cakes. 129: They have a witty and flirtatious exchange. 130: Stays behind to talk to Sei Shōnagon when his companions flee.

Appendix 3
Time

The months of the old Japanese calendar did not coincide with the western calendar. The old Japanese calendar was largely based on the lunar cycle, and the full moon was the fifteenth day of each month. The new year began on the first day of spring (still celebrated in China), generally February in the Julian calendar. The Japanese calendar was borrowed from China, together with a complex application of the twelve zodiacal signs (rat, ox, tiger, rabbit, dragon, snake, horse, ram, monkey, cock, dog, boar) that designated not only years, but also the days of each month, directions and hours, and that was often used for divination.

The months had individual names, but were frequently referred to by number, as in this translation. The four seasons were: spring 1–3, summer 4–6, autumn 7–9, winter 10–12. (A lunar month is between one and two months ahead of the number of that month in our Julian calendar, i.e. the first Japanese month falls in our February–March, etc.)

There were several ways to refer to the days of the month. The most usual method by number. Thus the fourth day of the seventh month of 998 is written as 998.7.4.

The day was divided into twelve hours, named after the zodiacal signs, each approximately 120 minutes long. The day began at midnight with the Hour of the Rat (11 p.m.–1 a.m.), and proceeded through the zodiac cycle to end with the Hour of the Boar (9–11 p.m.). Noon was at the Hour of the Horse.

A child was deemed to be one year old at the first new year after its birth. Thus, given ages differed by between one and twelve months from the method of calculation with which Westerners are familiar.

Zodiac Hour Names and Associated Directions

Outer Circle: Zodiac Names, Quarters, Semi-quarters
Second Circle: Modern Hours

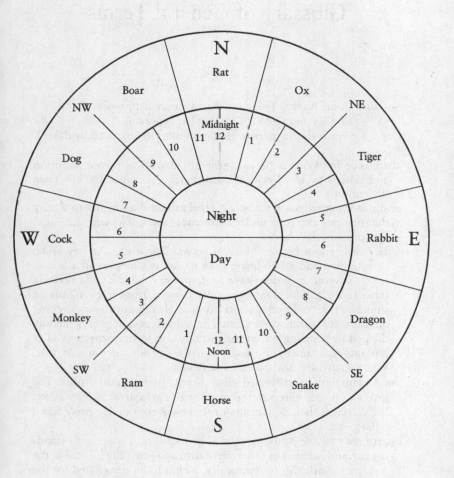

Appendix 4
Glossary of General Terms

See also Court Ranks, Titles and Bureaucracy (Appendix 5) and
Clothes and Colour Glossary (Appendix 6)
Dates for Festivals are given with month number followed by day.

abstinence *monoimi* A period (generally a day) of forced seclusion and taboos to avoid evil influences, etc., prescribed by **Yin-Yang** divination.

abstinence tag *monoimi no fuda* A label attached to the hat to signify that one was currently under **abstinence** taboo, if leaving the house for some special reason.

aisle / aisle room *hisashi / hisashi no ma* The area, one bay wide, surrounding and a step lower than the **Inner Chamber** of a house. It was covered by a deep-eave roof, and beyond it lay the **veranda** (also roofed), which was generally divided from it by **blinds** or shutters. It served both as corridor and also frequently as sleeping quarters for gentlewomen, etc., in which case it was generally divided by **standing screens** or **curtains** into sections that served as separate **apartments**, leaving a narrow corridor down one side. When so divided also called **Long Room**.

aoi A plant with heart-shaped leaves, sacred to the Kamo shrines. The leaves were used extensively during the **Kamo Festival** as decorations for carriages, hair ornaments (traced back to a divine precedent), pillars, etc.

apartment *tsubone* A 'room' created by enclosing a space with **standing curtains**, **screens** or other partitions, and generally located in the residence's **aisle**. More specifically, such a room designated for the personal use of one or more gentlewomen when not on duty: see also **Long Room**.

Appointments List *jimoku* Imperial appointments to new posts were announced twice a year. Those for **Provincial Governorsh** (Appendix 5) and other provincial appointments were made in spring (the first three days of the year), and those for palace positions in autumn.

archbishop *sōjō* Effectively the supreme head of the hierarchy of a Buddhist sect.

attendant *toneri* A serving man in ranking households, who performed a variety of duties.

basketwork carriage *ajiro* Woven of reeds or bamboo strips, this carriage was less elaborate than the formal **palm-leaf carriage**, and was used by people of lesser rank or by senior nobles on less formal occasions.

baton *shaku* A long, flat, tapering piece of wood, rounded at the top, that a court official held upright before him on ceremonial occasions.

bay *ma* The space between two structural pillars of a building used as a more or less standard unit of length (about 10 feet). It could also denote a room.

bishop *sōzu* Immediately below the archbishop in a Buddhist sect's hierarchy.

biwa A four-stringed instrument of the lute family, played by plucking with a wide plectrum. (In Chinese, *pipa*.)

Black Door The door at the north-east corner of the **Seiryōden**. When Teishi was visiting the Emperor, her allotted room was next to this door, and her gentlewomen spent much of their time in the **Long Room** adjacent to it.

blind *sudare / misu* Fine hanging blinds of reed or split bamboo that could be rolled up. They were hung from the upper lintels at the outer sides of the **Inner Chamber** and the aisle. See p. 28.

Blue Roans Festival *aouma no sechie* (1.7) This **palace festival** originated in China. Special white horses (originally rare blue roans) were paraded before the Emperor and his entourage in the palace grounds. The sight of these horses was believed to protect against evil influences in the coming year.

Bo Juyi *Hakurakuten* Chinese poet (772–846) whose work was immensely popular in Japan during this period. See also *Song of Everlasting Sorrow*.

bound book *sōshi* A collection of folded pages sewn together along one edge to form a book (as distinct from the rolled paper scroll).

brazier *hioke* A wooden tub lined with metal, which held a charcoal fire in a deep bed of insulating ash. Its outer surface was often highly decorated. The only method of heating in buildings. Varieties included footed (*hibitsu*), long or rectangular (*nagasubitsu*), and square (*subitsu*).

Breakfast Room *asagarei* Room to the north of the **Table Room** in the Emperor's residence, where his breakfast was served.

bridgeway *watadono* A short roofed **gallery** that connected the main building and a wing. It could be either open or walled, and sometimes included **apartments**, such as those for gentlewomen.

bush clover *hagi* A bush, commonly found in gardens, with delicate hanging branches, clover-like leaves and racemes of reddish purple or white flowers from late summer to autumn. See also Appendix 6.

cabinet *(mi)zushi* An elegant storage chest with hinged doors, sometimes topped with one or more shelves.

capital *miyako* The usual term for Heian-kyō (present-day Kyoto), whose centre was the imperial palace, site of the Emperor's residence and the seat of government in Japan.

carriage *kuruma* The usual form of transport, consisting of an enclosed box on two large wheels, generally seating up to four, which was boarded from the rear, with front and sometimes side windows covered by blinds, beneath which a lady's sleeves or train could be displayed. It was drawn by an ox. See also **basketwork carriage**, **Chinese-style carriage** and **palm-leaf carriage**.

Chinese eave *karabisashi* An eave whose wide fronting board was curved in imitation of the Chinese style.

Chinese-style carriage *karaguruma* The largest and most ornate carriage reserved for the use of the imperial family and high-ranking dignitaries. It had Chinese eaves, and the inner blinds and other furnishings were also decorated in the Chinese style. See p. 223.

Chrysanthemum Festival *kiku no sekku* (9.9) A **palace festival**. Chrysanthemums were associated with long life and good fortune. The Emperor offered ritual chrysanthemum wine to his courtiers on this day. Among the general populace, cotton wadding was spread over chrysanthemum flowers the night before, and the dew thus collected was wiped over the body to protect from the ills of old age.

clubmoss *hikage* A small, moss-like fern whose long stems spread over the ground. It was used as a hair decoration during the banquets associated with **Season-change days**.

Complete Sutras *issaikyō* The entire Buddhist canon (1,597 scrolls all told) was copied and dedicated as a pious gesture on special occasions.

Crafts Workshop *tsukumodokoro* A subsidiary of the **Chamberlains' Office** (Appendix 5), responsible for making furniture and other household objects.

curtained dais *michōdai* A raised dais, roofed and hung with curtains on three sides, that stood in the **Inner Chamber** of the house. It served as both bed and sitting area for the household head.

cushion *shitone* A square of padded cotton or soft straw matting, often edged with decorative cloth, that was placed on the floor for sitting or sleeping. See also **straw cushion**.

Dance of the Heavenly Maidens See **Gosechi Festival**.

darani **incantations** *darani* Phrases endowed with magical and thus mystical powers, chanted during Tantric Buddhist ceremonies, invoking various deities. They derived from Sanskrit words, and were thus incomprehensible to everyone, the intoner included.

decorated paper *shikishi* Paper dyed or printed in a pale colour (including white), which was used for writing poetry and letters.

dedicatory prayer *ganmon* A petition stating the intention of a ritual ceremony, either Buddhist or dedicated to a native deity.

deutzia *u no hana* A shrub frequently used in hedges. It has sprays of white flowers in early summer. See also Appendix 6.

directional taboo *katatagae* **Yin-Yang** divination dictated that at specific times, certain directions must be avoided. This meant that, in the case of travel, a direction was temporarily 'blocked' and one must change one's course and spend time elsewhere (perhaps as a guest who was to be treated generously) until the taboo no longer pertained. Particular directional taboos were associated with the **Season-change** times of year.

double doors *tsumado* Double-panelled wooden doors opening outwards near the four corners of a building. They were held closed with metal latches on the inside. See p. 56.

drapes *katabira* The trailing cloth pieces of **standing curtains**. The same word was used for **summer under-robe** (Appendix 6).

Eastern Dances *azuma asobi* Dances and musical accompaniment originating in the Eastern Provinces but adopted and modified by the court. Four or six dancers performed to the accompaniment of flutes and **koto**. These performances played an important role in Shinto festivals, most importantly the **Kamo** and **Yahata Provisional Festivals** (see **Provisional Festivals**).

escort guards *zuijin* Attendants who accompanied the carriage of a prestigious person.

exorcism See **spirit**.

exorcist priest *genza* A practitioner, often a **mountain ascetic** associated with Tantric (esoteric) Buddhism, who played an important role in Heian life by performing incantations and prayers to avert disaster or cure illness (see also **spirit**).

fasting *sōji(n)* A form of religious practice that constituted abstinence from meat and alcohol, together with chanting of Buddhist sutras.

Festivals The main events that delineated the year at court were the numerous festivals and observances. There were many more than appear in *The Pillow Book*, often consisting of rituals centring on the Emperor, but which did not impinge on the lives of gentle-women. Some of the festivals were connected to the great Shinto shrines. Others were based on what were originally folk beliefs, often inherited from China, concerning the pervasive presence of evil spirits that could cause illness and misfortune. Observances were strongly associated with the seasons and particularly with season-change days, which were held to be inauspicious.

fire hut *hitakiya* A small hut in the palace courtyard used by the palace guards for their fire.

fire tongs *hibashi* A pair of long metal chopsticks used for arranging charcoal and tending the fire in braziers.

First Fruits Festival *niinamesai* (mid-11) An important festival occurring over several days and commencing on the second Day of the Hare. Its ritual importance was for the Emperor to make dedicatory offerings of the first fruits of the harvest and partake of them. Its main attraction for those at court was the **Gosechi Festival**.

folded paper *tatōgami* All-purpose paper folded in half and carried by men and women in the breast of the robe, for everyday use.

Fubokushō A private poetry collection completed around 1310, which includes many poems whose source is otherwise unknown. Title in full: *Fubokuwakashō*.

gagaku Courtly song and music, derived from early folk songs.

gallery *rō* A roofed passageway, that linked buildings, and sometimes contained rooms.

gentlewoman *nyōbō* A woman from a good family who served in a great household or in a palace court. Also called simply 'ladies' in this translation.

go A popular board game, played with numerous small black and white counters or 'stones' by two people seated at a low *go* table.

Gosechi Festival A popular court event in which four or sometimes five young girls, usually chosen from court noble and senior courtier families, performed dances before the court. They and their attendants were housed in special rooms in the Jōneiden during the elaborate ceremonies, which included a formal rehearsal before the Emperor several days before the culminating performance of the Dance of the Heavenly Maidens at the final banquet, on the last day of the **First Fruits Festival**.

Gosenshū An imperial poetry collection compiled in 1312, which is the only source for a number of poems. Title in full: *Gosen-wakashū*.

Greater Sutra on the Perfection of Wisdom *daihannya-kyō* A compilation of the *hannya* (wisdom) sutras consisting of 600 fascicles.

Great Sutra Readings *midokyō* A ceremony held biannually (spring and autumn) in the palace and at other great households, in which a large gathering of monks chanted the **Greater Sutra on the Perfection of Wisdom** over the course of four days. An imperial abstinence was observed at court on the eve of the final day.

half-panel shutter See **lattice shutter**.

hare-mallet *uzuchi* A four-inch stick of peach wood decorated with long coloured threads, hung in rooms on the first Day of the Hare in the new year to ward off evil spirits. Hare-wands (*uzue*) were similarly decorated poles about 5 feet long, also used for the same magical purpose on this day.

hare-wand See **hare-mallet**.

Hase (Temple) *hase / hatsuse / hasedera* An important temple south of Nara, devoted to the worship of Kannon, and a very popular pilgrimage destination. It is on a hill, and the approach, today as in the Heian period, is a long, steep covered stairway.

Heian period *heian jidai* The name of the historical period from 794 to roughly the end of the twelfth century.

herbal balls *kusudama* Small bags containing herbs and decorated with flowers and coloured threads, that were hung in rooms for the **Sweet Flag Festival**, as protection against evil spirits. See p. 88.

hichiriki A small, shrill reed flute.

high tray *tsuigasane* A footed tray with shelf beneath, for serving food.

Holy Adept *azari / ajari* A distinguished priest of one of the Tantric (esoteric) Buddhist sects, expert at performing rites to avert disasters and to cure illness with the power of incantation and ritual.

hototogisu A small cuckoo (*Cuculus poliocephalus*), whose call is associated with early summer. There was a particular poetic pleasure in hearing its first call of the season, and expeditions were sometimes organized to this end.

Ichijō Palace *Ichijō-in* This temporary palace was set up after a fire in the imperial palace in 999; also known as the Temporary Palace (*imadairi*.) Its different orientation caused confusion in palace naming conventions that used directional terms.

imayō Literally 'songs in the modern style'. Popular in the court at the time, they generally consisted of four verses in the seven–five syllable style.

Imperial Day Chamber *hi no omashi* The room in the Seiryōden which the Emperor occupied during the day.

inauspicious days *kuenichi* Days deemed unlucky by **Yin-Yang** divination, during which a number of taboos applied. Between three and fourteen days in any month were deemed 'inauspicious', too many for people to keep thorough track of them.

inkstone *suzuri* A utensil made of fine black stone on which the inkstick (*sumi*) is ground with water to produce ink for brush writing. The inkstone was part of a set of calligraphy implements contained in a decorated lacquer box (*suzuribako*).

inner blinds *shitasudare* Long blinds that hung inside and protruded beneath the blinds at the front and rear of a carriage.

Inner Chamber *moya* The large central area of a building, a step higher than the surrounding **aisle**, was the main residential space, and could be divided into a smaller and a larger room. The perimeter could be partially or completely partitioned off from the aisle with **blinds**, **standing curtains** or **sliding panels**.

Iwashimizu Hachiman Shrine *iwashimizu hachimangū* A large shrine in Yahata, to the south of the city, associated with the imperial family. Site of the Yahata Provisional Festival (see **Provisional Festivals**).

Iyo blinds *iyosu* Rough blinds made of woven bamboo.

kagura A combination of music and dance performed as a sacred Shinto rite to celebrate the gods.

Kamo Festival / the Festival *kamo matsuri* (mid-4) The main Shinto festival of the year, held on the second day of the Bird in the fourth month. Often referred to simply as 'the Festival'. The great procession, which wound through the streets to the Kamo Shrine, where ceremonies were performed, was hugely popular, and members of the court flocked in their carriages to observe it. The following day, people could observe the procession for the Return of the High Priestess of the Kamo Shrine (*matsuri no kaesa*), who returned to her sacred residence after the ceremonies were over.

Kamo High Priestess *saiin* The High Priestess of the two Kamo Shrines in the capital, chosen from among the Emperor's virgin daughters and other close relations. In *The Pillow Book* the title refers to Emperor Murakami's daughter **Senshi** (Appendix 2).

Kannon A bodhisattva (a form of buddha dedicated to the salvation of all) who embodies compassion. The temples at Kiyomizu and **Hase** were important centres of worship for Kannon.

Kazuraki (god of) *kazuraki no kami* The god Hitokonushi, local to the Kazuraki area (near present-day Nara). According to legend, he would only agree to a holy ascetic's request to build a stone bridge between two holy mountains if he could work at night, in order to hide his ugly face.

kin A seven-stringed version of the *koto* from China, particularly difficult to master. It was somewhat unfashionable by the time of *The Pillow Book*.

Ki no Tsurayuki An important early poet (868?–945?), who helped to compile the *Kokinshū*.

knotted letter See letter.

Kokin rokujō A large poetry collection compiled in or before 987, which is the only source for many of the poems quoted in *The Pillow Book*. Title in full: *Kokin waka rokujō*.

Kokinshū An important collection of approximately 1,100 'poems old and new', compiled at imperial command in the early tenth century. Deep familiarity with it formed the basis for the important skill of poetic allusion at the court in subsequent periods. Title in full: *Kokinwakashū*.

Kōrai matting *kōrai(beri)* A thin woven mat whose decorative cloth edging consisted of a white ground with a cloud or chrysanthemum design woven through it in black.

Korean dogs *komainu* A pair of statues of fancifully ornate lion-like dogs, believed to repel demons, were placed as guardians on either side of Shinto shrine gates, and also before such places as the **curtained dais** in important households.

koto The general term for a stringed instrument much like the modern instrument of that name. It consisted of a long wooden sounding-board with a varying numbers of strings, which the player knelt on the floor to play. Versions of the *koto* were named according to the number of their strings (see **kin**, **thirteen-stringed koto** and **wagon**).

lacquer design *makie* Lacquer over which is sprinkled gold or silver powder to create elegant pictures and designs, commonly seen on boxes and other household utensils.

lattice fence *tatejitomi* Free-standing open-work panels backed with wood, which were generally used as a screen between house and garden. See p. 61.

lattice shutter *kōshi* Lacquered, open-work wood panels stood between pillars to divide off living areas or along the outside of a building. The upper half, hung from a lintel, could be hooked back or removed entirely. The half-panel shutter (*hajitomi*) was the upper half of a lattice shutter, which could be independently lifted and hooked up.

Left Division guardhouse *saemonfu* The guardhouse of the Left Division **Palace Guards** (Appendix 5) was situated directly outside the **Office of the Empress's Household.**

letter *fumi* Letters varied from official documents to private messages between acquaintances or lovers, and were delivered by messenger. Private ones frequently contained or consisted of a poem, and were commonly attached to a sprig of an appropriate plant or other object (see also **next-morning letter**), and sealed with a covering brush stroke. The choice of paper was important, as was calligraphy. They were folded when sent: the knotted letter (*musubibumi*) was knotted in the middle, while the formal straight-folded letter (*tatebumi*) was wrapped in white paper whose ends were bent.

lintel cloth *mokō* A narrow cloth panel that hung from the upper lintel (*uwanageshi*) or along the top of a blind.

Litany of Buddha Names *butsumyō* A service held 12.19–21, when the names of the buddhas of the three worlds were chanted, to pray for the extinction of sins.

little aisle *kobisashi* A small anteroom aisle that was part of the aisle.

long box *nagabitsu* A large, rectangular, legged box with lid. See p. 95.

Long Room *hosodono* The name sometimes given to the aisle or gallery containing the apartments of the gentlewomen.

Lotus Discourses *hakō* / *hoke hakō* A ceremonial series of discourses held over four days, in which a succession of priests held formal debates on the eight fascicles of the *Lotus Sutra*. This could also be arranged by a member of the nobility on a special occasion such as the dedication of a new building.

Lotus Sutra *hokekyō* The most important of the Buddhist texts in Tendai Buddhism. Its full title is 'Sutra of the Lotus of the Marvellous Law'. The sutra itself and its numerous parables played a key role in lay understanding of the Buddhist teaching.

Manyōshū The earliest of the imperial poetry collections, in 20 volumes, whose final compiler is believed to have been Ōtomo Yakamochi (d. 785).

mat *tatami* A large, thick woven straw mat, edged with decorated cloth, that was placed on the floor for seating. See p. 112.

meal-stand *kakeban* A low, four-legged individual lacquer table used for serving meals.

Michinoku paper *michinoku(ni)-gami* Soft, thick high-quality paper from Michinoku (northern Japan), made from mulberry bark, and used for letters and notes, or for wrapping.

Miyanobe Festival A Yin-Yang festival to ensure long life and prosperity, celebrated twice a year, in the twelfth and the first months.

morning letter See **next-morning letter**.

'Motomego' From the **Eastern Dances**. See p. 185.

mountain ascetic *yamabushi* A Buddhist practitioner who performed rigorous ascetic practices in sacred mountain areas. See also **exorcist priest**.

mudguards *ōri* Long leather flaps that hung on each side of a saddled horse.

New Year's Day *gantan* (1.1) The first day of the year coincided calendrically with the first day of spring. Important ceremonies were held at court, and there were formal exchanges of New Year felicitations.

next-morning letter *kinuginu no fumi* It was customary for a man who had spent the night with a woman to send her a letter, generally consisting of a poem, the following morning. This was attached to a suitable seasonal spray of flowers or leaves, etc., frequently one which echoed or added a further dimension to the imagery of the poem. See p. 177. See also **letter**.

night watch *tonoi* Remaining on guard duty through the night to guard the premises and its occupants.

'nine-fold palace' *kokonoe* A poetic term for the imperial palace that suggests its vast expanse.

nurse *menoto* The child of an important family was put in the charge of a nurse, or wetnurse. Their close relationship generally continued into adulthood.

Office of State *kan no tsukasa* An administrative building (also known as *daijōkan-chō*) in the greater palace grounds.

Office of the Empress's Household *shiki no mizōshi* The living quarters in the building that housed the office devoted to the needs of the Empress and her court (*chūgūshiki*). Teishi made frequent use of it as a temporary residence. It was situated directly outside the eastern gate of the inner palace compound, through which senior courtiers, etc., frequently passed.

Old Bamboo Cutter, The *taketori monogatari* An early tale (*c.* 960) of a bamboo cutter who finds a tiny girl in a bamboo stem. She grows up beautiful, is wooed by the Emperor and other nobles and returns to her home, the moon.

onion-flower finial *nagi no hana* A ball with pointed tip, resembling the bud of an onion flower, that frequently crowned the roof of a palanquin. See p. 225.

Ōsaka barrier gate *Ōsaka no seki* The first barrier gate to be crossed when leaving the capital travelling east. Important in poetry for the traditional association of the name (literally 'meeting slope') with lovers' meetings – generally ones that were fraught with difficulty.

page boys *kodoneri warawa* Boys under the age of about thirteen who accompanied and served important men.

palace *dairi / uchi* A general term referring to the walled compound of buildings that comprised the imperial court and its administrative and ceremonial functions. The 'inner palace' (also called *dairi*) contained the residences of the Emperor and his consorts, while the 'greater palace' (*daidairi*) surrounded it and consisted of administrative buildings.

palace festivals *sechie* Occurred at the change of season and at other times. A public banquet was held, at which the Emperor made ritual gifts of food and drink to his courtiers. They include: **New Year's Day**, **Blue Roans**, **Peach**, **Sweet Flag** and **Chrysanthemum Festivals**.

palanquin *mikoshi* A conveyance consisting of a box held aloft on poles borne by porters, in which a god is transported during a shrine festival. It was also the customary mode of travel for the Emperor or other high-ranking members of the imperial family. See p. 225.

palm-leaf carriage *birōge* An elegant carriage thatched with fine strips of palm leaf, used by the nobility on official occasions. See p. 31.

Peach Festival *momo no sekku* (3.3) Held at high spring. Observances included the **Winding Waters Banquet** and a display of dolls.

plume grass *susuki / obana* A grass that produces a tall plumed seed-head, similar to that of the pampas grass, in early autumn.

Privy Chamber *tenjō no ma* The room in the **Seiryōden** where the senior courtiers and court nobles gathered when on duty.

Provisional Festivals *rinji no matsuri* Shrine festivals at the Kamo Shrine (11) and the Iwashimizu Hachiman Shrine (known as the Yahata Provisional Festival) (3). The name was used to distinguish the first from the main **Kamo Festival**. Both included music and dance performances by court nobles, which were viewed by the Emperor and others at the palace in the Rehearsal of Performance.

provisions bag *ebukuro* A bag used for carrying food when travelling.

railing *kōran* A low railing that ran along the outer edge of the veranda.

Records of the Historian **shiki** (Chinese *Shiji*) The official history of China through the Early Han dynasty, completed by Sima Qian in 91 BC. It played an important role in the education of the Heian aristocracy.

reed blinds See **blind**.

Rehearsal of Performance See **Provisional Festivals**.

Retreat Room *nurigome* A small walled room within the **Inner Chamber** that served as a storeroom or occasionally for sleeping.

Return of the High Priestess See **Kamo Festival**.

saibara Folk songs from the eighth century adopted by the Heian aristocracy as part of its musical repertoire.

sakaki A low evergreen tree with glossy leaves, sacred to **Shinto** shrines.

saké pot *hisage* A lacquered pot with a handle, similar to a teapot, used for serving *sake*.

screen *byōbu* A folding type of movable partition used inside buildings, with two to six hinged wooden panels whose surface was covered with paper or silk and decorated with paintings. See p. 107. See also **standing curtains**.

screening fence *suigaki* / *suigai* An open-weave fence of wood or bamboo slats, which afforded a limited view.

Season-change days *setsubun* The day when a new season was calendrically determined to begin was considered to be particularly inauspicious. It was associated with directional taboos and other rituals to protect from evil influences.

secondary aisle *magobisashi* / *matabisashi* A smaller aisle that was sometimes added on the outside of the main aisle.

Seiryōden The Emperor's private residence, linked by **galleries** to the other buildings of the inner palace compound, including the residences of the Empress and other consorts.

serving table *daiban* A low, footed lacquered tray-table, on which food on **meal-stands** was served.

serving tray *oshiki* A flat, square serving tray with a low rim.

shaft stand *shiji* A stool on which carriage shafts were rested when the **carriage** was parked, and also used as a step when boarding.

Shinto *shintō* A general term signifying the worship of native Japanese gods, associated with **shrines**, as distinguished from the Buddhist religion, associated with **temples**.

shō A wind instrument similar to a panpipe, with a varying number of pipes, that was played in court music.

shrine *yashiro* A place of worship for one or more of the **Shinto** gods.

Shūishū A mid-Heian imperial poetry collection, compiled 1005–1011. Title in full: *Shūiwakashū*.

shutter See **lattice shutter**.

sliding door *yarido* A single-panelled sliding wooden door. See p. 202.

sliding panel *sōji* / *shōji* A light sliding partition between rooms, usually covered with paper. Equivalent to the modern *fusuma*. See p. 10.

Song of Everlasting Sorrow chōgonka (Chinese *Changhenge*) A long poem by Bo Juyi. See also Section 34, note 2.

spirit *mononoke* The tormented spirit of someone living or dead was believed to be capable of possessing a person and causing illness or madness. This could be cured by exorcism, in which an **exorcist priest** used incantations to draw the spirit out into a medium, force it to express its grievance and banish it.

standing curtain *kichō* Trailing drapes hung from a portable frame, in several different heights. They were the most common of the movable temporary partitions (see also **screen**) used to delineate living spaces within a building. See p. 52.

standing lamp *tōdai* An oil lamp on a thin stand of varying height. See p. 116.

standing screen. See **screen**.

standing tray *takatsuki* A flat tray raised on a central leg and wide base.

straight-folded letter See **letter**.

straw cushion *warōdo / warōda* A round flat cushion of woven straw.

sugoroku A board game with two players; its primary aim was to remove all a player's pieces (known as 'horses') from the board as quickly as possible with throws of the dice. See p. 147.

summer fan *kawahori* Literally 'bat', owing to its wing shape. A hinged fan of folding paper on plain bamboo or lacquer ribs.

sutra *kyō* A Buddist text, which could be treated as having magical powers when intoned.

sweet flag *sōbu* A water reed with long, iris-like strap leaves. See also **Sweet Flag Festival**.

Sweet Flag Festival *ayame no sekku / tango no sekku* (5.5) An important **palace festival** held on one of the inauspicious **season-change days**. Leaves of the sweet-flag plant, as well as wormwood, were spread on roofs and used decoratively to ward off evil, and a special banquet was held. **Herbal balls** were also hung in buildings as further protection.

Table Room *daibandokoro* Room used by gentlewomen for preparing food to be served to the Emperor, and also as a general sitting room.

Tale of the Hollow Tree, The utsuho monogatari A lengthy (20 volumes) and very popular anonymous tenth-century tale, which centres on the fortunes of the two rivals, Nakatada and Suzushi. Much of the tale concerns the possession of extraordinary skills in playing the *kin*. See also Section 78, note 5.

Tales of Ise Ise monogatari An influential early-tenth-century anonymous collection of tales of a lover's exploits. It is built around poems, many of which were composed by Ariwara Narihira (825–880).

Tanabata Festival *tanabata-sai* (7.7) A palace festival, inherited from China, celebrating the yearly meeting in the heavens of the celestial lovers, the Weaver Star (Vega) and the Herdsman Star (Altair), who cross a bridge to meet briefly on this night.

temple *tera* A building or group of buildings devoted to Buddhist worship. Temples were frequently sites of pilgrimage, and the larger ones could contain accommodation for pilgrims.

Temporary Palace See **Ichijō Palace**.

thin paper *usuyō* A thin, delicate paper often used for letters.

thirteen-stringed *koto* *sō/shō no koto* A thirteen-stringed version of the *koto*.

threshold *nageshi* A long wooden beam which formed the step down from the **Inner Chamber** to the surrounding **aisle**, and another from aisle to **veranda**. *Nageshi* was also used for the equivalent panels that ran between pillars at ceiling level.

thunder guards *kaminari no jin* Guards assigned to defend the Emperor's residence if there were three claps of thunder.

Tōkaden The usual residence of Teishi and her court inside the inner palace grounds.

tonsure, taking the *shukke* Literally 'leaving the world', an act of formal dedication to the religious life, which involved either shaving the head completely or cutting the hair symbolically short, and donning religious robes. Although this could signify a heartfelt commitment and entry into a temple or monastery, in court circles it was more often the equivalent of a retirement from worldly duties, either owing to advancing age or to a crisis in one's career, and did not necessarily involve total retreat from the world.

uguisu A small bird whose beautiful spring song played a prominent role in poetry. In summer, the song becomes a drawn-out, wavery repetition of three notes.

vajra, **single-pointed** A short carved metal stick with pointed ends, associated in tantric Buddhism with the power to defeat evil delusions and induce salvation, and commonly used for spirit transference. See p. 253. Other variants, have three or more prongs at, both ends.

veranda *sunoko* A narrow balcony of wood or bamboo, generally enclosed by a railing, that comprised the outer edge of a building, over which the eave extended. A **threshold** put it on a lower level from the aisle.

wagon A six-stringed version of the *koto*.

Wakan rōeishū (*Japanese and Chinese Poems to Sing*). A collection made *c.* 1012 by Fujiwara Kintō (966–1041), of Chinese and Japanese poetry. It was the primary source for quotations of Chinese poetry in the court. The poems could be intoned in a specific poetry-chanting style.

water iris *kakitsubata* An iris that grows in shallow water. It bears purple or white flowers in early summer.

Winding Waters Banquet (3.3) This ceremony included the ritual of floating cups down a winding stream in a garden, while the participants seated beside it composed a poem before a floating cup reached them.

wing *tai* A separate building connected to the main house by **bridgeways**. Typically, there were east and west wings.

wood-grain pattern *kuchiki kata* A formalized dye pattern that imitates the rough grain of water-weathered wood. It was commonly seen in the decorative cloth used in furnishings, such as the drapes of **standing curtains**.

wormwood *yomogi* A weed commonly found in an overgrown garden. Together with sweet-flag leaves, it was strewn during the **Sweet Flag Festival**.

Yahata Provisional Festival See **Provisional Festivals**.

Yin-Yang master *onmyōji* A professional practitioner of geomantic and other Yin-Yang divination (*onmyōdō*), based on a complex system inherited from China. See p. 239.

Young Herbs, Festival of (1.7) Seven types of 'herb' were gathered and eaten in a ritual meal to ward off evil and illness. The tradition originated in China. This was also the day for the official Conferment of one of the twice-yearly promotions at court. On the following morning the recipients did the rounds of associates and benefactors in their carriages to thank them officially for their support, and to receive congratulations.

Appendix 5
Court Ranks, Titles and Bureaucracy

A courtier's rank and title were of vital importance. Men were commonly referred to by title rather than by name, except by their superiors. (I have considerably modified this usage to avoid confusion for the reader.) Ladies at court were generally referred to by the title of a male relative, although they had a very limited ranking system.

Rank began at the top with the first, the bottom rank being the ninth. Ranks were subdivided into senior and junior, and (below the third rank) upper and lower grades of these. The three highest ranks were designated **court nobles**, and were members of the **Council of State**. Fourth- and fifth-ranking men comprised the group known as senior courtiers. Some among these (along with the court nobles) were generally granted the prestigious honour of access to the **Privy Chamber** (see Appendix 4) in the Emperor's residence. Senior courtiers were the men with whom gentlewomen at the palace most frequently consorted. Special access to the Privy Chamber was also granted to **Chamberlains** of the sixth rank, whose role it was personally to attend the Emperor. Men of the sixth to ninth ranks were designated as 'lower-ranking' (*jige*), and were considered insignificant. Rank was to a great degree dependent on birth, although promotion also sometimes involved a rise in rank, since offices were generally associated with specific ranks.

Offices, and their attendant titles, were the focus of intense competition in the twice-yearly **Appointments Lists**, although their importance was entirely a matter of prestige, and the actual work was largely performed by lower-ranking men. One peculiarity of the system was that certain more high-ranking offices commonly involved dual appointments: thus, the title Secretary Controller identified the holder as both **Secretary** in the **Chamberlains' Office** and **Controller** in the **Controllers' Office**.

The titles 'Left' and 'Right' also frequently occur. These mirror the traditional categories inherited from the Chinese system, which pictures those who serve the Emperor as seated to his left (east) and right (west) as he faces south surveying the nation. Left was considered slightly more prestigious than Right. (The left/right system of categorization can also be seen in many other situations, such as poetry and other competitions.) Most offices were held by more than one man.

The translation of titles is necessarily arbitrary, since no similar system exists in English. I have largely followed Royall Tyler's terms, with certain modifications. For a detailed treatment of the full complexities of rank and office, see *A Tale of Flowering Fortunes*, trans. William H. and Helen Craig McCullough, Appendix A.

Acting *gon* An addition to the names of certain offices (Counsellor, etc.), in order to increase the number of possible incumbents.

Adviser *jijū* A junior official of the lower fifth rank under the **Bureau of Central Affairs**.

Aide of Ceremonial *shikibu no jō / zō* A posting of the third level in the **Bureau of Ceremonial**. If a man of the fifth rank occupied this usually sixth-ranking post, his title was Commissioner of Ceremonial (*shikibu no taifu*).

Appointments List See Appendix 4.

Board of Censors *danjōdai* Officially monitored the conduct of those employed at the palace.

Bureau of Central Affairs *nakatsukasashō* The most important of the bureaus, in charge of general administration of the palace. Its minister was in particularly close contact with the Emperor, and was frequently an imperial prince.

Bureau of Ceremonial *shikibushō* The administrative Bureau that dealt with procedures at court ceremonies.

Bureau of Clothing *nuidono* The office that provided the clothing for the inhabitants of the palace.

Bureau of War *hyōbushō* The administrative bureau for military affairs and equipment, which in practice did little beyond training contestants for the court's archery competitions.

Captain of the Left Gate Watch *sahyōe no kami* A fourth-ranking post in the **Gate Watch**.

Captain of the Palace Guards *chūjō* Literally 'Middle Captain', the second of three ranks of Captain. A prized title usually held by a young man of high-ranking family, concurrently with another office such as **Secretary**.

Captain Third Rank *sanmi no chūjō* A special designation for a Captain whose rank was third rather than the usual fourth.

Chamberlain *kurōdo* An official in the **Chamberlains' Office** of the fifth or sixth rank, who personally served the Emperor and thus was afforded special privileges above his rank. These included entry to the **Privy Chamber** (Appendix 4) and permission to wear forbidden fabrics and colours, particularly the special olive-green reserved for the Emperor. When acting as message-bearer, etc., for the Emperor, a Chamberlain was treated with a reverence quite out of proportion to his lowly rank.

Chamberlains' Office *kurōdodokoro* The office which dealt with matters relating directly to the Emperor, including care of his falcons, musical instruments, etc., headed by two Chief Chamberlains (*kurōdo no tō*).

Chief Equerry *muma no kami* The senior officer, of the fifth rank, in charge of the Left [*sama no kami*] or Right [*uma no kami*] Imperial Stables [*meryō / uma no tsukasa*].

Chief Gentlewoman *naishi* The highest rank of gentlewoman.

Commander *taishō* One of the Right and Left commanding officers of the **Palace Guards**.

Commissioner *taifu / daibu* A general appellation for anyone of the fifth rank.

Commissioner of Ceremonial See **Aide of Ceremonial**.

Constable *udoneri* A man attached as guard to a **court noble** and affiliated with the **Bureau of Central Affairs**. They were notorious for their overbearing ways.

Consultant *sangi / saishō* A post ranked below **Counsellors** in the **Council of State** hierarchy.

Controller *ben* One of the heads of the two Controllers' Offices (*benkankyoku*), which supervised certain government bureaus. They were divided into Major (*dai*), Middle (*chū*) and Lesser (*shō*).

Controller Chamberlain *kurōdo no ben* A dual post. See **Controller** and **Chamberlain**.

Council of State *daijōkan* The highest governmental organ above the bureaus, comprised of **Grand Counsellors**, **Counsellors** and **Consultants**.

Counsellor *chūnagon* Literally 'Middle Counsellor'. A prestigious title, either regular or acting, frequently held by high-ranking young men.

court noble *kugyō / kandachime* A general term applied to men of the highest three ranks and holding office above a certain level.

Deputy (Governor, etc.) *suke* A general designation for the second in command, below Captain or Provincial Governor.

Deputy of the (Right) Gate Watch *emon / yugei no suke* Second in command of the Gate Watch.

Deputy Officer of Grounds *tonomo no suke* Second in command in the Office of Grounds.

Empress Dowager *nyōin* The mother of the Emperor. In *The Pillow Book* the title refers to Ichijō's mother, Senshi (Appendix 2).

Empress's Office *miyazukasa/ chūgūshiki* The office which dealt with matters pertaining to the Empress.

Gate Watch *e(mon)fu / yugei* The guards of the gates of the palace compound, divided into Left and Right.

Governor See **Provincial Governor**.

Grand Counsellor *dainagon* The highest ranking of the three degrees of **Counsellor**, second in importance to **Ministers**.

groundskeeper *tonomo(ri)zukasa* Women or men employed by the Office of Grounds to look after the palace grounds as well as to see to the provision of lamps, charcoal, etc. for the palace. They were often used as messengers.

High Consort *nyōgo* A high-ranking consort of the Emperor, from among whom the Empress was chosen.

High Gentlewoman *naishi no suke* A relatively high-ranking gentlewoman, privileged to attend personally on the Emperor.

Housekeeping Office *kanmorizukasa / kamonzukasa* An office in the Bureau of the Treasury, responsible for upkeep of palace furnishings and gardens.

Imperial Attendant ladies *himemōchigimi* Ladies who attended the Emperor on horseback during imperial processions.

Junior Counsellor *shōnagon* A lower-level officer (fifth rank) in the Council of State.

Lady Chamberlain *onna kurōdo* Low-ranking women who performed general duties at the court.

Lieutenant *shōshō* A third-level officer in the **Palace Guards**.

Lord *ason* A hereditary title.

lower-ranking gentlemen *jige* A general term for courtiers holding ranks below the fifth, and thus denied access to the **Privy Chamber** (Appendix 4).

Major Controller See **Controller**.

Master (of the Household) *betō* The director of a household of a member of the imperial family. *Betō* was also the name of the Head Abbot of a temple.

Minister *daijin* / *ōitono* The highest office in the **Council of State**. There were Ministers of the Left (*sadaijin*) and Right (*udaijin*).

Minister of Ceremonial *shikibukyō* Head of the **Bureau of Ceremonial**.

Minister of the Treasury *ōkurakyō* Head of the Bureau of the Treasury (*Ōkurashō*), a fourth-rank post.

Mistress of the Imperial Wardrobe *mikushigedono* The head of the Office of the Imperial Wardrobe, which saw to the sewing of the Emperor's clothes. Her position was a powerful one, since she was in practice an imperial wife. In *The Pillow Book*, the title refers to Teishi's sister (Appendix 2).

Myōbu A title given to women belonging to the fourth and fifth ranks of gentlewomen. It frequently served as a name.

Office of Grounds *tonomo(ri)zukasa* The office responsible for the maintenance of palace grounds and supply of such items as charcoal and wood.

Officer of the Left Gate Watch See **Gate Watch**.

Palace Guards *konoefu* A body of guards whose role was to guard the Emperor and his palace, and act as imperial bodyguards during processions. They were ranked higher than the **Gate Watch** guards. See also **Left Division guardhouse** (Appendix 4).

Palace Maiden *uneme* A young woman employed to serve at table, etc., in the palace.

Palace Minister *naidaijin* / *uchi no otodo* The most junior of the three **Ministers** in the **Council of State**.

Provincial Governor *kami* / *zuryō* A man of the fifth or sixth rank appointed to oversee one of the provinces, but a position looked down on in court circles. The prestige of the post depended on the rank of the province. Gentlewomen (such as Sei) were often drawn from among the daughters of Provincial Governors.

Regent *kanpaku* A role outside the bureaucratic hierarchy. The Regent effectively wielded supreme power, being appointed to act on behalf of the Emperor, often a child, who generally delegated complete authority to him. In *The Pillow Book*, the title refers to Michitaka (Appendix 2).

Second of the Watch *hyōe no suke* Second in command of the **Gate Watch** guards.

Secretary *kurōdo no tō* Second in command in the **Chamberlains' Office**.

Secretary Captain *tō no chūjō* A dual post, combining **Secretary** in the Chamberlains' Office with **Captain** of the Palace Guards.

Secretary Controller *tō no ben* A combined post of Secretary in the Chamberlains' Office and Controller.

senior courtier *tenjōbito / uebito* A man of the fourth or fifth rank, who was given express permission to enter the Privy Chamber (Appendix 4).

Senior Steward *daijin* A third-level post in the Office of the Empress's Household (Appendix 4).

Sixth-rank Chamberlain See **Chamberlain.**

Appendix 6
Clothes and Colour Glossary

Clothing played an extremely important role in court life. People were perceived and assessed in terms of what they wore quite as much as for their physical attributes and personality. The subject of clothes and colours was of immense interest to both men and women, and involved a large and subtle vocabulary. As much as possible, the translation of clothing terms below attempts to convey some idea of how the items are worn, but words such as 'cloak', 'jacket', 'shift', etc., inevitably are inclined to evoke very different images for the twenty-first century reader, so consult the illustrations here and in the text.

Women's and men's clothing was largely prescribed by situation and degree of formality, but individual expression was revealed in choice of colour, cloth design and fabric, as well as in combinations of these. Clothes were sometimes worn in numerous layers; each layer arranged to reveal itself with an edge of sleeve, with the longest sleeve being the innermost. Colour was of primary concern in choosing these combinations, and within the seasonal prescriptions for colour, choice could be inventive. Frequently some or all of the robes themselves combined two colours through an outer layer and an inner lining, the latter revealing itself as an edging to the robe at sleeve and elsewhere. Such combinations, both of robes and of robe-plus-lining, were known as *kasane* (literally 'layering'), and the art of *kasane* was at the centre of the vitally important art of clothing selection for both women and men. *

The concept of *kasane* is also present in colour terms. Many colour names express a colour achieved through a *kasane* effect; for instance, *fuji* (wisteria) expresses the effect achieved by layering a pale violet-grey over a green reminiscent of the vivid green of spring leaves, known as *moegi* (spring-shoot green). This example also reveals the strong tendency for simple and combination colours, and their names,

* The kimono as we know it today was developed in the late nineteenth century.

Courtier in Everyday Court Costume

1. Lacquered cap
2. Shift
3. *Ákome* gown
4. Cloak
5. Fan
6. Gathered trousers
7. Lacquered shoes

Court Lady in Normal Formal Dress

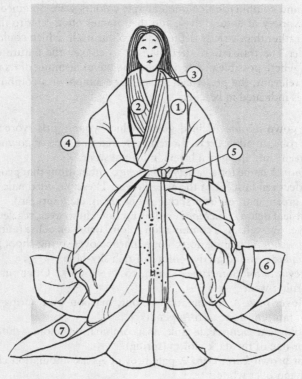

1. Chinese jacket
2. Layers of gowns
3. Shift
4. Folded paper
5. Fan
6. Train
7. Skirted trousers

to express elements of the natural world, usually plants and flowers. There was often considerable variation in defining and naming both simple and combination colours. Simple colours were obtained from a wide variety of natural dyes, and their names often refer to the dye source rather than strictly defining the colour itself, which could vary in shade. The translation attempts first to convey the nature of the colour, where possible preserving also the literal meaning of its name. Where relevant, the prescribed season for a simple or a combination colour is indicated in brackets.

akomé gown *akomé* A lined gown, which young girls wore as an over-robe. In adult dress, the term referred to a type of gown worn between shift and gown layers in formal wear.

aster *shion* A name for a variety of *kasane* combinations that produced an effect reminiscent of the aster flower. These included pale violet over green, maroon over spring-shoot green, etc. (autumn).

autumn-leaf ochre *kikuchiba* A reddish yellow. In weaves, scarlet warp and yellow weft. As a combination colour, ochre on ochre (autumn).

azalea *tsutsuji* A combination colour, maroon over spring-shoot green.

azure *hanada* An indigo dye colour of rich sky-blue.

blue-grey *aonibi* Sometimes closer to green-grey. Often used in mourning-wear.

bush clover *hagi* A combination colour, maroon over spring-shoot green (autumn). See also Appendix 4.

cherry blossom *sakura* Pale pink. As a combination colour, white over red or one of the dark violets (spring).

chestnut brown *kurumi-iro* A pale brown. As a combination colour, clove-tan over white.

Chinese jacket *karaginu* A short jacket worn with the train as the top layer in women's formal wear. It could be brocade, embroidered or woven silk, depending on rank. See p. 18.

cloak *nōshi* A lined (winter) or unlined (summer) men's cloak, tied with a circular band at the neck, generally worn over gathered trousers as normal full dress at court or at home. See p. 7.

clove-tan *kōzome* A warm tan achieved with a clove dye. As a combination colour, two layers of this.

combination See introduction to this appendix.

damask *aya* Twill weave silk. Forbidden to those below the sixth rank, with the exception of Chamberlains.

dapple-dye *murago* Cloth dyed with dappled shadings of a single colour.

dark leaf-green *aokuchiba* In dyed colour, a blackish-green. As a weave name, the colour achieved with green warp and yellow weft. As a combination colour, green over fallen-leaf ochre (summer/autumn).

decorative sashes *hire, katai / kutai* Cloth sashes that hung from the shoulders (*hire*) and the waist (*kutai*) as part of women's formal wear.

deep green *midori* A variable colour, ranging from blue-green through to deep blue. The prescribed colour for the formal cloak of the sixth rank.

deep (scarlet-)purple *koki* A highly esteemed colour.

deutzia *u no hana* A combination colour, white over spring-shoot green.

display *idashiginu* Literally 'putting out the robes'. The formal display of women's sleeves and hems from beneath screens in buildings or carriages. Also, displaying the hem of under-robes (*akomé* gown, etc.) from beneath the outer clothing.

dried grass *kareno* Literally 'withered field'. A combination colour, yellow over light green (autumn, winter).

fallen-leaf ochre *kuchiba* Literally 'rotting leaf'. An orange yellow produced with saffron and gardenia dye. As a combination colour, fallen-leaf ochre over yellow (autumn).

figured (silk) *orimono* Silk with a patterned weave.

formal cloak *hō* The top layer of men's formal court attire (*sokutai*), an unlined cloak whose colour reflected the wearer's rank, from varying depths of purple through scarlet to green. It was worn over a white gown, possibly a summer gown of silk gauze in Section 2.

formal lacquered cap *kanmuri* A stiff lacquered cap with raised section at the back and stiff gauze tail or other attachments, worn with full civil dress.

formal over-robe *kouchigi* A shorter patterned robe that was worn over the layers of gowns (*uchigi*) when a little more formality was required in women's wear.

full civil dress *sokutai* A nobleman's formal costume worn or special occasions. It consisted of **formal lacquered cap, formal cloak** over **train-robe** and **gowns**, and two pairs of **skirted trousers**. A **stone belt** and **baton** (Appendix 2) completed the outfit.

fulled See **glossed silk**.

gathered trousers *sashinuki* Long, voluminous men's trousers tied at the ankle. Worn with cloak or hunting costume.

girl's over-robe *kazami* A long, loose over-robe worn by girls on formal occasions.

glossed silk *uchimono* Silk was glossed by being beaten on a fulling block (*kinuta*).

gloss-yellow *neriiro* A pale yellow produced by glossing white silk.

gossamer silk *suzushi* A very thin silk.

gown *uchigi* / *uchiki* / *kinu* Generally in several layers, gowns were worn between the outer clothing and the shift in everyday men's and women's wear.

graded dye *susogo* Cloth dyed a deeper colour at the top shading to paler at the hem.

grape *ebizome* A dye colour varying from grape purple to reddish brown. As a weave name, red warp and pale lavender or grape weft. As a combination colour, maroon over azure.

green *ao* A colour with a wide range across the blue-green spectrum and into yellowish green.

hair-binding cord *motoyui* A cord of cloth or twisted paper used to bind up men's and women's hair.

hanpi **jacket** *hanpi* A short-sleeved, thigh-length jacket worn under the **formal cloak** and over the **train-robe** as part of the courtier's formal costume.

hay-dye yellow *kariyasu-zome* A yellow dye made from the stems and leaves of dried grass.

heavy brocade *katamon* A tight weave brocade with unraised pattern. Cf. **raised brocade**.

high clogs *keishi* Open-toed thonged shoes, similar to the modern *geta*, raised on a high bridge. See p. 15.

hunting costume *kariginu* A kind of cloak with open shoulders and drawstrings at the sleeve cuffs. It was originally hunting attire, but later became everyday wear for courtiers.

indigo-on-white *jizuri* Indigo-blue print patterns on a white ground.

indigo-print *aozuri* A printed dye pattern from the mountain indigo plant.

kasane See introduction to this appendix.

kerria-yellow *yamabuki* A golden yellow. As a combination colour, usually fallen-leaf ochre over yellow (spring).

lacquered cap *eboshi* A stiff, peaked, rimless lacquered hat, worn by men as an integral part of their everyday wear. For more formal occasions, it was replaced by the more elaborate **formal lacquered cap**.

lapis lazuli blue *ruri* A rich purplish blue.

lavender *futaai* A light or darker purple achieved by dyeing in safflower (scarlet) followed by indigo. As a weave colour, indigo weft and scarlet warp. As a combination colour, a double layering of lavender, or lavender over white. This could extend from almost all safflower to almost all indigo, depending on season and age (summer).

light blue *asagi* A colour obtained with light dipping in indigo.

light grey *usunibi* Used in mourning, or for nun's robes.

long divided robe *hosonaga* A narrow outer robe, with two long trailing panels. It was formal wear for high-ranking women.

maroon *suō* A dark, rusty reddish-purple. As a combination colour, a lighter over a darker shade of maroon.

night-service wear *tonoi sugata* An abbreviated form of the formal court-service wear worn by courtiers on night duty.

olive-green *kikujin* A special imperial colour which **Chamberlains** (Appendix 5) were permitted to wear.

overcloak *ao* A kind of formal cloak worn by officials, whose colour was determined by rank.

pale violet-grey *usuiro*

pine-leaf green *matsu no ha* A combination colour, spring-shoot green over lavender.

plum *mume / ume* A combination colour, variously deep scarlet over plum pink, white over maroon, or a double layer of maroon.

plum-pink *kōbai* A rich pink. As a combination colour, scarlet over maroon. (late winter/early spring).

raised brocade *ukimon* A brocade weave in which the pattern is woven in relief. Cf. **heavy brocade.**

red *akaki*

red-purple weave *akairo* A weave colour obtained by using a red weft and a purple warp.

scarlet *kurenai* A bright, pinkish red. Also sometimes referred to as *koki* (elsewhere, deep scarlet-purple). As a combination colour, scarlet over scarlet.

shift *hitoe* The unlined gown, usually white, that was worn next to the skin. It was generally cut longer than other gowns, and showed prominently at hem and sleeve cuffs. The term could also refer to any unlined gown.

short boots *hanka / hōka* Ankle-length lacquered shoes for men, turned up at the toes.

short hunting trousers *suikan no hakama* Less elaborate than **hunting costume.** The trousers were mid-calf length.

silk gauze *usumono* A very light silk weave, typically used in the summer gauze gown (*usumono no uwagi*).

sixth-rank cloak *rokuō / rokusō* The dark green formal cloak worn by men of the sixth rank.

skirted trousers *hakama* Wide-bottomed trousers worn under the gowns by men and women. They came in several types, such as white over-trousers (*ue no hakama*) in men's formal wear, or women's scarlet trousers that extended beyond their feet.

softened silk *kaineri* Silk softened and glossed by being boiled with lye, as distinct from raw gossamer silk (*suzushi*). In *kasane* combination, both upper and lower layers are glossed scarlet.

spring-shoot green *moegi* A yellowish or deeper green, of indigo over-dyed with a yellow.

stone belt *sekitai* A black leather belt the back of which was embedded with gemstones. It was worn with the **formal cloak** as part of men's formal wear.

straw coat *mino* A sleeveless rain-cloak of woven straw worn over the shoulders.

summer under-robe *katabira* A short unlined robe worn under the cloak in summer. Also, a woman's unlined summer robe, of hemp or cotton. (The same term was also used for the **drapes** (Appendix 4) of a standing curtain.)

surplice *kesa* A priest's long cloak, worn draped from the left shoulder over the right thigh.

tail *ei* The long stiff lacquered tail that hung from the back of men's **formal lacquered caps**.

train *mo* A long apron-shaped garment tied at the waist and worn at the back. It was worn over the outer robe (*uwagi*) and under the Chinese jacket as an essential part of women's formal or court-service wear.

train-robe *shitagasane* A jacket whose back extended to a long full train that trailed on the floor. It was an essential part of men's formal wear, the train protruding from beneath the formal cloak. Its length was prescribed by rank.

travelling attire *tsubo sōzoku* A special costume worn by women, generally of lesser rank, when travelling on foot or horseback on pilgrimages, etc. It consisted of a cloak and a broad-brimmed, high, bell-shaped travelling hat (*ichimegasa*).

unlined gowns *hitoegasane* Women's formal summer attire, a layering of shifts.

violet *murasaki* A deep purple, named from its dye-plant, the gromwell (*Lithospermum erithrorhizon*).

wild indigo *yamaai* A particular bluish-green dye colour obtained from the wild indigo plant.

willow *yanagi* As a weave colour, white weft and light green warp. As a combination colour, white over green (spring).

wisteria *fuji* A combination colour, pale violet-grey over spring-shoot green (summer).

Notes

The probable date of an episode is provided in brackets after the title where it is known. The order given is year, month (or season), day. Month number follows the Japanese calendrical year (see Appendix 3). Translations of the poems are my own.

The author is referred to as 'Sei' throughout these Notes.

1 In spring, the dawn

This section establishes the theme of listing moments, experiences or objects that give particular pleasure, beginning here with seasonal categories.

1. *even the crows*: Mundane birds such as crows would not normally be considered a moving sight.

2 Times of year

The seasonal pleasures of the calendar year were intimately bound up with the great round of court rituals and festivals. Here, Sei describes some of the festivals of the first four months.

1. *people pluck ... herbs*: See Appendix 4, Young Herbs, Festival of.
2. *It's fun*: This description seems to be a personal recollection from a time before Sei joined the court.
3. *gruel sticks*: To mark the first full moon, a special gruel made up of seven grains was served, to avert evil influences. Sticks made from the unburned wood retrieved from the fire that cooked this gruel, if struck on a woman's thigh were considered in folk belief to produce a male child.
4. *call on his new wife*: It was a common custom for a husband to be adopted into his wife's family, and for him to visit her at her home during the early stages of a marriage, rather than the couple living on their own. He often continued to maintain a separate establishment, but her family home became his official base.

5. *the Festival*: The Kamo Festival.
6. *rolls of . . . fabric*: These are to be used for making up the robes worn at the Festival.
7. *Chamberlain's green formal cloak*: Lesser ranking members of the Chamberlains' Office, who took up the head of the procession in the Kamo Festival, were allowed to wear the Chamberlain's forbidden colour for the occasion, but their cloaks were not made of damask.

4   It breaks my heart to think

An important role of priests in Heian society was magical, as protectors against the pervasive danger of the evil spirits that cause illness and disaster. Despite the ritual importance of Buddhism, priests were generally held in low esteem, as Sei demonstrates in Sections 22 and 25.

1. *Exorcist priests*: If the possession was a tenacious one, the priest must throw himself into his incantations for long, exhausting hours.

5   When the Empress moved to the home of Senior Steward Narimasa (999.8)

These scenes, late in the period covered in this book, occurred when Teishi had moved to Taira Narimasa's house, Sanjō Palace, on the Third Ward, to avoid ritually defiling the Emperor's palace in giving birth there. Narimasa had quickly to get permission to add two pillars for the imperial visit.

1. *that man . . . grand and tall*: A story in the Chinese classics about a man of the Early Han dynasty, who ordered that an especially large gate be built for his house in anticipation of the impressive retinue he believed his son, Yu Dingguo, would one day command. Dingguo did indeed go on to achieve great things. In fact, Narimasa gets the reference wrong, since Sei was referring to the father (Yu Gong), not the son.
2. *the young princess . . . "akomé gowns"*: The Empress's two-year-old daughter, Princess Shūshi, had come with her. Narimasa reveals his ignorance of the intricacies of the names for little girls' clothes. (He refers to *kazami*, a girl's (formal) over-robe, as *akomé*.)
3. *leetle*: Narimasa's odd pronunciation is either regional dialect or an affectation from his student days.
4. *the Counsellor*: Taira Korenaka, Narimasa's older brother, a very talented man whom Narimasa greatly admired.
5. *one of the outer rooms*: The gentlewomen were serving the

Empress in her quarters in the Inner Chamber. Sei had to go
to the outer edge of the aisle room (see Appendix 1) to meet
Narimasa.

6   The Emperor's cat (1000.3?)

1.   *Myōbu . . . Muma no Myōbu*: Only cats of fourth and fifth rank
were permitted in the Emperor's palace. *Myōbu* is the title for a
gentlewoman of the fifth rank. The cat's carer was also of this
rank, and so shared the name.

2.   *Dog Island*: This appears to have been an island where stray and
unwanted dogs were sent.

8   The Offering of Official Thanks

This refers to the ceremony in which those newly promoted present
themselves to the Emperor. The ceremony involved dance and highly
stylized gestures expressing joy and gratitude.

9   The eastern side of the Temporary Palace

This replacement palace was built in a different directional orientation,
facing south instead of east. However, conventional names – such as
'the northern guardhouse' – remained, even though the gate that
housed the guardhouse was now located in the east. (Sukuse no Kimi
is unidentified.)

1.   *branch fan*: It is unclear what this is. It seems most likely that
the tree's branches formed a natural fan shape, so the tree suggested itself as a giant's fan. Bishop Jōchō was unusually tall.

2.   *Yamashina Temple*: An alternative name for Kōfukuji in Nara,
the clan temple of the Fujiwara family.

10   Mountains

This and Sections 11–17 list place names that Sei finds particularly
attractive or intriguing. Their charm most frequently lies in the poetic
associations of the name, and/or its meaning. The place itself as a
geographical entity is not the point. Space precludes explanation of
the likely reasons for each name's inclusion, but a few important
references are noted below.

1.   *I wonder how it stands aside*: *Katasari* can mean 'stand aside'.

2.   *'now looks askance at me'*: A quotation from *Fubokushō* (8766):
'She who long ago / would look upon me favourably / now looks
askance at me – / for she dwells far above me / on Asakura's
cloudy heights.'

3.   *the dancers . . . Festivals*: The dancers at these two great festivals

sang a folk song which included 'Ōhire' as they left at the end of the dances.

14   River Pools

1. *to give it such a name*: *Kashiko* can mean 'awe'.
2. *who told whom not to enter*: *Nairiso* can mean 'don't come in'.

18   Large Buildings

This and Section 19 list names of impressive buildings in the capital. Some belonged to important men, or the families of members of the imperial family, while others are unidentifiable today.

20   The sliding panels that close off the north-east corner (994, spring)

This (possibly a combination of different occasions) probably took place when the Emperor was 15 and Teishi 18. Her brother Korechika was then Grand Counsellor. Teishi was temporarily residing in the Emperor's Seiryōden Palace, ensconced in the room in the north-east corner set aside for visiting empresses. See Introduction, pp. xiv–xv.

1. *the north-east corner ... long arms and legs*: The north-east direction was considered unlucky in Chinese geomancy (a kind of *feng-shui*), and the frightening scenes on these panels were a protective device. The 'terrifying creatures' (*tenaga ashinaga*) from Chinese legend had grotesquely long arms and legs.
2. *The months ... Mount Mimuro*: *Manyōshū* (323). Korechika omits the last line, which specifies that the poem refers to the imperial palace, thereby allowing it to be interpreted as directed to the Empress. Sei later manages a similar shift that cleverly echoes his.
3. *With the passing years ... age and time*: Fujiwara Yoshifusa (804–872), *Kokinshū* (52). It is particularly appropriate because it was written by an admiring father to his daughter, who had become the Emperor's consort, and its introductory headnote states that it was composed while viewing a vase of cherry blossoms.
4. *Retired Emperor Enyū*: The present Emperor's father. Enyū (959–991), reigned 969–984; son of Emperor Murakami, and husband of Fujiwara Senshi.
5. *Our present Regent*: Michitaka, father of Teishi and Korechika.
6. *"As the tide ... think of you"*: No record of this poem has survived, but it was no doubt well known at the time.
7. *that poem of mine ... come up with*: As well as putting her

cleverness down to her advanced age, Sei may be suggesting that, as a woman of nearly thirty, her poem of old age was appropriate.

8. *Senyōden Consort*: Thus named because Hōshi, daughter of Fuji-wara Morotada, normally resided in the building of that name in the imperial palace. This story takes place during the reign of Murakami (reigned 946–961).

9. *he ordered ... for her*: He engaged a priest to chant sutras as a form of incantation to ensure her success.

22 Dispiriting things

1. *a trap ... daughters*: A barrier of woven sticks built across a river in autumn and winter to trap whitebait. The season for the plum-pink combination (scarlet over maroon) was from the eleventh to the second month. Owing to a pollution taboo, child-birth took place in a separate birthing hut set aside for the purpose. The tradition of scholarship often ran in families, but girls did not become scholars.

2. *a woman fails to visit him*: It was usual for a man to visit the woman, but under special circumstances the roles could be reversed.

3. *the medium ... Guardian Deity*: The transference of the spirit that is causing the illness is effected with the help of a Guardian Deity, who possesses the medium.

4. *an excursion ... as they wait*: Under the circumstances, he would probably be making a pilgrimage to a shrine or temple to pray for success. The former retainers have gathered to fawn, hoping for a windfall of gifts from him. The appointments were announced over a three-day period.

5. *a man you care for*: Failure to respond in kind to a love poem usually signified rejection.

6. *something ... painted on it*: It seems that the person is asked to decorate the fan, and paints something inappropriate or tasteless.

7. *'daytime nap'*: It is likely that this is a euphemism for midday sex (see also Section 104, note 2).

8. *'a single day of purificatory abstinence'*: The meaning is unclear, but some commentators believe that the last two sentences con-tinue the theme of sex.

24 Things people despise

1. *A crumbling earth wall*: Such a wall around a house is a sure sign that the family fortunes are in decline.

25 Infuriating things

1. *tuck . . . their knees*: The front of a man's hunting costume should be spread out when the wearer is seated.
2. *'Going to See the Governor'*: Unidentified, but presumably a children's song accompanied by certain gestures and expressions.
3. *fine reed blinds*: An elegant kind of blind, with a wide strip of decorative lintel cloth along its upper edge.
4. *if they sneeze*: Sneezing was considered to invite bad luck, and was countered with a quick spell or auspicious phrase. It is unclear what Sei was objecting to here – perhaps a person who considers that merely saying the words makes a loud sneeze socially forgivable.

26 Things that make your heart beat fast

Most of these examples depict situations that evoke a hazy, romantic atmosphere of dreamy expectancy.

28 Things that make you feel cheerful

1. *the female style*: A painting done in the softer, sometimes tinted, 'Japanese' style, as distinct from the bolder 'Chinese' style known as the 'male style'. Here it is presumably part of an illustrated tale.
2. *viewing expedition*: Going on expeditions to view festival processions, etc., was one of the favourite entertainments of women of quality. They remained largely invisible behind the carriage blinds, but it was the custom to hang their sleeves out in decorative display from beneath the blinds.
3. *dice-matching*: Probably a game in which several dice are rolled to try to achieve matching numbers.
4. *to rid . . . curse*: Although purification (*harae*) is essentially a Shinto practice, practitioners of the Chinese divinatory art of Yin-Yang sometimes performed it. The dry bed of the Kamo River was considered particularly suitable for this.
5. *some prayer of yours*: A request to the gods or Buddhist deities.

29 A palm-leaf carriage

The various types of ox-drawn carriages differed according to rank and use. See also Section [s22].

30 A priest who gives a sermon should be handsome

Sermons based on an exposition of the sutras were often held in conjunction with some pious occasion, such as the dedication of a newly copied sutra, and were frequently attended by members of the court. Ladies of rank listened from within their screened carriages, which were backed in close to the edge of the building. The event was often an excellent opportunity to socialize. The Lotus Discourses was the most famous and important sermon series.

1. *An ex-Chamberlain*: The four Chamberlains of the sixth rank held their post for six years, after which they were promoted to Chamberlains of the fifth rank and usually received a Provincial Governorship. See also Section 83, note 3. However, if there were no vacancies for fifth-rank Chamberlains, they were retired and were known as 'Chamberlain fifth-rankers' (*kurōdo no goi*), such as those depicted here.

31 While I was visiting Bodai Temple

1. *While I was visiting ... Salvation Lotus Discourses*: Bodai Temple was in the eastern hills of the capital. The Salvation Lotus Discourses were a set of Lotus Discourses specifically intended to provide listeners with merit that will draw them to salvation.
2. *You long ... other world*: Sei's poem is built on a play of words: *motomete* ('you desire of me' and 'I desire for myself'), *kakaru* ('the fall of dew' and 'this') and *okite* ('to lie [on the lotus]' and 'to leave behind').
3. *Sōchū*: In the Chinese story, Xiangzhong Laoren (Japanese *Sōchū*) became so absorbed in reading a Daoist text that he failed to return home, forgetting those who anxiously awaited him.

32 The place known as Koshirakawa (986.7.22)

The early date established by scholars for this event makes Sei's memory for detail all the more remarkable. Michitaka became Regent in 993, so she is writing after that. She would have attended as a young woman from a private household.

1. *the Koichijō Commander*: Fujiwara Naritoki, Commander of the Palace Guards at the Koichijō Palace. Shirakawa, in the eastern foothills near the city, was a popular place for the country villas of noblemen, but the exact location of Koshirakawa is not known.
2. *the first three rows*: See headnote to Section 30.
3. *Consultant Sukemasa*: Fujiwara Sukemasa. He would have been

43 at the time. (Not the same man as the Chief Equerry in Section 85.)

4. *above the threshold ... Next in line*: The nobles were seated at the outer edge of the Inner Chamber, with the senior courtiers, etc., seated behind them in the aisle, below the dividing threshold.

5. *Second of the Watch Sanekata and Adviser Chōmei*: Respectively Naritoki's nephew and son.

6. *Counsellor Yoshichika*: The Emperor's nephew, who was 31 at the time. Six days after this event, Emperor Kazan suddenly took the tonsure, and Yoshichika (whose power base was thereby destroyed) chose to follow him, tragically cutting off his career at its height. Sei's audience would have been aware of the poignancy of this scene.

7. *The Fujiwara Grand Counsellor*: Possibly Fujiwara Tamemitsu, Michitaka's grandfather.

8. *rather bent*: The lady's imperfections have betrayed Yoshichika's high expectations. This is apparently a witty reference to a poem (*Gosenshū* 1155): 'The tree may seem straight / but you will find bent branches. / So it is pointless / to blow back the hair that hides / and then lament the faults you see.'

9. *Well, well ... five thousand*: Yoshichika is aptly quoting from the *Lotus Sutra* (which was being expounded in the discourse from which the ladies were withdrawing), in which the Buddha gently rebuked the 5,000 who proudly believed that they were enlightened and thus did not need to hear him preach, and left early. Sei's response not only demonstrates that she has caught the reference, but implies that Yoshichika, by putting himself in the Buddha's place through his quote, is revealing his own arrogance.

10. *'the dew fell on him'*: A reference to a poem by Minamoto no Muneyuki (*Shinchokusenshū* (an imperially-ordered poetry collection, completed 1235) (820): 'The morning glory / shows its face only until / the white dew falls. / Better the flower's beauty / were never seen at all.' The implication of Sei's words is that Yoshichika's retirement is even more to be lamented than the brief flower.

33 In the seventh month, when the heat is dreadful

This section quickly shifts to an imaginary scene written in the mode of the popular romantic tales of the period. These were usually read aloud, while listeners looked at illustrations of the scenes; hence the strongly visual nature of this description.

1. *mat*: A mat was spread on the floor wherever it was needed, for sleeping, sitting, etc. *Tatami* mats were used as permanent floor covering later.

2. *a quite unseemly way*: The function of the standing curtain is to shield one from view, but the woman is apparently sleeping exposed to the eyes of the outer world because of the heat.

3. *a robe ... over her head*: This robe is being used as a cover for sleeping, functioning much like a quilt.

4. *Nearby is a gentleman*: This shift of focus is not made explicit, but it seems that this man is returning from a tryst with another woman. The Nōinbon text introduces him, as 'returning from who knows what tryst, through a thick dawn mist'.

5. *morning glory*: There is a debate over whether the word *asagao* refers to what we now call a morning glory. It may have been a generic term for flowers that fade as the day advances.

6. *'the ferns in the flax field'*: *Kokin rokujō* (2999): 'In the flax field / the ferns below the cherry flax / are moist with the dew / so I will stay with you till dawn / though our parents will know.' 'Dew' probably carries erotic overtones.

7. *attaching ... bush clover*: On such an attached spray, see next-morning letter (in Appendix 4).

34 Flowering trees

1. *close association with the hototogisu*: The *tachibana* (a kind of orange tree) is conventionally depicted in poetry as having a strong affinity with the *hototogisu*, which is drawn to perch in its branches.

2. *the weeping face ... pear*: A reference to the famous story of the tragic infatuation of the Chinese Emperor Xuanzong (685–762) with his beautiful concubine Yang Guifei, which led him to neglect affairs of state and thereby cause a mutiny during which she was killed for her part in his negligence. The quotation is from *The Song of Everlasting Sorrow*, where Bo Juyi describes the Emperor's messenger, sent to find her after her death, being greeted by her weeping spirit.

3. *being purple*: Purple is associated with nobility.

4. *that fabulous bird ... perch*: The phoenix-like bird of Chinese fable is said to live in paulownia trees.

5. *the melia ... the fifth month*: *Melia japonica* has small purple flowers clustered in racemes. The Sweet Flag Festival was one of the important palace festivals, and melia branches were used to dispel evil influences.

35   Ponds

This section continues the theme of Sections 10 to 17 of interesting place names. Here too, the primary focus is on places with poetic associations and/or punning or meaningful names.

1. *had drowned herself there*: According to legend, a girl in service to the Emperor when Nara was the capital drowned herself when his love for her waned. When he learned of her death, the Emperor visited the pond and had those accompanying him compose poems for the occasion. Sei quotes what was believed to be one of these (*Shūishū* 1289), by the famous poet Hitomaro (d. *c.* 710): 'I grieve to see / her hair tangled as in sleep / floating there now / like jewelled waterweed / on Sarusawa Pond.'

2. *because of the poem*: Kokin rokujō (3955): 'Though you drag out the burr reed / from the bed of "loving" Sayama Pond / it will not break – / but drawn from my lover's bed / ah I break.'

3. *'Oh do not cut the jewelled weeds'*: A popular song from the provinces that mentions this pond.

37   Trees that have no flowers

Botanically speaking, this is not a precise description. Sei's meaning is rather that these trees have no flowers worthy of attention.

1. *the clinging vine . . . the Provisional Festivals*: The name *yadorigi* (literally, a plant which depends on others) is a general term for parasitic plants, although the reference here seems to be to a specific plant. A *sakaki* branch is used in the *kagura*, such as the dances of the two important festivals of the Kamo and Iwashimizu Hachiman shrines.

2. *this palace . . . fifth month*: From a popular song. Cypress is above all associated with the construction of buildings, and the poetic conceit of its imitation of the sound of rain at the start of the rainy season derives from Chinese poetry.

3. *asuwa cypress . . . promise of a name*: This cypress grows in deep mountain country. Mitake is a sacred place in the rugged mountainous area in Nara prefecture behind Yoshino, and was a popular pilgrimage site at this period (see also Section 114, note 1). The name *asuwa hinoki* can be read as meaning 'tomorrow (it) will be a cypress'.

4. *are being dyed . . . the land of Izumo*: It was a different plant that was used to dye the deeper colours of the cloaks for these ranks, but the white colour of the white oak's leaves may have led to Sei's confusion. The end of this sentence appears to refer

to Hitomaro's poem (*Shūishū* 3): 'The paths are lost / upon the foot-dragging mountain / for snow has fallen / on every leaf and branch / of the white oaks.' Although it has no connection with the myth of the storm god Susanoo's journey to Izumo in the west, a late Heian text claimed the poem to be his work, which may have provoked the legend to which Sei seems to be referring.

5. *the food of the dead ... reddens the yuzuriha*: It was believed that the souls of the dead returned at noon of the last day of the year, and departed the next morning. Special food such as *mochi* (glutinous rice cakes) placed on the evergreen *yuzuriha* leaves was served on the second day of the new year, to ensure longevity. The poem referred to is *Rokkashū* (*c.* 1346) (27): 'On the day when autumn reddens / the wild *yuzuriha* of Kasuga, / that traveller's lodging, / on that day, / I may forget you.'

6. *The oak ... given its name*: The leaves of the *kashiwa* turn brown in autumn but remain on the tree, and the god was said to protect them from falling till spring. *Kashiwagi* (*Kashiwa* Tree) was the name given to certain ranks of officer in the Gate Watch, perhaps because such a tree once grew by their guardhouse.

38 Birds

1. *reaches the very heavens*: A reference to an ancient Chinese poem in the *Book of Songs* (*Shijing*, Japanese *Shikyō*): 'The crane stands in the winding stream, / his voice is heard in the heavens.'

2. *'and will not sleep alone'*: *Kokin rokujō* (4480): 'Though even the herons / of the woods of Yurugi / in Takashima / vie loudly for a roosting mate / and will not sleep alone ...' (I remain solitary).

3. *brush the frost from each other's wings*: *Kokin rokujō* (1475): 'Left to sleep alone / how sad the mandarin duck / who cannot have the frost / brushed from his freezing wing / by his adoring mate.'

4. *'nine-fold palace'*: Sei uses the poetic name because she is making a judgement based on poetic aesthetics, in which it would be pleasingly appropriate to have the elegant *uguisu*'s song associated with the palace precincts.

5. *wavery old voice*: The summer call of the *uguisu* changes to a long, repetitive, monotonous song that slowly trails away.

6. *after the Kamo Festival*: The day after the festival in the fourth month, the High Priestess returned in a procession that passed these temples near her residence at Murasakino. See also Section 205.

40 Insects

1. *The bagworm . . . for her*: A small insect that lives inside a sac made of tiny twigs and was thought to resemble a demon. It was believed to cry *'chichiyo! chichiyo!'*, seeming to be crying for its parent.
2. *used in people's names*: In earlier periods, and possibly also at this time, the word *hae* (fly) was sometimes used in the names of people of the lower classes.
3. *Summer insects*: A general term for the insects that fly into flames in summer, here probably referring to certain delicate moths and mayflies.

41 In the seventh month when the wind blows hard

The beginning of autumn, when typhoons blow in to replace the summer heat with coolness.

42 Unsuitable things

This section begins by listing scenes whose inappropriateness derives from the unsuitable combination of the poetically beautiful (snow, moonlight, etc.) with the unpoetically common.

1. *an auburn-coloured ox*: Oxen of this colour were especially prized by the aristocracy.
2. *crimson skirted trousers*: Worn by the more menial women serving in the palace and important houses, but inappropriate for commoners.
3. *on night patrol . . . beyond belief*: Perhaps because night patrol is a demeaning role for a person of his rank. See also Section 291.
4. *It looks terrible . . . Captain Yorisada*: It is unclear why this role is particularly unfortunate. It may have to do with the ugliness of the prescribed clothing. Minamoto Yorisada, who had a great reputation as a dashing ladies' man, held the position 992–998.

43 A lot of us are gathered in the Long Room

1. *The Long Room*: The gentlewomen are gathered in a temporary 'room', with much traffic of passing people close by.

44 No menial position could be finer

Palace groundswomen frequently played the important role of carrying messages. It had become a quite sought-after position by this period.

46   Secretary Controller Yukinari was standing by the lattice fence

Although Sei was married, one of the men she was closest to while at court was Fujiwara Yukinari. This section depicts the delicacy and intimacy possible in a relationship that seems to have remained a flirtation carried on through the customary intervening curtain or screen, until the final line.

1. *that old Chinese saying*: A free translation from a passage in the *Records of the Historian*.
2. *"inseparable as the willow of Tōtōmi"*: *Manyōshū* (1293): 'The willow tree that grows / on Tōtōmi's Ado River / where the thick hail falls – / cut it and it will come again / that Ado River willow tree.' There is a pun on *karu* ('cut' and 'part').
3. *'in all you do . . . correct an error'*: Sei and Yukinari here are cleverly capping each other's references to Chinese quotations: she restates a sentence from *Ikai* (*Advice*) by Fujiwara Morosuke, he refers to a line from a poem by Bo Juyi, and she responds by referring to a passage in the *Analects* of Confucius.
4. *show me your face*: A woman would show her face to a male only if he was her husband or a close family member.
5. *only the formal cloak*: I.e. they had removed the train-robe normally worn in formal court attire.
6. *Noritaka*: The younger brother of Sei's husband Norimitsu, and hence 'family'. He was at this time Chamberlain to the Emperor, so would naturally have been in the vicinity. The poor lighting would make his face hard to distinguish even when he showed himself.

47   Horses

1. *'wand paper-white'*: The mulberry bark paper referred to in this expression (*yū*) was used for the wand of paper ribbons used in Shinto ritual, to which Sei likens the horse's white mane and tail.

50   Carriage runners and escort guards

1. *Carriage runners*: Rankless men employed in various parts of the palace and great houses to do odd jobs, which included accompanying carriages. On escort guards, see Section 45.

52   Ox handlers

1. *Ox handlers*: Generally boys under the age of about thirteen, who tended the carriage oxen.

53   The nightly roll call

At 9.30 each night, those on duty would gather in the aisle of the
Privy Chamber, at the southern end of the Emperor's quarters, and
announce their name one by one for the Chamberlain to record. This
completed, they left in a body, and the Chamberlain proceeded down
the east aisle and recorded the names of the guards who were gathered
in the garden. Whenever the Empress and her ladies were residing in
the Emperor's palace, this took place very close to their quarters.

1.   *Masahiro*: Minamoto Masahiro, a Chamberlain 996–999, was
     a notorious bumbler.
2.   *the ledge where the Emperor's food is placed*: A shelf which held
     the Emperor's meal while it was waiting to be served. Masahiro
     mistook this for a similar shelf in another place, where the Cham-
     berlains placed their shoes. Shoes are ritually defiling objects.

54   It's digusting when a well-bred young man

1.   *someone inconsequential, or a young girl*: The nuance of 'some-
     one inconsequential' (*hashitamono*) is unclear, but the suggestion
     seems to be that in both these cases there can be no suspicion
     that the man is calling on her as a lover.

56   Little children

1.   *incense from their clothes*: Robes were customarily scented by
     being draped over a lighted incense burner.

57   The central gate of a grand house

We are looking in from the street through the outer gate of one of the
great houses, at the scene in the courtyard where high-ranking guests
have come visiting. The central gate is an entry midway along the
east and west galleries of the house. The accompanying courtiers are
dressed in formal wear, which included carrying a baton, a thin flat
length of white wood or ivory.

58   Waterfalls

1.   *Furu Falls ... paid a visit there*: The falls are behind Isogami
     Shrine in Tenri. There is no record of a Cloistered Emperor (one
     who has retired and taken the tonsure) visiting them. *Kokinshū*
     refers to a visit by Emperor Kōkō (reigned 884–887), which is
     probably Sei's source.
2.   *Nachi Falls ... in Kumano*: The falls, in the Kumano area of

present-day Wakayama prefecture, were and are an important focus of worship in the great Kumano pilgrimage.

3.   *thunder*: *Todoroki* literally means 'thundering'.

59   Rivers

1.   *Asuka River . . . the poem says*: The river is in the Yoshino area. The poem is *Kokinshū* (933): 'What in this world of ours / is sure and unchanging? / In Asuka River / the deeps of yesterday today / shift to running shallows.'

2.   *Mimito River . . . quick ear caught*: *Mimito* literally means 'sharp-eared'. Ki no Tsurayuki in *Kokin rokujō* (1561): 'Mimito River / that flows by the great stone walls / of towering Ōmiya, / has caught with its quick ears / the echo of your voice, my love.'

3.   *what sort of 'name' it had*: *Natori* means 'name-taking', or by extension, 'of famous name'.

4.   *poem of Narihira's . . . Weaving Maid*: Ariwara Narihira's poem (*Kokinshū* 418) is: 'Hunting all the day, / at Heaven's River plain / I have arrived. / And so let me beg shelter / from the Heavenly Weaving Maid.' (See Tanabata Festival in Appendix 4.)

62   Villages

These village names are almost all chosen for their unusual literal meanings, most of which are associated with the image of a love affair.

1.   *his wife stolen . . . someone else's*: *Tsumatori* literally means 'wife-taking'.

63   Plants

While this section occasionally mentions flowers, its focus is on the plants themselves. The following section lists plants whose main interest is their flowers. Many of the names given are approximate translations only, and where the identity of the plant is unclear, the Japanese name is preserved.

1.   *an interesting name*: *Omodaka* literally means 'lifted face'.

2.   *Rootless plants . . . cliff edge*: *Ayafugusa*, which is thought to denote rootless plants, literally means 'precarious plants'. The *itsumade* creeper is depicted in poetry as growing on earth walls, which crumble easily, unlike plastered walls. Its name, which literally means 'until when?', is poetically associated with the uncertainties of love.

3.   *The kotonashi plant . . . wayside grasses*: *Kotonashi* literally means 'succeed in doing something'; the plant is unidentified.

Shinobu means 'to suffer in silence'. 'Wayside grass' is a highly evocative poetic expression.

4. *when other plants . . . Chinese poem*: The lotus blooms in mid-summer, when other flowers are rare in Japan. As with many of the plants mentioned in this section, the poetic reference is a poem in *Wakan rōeishū*, by Xu Hun (791–854?): 'Emerald fans part the mist, in dawn's clear breeze. / On the water float crimson cloaks, draped in autumn's dews.'

5. *its colour fades so easily*: Dye made from the dew plant is quick to fade.

64   Flowering plants

1. *the kamatsuka . . . 'wild geese arriving'*: *Kamatsuka* literally means 'sickle handle', and the word seems to have applied to various flowers. The flower whose Chinese characters express the meaning 'wild geese arriving' is a kind of amaranth, but does not fit the description here.

2. *the stag seeks it out*: Ki no Tsurayuki (*Gosenshū* 306): 'Like the dew that lies / on Ono's autumn bush clover / where the stag seeks it out / I too must disappear / and return to nothing.'

3. *speak of the two together*: The names for moonflower (*yūgao*, 'evening face') and morning glory (*asagao*, 'morning face') form a natural pair.

4. *not to include plume grass here*: *Susuki*, a kind of low pampas grass commonly seen in open plains and along riverbanks, is considered the quintessential autumn grass. Sei seems to have added this passage after her work was first circulated.

66   Topics of poetry

Poems for public occasions, such as poetry competitions, were generally composed on a pre-determined topic. Sei does not name any of the more common topics, such as the moon, cherry blossoms, love, etc.

67   Disturbing things

1. *embarked on the twelve-year mountain retreat*: When a monk was ordained at the great temple of Enryakuji on Mt Hiei, he was forbidden to leave the mountain for twelve years.

70   A man comes calling

1. *till the very axe rots*: A reference to the Chinese legend of Wang Zhi, who went into the mountains to cut wood, and came upon

two immortals playing a game of *go*. He was held entranced by the sight until he suddenly returned to earthly time and discovered he had stood so long that the handle of his axe had rotted away.

2. *'stays seething deep below'*: *Kokin rokujō* (2648): 'Greater the feeling / that in the waters of the heart / stays seething deep below / and never rises into words / than that which can be spoken.'

72   Our apartments in the Long Room

Since the temporary 'rooms' were merely screened-off parts of the aisle, at night male visitors could be heard calling on their lovers.

1. *children ... make a noise*: Presumably, close proximity to the Empress's quarters would inhibit their behaviour.

2. *quite unexpected men hovering outside*: The scene has shifted to a visit by a number of gentlemen to the ladies' quarters.

3. *a brightly-coloured standing curtain ... gaping at the back*: The ladies inside the room have arranged their flowing hems for display outside the standing curtain. The description of the men's clothing is obscure, but seems to be a style of cloak.

4. *Or again ... he standing without*: The lintel cloth at the top of the blind, and the standing curtain behind which she sits, both restrict their view of each other, but a small gap allows them to see each other dimly through the blind itself. She is sitting a step above where he stands. The two scenes in this paragraph are such as might be found in a romantic tale.

5. *Provisional Festival*: The Provisional Kamo Festival.

6. *'Oh let us pluck the rice flowers'*: An old folk song which had become a court song: 'Oh let us pluck the rice flowers from the fallow fields / and carry them to the palace and present them to our lord.' It was traditionally sung as the singers and musicians emerged.

7. *"Why do you hasten thus to relinquish this night"*: This is evidently a quote, but its origins are unknown. There is probably a pun on *yo* ('night' and 'this world').

73   When Her Majesty was in residence (997, summer)

This episode probably took place when Teishi had just moved to her temporary quarters in the Office of the Empress's Household. Her power had been eclipsed, and the circumstances were in fact dismal, but Sei paints a rosy picture.

1. *that Chinese poem about the voice of autumn*: The men were

chanting, as they made their way back, a poem by Minamoto Fusaakira (d. 939): 'The pond is chill, the last of summer's heat is gone / and high in the pines the wind carries the sound of autumn.'

75 Things that look enjoyable

1. *The hare-wand priest*: This seems to have been a priest who walked about the town with hare-wands offering celebratory words on the festival day.
2. *The conductor . . . in the kagura procession*: At the end of each piece, the conductor performs a dance. The reference to a banner is obscure.

76 The day after the Litany of Buddha Names (994?)

During this event, special screens depicting scenes from hell were placed in the Seiryōden. Sei was probably still new to the court at the time when this scene took place.

1. *'The sound . . . would not speak'*: From Bo Juyi's 'Song of the *Pipa*'. The line depicts a moment when the poet hears across the water the sound of a mysterious *pipa* (*biwa*), and longs to learn the player's name.

77 When Secretary Captain Tadanobu (early 995)

This section concerns another man to whom Sei was close, Fujiwara Tadanobu. Near the end we meet Tachibana Norimitsu, who is generally believed to have been her husband before she came to court, though by now the relationship is merely that of brother and sister.

1. *as part of an imperial abstinence*: It was the custom for senior courtiers to join the Emperor's observance of an abstinence by secluding themselves in the Privy Chamber.
2. *a writing game*: This seems to have involved supplying the missing parts of Chinese characters.
3. *the line from Bo Juyi*: From 'Alone at Night in a Grass-thatched Hut beneath Lu Shan Mountain', sent to a friend in the capital: 'You are there in the flowering capital, beneath the Council Chamber's brocade curtains / while I sit on a rainy night in my grass-thatched hut beneath Lu Shan Mountain.' Sei knows the poem, but her dilemma is that it would be unladylike to respond in Chinese. Furthermore, simply to supply the next line would be a poor response. Her solution is to turn the second line of Bo's poem to her own purposes by creating the final two lines of a new poem in Japanese that alludes to Tadanobu's failure to call on her (written with charcoal, to reinforce the suggestion of

a simple life in a bare hut). This in turn means the recipient should supply the first three lines, which Tadanobu and his friends find they cannot do.

4. *the Minamoto Captain*: Minamoto Nobukata.

5. *"Jewelled Palace"*: A phrase derived from the Chinese; the immediate reference is probably *Shūishū* (110): 'Today when I look / I find no jewelled palace / but see here only / this lowly hut / thatched with iris leaves.'

6. *in no position to appreciate these poetic refinements*: Sections 79 and 126 also demonstrate Norimitsu's lack of appreciation for poetry.

78 The following year, towards the end of the second month (996.2)

Teishi's brothers Korechika and Takaie had been disgraced and exiled the month before the events of this section, and she and her gentlewomen were in mourning for her father Michitaka, whose recent death had brought about her eclipse at court. All this is conspicuously absent from Sei's account.

1. *the Mumetsubo*: Also called Gyōkasha, where Teishi had been residing. 'Mumetsubo' literally means 'plum-tree tub', a name derived from the flowering plums that grew on either side of the front steps.

2. *a directional taboo this evening*: Tadanobu had learned that south was a 'blocked direction' that evening, so he left after midnight and came to the capital from the west.

3. *that is where I spent the night*: Although the Mistress of Imperial Wardrobe normally resided in another building, she may have moved to the Mumetsubo when Teishi left.

4. *hair not even my own*: Sei seems to have worn a hair insert.

5. *the two heroes ... the Emperor's daughter*: Suzushi and Nakatada were rivals for the hand of the Emperor's daughter in *The Tale of the Hollow Tree*. Nakatada and his mother had earlier fallen on hard times and were forced to live in the forest, taking shelter in a hollow tree vacated by bears who were impressed with his filial piety. Nakatada's skills on the *kin* were literally magical, but there is one scene in which a heavenly maiden appears and dances when Suzushi plays the *kin* (see also Section 81 and note 2). It is Nakatada, however, who wins the daughter.

6. *the tiles ... the city's western gate*: Saishō quotes from Bo Juyi's 'A palace stands high upon Mt Li', lamenting the desolation of the palace (which was to the west of the Chinese capital):

'the walls are cloaked in moss, and the tiles pine-smothered'.
Tadanobu continues the quotation.

79   When one's returned home on a visit

1. *Captain Consultant*: Probably Tadanobu, who attained this dual
    position in 997.
2. *The silent seaweed ... these hidden depths*: The poem cleverly
    explains the meaning behind the piece of seaweed by an elaborate
    series of sea-related images and puns (*soko* means both 'the place
    where she is' and 'depths [of the sea]', *me kuwase* means both
    'make you eat seaweed' and 'send a silent message with the eyes').
3. *Brother and Sister Hills ... used to be*: Sister (*imo*) and Brother
    (*se*) Hills are mountains in Yamato province, and the Yoshino
    River flows between them. If they crumble, the river (which in
    the poem becomes the love that once flowed between them)
    would be buried and disappear. There is a pun in *kawa* ('river'
    and 'he is the one'). Her poem also refers to one in *Kokinshū*.
4. *Deputy Governor of Tōtōmi*: A promotion to the fifth rank.
    Tōtōmi was a province close to the capital, and thus one of the
    more prestigious Provincial Governorships.

81   After our visit to the Guard Office (997)

This section seems to follow on from Section 73. It contains a tangle
of references and possible interpretations, and its point remains somewhat obscure.

1. *the writer*: One of the gentlewomen had written relaying Her
    Majesty's official message and added her private message.
2. *"a heavenly maiden hovering" ... Nakatada's reputation*: Sei
    quotes from the scene in *The Tale of the Hollow Tree* in which
    a heavenly maiden descends to dance when Suzushi plays the
    kin, already mentioned in Section 78. Teishi's reply probably
    implies Nakatada is portrayed in this scene as inferior to Suzushi.

82   Once when Her Majesty was in residence
(late 998–999.1)

A woman whom everyone at first takes for a beggar nun arrives and
proceeds to intrigue the gentlewomen with her clever antics. From her
bawdy songs and general demeanour, they slowly realize that she is in
fact a wily itinerant entertainer.

1. *Continuous Sutra Reading*: A type of recitation that continued
    without pause day and night, generally performed by a group of
    twelve monks who took turns at each change of watch.

2.   *distribution of the offerings*: The offerings of food made at the
      Buddhist altar were generally handed out after the ceremony.

3.   *'Who oh who ... quite a name'*: Hitachi no Suke is literally
      the Governor of Hitachi Province'. 'Man Mountain' (Otoko-
      yama) is a mountain south of the capital, that was famous for
      its autumn colours. The word 'colour' (*iro*) also signifies the
      erotic, so the song produces the double entendre that the man/
      his penis (the mountain) is famous for erotic adventures (autumn
      colours).

4.   *Give her this gown*: Clothing was the usual form of gift or
      payment at this time.

5.   *drape the gown ... a dance*: She is cheekily imitating the courtly
      ritual dance of gratitude performed on receiving an official gift
      of clothing.

6.   *Kannon of White Mountain*: Hakusan (White Mountain) is a
      sacred mountain in present-day Ishiyama prefecture (Koshi),
      famed for its perpetual snow, on whose summit is an important
      shrine to Kannon, the Bodhisattva of Mercy.

7.   *Kōkiden and Kyōgokudono*: Respectively, the Empress's quar-
      ters, inhabited by Teishi's rival Shōshi, and the home of the
      Minister of the Left, Michinaga at this time.

8.   *'Alas ... things are given'*: Hitachi no Suke's poem is boringly
      straightforward, relying only on a hackneyed pun on *ama* ('nun'
      and 'fisher girl').

9.   *When I went ... this day*: On the first Day of the Hare, when
      it was traditional to send a gift of decorative hare-wands or
      hare-mallets, the Kamo High Priestess has devised the conceit of
      dressing the tiny hare-mallets to look like large hare-wands, and
      decorating them with sprigs of mountain plants to suggest that
      they have come fresh from the scene depicted in her poem.

10.   *Koshi's famous snowy mountain*: See note 6 above.

11.   *the night of the thirteenth*: The translation of the date (13th)
      follows the Nōinbon version, which accords better with the
      story's chronology.

12.   *that wandering performer's ... his hat*: This rather confusing
      description appears to refer to a comic act by an itinerant per-
      former 'priest' that is based on a well-known tale: the Buddha,
      who is performing austerities on Snow Mountain, throws himself
      from the mountain in exchange for receiving from a demon the
      second half of the teaching that will enlighten him. The connec-
      tion with the lid lies in a pun on *mi* ('body' and 'the bowl section
      of a container').

13. *The fellow*: The Sankanbon text has 'woman' at this point. I follow the Nōinbon text.

83 Splendid things

1. *Ornamental swords. Tinted Buddhist images*: These swords, with scabbards richly decorated with gold and silver, lacquerwork, etc., were only worn on special occasions by noblemen above the fifth rank. The Buddhist images were probably relief carvings with details accented with colours.

2. *great ministerial banquets*: Such banquets traditionally received a gift of dried chestnuts and milk curds from the Emperor, which it was the sixth-ranking Chamberlains' role to present on his behalf.

3. *such a shame . . . among the Provincial Governors*: Sei's relishing of the splendid robes and special colour that were a Chamberlain's prerogative cause her to regret the fact that Chamberlains often preferred to dress in more usual clothing. Although the position of Chamberlain was nominally for six years, it was commonly held for only three or four. See also Section 30, note 1.

4. *as their tutor*: Besides being employed as official scribes, scholars from the university were tutors in the Chinese classics to the sons of great families as well as imperial princes and Emperors.

5. *Kasuga Shrine*: This important shrine in Nara was the tutelary shrine of the Fujiwara family.

6. *the violet in his clothes*: The Chamberlain wore violet gathered trousers on night watch.

84 Things of elegant beauty

1. *A three-layer fan*: The usual ('single layer') fan consisted of 8 ribs. The three-layer had 24, and the extra-thick five-layer had 40.

2. *Long stems of sweet flag . . . cypress-bark roof*: As part of the Sweet Flag Festival.

3. *The Sweet Flag Chamberlains . . . Sweet Flag Festival*: These women delivered the gifts of festive herbal balls for the festival. See also Section 205 and note 4.

4. *the red abstinence cords of the First Fruits Festival*: Worn on the shoulders of participants in the rites of the festival.

5. *The young gentlemen . . . the Lesser Abstinence*: These young men, who officiated in the religious ceremonies, wore special Lesser Abstinence (ritual purificatory abstinence for Shinto festivals, etc.) robes, white with a design in mountain indigo dye.

85   When Her Majesty provided the Gosechi dancers (993)

This event seems to have occurred early in Sei's career at court, during the First Fruits Festival and its accompanying four-day Gosechi Festival. Occasionally the Gosechi dancers were chosen from one of the palace households, as here; their attendants were usually no more than eight.

1.   *the Day of the Dragon*: The final day of the Gosechi Festival, when the dancers performed the Dance of the Heavenly Maidens.
2.   *red cords*: These Gosechi robes with their red cords are a variant of the Lesser Abstinence robes in Section 84. The men would have been wearing clothes of the same sort.
3.   *serving ladies*: Ladies-in-waiting whose role was to provide general background support for the dancers.
4.   '*A wintry indifference . . . its icy knot*': This laments Kohyōe's indifference to him, through a play on the image of the special indigo-dye robes (*yamaai* meaning both 'mountain well' and 'mountain indigo'), and on *himo* ('cord' and 'ice').
5.   *sat there, saying nothing*: It was common for a poem to be composed by others on someone's behalf, if the composition proved difficult.
6.   '*The cord's knot . . . in the hair*': Sei's poem picks up Sanekata's punning imagery of ice (loosening/melting) and the ceremonial cord, here extended to the ceremonial garland of creeping fern (*hikage*, which also means 'sunlight') that the young gentlemen wear for this occasion.
7.   *had to be carried out*: It was apparently common for some of the young girls to succumb to stress and exhaustion of the occasion.

86   Another elegant sight

1.   *narrow-bladed sword . . . cord attached*: The sword and special ribbon are both accoutrements of formal ceremonial occasions. This section seems most properly to belong with Section 84.

87   At the time of the Gosechi Festival

An apparent mixture of general reminiscence on this yearly event and further recollections of the specific occasion described in Section 85.

1.   *the groundswomen . . . the arched bridgeway*: The groundswomen were employed on this occasion to light the way for the dancers. The bridgeway connected the Senyōden with the Jōneiden, where the dancers' temporary retiring rooms were set up.

2. *'messengers in waves come swelling our rank'*: Probably a cel-
    ebratory song, a version of one now preserved in the *Ryōjin
    hishō* collection (*c.* 1169), which describes the courtiers' continu-
    ous rising in rank. This scene takes place after the Emperor's
    private viewing of the dancers on the Day of the Tiger.
3. *on the first night*: A ceremony in which the Emperor was given
    his first preview of the dancers, at the Jōneiden.
4. *The sight . . . most enchanting*: The young dancers would have
    dozed off from the exhaustion of the occasion.

88   One day His Majesty brought along a biwa

It was common to give a name to precious objects such as swords or
musical instruments. The two names of importance in this section are
Mumyō ('Nameless') and *Inakaeji* ('Irreplaceable', literally 'No I Will
Not Replace It').

1. *The Secretary Captain . . . Giyōden's top drawer*: The Secretary
    Captain is probably Tadanobu. The Giyōden was the building
    in which the imperial treasures, including instruments, were
    housed. The top drawer would have held the most precious of
    these.

89   I remember an occasion before the blinds of
Her Majesty's apartment

1. *The maiden who 'half hides her face' . . . his feelings on 'parting'*:
    Sei refers to 'The Song of the *Pipa*' by Bo Juyi, which describes
    a girl he met on a boat, who 'takes up her *biwa* and half hides
    her face'. Teishi's reply is generally considered to refer to a
    subsequent scene, in which the poet laments having to part from
    the maiden – perhaps with the implication that since Sei's com-
    parison had placed herself in the male role, she should identify
    with the departing senior courtiers.

90   Infuriating things

1. *the Southern Residence*: A detached palace, the residence of
    Teishi's father Michitaka.
2. *there you have to stop*: A woman would not emerge from behind
    the blinds if a man was present.
3. *retrieve it*: See also Section [s27] and headnote.

93   Regrettable things

1. *women or men*: The Sankanbon text incongruously adds priests
    to this company. I follow Nōinbon here.

94   At the time of the Abstinence and Prayer of the fifth month (998.5)

This section illustrates the important role played by both occasional and formal poetry composition in the court. The surprising nervousness that Sei reveals stemmed in part from the fact that her father Kiyohara Motosuke and her family in general were known for their poetic talent.

1. *the Abstinence and Prayer*: A period set aside in the first, fifth and ninth months for strict observation of the Buddhist injunctions concerning fasting and prayer.

2. *that place called ... but not as pleasant*: The bridge that the Tanabata lovers must cross is Kasasagi, which sounds not dissimilar to the name Sei is obliquely referring to, Matsugasaki (Pine Point). Its unpleasantness presumably stems from the alternative meaning, 'Waiting Point', suggesting by association that the lovers would have to wait rather than be reunited there.

3. *cicadas*: Since the cicada (*higurashi*) does not begin to sing until summer (and its song is quite unlike that of the *hototogisu*), we should assume that this is a witty literary reference. One suggestion is that it is a complex pun whereby '*matsu*' in the place name (note 2 above) is associated with a well-known poem of waiting which is based around a pun involving the word '*higurashi*'.

4. *the Riding Ground*: One of two areas at the northern verge of the city which were devoted to riding practice and associated activities. The event the ladies witnessed was part of a series of ceremonial archery competitions held over a number of days.

5. *delightfully reminiscent ... Lord Akinobu*: They were travelling the same road along which the Kamo Festival procession moved. This house, being beyond the city limits, would have been the second or country residence of Teishi's uncle, Lord Akinobu.

6. *something called 'rice heads' ... some unfamiliar machine that revolved*: The word for rice plant (*ine*) is not the same as the word used for rice as a food, so the ladies are being introduced to something that may in fact be new to them. What they were probably shown was a sheaf of rice heads from last year's harvest, perhaps an unfamiliar sight to court ladies, although Sei may well be elegantly feigning her ignorance of rustic matters. The 'unfamiliar machine' was probably a device for milling the rice.

7. *used to the face-down pose*: Akinobu seems to be teasing them about their role of service at court, where they would be frequently on their knees bowing low.

8. *the Ichijō mansion ... Adviser Kiminobu*: The mansion, by the north-east corner of the imperial palace grounds, was at this time the home of Fujiwara Tamemitsu. Kiminobu was his sixth son.
9. *the Tsuchi Gate*: The north-east gate of the palace compound.
10. *my lacquered cap*: This cap was worn with everyday wear, and was inappropriate dress for the palace.
11. *Three Worms Night*: A belief going back to Taoism, that at a certain conjunction in the calendar (the coincidence of the Elder Metal with the Monkey sign, or *kōshin*) the three worms that dwell in the body and know our secret sins will ascend to heaven and reveal them while we sleep, thereby shortening our life. To prevent this, people spent the night keeping themselves awake with entertainments such as games and poetry competitions.

95 It was while we were in the Office of the Empress's Household

1. *I'm simply ... the spirit of the moonlight*: Behind this statement lie a number of possible poetic references. The most apt is from Bo Juyi's 'Song of the *Pipa*', where the listeners who have been listening to the *pipa* 'are left silent, simply gazing / into the river and the whiteness of the autumn moon'.

96 There was a large and distinguished gathering

1. *there can be no other Law ... even the lowest*: The teasing name refers to the *Lotus Sutra*'s claim for itself (in the 'Expedient Devices' (*Hōben*) chapter) that 'there is but one vehicle of the Law, there are not two or three'. Sei's response cleverly refers to current Buddhist teaching, which divided rebirth in Paradise into nine ranks; she says that, in the case of Her Majesty, she will gladly accept even the lowest rank if it will allow her to enter the exalted presence.

97 The Counsellor paid a visit

1. *The Counsellor*: Teishi's brother Takaie.
2. *the ribs of a jellyfish*: Sei's point is that if no one has ever seen the ribs, they must be non-existent.

98 One wet day during the endless rains

1. *Aide of Ceremonials Nobutsune*: Probably Fujiwara Nobutsune, who was given this post in 998.
2. *let's say it's your footman*: There is much uncertainty over the meaning of Sei's reply, translated freely here. It seems to have

involved a no-longer-understood pun, to do with wiping the feet.

3. *Enutaki . . . when you look*: 'Enutaki' is an odd name, variously interpretable as 'dog-hugger' or 'dog's vomit', and her witty reply involves a pun that turns the play on names back on to Tokikara, which can be interpreted to mean 'depending on the time'. (The Empress in question was consort to the previous Emperor, Murakami.)

99 There could be no more splendid celebrations conceivable (995.2)

Sei records in vivid detail a scene of Teishi's family in the final moments of its glory, as two months later her father Regent Michitaka died suddenly. Present are Michitaka and his wife Kishi, his sons (in descending order: Yamanoi, Korechika, Takaie and Chikayori), his second daughter Genshi (the Shigeisa), who had just become consort to the Crown Prince (she was 15 at the time) and a grandson. See also Section 259, note 7.

1. *they hadn't yet met in person*: I.e. in Genshi's new exalted capacity as the Crown Prince's consort. This is the official first encounter, at which the other members of their family are also present.

2. *Plum-pink . . . awful*: Teishi's primary concern is to do with the prescribed colour combinations for the time of year.

3. *in the style of a gentlewoman*: Although she was in the presence of her own children, on this formal occasion Kishi was ranked below them in station, and hence dressed with suitable humility.

4. *the washing of hands*: Since it was morning, the usual morning ablutions took place. (The visit began at night and extended into the evening of this day.)

5. *via the Senyōden . . . the Chinese roof section*: The Senyōden and Jōganden lay between the Empress's present residence and the Shigeisa's residence, from which her water was brought; all were connected by galleries. The central part of the gallery was covered by a deep-eaved roof which turned up in the Chinese style.

6. *put up Her Majesty's hair*: For the meal.

7. *draped them on the Lieutenant's shoulder*: It was customary to accept gifts of clothing by putting them on one's shoulder. See also Section 82, note 5.

8. *rolling out the mat*: When the Emperor paid a visit on foot, a long woven mat was placed on the ground for him to walk on.

9. *retired to the curtained dais*: The Emperor's apparently high-

handed interruption of this important gathering to assert his sexual prerogatives was probably interpreted as auspicious by the family, since it was a reassuring demonstration of Teishi's position as imperial favourite.

10. *the Director of the Court Repository*: Probably Michitaka's fifth son, Yorichika, who took this position in 1005 (which provides a possible date for the writing of this present section).

11. *the temporary bridgeway*: A bridge between buildings had evidently been set up for the occasion.

100   A branch of plum from which the blossoms had fallen

1. *What do you make ... already scattered*: Sei is being invited to respond poetically on the subject of the plum branch. Her response is the Japanese rendering of a quotation from a Chinese poem by Ōe no Koretoki (888–963): 'The flowers have already scattered from the plums of Dayu Ridge. / Who now inquires after their powdered faces?'

101   Around the end of the second month

1. *Consultant Kintō*: Fujiwara Kintō (966–1041) was considered the finest poet of his day.

2. *a piece of notepaper ... touch of spring*: Notepaper kept tucked into the breast of one's clothes, for jotting down notes; hence not formal paper of the sort usually used for letters, and signifying that the message was a passing thought. Rhythm and diction make it clear that these 'lines' are the closing section of a poem. There is a hidden reference to a poem by Bo Juyi: 'At the third hour a great snow comes tumbling from chilly clouds. / The second month brings a tiny touch of spring to the mountains.' Sei's response echoes elements of the first of these lines, her trembling calligraphy echoing the theme of coldness.

3. *Who is there to hear it*: As Section 100 shows, an ostensibly private response would generally be shared around and savoured if others were present.

4. *Captain of the Left Gate Watch*: Fujiwara Sanenari became Captain of the Left Gate Watch in 1009, which means that this section was written about ten years after the event.

102   Things with far to go

1. *the long cord of a hanpi jacket*: This jacket was worn with a long, thick cord over three metres in length around the waist, which required considerable work to twist and paste.

103   Masahiro is a great laughing-stock

1.   *tossing his beans in the oven like this*: This is probably a muddled reference to a Chinese saying (roughly, 'jumping up and down like beanskins in an oven') expressing impatient haste.

2.   *"your bodily appendages"*: This passage is obscure. The point appears to be that instead of using the more usual word for 'body' this person, perhaps hoping to sound more learned and impressive, used the Buddhist term *gotai*, which in fact refers to the five appendages (head, arms and legs) of the body. It may also be that the passage has become garbled, and these are in fact the words of someone reporting Masahiro's own mistake.

3.   *terra firma literally trembled at his tread*: Sei seems to be mocking him with a Masahiro-like absurdly grandiose Sinified phrase.

104   Things that are distressing to see

1.   *A priest ... stuck on his forehead*: Presumably Sei's objection is to the incongruity of a Buddhist priest donning the little hat of the Yin-Yang master in order to perform a Yin-Yang ceremony.

2.   *I do hate ... sprouting from his face*: The term 'daytime nap' (*hirune*) may have had connotations of lovemaking, but it seems that Sei's primary objection is to the way these people look, not to their behaviour.

105   Things that are hard to say

1.   *It's very difficult ... some high-ranking person's words*: Presumably because particular care must be taken to relay the words correctly, and to use the appropriate honorific language.

106   Barrier gates

These gates were set up at the boundaries of provinces, etc., to levy tolls and generally keep a check on travellers. Their names frequently appeared in poems, in which certain landmarks and place names carried specific poetic associations, often related more to the name than the actual characteristics of the place. This list moves progressively from west (close to the capital) to east.

As well as poetic associations, Sei chooses names for the interest of their literal meaning, e.g., *Tadakoe*: 'crossing at full tilt'; *Habakari*: 'fearfully'; *Yokohashiri*: 'running sideways'; *Kiyomi*: 'pure seeing'; *Mirume*: 'seaweed', also 'the seeing eye'.

1.   *Yomoyomo ... thought better of*: Yomoyomo is similar to a word meaning 'definitely not'.

107   Forests

1. *Iwase ... Tachikiki*: Meaning both 'stony rapids' and 'to make speak' and 'standing and overhearing', respectively. This section is a variation on 193.

109   Around the end of the fourth month

1. *boats loaded with reeds ... Takase Pool*: The reeds were being harvested to be used in weaving mats. The quote is from an old song accompanying a *kagura* dance, included in *Kokin rokujō* (3810): 'On this reed pillow – / made of the severed reeds / cut from Takase Pool / though severed they may be / – yet will I place my trust.' Takase was not far from the Yodo Crossing.

2. *gathering sweet flag*: For use in the Sweet Flag Festival.

110   Common things that suddenly sound special

1. *An ox cart on the first day of the year*: Presumably because it heralded the traditional visits people paid each other on this day.

114   Moving things

1. *Mitake austerities:* A sacred place where rigorous austerities were undertaken by practitioners of the mountain ascetic (*yamabushi*) austerities. See also Section 37, note 3.

2. *Nobutaka*: Fujiwara Nobutaka was the husband of Murasaki Shikibu, author of *The Tale of Genji*.

3. *dressed in deep black*: Mourning clothes. The deeper the shade, the closer the relation to the person who had died.

4. *preventing it*: See also Section [S25] and headnote.

115   It's delightful to be on retreat

Pilgrimages to temples were an important aspect of court life, and frequently involved a 'retreat' at the temple, of varying duration. Despite the ostensibly religious purpose, we learn here how the sense of adventure and occasion could also make it an enjoyable event. This section shifts between generalized description and personal reminiscence. Although the Sankanbon text gives the temple as Kiyomizu, other texts name it as Hase Temple. See also Sections 211 and [S27].

1. *little waist-robes*: Literally 'wearing only waist sashes'. The meaning is unclear, but may refer to short robes tied simply at the waist, which were the most abbreviated form of monks' clothing and could be half stripped to hang from the waist sash.

2.   *the four-word verses of the Kusha Sutra*: This sutra was divided into 600 'verses' (*ge* or *zu*) of 4 words each, to aid in recitation.

3.   *the sacred image*: The image (a large, gilded sculpture) enshrined at both Kiyomizu and Hase Temples is Kannon bodhisattva.

4.   *a monk approaches . . . star anise leaves*: The reference is unclear. It may be that the priest is offering the incense water in a pot with a sprig of the highly-scented star anise in it.

5.   *a conch horn*: The conch shell, fashioned into a horn, was blown to announce the hours in the temple.

6.   *over the lattice of the inner sanctum*: Possibly to shield their rooms from the inner sanctum, since they have not yet presented their prayers.

7.   *the prayer gong*: A flat, round metal gong that hangs at the entrance of the worshipping hall is beaten briefly before prayers are offered.

117   Miserable-looking things

1.   *its rain cover*: A piece of straw matting, also put on a carriage when the occupant was in mourning.

118   Things that look stiflingly hot

1.   *The hunting costume . . . escort guard*: Perhaps because he has to stand guard for long periods in blazing sun.

2.   *A Lieutenant . . . the imperial games*: He must sit in formal posture before the games (archery, etc.) for many hours in the hot sun.

119   Embarrassing things

Specifically, people or situations that embarrass by exposing what is normally private or hidden.

1.   *The heart of a man*: The suggestion is that a man can see into a woman's heart, though he remains inscrutable to her.

2.   *A night-priest*: A priest employed to stay up all night to perform prayers and incantations for a household. The embarrassment may have to do with the fact that, being next door, he overhears things said (and done) when people assume he is napping (see also Section 127).

121   Prayers and incantations

1.   *the protection mantras*: Mantras performed at the beginning of the Shingon and Tendai sects' Tantric ceremonies to invoke protection for the priest himself. Evidently the invocations used

in the older Nara temples differed in style from those of the capital.

122   Awkward and embarrassing things (995.10.21)

1. *On the way back*: This recollection of a moving moment Sei witnessed during an imperial procession to Iwashimizu Hachiman Shrine is treated as a separate section by some editors.
2. *the viewing stand*: An elaborate stand specially erected for the viewing of a procession.

123   The Regent was to emerge (994?)

Michitaka has paid a formal visit to the Emperor in the Seiryōden, where Teishi also happens to be staying, and she and her gentlewomen are there to welcome him as he emerges triumphantly, together with other members of his family. (See also Section 99.) The brief appearance of his rival (and brother) Michinaga, who was soon to oust his family from power, registers here only as a small, uneasy moment between the two.

1. *from the Fujitsubo wall . . . Tōkaden*: I.e. the line stretched north from the western side of the gallery into which Michitaka emerged, towards the rear of the palace compound.

125   When we gathered the herbs

1. *the No-ears plant*: A literal translation of the name *miminagusa*, a member of the carnation family with edible leaves.
2. *Though you . . . chrysanthemum*: This clever poem hinges on two puns: the verb *tsumu* (to pluck flowers/pinch an ear, etc.) and *kiku* (chrysanthemum/to hear or listen).

126   In the second month, an event called The Selection

The following teasing exchange is based on the name 'Shōnagon', which is the name of a post (Junior Counsellor), apparently deriving from the post Sei's father held.

1. *an event called The Selection . . . called sōmé*: Sei here manages to confuse not only the names of events, but their times and their associated ceremonies as well, displaying the ignorance of such matters typical of the women at court.
2. *heitan cakes*: Square rice cakes with a filling of eggs, vegetables, etc., that were presented to the court nobles and senior courtiers the day after the Preselection and Selection Ceremonies.
3. *'Mimana Nariyuki'*: A false name which includes the characters for Yukinari's name in reverse. Mimana was the name of a low-ranking family, hence a typical retainer's name.

4. *he refrains ... his ugly appearance*: A reference to the shy, ugly god of Kazuraki.

5. *this kind of protocol*: Sei wants to continue the game by responding as would befit a Junior Counsellor.

6. *Korenaka's voice*: Taira Korenaka, who was in charge of the present ceremonies.

7. *looking terribly smart and proper*: He is under the impression that Sei has called him in order to relay something from the Empress herself.

8. *Such handsome cakes ... himself*: The wit lies in the similarity between the name of the cakes (*heitan*) and the word for rude or callous (*reitan*).

127   One day someone idly said

This discussion centres around the literal or apparently meaningless names of items of clothing. Elsewhere I use explanatory names for many of them, but give the literal meanings here.

1. *"thin-long" ... "sweat-garment"*: *Hosonaga*, long divided robe. *Kazami*, girl's over-robe, and originally an undergarment.

2. *"long-bottom"*: *Shiranaga*, an unidentifiable item of clothing worn by boys.

3. *"Underlayer" ... "wide-mouth"*: *Shitagasane*, train-robe. *Ōguchi*, short, wide-bottomed skirted trousers.

4. *"sew-and-pull"*: *Sashinuki*, gathered trousers.

128   After the late Regent's death (995.9)

1. *Once more the moon ... loved it then*: From a Chinese poem by Sugawara Funtoki (899–981), included in *Wakan rōeishū*.

2. *her teasing reply*: Teishi is referring to Sei's special fondness for Tadanobu.

129   One evening, Secretary Controller Yukinari

1. *the Hour of the Ox*: Between 2 and 4 a.m.

2. *the false cock of Lord Mengchang*: According to legend, when trying to escape capture, Mengchang arrived at the Hangu barrier gate in the middle of the night and found it closed. His enemy was close at his heels, and in desperation he had one of his followers imitate the rooster crow that was the signal for the gates to be opened. Sei is suggesting that the 'cock's crow' that Yukinari claims he heard was in fact contrived to help him escape.

3. *Kanko ... barrier gate of Ōsaka*: Yukinari takes up Sei's reference to the Kanko barrier gate and teasingly twists it to the

Ōsaka gate, the latter a symbol of the difficulty of lovers' meeting.

4. *was quite overawed by it*: Yukinari's calligraphy was famous, and presumably it was this rather than the poem itself that awed Ryūen.

130   One dark, moonless night in the fifth month

1. *"this gentleman"*: Sei responds to the joke with a neat reference to a Chinese poem on bamboo by Fujiwara Atsumochi (d. *c.* 793) in *Wakan rōeishū*, which quotes an early Chinese poet as referring to the bamboo he planted as 'this gentleman'. The senior courtiers quote the appropriate line when they return.

131   When the year of mourning (992, early summer)

Emperor Ichijō's nurse, the powerful and high-ranking Tōsanmi (Fujiwara Shigeko), has a trick played on her by the twelve-year-old Ichijō and Teishi. Although narrated with all the detail of a witnessing voice, this happened before Sei came to court.

1. *a presentation stick*: A long stick to which a formal letter delivered to a high-ranking person was attached.

2. *over the top of the lower shutter*: The lower half-shutter remained closed, while the upper one was raised to take in the letter.

3. *Record of the Readings ... white-backed walnut-brown paper*: Tōsanmi assumes that the official-looking message contains the Record of the Readings – a list of the sutras, etc., and number of times performed – which is sent to the petitioner after scripture readings have been performed on their behalf. However, this would have been on a plain white sheet of paper.

4. *These deep-dyed clothes ... forgot him*: The evergreen oak (*shii*) produces a dye for mourning clothes. The poem's conceit is that the priest lives in the mountains, among the evergreens, while down in the city the season has advanced and the trees bear new leaves (i.e. have changed to bright new clothes). A strong rebuke is implied.

5. *the Abbot of Ninnaji ... Fujiwara Grand Counsellor*: Ninnaji (Niwaji) was a temple to the north of the capital, whose abbot was chosen from among the members of the imperial family. The Grand Counsellor is Fujiwara Asateru.

6. *some demon from the past*: The straw raincoat, worn by the messenger, is a garb frequently associated with demons.

7. *shook her ... happy pride*: Tōsanmi can treat the young Emperor and Empress with such astonishing familiarity because she is the

Emperor's nurse. Her pride would have derived both from the special intimacy that allowed her to take such liberties, and from the honour of having a trick played on her by the Emperor and Empress.

134 Worthless things

1. *Clothing starch that's gone bad*: Starch was made from rice paste, which has a foul smell if left too long. There seems to be a textual corruption at this point, and this translation follows one possible interpretation.
2. *the fire tongs ... post-funeral fire*: After a funeral, a fire was lit at the gate of the house, and the bamboo fire tongs used to build the fire were immediately thrown on to it.
3. *After all ... strange or unpleasant*: This section, which keeps pausing to justify and defend itself, is generally considered to have been added after parts of the *Pillow Book* had come to be read (and presumably criticized) by others.

135 Things that are truly splendid

What begins as a list quickly becomes a lovingly detailed description of the Provisional Festivals: the Rehearsal of Performance for the Yahata Provisional Festival in spring, and the winter Provisional Kamo Festival. It is narrated as a vivid 'present', although evidently largely based on specific past memories.

1. *here ... towards the Emperor*: Although Sei is describing the Yahata Festival, her directions are mistaken: the envoys face south for this festival, towards the Iwashimizu Shrine, and north towards the Kamo shrine for the Kamo Festival.
2. *'Udohyō'*: A folk song in the Eastern Songs (*Azuma-uta*) cycle, part of the Suruga Dance.
3. *Their hands ... 'Mount Koma'*: The hand movements seem to have been part of the dance, a miming of the song's words ('come let's relax, let your sleeves hang loose, let the glossy cords dangle'). The title is an amalgam of an Eastern Dances song and another which would not have been sung on this occasion.
4. *Returning Dance*: When the rituals at the Kamo Shrine are over, the dancers return to the palace at night to dance again.
5. *the Secretary Captain*: The title reference is confusing, but the legend is associated with the name of Fujiwara Sanekata, who died in 998.
6. *the trains caught up on their heads*: The ladies had apparently picked up their trains and slung them over their shoulders in

order to hasten, and the trains had accidentally caught on their heads.

136   After the Regent had departed this life (996, autumn)

With Michitaka's death followed by the exile of two of her brothers (see Introduction, p. xv), Teishi was obliged to leave the palace in 996; she went first to Korechika's Konijō mansion, where she took holy orders, but when it burned down a few months later she moved to her uncle Akinobu's home, the setting for this section. Sei was known to admire Michinaga, so felt she was under suspicion of being in league with him, and seems to have spent about four months in voluntary retirement at home.

1.   *The gentlewomen were all . . . to see the dew on it:* There is a poignancy in the fact that they are maintaining court standards despite their exile. The colours they wear make it clear that it is autumn, a season that deepens the effect as does the neglected garden. Dew is poetically symbolic of worldly transience.

2.   *lovely peonies:* It is late for peony flowers, so perhaps it was their autumn leaves that Minamoto Tsunefusa praises.

3.   *a single kerria petal . . . never rises into words:* The kerria petal, which is poetically associated with unspoken thoughts, would probably have been made of paper. See Section 70, note 2 for the poem. The message is that Teishi's love for Sei is the greater for being silent.

4.   *game of Riddles:* A courtly pastime in which two teams (left and right) were selected to prepare a series of riddles. On the day, the participants would be paired off to answer each other's riddles. Points were recorded by placing tokens in a container.

5.   *"A bow drawn in the heavens":* The answer would be immediately evident to everyone, since the expression 'bow-drawn moon' was a well-known figure of speech for the 'new moon'.

140   Alarming-looking things

1.   *Thorny acorn husks . . . Water chestnuts:* The husks of the *kunugi* oak's acorns are thorny, and were used as a dye. The next three items are all foods that are either hairy (the mountain yam) or spiked (the prickly water lily and the water chestnut).

141   Things that look fresh and pure

1.   *Earthenware cups:* These were discarded after each use.

142 Distasteful-looking things

1. *The baton ... lined with simple cloth:* A ceremonial baton was sometimes used for holding memos concerning ceremonial details, etc., and the baton of an Aide of Ceremonial (which was wood, unlike the ivory batons of those of higher rank) was apparently put to particularly frequent use. A standing screen would usually be silk.

2. *A cabinet ... Izumo matting:* Perhaps such a cabinet is felt to be vulgar because sliding doors, rather than the usual hinged doors, were cheaper. Probably this matting was coarse-woven and originated in the province of Izumo (present-day Shimane prefecture).

143 Things that make the heart lurch with anxiety

1. *Watching ... hair-binding cord:* Horse races were held as part of various festivals. The hair-binding cord may snap as it's twisted.

144 Endearingly lovely things

1. *'nun's cut' hairstyle:* The hair of all children was cut to the shoulders with a long fringe, as was the hair of women who took the tonsure.

146 Things with terrifying names

1. *'Scale-board' walls ... 'Arm-umbrella' rain:* A wall made of overlapping slats, which look like a fish's scales. A downpour fierce enough to force people to shield themselves with a bent arm.

2. *Living spirit possession ... A bull-demon:* The spirit of a living person consumed with anger and resentment attaches itself to the person who is its object and causes illness and death. Possibly a legendary demon with a bull's head. (*Kanamochi* is inexplicable.)

147 Things that look ordinary but become extraordinary when written

Many names even for common objects were or could be written with Chinese characters that, when interpreted literally, often produced strange or incomprehensible meanings, as are most of the items here. (See also Section [s4].

1. *strawberry ... dew plant ... chestnuts:* Respectively, overturned tray child; sole of duck's foot grass; barbarian peach.

148   Repulsive things

1. *The seams ... added*: This presumably follows the theme of hairiness, as the animal hair would show on the inside of the seam until the garment was lined.

149   Occasions when something inconsequential has its day

All these examples are of people/things that normally play a humble role, but become briefly important at a particular ceremonial event.

1. *the Bamboo Breaking ceremonies*: Twice a year, the Lady Chamberlains performed a ceremonial measuring of the Emperor's height with a piece of bamboo, which was then broken to that length.

2. *The foodtaster ... new year*: A young girl is designated to taste the ceremonial spiced *saké* before it is drunk by the Emperor.

151   People who seem enviable

1. *Inari Shrine*: A large mountain shrine just beyond the south-east edge of the capital.

2. *none of her ladies ... chicken scrawl*: The lady would ask one of her gentlewomen to write the message on her behalf, as the artistic standard of her court would be assessed by the calligraphy.

3. *who have the freedom ... imperial wives*: Gentlewomen in service in the various households of the imperial wives were not in this position, since they were rivals.

152   Things whose outcome you long to know

1. *When one of the various forms ... is in process*: These methods (known generally as *shibori*) involve creating patterns by tying off parts of the cloth in various ways; the pattern is only revealed when the tie-threads are removed.

154   When Her Majesty was in mourning for the previous Regent (995.6–7)

Owing to the pollution associated with death, members of the family had to remove themselves from the palace during the Shinto ceremony of the Great Purification, which took place in the sixth and twelfth months. The Aitadokoro was a building in the greater palace compound used for banquets and other formal occasions but not designed as a residence.

1. *The Timekeeping Office ... watch-drum*: Part of the Bureau

of Divination. A drum or a bell was sounded at each change of watch. In the next paragraph, the Left Gate Watch is the Kenshunmon Gate, which was to the north of the Aitadokoro and the Bureau of Divination.

2. *centipedes*: These centipedes, known as *mukade*, appear in the summer months in Japan and can inflict an extremely painful bite.

3. *Who ever ... nightly trysts*: Apparently improvised for the occasion in the Chinese manner, lightheartedly imitating the venerable poetic tradition of lamenting a place's fall from past grandeur.

4. *'one-side breeze'*: A passing quotation from *Kokinshū* (168): 'Up there in the sky / where summer and autumn now / cross paths as they pass / the breeze must be blowing cool / down one side of that heavenly road.'

5. *we seemed to have ... less spacious*: This may refer to the table of offerings traditionally set up by the front steps for this festival.

6. *Michikata ... world of humans*: Minamoto Michikata, Nobukata's younger brother Tadanobu's apparently incomprehensible reply is explained by Sei later (see note 8).

7. *'Dew ... part at dawn'*: From a poem in Chinese by Sugawara Michizane, found in *Wakan rōeishū*, which describes the tears of the heavenly Weaver Maid when she must part from her Herdsman lover star after their Tanabata meeting.

8. *picked up on my reference*: Tadanobu's reply (see note 6) had been a cryptic statement that his Tanabata poem the next day would inappropriately refer to the human (as opposed to the heavenly) realm and the fourth instead of the seventh month, to balance his earlier gaffe.

9. *breaking up the board*: I.e. a victory has been achieved and the players are now removing their tiles.

10. *"playing a round"*: Sei uses a term meaning 'infidelity' (*sadame naku*), which contains an internal pun on the word for a *go* stone (*me*).

11. *"Magistrate Hsaio ... ancient shrine"*: From a poem in Chinese by Ōe no Asatsuna (866–957). Its theme, the bond of friendship, is on Sei's mind as she contemplates the fact that Tadanobu's new appointment will mean he has less opportunity to visit because he will have ceremonial obligations and new duties.

12. *"He had not ... his thirties"*: From a poem in Chinese by Minamoto Fusaakira, lamenting his passing years and comparing himself with earlier poets who had achieved greatness relatively early.

13. *I believe that ... admonished his wife*: It seems Nobukata was
close to forty. Sei refers to the Chinese tale of a man who admon-
ishes his wife when she threatens to leave him because of his
poverty, and tells her that although he is already in his forties
(or thirty-nine, in the version Nobukata later refers to), he will
be rich by his fifties, a vow which he fulfils.

155   The name 'Kōkiden' (998?)

1. *Kōkiden ... the Left*: The name of the palace where she normally
resided was commonly used to refer to her. She was Fujiwara
Yoshiko, daughter of Fujiwara Kinsue.

2. *'Lie-down'*: This is perhaps the person of the same name (Uchifu-
shi) who appears in records of the time as an accomplished shrine
priestess, whose nickname derived from the fact that she would
always prostrate herself when speaking.

156   Things now useless that recall a glorious past

1. *A fine embroidery-edged mat*: Such a mat, whose edging was
woven in elegant coloured patterns, was reserved for important
use only.

2. *Grape-coloured fabric ... turned*: The dye used for purple and
grape-coloured cloth had camellia lye added. When the dye
faded, the lye was said to have 'turned'.

158   Sutra readings

1. *Continuous Sutra Readings*: See Section 82, note 1.

159   Things that are near yet far

1. *The Miyanobe Festival ... Kurama Temple*: The second of the
biannual Miyanobe Festivals, in the twelfth month, was both
near (one month distant) and far (a year apart) from the first.
Kurama Temple, in the mountains north of the capital, is not far
up the mountain, but the path to it describes large zigzags.

160   Things that are far yet near

1. *Paradise. The course of a boat*: Buddhism teaches both that
Paradise (*gokuraku*) is countless *kalpas* distant and that Amida
Buddha, who welcomes one to Paradise, is close at hand for
those who call on him. In a boat one travels straight and com-
paratively fast to a destination, which makes it seem surprisingly
close. (*Kalpa* is a Buddhist term indicating an undefined but
extremely long period of time.)

161   Wells

1. *mountain well*: A reference to an early poem (*Manyōshū* 3807): 'The shallow waters / of the mountain well can hold / vast Asaka Mountain / yet far from shallow is this heart / that holds such loving thoughts of you.' Most names in this list are chosen for their poetic associations.
2. *Asuka Well*: The reference is to a quotation from a popular *saibara*, whose charm lies in its use of an archaic word for 'water'.
3. *Shōshō Well*: Shōshō means 'Lieutenant'.

162   Plains

Poetic associations lie behind all these names. Saga, Ono and Murasaki Plains are close to the capital and would have been known to Sei.

164   Nobles

While the court nobles (*kandachime*) of Section 163 were generally men who held the third rank or higher, these 'nobles' (*kindachi*) were the sons of one of the great houses. Many of the titles listed here are dual posts. See Appendix 5.

165   Acting Provincial Governors

1. *Kai . . . Awa provinces*: These were among the most prestigious provinces, in part because they were close to the capital.

166   Commissioners

These titles would normally be considered sixth-ranking, but have been raised a rank to fifth.

169   Sixth-rank Chamberlains

1. *The post . . . aspire to*: This sentence bears little relation to the rest of the section, and some consider it belongs with Section 164 or 165.

170   A place where a lady lives alone

The situation is typical of certain touching heroines in romantic tales of the period. 'Alone' of course does not take into account the various people in her service.

171   The home of a lady in court service

1. *various ladies . . . visitor*: Here, gentlewomen from different households are all gathered together in someone's home.

172   One day in the ninth month

This section takes the form of a romantic scene typical of the old tales. According to some views of how the sections fit together, it is a continuation of the previous section, a tale told by one of the ladies.

1. *'though there ... hangs bright'*: From a poem by the seventh-century poet Kakinomoto Hitomaro (*Shūishū* 795).
2. *The woman ... slip quietly away*: The passage is difficult to follow, and some have suggested that her wig slipped when she bent forward, and her bare, shiny head is lit with the moonlight, which would indeed astonish the gentleman. In that case, the section becomes a spoof of the romantic tale genre.

173   It's quite delightful when the snow is falling

1. *'The man ... today'*: A poem by Taira no Kanemori (d. 990) (*Shūishū* 251): 'Snow falling thickly / here in this mountain village / and the path is gone. / The man who comes to call today / would truly move my heart.' This visitor is wittily suggesting that they should find his visit moving.
2. *'snow ... certain mountains'*: From a Chinese poem 'To Yin Hsieh-lii', of uncertain provenance, in *Wakan rōeishū*: 'At dawn when I entered the garden of the King of Liang / the snow lay thick upon the heaped mountains. / At night when I climbed the tower of the Duke of Yü / the moonlight lit the land a thousand miles about.' 'The heaped mountains' refers to the snow mountains that the King of Liang reportedly built in his garden, but the visitor is intentionally obscuring the specific reference.

174   Once, during the reign of the former Emperor Murakami

1. *'at times ... blossom'*: From a poem by Bo Juyi. The relevant lines are: 'My companions of lute and wine / All have left me and scattered. / At times of snow, moonlight and blossom / Above all other times, I think of you with love.'
2. *'When I went ... with it'*: The puns are *kogeru* ('to row' and 'to burn or singe') and *kaeru* ('to return' and 'frog').

175   The lady known as Miare no Seji

Her name refers to her role as imperial messenger to the Kamo High Priestess. This episode occurred during the reign of a previous Emperor.

1. *mizura style*: Parted at the crown and bound on either side of the head.

176   When I first went into court service (991–993)

1. *by the light ... standing tray*: The oil lamp has been placed on an inverted standing tray, making it lower than usual and illuminating what is beneath in more detail.

2. *The head of my room*: Several women usually shared an apartment. The one who had been in service longest acted as the head.

3. *His Excellency*: Teishi's father, Regent Michitaka. He is probably the 'glamorous' joking man who arrives later.

4. *"the path is gone" ... "truly moved"*: See Section 173, note 1.

5. *free calligraphic style*: A calligraphic script (also known as 'grass style') in which Chinese characters were written in flowing and abbreviated form, a precursor to the development of the phonetic *hiragana* (see Introduction, p. xxvii).

6. *I see you've lied to me*: Superstition had it that a sneeze indicated that something bad was afoot. An exception was the sneeze at New Year (seen in the following section), which was a sign of long life.

7. *How could I ... Her Majesty feels*: The poem puns on *sora* ('sky' and 'untruth') and *tadasu* ('to arraign and judge', and the name of the sacred wood at the entrance to the lower Kamo Shrine). Teishi dictated the poem to a gentlewoman, who added her own message.

8. *We may judge ... misjudged misery*: The central pun is on the word *hana* ('flower' and 'nose') and its associated words *ususa* and *kosa* (respectively 'paleness' and 'richness' of colour, also applicable to shallowness or depth of love).

9. *The god ... awe of him*: Sei is implying that the god from whom the Yin-Yang masters receive their information, rather than the god of Tadasu, knows her heart.

177   People who feel smug

1. *A Provincial Governor ... a noble family*: A young noble would rise through the ranks via more prestigious appointments such as Captain of the Palace Guards.

178   Nothing is more splendid than rank

Sei is referring specifically to high rank, rather than the institution of ranking itself.

180 Illnesses

The focus is on illnesses that provide an engaging and moving scene for the viewer, presented as if one were witnessing it in an illustrated tale.

1. *Internal illnesses . . . spirits*: The first appears to cover a variety of illnesses, including those of heart and lungs. Spirits were thought to cause a number of illnesses and derangements, which could be cured by exorcism.

181 It's delightful to see someone who's a great ladies' man

1. *the crumpled sleeve . . . shift*: The implication is that it has been wrung, perhaps with the tears of parting. This image may have been woven into his next-morning poem.
2. *the sixth volume of the Lotus Sutra*: This includes the important chapter named *'juryōbon'* ('The Life-span of the Thus Come One').

184 It's enchanting to overhear

1. *'The wanderer . . . waning moon'*: From a poem attributed to Chia Sung in *Wakan rōeishū*: 'The lovely lady has finished adorning herself / the bell resounds in the palace of Wei. / The wanderer sojourns on beneath a waning moon / while at Han-ku Pass a cock crows.'

185 Things that prove disillusioning

1. *You instantly . . . gonna go home*: Sei's criticism is of a shift in spoken language, in which the particle *to* became elided, so that, for example, the expression *iwan to su* (I'm going to say it) became *iwanzuru*.
2. *'a single cawidge' . . . 'lek for'*: Her examples are *hitotsu* pronounced *hitetsu*, and *motomu* pronounced *mitomu*.

186 It's very unseemly for a man

1. *the northern quarters*: The kitchen and servants' quarters were on the northern side of the house.

187 Winds

1. *summer's padded robe . . . sleep under*: The padded robe is hung up to air during the day. It has been used for sleeping during the summer (see Section 41). When a typhoon brings in the first cool air of autumn, another layer is added.

188   The day after a typhoon

1.   *'I see why the word "storm"'*: Funya no Yasuhide (*fl.* 858–888), *Kokinshū* (249): 'I see why the word "storm" / becomes in writing "mountain wind", / for autumn's trees and plants / all bend and wither in the force / of this wind from the mountain tops.' (The character for *arashi* (storm) is a combination of the characters for mountain and wind.)

189   Elegantly intriguing things

These scenes, auditory as much as visual, share the quality of arousing interest by their elegant suggestiveness of situations that can only be guessed at.

1.   *Hair tossed back ... splendid length*: The woman would be seated, and the end of her hair would lie piled on the floor.
2.   *The metal clasps ... trefoil cords*: The blinds are rolled up to the lintel cloth, with braided cords in a trefoil design at their upper edge, and held in place by metal clasps.
3.   *The scent of incense ... Little Door*: Incense is used to scent clothes; creating incense blends was a highly cultivated art. The Little Door is the room's northern door, probably a small wooden double door.

190   Islands

Poetic association is the primary reason behind Sei's choice of place names in this and the next two sections.

1.   *Yaso and Uki Islands*: These mean respectively 'numerous islands' and 'floating island'.
2.   *Taware*: *Tawaru* means 'play', and has sexual overtones.

191   Beaches

1.   *Fukiage ... Uchiide ... Moroyose ... Chisato*: Literally, 'waves blown up by wind'; 'going out'; 'bringing together'; 'a thousand miles', respectively.

192   Bays

1.   *Korizuma Bay*: An invented place name, located in Suma, which plays on that name plus the word *korizu* (not to become obsessed, as by a failed love affair, etc.).

193 Woods

This is a lengthier version of Section 107. Many of these names are
not geographically traceable. Most have poetic associations and are
primarily interesting for their meanings.

1.   *Utatane . . . Tareso . . . Kurubeki . . . Tachigiki*: Literally 'nap';
     'who goes there?'; 'expected to come'; 'eavesdropping', respect-
     ively. For Iwase, see Section 107, note 1.
2.   *one tree*: The reference to the single tree is unclear.

194 Temples

These were all situated in and around the capital.

1.   *Ryōzen . . . the Buddha*: Ryōzen is an abbreviated form of the
     name Vulture Peak, where the Buddha was said to have preached
     the *Lotus Sutra*.

196 Buddhas

Buddhas exist in numerous manifestations, those listed here being
among the most well known. Their primary characteristics are given
below.

1.   *Nyoirin. Senju . . . Kannons*: Nyoirin: Saves sentient beings from
     suffering. Senju is the thousand-armed form of Kannon, bodhis-
     attva of mercy, who also takes five other forms, including that
     of Nyoirin.
2.   *Yakushi . . . Fugen*: Yakushi: The healing buddha. *Shaka* is the
     historical buddha (Guatama). Miroku is the bodhisattva of the
     future. Jizō is specifically associated with the salvation of chil-
     dren. Monju: is the bodhisattva of wisdom. Fudō Myōō: a fierce
     guardian deity of great importance in the Shingon sect. Fugen: a
     bodhisattva associated with meditation and wisdom.

197 Chinese writings

The list begins with classic Chinese literary texts, and ends with some
of the kinds of formal religious and court documents that were traditionally written in Chinese in the Japanese court.

1.   *Monju . . . Goteihongi*: Monju: (Chinese *Wenji*), a collection of
     the poems of the popular Chinese poet Bo Juyi (Hakurakuten).
     Monzen: (Chinese *Wensuan*), a compendious collection of prose
     and poetry down the ages. *Shinbu*: (Chinese *Xinfu*), reference
     unclear, possibly a name given to part of *Monzen*. *Shiki*: (Chinese
     Shiji), *Records of the Historian*; its first volume is *Goteihongi*
     (Chinese *Wudi benji*).

198 Tales

A partial list of the large number of tales that were being read at this time, of which only two survive. On Komano and Katano, see Section 273 and notes 4 and 5.

1. *Sumiyoshi*: A tale of the persecution of a stepchild. It exists in a form modified at a later period.
2. *The Tale of the Hollow Tree*: See Appendix 4. *Changing Residence* (*Tonoutsuri*) and *Yielding Up the Country* (*Kuniyuzuri*) probably refer to sections of it, although the names are not in existing versions of the work.

201 Games

1. *Court kickball*: A popular courtly game played with four, six or eight men.

202 Dances

The first two dances listed were part of the Eastern Dances. The others originated in China or India.

1. *'Taiheiraku'* ... *Bird Dance*: A sword dance, and a dance in which dancers were costumed in wings and headdresses, respectively.
2. *Batō Dance* ... *the ground*: A dance in which the dancer wore a fierce blue mask and long blue wig; *batō* means literally 'head-pulling'. The Crouch a Dance was performed in the squatting position.
3. *Lion Dance*: Probably related to the Chinese Lion Dance. See also Section 205 and note 6.

204 Wind instruments

1. *as for the face of the player*: He must blow out his cheeks and distort his mouth to produce a sound.

205 Spectacles

1. *broad spotted sheaths*: Made of leopard skin.
2. *'As the shrine priests will bind their robes'*: An anonymous poem, *Kokinshū* (487): 'As the shrine priests will bind / their robes with mulberry sashes / for the mighty gods / so, my lord, no day goes by / when my thoughts are not bound to you.'
3. *Rope Escorts*: The palanquin is pulled along by ropes, and beside the rope-drawers walk their more splendid escorts.
4. *Most incomparably ... the Butokuden*: This description is of the

imperial progress to the Butokuden (Hall of Military Accomplishments) to view the horse racing associated with the Sweet Flag Festival. Festive herbal balls and sweet flag were distributed to the courtiers by the Lady Chamberlains. The tradition was abolished in 968. See also Section 84.

5. *The Ebisu Residence Move . . . arrows*: The text is very confusing. I have followed the interpretation that it refers to certain apparently farcical entertainments that took place the day after the Sweet Flag Festival.

6. *lion and dog dances*: As the dancers performed the lion (*shishi*) dance, two children costumed as Korean dogs (*komainu*) danced playfully among them.

7. *it's a shame . . . down the road*: The nobles are taking part in the procession, so are not mingling with the audience.

8. *The procession . . . carrying the empty palanquin back*: See also Section 38. The Kamo High Priestess returned by ox-drawn carriage, so the palanquin was no longer needed.

9. *you almost expect . . . hidden there*: The *hototogisu* is often poetically described as singing hidden in a hedge of flowering deutzia.

10. *'parted by the mountain peak'*: A poem by Mibu no Tadamine (*fl.* 898–920), *Kokinshū* (601): 'White clouds in the wind / are parted by the mountain peak / and are seen no more – / as your cold heart at parting / holds no traces of regret.'

206 Around the fifth month

1. *In swampy ground . . . human tread*: The feet of the men leading the carriage the women travel in. Woven into this description is a strong echo of an anonymous love poem, *Kokin rokujō* (1688): 'The reed-tangled mud / makes a beguiling surface / but hidden there below / the unexpected water lies / like hidden feelings of the heart.'

208 On the evening of the fourth day of the fifth month

1. *the fourth day of the fifth month*: The day before the Sweet Flag Festival, when underlings are bringing in the sweet flag leaves to strew.

209 On the way to the Kamo Shrine

1. *'Yah! You there . . . planting'*: The time of the *hototogisu*'s song coincides with the season of rice-planting. A version of this folk song still survives.

2. *'Hototogisu ... so loud'*: Several poems are possible references for this quotation, e.g. *Shūishū* (120): *'Hototogisu /* please do not sing so loud. / Wait till your long calls / can be threaded through the jewels / of the fifth month's herbal balls.' The *hototogisu*'s call also heralds the time of the Sweet Flag Festival and its decorative herbal balls.

3. *just like ... Nakatada's childhood*: For Sei's preference for Nakatada, see Section 78 and note 5.

210 At the end of the eighth month

A seasonal contrast to the previous section, describing a memory of a specific pilgrimage to Kōryūji, a temple to the north-west of the capital in the Uzumasa area.

1. *How recently ... rice plants*: An anonymous poem, *Kokinshū* (172): 'How recently it was / that they took up the young rice plants – / only yesterday, / and now the autumn breezes blow / through the ripened ears of rice.'

2. *the little huts in the fields*: Used by people set to guard the rice fields.

211 Soon after the twentieth day of the ninth month

1. *pilgrimage to Hase*: This may be the same pilgrimage as that described in detail in Section 115 (identified in some texts as Hase Temple).

212 Setting off to climb the slope

1. *to climb the slope ... burning firewood*: Kiyomizu, like many temples, is approached by an uphill path. The smoke was probably from the houses of the village outside the temple gates.

213 The sweet flag leaves from the fifth month

1. *The sweet flag leaves ... winter*: The leaves used in the Sweet Flag Festival seem to have been left in place until the following year.

214 A well-scented robe

1. *A well-scented robe ... scenting frame*: Robes were scented by being draped over a frame, which formed a small tent within which incense was burned.

216   Things that should be big

1. *Provisions bags*: Used for carrying food when travelling.
2. *great glaring eyes*: Literally 'eyes like metal bowls', a reference to the glaring metal eyes of fierce guardian deities, etc., in Buddhist sculpture.
3. *Winter cherries*: Large *Physalis alkekengi* were used medicinally, or in children's games.

217   Things that should be small

1. *small*: The word *mijikaki* includes the meanings of both 'small' and 'short'.

218   Things that a house should have

1. *An elbow-shaped corridor*: The precise meaning is unclear, but probably a corridor with a bend would give an impression of depth.
2. *Oharaki and kakiban*: References unknown, but *kakiban* was probably a board used either for sewing or for writing on.

219   On your way somewhere

1. *piled in a lid*: Large lids were often used as trays to carry objects.

221   I heard people saying there'd been a man in the Long Room

1. *Dawn ... morning had arrived*: The second and third 'lines' (7, 5) of Teishi's poem, which has a picture as the first 'line'. (Other texts have *mikasayama*, 'Umbrella Mountain', for the first line which clarifies the poetic intent.) The implicit pun is on the phrase *nureginu wo kiseru*, (literally, 'to be made to wear wet clothes'), which meant 'to be the butt of false rumours', with the umbrella providing the unspoken connection. Sei's answer, which also uses a picture to substitute for a word, draws on this allusion.

222   When Her Majesty was in the Sanjō Palace (1000.5)

Another fire had caused Teishi to move temporarily again to Taira Narimasa's home. She was pregnant with her third child, and Michinaga's growing power was threatening her position in the court.

1. *the fifth day*: The day of the Sweet Flag Festival.
2. *the little Prince and Princess*: Teishi's children, Atsuyasu and Shūshi, were respectively two and five years old at the time.
3. *green-wheat cakes ... across the fence*: The cakes are made from

unripe wheat. 'Across the fence', was probably intended as an allusion to *Kokin rokujō* (1427): 'The horse in his field / stretches to reach the green grass / that grows across the fence – / so my heart too yearns over / to where you lie out of reach.'

223   When Nurse Taifu

1.   *went off to Hyōga … gave her*: Taifu was probably accompanying her husband when he was posted to Hyōga as Governor. It was the custom to give a gift of a fan to someone departing on a journey.
2.   *Face … in the capital*: The pun turns on the name Hyōga, which is written with characters meaning 'sun' and 'turn or go towards'.

224   Once when I was in retreat at Kiyomizu Temple

1.   *red-tinted Chinese paper*: Paper of very high quality, which causes Sei to be at a loss for suitable paper for her reply.
2.   *a violet lotus petal*: Probably an artificial petal such as were used decoratively in temple services.

225   Posting stations

There were stations, often with an inn attached, roughly every thirty miles along major roads, for exchanging horses on a journey. This section seems to include wayside inns generally in the term.

226   Shrines

1.   *Sacred resting shrines*: A shrine which the god temporarily inhabits when it is carried in a palanquin during a shrine festival.
2.   *Cedar Shrine … poem says*: Ki no Tsurayuki, *Tsurayukishū* (226): 'This is no lost tale / from the world of far-off days – / the cedar at the gate / of Miwa's Shrine still stands to mark / its sacred power to all who cross that hill.'
3.   *Kotonomama … every prayer*: The name means literally 'just as the words say', i.e. a promise to answer every prayer to the letter. The reference is to *Kokinshū* (1055): 'This shrine's diligent god / will answer each and every prayer / with such a zealous will, / surely it makes the very woods / at last lament the fearful task.'
4.   *Aritōshi Shrine … fall ill*: It was said that when Tsurayuki's horse became ill on a journey, the local people told him it was the doing of the local god, who was unhappy at lacking a shrine. Tsurayuki composed and dedicated a supplicatory poem to the god, and the horse was cured. The name 'Aritōshi' literally means 'putting ants through'.

5. *The parents . . . as a son*: If his father had been a noble, the son
    would have risen above this rank by the time his parents were old.

227   The Ichijō Palace went by the name of 'The Temporary
          Palace' (1000, spring)

1. *resided in the Seiryōden*: The name of the Emperor's palace was
    transferred to a building at the Ichijō palace during his residence
    there.
2. *Takatō . . . 'Takasago'*: Fujiwara Takatō, Minister of War,
    992–996. A *saibara* song.
3. *we felt . . . as we gazed*: The reference is to an old song and its
    associated legend, wherein a forlorn lover picks wild parsley in
    a vain attempt to assuage his longing for a maiden he has seen
    doing this. Sei refers to the unassuaged sorrows of their present
    situation.

231   Hills

1. *Funa Hill*: A famous burying ground to the north-west of the
    capital.
2. *the song's bamboo grass . . . Tomo Hill*: The bamboo grass
    appears in the sacred *kagura* song: 'Oh where does it grow, / the
    bamboo grass that serving men / dangle from their belts? / That
    is the same bamboo grass / that grows upon Tomo Hill.'

235   Stars

1. *Altair . . . Shooting stars have a certain interest*: Altair is the chief
    star in the Aquila constellation; the Herdsman star in the legend
    on which the Tanabata Festival is based. The interest in shooting
    stars probably comes from their name, '*yobaiboshi*', meaning
    'courting star'.

236   Clouds

1. *a Chinese poem . . . morning*: Nothing approximating these
    words has been identified in Chinese poetry.

237   Things that create a disturbance

1. *the offering portion . . . morning meal*: Monks set aside a portion
    of the day's main meal as an offering to all sentient beings. It
    may have been placed on the roof.
2. *Kiyomizu Temple . . . the retreat*: The eighteenth day of each
    month was dedicated to Kannon bodhisattva.

238   Slovenly-looking things

1.   *The rear view ... holy men*: Unlike in Japan, the Chinese dress
style was to wear the decorative part of the belt at the front, thus
leaving the back view as bare leather. Holy men were generally
eccentric recluses.

240   People who are smug and cocky

1.   *The woman ... painful belly*: She may have been a midwife, but
was primarily employed for her shamanic skills.
2.   *splits open ... toothed object*: Probably a saw. The bamboo was
to be used for suspending the sacred paper strips used in Shinto
ceremonies.

243   I particularly despise people who express themselves
poorly in writing

Sei is concerned here with the fraught question of correct use of respect
language, a complicated set of linguistic choices that affected every
social communication.

1.   *when you hear ... neutrally polite*: The retainer, who should
normally use honorific expressions when speaking to or of his
master, is here speaking in front of a guest and should thus not
elevate his own master relative to the guest, but use a neutrally
polite verb.

244   Horrid filthy things

1.   *The bowls in the Privy Chamber*: Probably a reference to the
lidded lacquer cups there, which were reputed to be used as a
pillow by senior courtiers obliged to stay there on night duty.

247   A son-in-law is brought in

1.   *A son-in-law is brought in*: See Section 2, note 4.
2.   *the tailpiece of her carriage*: The opposite ends of the carriage
shafts projected out some way behind it.

254   Once, towards the middle of the tenth month

1.   *She looked ... 'Dolly'*: The meaning is unclear. It may be that
the effect of the great pile of hair she has drawn round her face
(perhaps because the night was cold) makes her shape in the
moonlight resemble a tall stupa. However, there is no obvious
connection with the nickname, whose meaning is itself obscure.

(A stupa is a mound or tower containing sacred Buddhist relics, sutras, etc.)

256   No one had sharper ears

1. *the Minister of the Treasury*: Fujiwara Masamitsu, who became Minister of the Treasury in 998.

257   Things that give you pleasure

1. *a puzzling dream . . . harmless*: Dreams were considered to portend future events. A professional dream interpreter was often called on to interpret their meaning.
2. *a matching game*: A kind of popular game in which objects such as shells, flowers or paintings were competitively matched.

258   I was talking with some people in Her Majesty's presence

1. *couldn't bear to relinquish it*: Sei refers to the Buddhist teaching to 'relinquish' all attachment to the illusory world of the senses.
2. *trifles console . . . Obasute Mountain*: Teishi is referring to an anonymous *Kokinshū* poem (878), set in the province of Sarashina: 'This sad heart of mine / can find no consolation – / ah, Sarashina, / I gaze at the moon above / sad Obasute Mountain.'
3. *magical formula for averting trouble*: A joking reference to the complicated gestures and incantations performed by priests in order to magically avert troubles and disasters.
4. *the Sutra of Longevity*: A sutra often copied as a prayer for long life and the averting of disasters. Teishi is making subtle reference to the ladies' teasing comments, as well as offering Sei comfort.
5. *Most inexpressible . . . longevity*: The punning conceit is on the double meaning of *kami* ('god' and 'paper'). The legendary crane lives for a thousand years. This image links back through Teishi's reference to the Sutra of Longevity, to Sei's earlier remark about paper giving her a renewed lease of life, as well as to the encouragement in her present circumstances.
6. *a bound book*: This *sōshi* may have been one origin of *The Pillow Book*.
7. *a letter*: The *fumi* could also be interpreted more generally as anything written, and some scholars believe that what Sei sent was an early form of her *Pillow Book*.

259 On the twenty-first day of the second month (994)

Sei was still a relative newcomer to the court, and Michitaka at the height of his power.

1. *Sakuzen Temple . . . Nijō Palace*: The occasion was the establishment of Sakuzen Temple at Hōkōin, a residence which had been converted to a temple and renamed five years earlier. The Nijō Palace had recently been built for Teishi, and was close to Hōkōin.

2. *all white with newness*: The new wood had not yet had time to age and darken.

3. *the Chinese lions and the Korean dogs*: Pairs of guardian animals, sculptures of which traditionally stood before the curtained dais.

4. *worn directly over*: I.e. without displaying the sleeves.

5. *I'll go back home*: Her father Regent Michitaka's home was more or less next door.

6. *a special occasion*: It would be more usual for the gift to be provided from Teishi's household, but she is there as Michitaka's guest.

7. *His Excellency's daughters . . . Your Highness*: Teishi's three younger sisters. Genshi (here called Nakahime (literally, middle daughter)), the eldest. The next (no name known) was the wife of Prince Atsumichi, so would be addressed normally as 'Your Highness', although she was present here in her role as Michitaka's daughter. The Mistress of the Imperial Wardrobe (Jōganden) was the youngest.

8. *because of the special circumstances*: They were returning in order to prepare themselves for the dedication ceremonies.

9. *the tear-wet face . . . dawn*: Anonymous poem in *Shūishū* (302): 'Seeing these faces / of the dew-soaked blossoms / I recall with love / the tear-wet face of she / whom I parted from at dawn.'

10. *'Let him scold if he will'*: Probably a reference to the poet Minamoto Kanezumi, although no such poem of his is known. The most likely source is, in fact, Sosei (*fl.* 859–897), *Gosenshū* (50): 'Let him scold as he will, / Takasago's mountain guard, / I will pluck a spray / of the Onoe cherry / and wear it in my hair.'

11. *"the rain of passing time"*: Teishi uses a rather hackneyed pun on the double meaning of *furu* ('to rain' and 'to grow old').

12. *the untimely 'morning glory' of my sleepy face*: Sei is playing with the name for the morning glory: *asagao*, literally 'morning face'. It is 'untimely' both because of the lateness of the hour and because the season is wrong for it to flower.

13. *"still earlier than I myself"*: Anonymous, *Tadamishū* (mid-tenth century) (101): 'Thinking to see / the blossoming cherry I went forth / in the moonlit dawn / but found the dew had come to it / still earlier than I myself.' Sei's glancing quotation is enough to alert Michitaka that she had witnessed the dawn removal of the cherry.

14. *"blamed the spring winds"*: Ki no Tsurayuki, *Kokin rokujō* (967): 'The season is so late / that even in the mountain fields / the rice is planting now – / No blame should lie on the spring winds / for the falling cherry flowers.'

15. *to cast her lie on the sky's spring winds*: Michitaka is playing with the pun on *sora* ('falsehood' and 'sky').

16. *apologetically*: Teishi feels obliged to play down politely Sei's skills to others. Her use of the word *tadagoto* (everyday statement) echoes the earlier wordplay on the poem's *kagoto* (blame) which shifted to *soragoto* (lie).

17. *Have the blossoms . . . nine times a night*: Teishi's message contains a phrase from a poem 'Endless Longing' by Bo Juyi, and Sei's reply also quotes it: 'The autumn night grows long with thoughts of you, my lord, / and my soul goes to your presence nine times a night.'

18. *On the night . . . Nijō Palace*: The narrative here reverts to Teishi's move to Nijō Palace. It leaps forward again (at p. 221 'I returned from my home'), to pick up from the previous episode in which Teishi urged Sei to hasten back.

19. *the South Hall*: Part of Michitaka's residence.

20. *sewing their gowns . . . formal trains*: They are securing the layers of the gowns to be worn at tomorrow's ceremony with judicious stitching, or threading braided cords to the waist area of the train.

21. *your fan*: The fan, an indispensable accessory with formal attire, would have been a special one for the occasion.

22. *swaggering about*: The Prince was making great play of being a member of this powerful family at such an impressive family event.

23. *the accompanying nuns*: Former gentlewomen who had taken the tonsure with her.

24. *the "special colours"*: The grape colour of Buzé's trousers resembles the purple which required special permission. Yamanoi is facetiously conflating her with her lover, and slyly referring to the special access that Shigemasa has been granted to the trousers.

25. *the same two accompanying gentlemen*: Korechika and Takaie.

26. *Michiyori*: Fujiwara Michiyori, Michinaga's eldest son.

27. *you should remove ... this particular gathering*: Michitaka is apparently referring to his wife's choice of formal over-robe, which is slightly less formal than the train and Chinese jacket combination, and jokingly telling her that it is Teishi's role to wear the less formal clothing in present company.

28. *we should have borrowed yours*: Priests' formal wear was of the same purple and red weave.

29. *Boddhisattva Jizō*: The most endearing of the bodhisattvas, associated with the salvation of children. He is portrayed as a monk, with shaven head and surplice. (Ryūen was 15 years old.)

30. *lotus flower ... dancing*: The lotus flowers were artificial. The dances were part of the Buddhist ceremony.

31. *Aide of Ceremonial Norimasa*: Minamoto Norimasa.

32. *'the close salt kilns of Chika'*: A shorthand reference to a situation in which, though close, two people cannot meet. The poem is anonymous, *Zoku gosenshū* (1251) (738): 'The salt kilns of Chika / in the distant land of Oku / may indeed be close / but there's no meeting of the people's / liking in that saltiness.' There are puns on *chika* (place name and 'close') and *au* ('to meet one's liking' and 'to meet').

33. *when compared with the present*: At the time Sei was writing, both Teishi and her father were dead, and power had shifted to the new Regent Michinaga.

260   Venerable things

1. *'Nine-Section Staff'*: When this sacred text is chanted, a staff with loose metal rings attached to its head is shaken to mark the end of each of its nine sections.

263   Hunting costumes

1. *green wisteria*: Probably a combination of green and yellow weave over a spring-shoot green lining. Most of the colours listed would be layering combinations.

264   Shifts

1. *gloss-yellow robes*: When white silk is glossed, it takes on a faint yellow. Sei is distinguishing this from discoloured yellowing.

265   Formal train-robes

1. *Formal train-robes*: Specifically as worn by men in full civil dress. The colours listed are layering combinations.

266   Fan ribs

1.   *hō tree ... colour*: A type of magnolia. The colours may refer to the paper rather than the ribs.

267   Cypress fans

1.   *Cypress fans*: More elaborately ribbed than other fans, with ribs made of cypress wood.

268   Deities

This section lists the native gods associated with various shrines, most of which were in or near the capital. (These shrines still exist.) It is still common to refer to a god by its shrine name.

1.   *the Emperor of this land*: There was a traditional identification between the deity of this shrine and an early Emperor, Ōjin. The procession is of the Yahata Provisional Festival.

2.   *'hold back the season's change'*: Ki no Tsurayuki, *Kokinshū* (262), composed 'on seeing autumn leaves on a shrine fence as he was passing': 'Even the kudzu vine / that clambers over the shrine fence / of the powerful gods / cannot hold back the season's change / and shifts to autumn's scarlet tinge.'

270   Huts

1.   *the 'thatched hut' ... poetry*: These two names are poetic words, both evoking lowly thatched huts. The 'eastern hut' (*azumaya*) appears in folk song poetry from the Eastern provinces.

271   The calling of the night watch is a wonderful thing

It was the general custom for the night watchman to twang his bow to ward off evil spirits, and beat a drum to mark the hour. A board on which the times were written was displayed in the garden outside the Privy Chamber. A peg was inserted at the appropriate place when the hour changed.

1.   *Countrified people ... 'Ox eight strikes'*: The night watchman beat the drum a specified number of times depending on the hour (nine times for the Hour of the Rat, eight for the Hour of the Ox, etc.), and this had evidently entered common parlance in this shorthand expression.

273   Captain Narinobu (1000)

Internal references (such as Narinobu's title, the two women sharing their little room) indicate the main episode occurred in 1000. Minamoto Kanesuke had become Governor of Iyo in 999.

1. *His Reverend ... War*: Emperor Murakami's son Prince Munehira, who had taken the tonsure.

2. *a very odd family name*: The portion of the text describing the nature of her name has resisted scholarly interpretation, although it appears to have something to do with its similarity to a food.

3. *Hyōbu*: 'Taira', who was evidently related to someone in the Bureau of War (*hyōbushō*).

4. *The Tale of Komano ... of old*: The same scene from this unlocated tale is mentioned in Section 198. The anonymous poem (*Gosenshū* 978) has the headnote 'sent to a forgotten lady': 'In the evening's dark / the road has grown invisible / but I ride homeward still / giving my horse free rein to walk / knowing he knows the way of old.'

5. *I like the hero ... the last two nights*: In *The Tale of Ochikubo* (anonymous, mid-tenth-century), Lieutenant Katano is a rival for the hand of the princess, and the hero speaks ill of him for being lascivious. Sei also refers to a scene in which the hero visits the princess for the third night (thus sealing the marriage), and must brave heavy rain to do so.

6. *'How could I forget her'*: A number of poems may be intended here, although no extant poem associates these words with a snowy scene.

7. *his Palace Guard costume instead*: The position of Chamberlain often doubled with that of Palace Guard. Palace Guard Chamberlains wore impressively long formal train-robes.

8. *'even if you do not share'*: Minamoto Nobuakira, *Shūishū* (363): 'Written to a lady on a bright moonlit night': 'Even if you do not share / the yearning that is in this heart / can it be that you / are not gazing as am I / at the moon this evening?' Her lover has evidently sent her the message.

274   You have a lover who always sends a next-morning poem

This could be considered a continuation of the previous section, carrying the theme of lovers' letters in varied weather into the realm of elegant vignettes.

1. *'the rising floods of rain'*: No extant poem matches this quotation. It may have used the image to express the rising force of a man's feelings for his lover.

275 Things of splendour and spectacle

1. *Peacock King Sutra:* This rite was held at the palace.
2. *The Great Purification*: A seven-day-long Buddhist ceremony held at the court from the eighth day of the first month, to ensure the safety of the country.
3. *The Rite of the Holy Star King*: The seven stars of the Ursa Major constellation were identified as a bodhisattva, and rites were performed invoking it for long life and protection from evil.
4. *The Rite of the Golden-Wheel Buddha*: A ceremony to protect the country from natural disasters and military insurrection.

276 When there are great thunderclaps

1. *by His Majesty's shutters*: The guards take up this post in thunderstorms to provide personal protection to the Emperor.

277 The *Kongenroku* screen is a fascinating thing

1. *The Kongenroku ... the Screen of the Months*: *Kongenroku* (Chinese *Kunyuanlu*), a book of Chinese geography, was the subject of an eight-panel screen in the palace. *Kanjo* (Chinese *Hanshu*), *The History of the Hans*, was a Chinese history. The Screen of the Months evidently depicted either a scene of each of the twelve months or of the major court ceremonies of the year.

279 The snow was piled high

1. *the snow of Kōro Peak*: This name appears in a well-known poem by Bo Juyi, the fourth of 'Five poems I jotted down on the east wall of my grass-thatched hut when first living under Xianglu Peak' (included in *Wakan rōeishū*), in which the poet lies in his warm bed on a winter's morning. The relevant lines are: 'I lift the blind to gaze out / at the snow on Xianglu [Japanese Kōro] Peak.'

281 In the third month, I left the court

1. *What a house ... all 'face'*: The slender willow leaf is a traditional metaphor for the eyebrows of a beautiful woman's face, with a further link being the punning meaning of *mayu* ('eyebrow' and 'silkworm's cocoon', which the catkins resembles). The connection with a beautiful face leads into another pun, where to shield

or hide the face means to 'lose face' (which the English expression for once aptly echoes).

2. *that Lieutenant*: This seems most likely to be a reference to the story of a Lieutenant Fukakusa, who wooed the famous poet Ono no Komachi by following tradition and going to her door every night for a hundred nights, but found he could not wait out the final night.

3. *The word "unbearable" ... unfortunate*: The word that Teishi finds fault with is *kanekeru*, which means literally 'could not'. It is unclear why this expression should be criticized. It may be that it doesn't suitably parry Teishi's poem, and rather conceitedly accepts that Sei's absence is indeed unbearable to the Empress.

282 On the twenty-fourth day of the twelfth month

The three-day ceremony usually began on the nineteenth day. The narrative point of view shifts rather disconcertingly between apparent personal recollection and imagined scene.

1. *the second service*: Each night was divided into three services, performed by different priests. The second would have ended at around 1.30 a.m.

2. *'The cold spreads crystal clear'*: From a Chinese poem in *Wakan rōeishū*: 'The cold spreads crystal clear / over the thousand miles of the Qin.'

283 When gentlewomen in the palace leave

This section appears to be written from the point of view of having left court service and yearning to stay in touch with that world and its gossip. Sei is perhaps imagining herself as the head of a household, still vicariously participating in court life through the gentlewomen who gather in her house.

284 Things that imitate

1. *Children*: This is generally interpreted to refer to children's propensity to copy what they see or hear. It may also be a humorous reference to women's tendency to have a child soon after a friend has done so.

285 Things one must be wary of

1. *what I believe is called the 'oar'*: Sei chooses to distance herself elegantly from the world of such workaday words. It is likely that the young man is poling the boat from the stern rather than rowing.

2. *rowed from the roofed end*: There is a small cabin area in the stern, where the main oarsman stands to row.
3. *'white retreating waves'*: A line from a famous poem by Priest Mansei (early eighth century) (*Shūishū* 1327): 'To what shall I compare / this transient world we live in? / White retreating waves / behind a boat that vanishes / rowing into the light of dawn.'

286 A certain Officer of the Right Gate Watch

1. *Touching indeed ... for his soul*: Offerings to or for the spirits of the dead were made in order to raise them from the sufferings of hell. Dōmei's poem may be ironic or a heartfelt expression of pity at human folly. Dōmei (d. 1021) was a priest of the Tendai sect who was also a skilful poet.

287 The mother of the Ohara gentleman

1. *The mother of the Ohara gentleman*: The poem's attribution in *Shūishū* makes it clear that she is the 'mother of Fujiwara Michitsuna'. Her reputation rests chiefly on her famous *Kagerō nikki* (*Gossamer Diary*, 954–974), a mournful record of her unhappy relationship with her husband, Fujiwara Kaneie. Michitsuna (father of Dōmei) was often referred to as 'the Ohara gentleman', from the name of the village north of the capital where he had a residence. See Section 286.
2. *We 'carried ... here at Ono*: The expression 'to carry firewood' (*takigi koru*) alludes to the description in the 'Devadatta' chapter, in which the Buddha carries firewood in service to a holy hermit, in order to hear from him the *Lotus Sutra*. For the axe handle, see Section 70, note 1. There is a pun on *ono* ('axe', and the name of the villa – the characters for 'Ohara' (see note above) could also be read 'Ono').

288 The letter Narihira's mother the Princess sent him

1. *'my longing grows the more intense'*: The scene containing this poem in *Tales of Ise* describes how Ariwara Narihira had been unable to visit his mother for some time, when he suddenly received the following (*Kokinshū* 900): 'Age grows upon me / and now our final parting / is surely drawing near. / My longing grows the more intense / to see you once again, my son.'

291   The Officers of the Left and Right Gate Watch

These men had the combined role of Officer of the Gate Watch and Vice-Superintendent of Police; as policemen they were powerful. See also Section 42.

1. *made a habit . . . green*: The Vice-Superintendent here is holding the concurrent post of (sixth-rank) Chamberlain.
2. *'the dawn that once I saw'*: No relevant poem is known.

292   Grand Counsellor Korechika presented himself one day (993 or 994)

1. *the hour of the Ox fourth quarter*: Around 2.30 a.m.
2. *'That sound awakens . . . sleep'*: From a Chinese poem by Miyako no Yoshika (834–879), in *Wakan rōeishū*: 'The cock-watchman announces the dawn; / that sound awakens the wise king from sleep.'
3. *hung my train and Chinese jacket*: Worn to accompany the Empress, Sei leaves her formal wear there for her return next morning to accompany Teishi back to her own residence.
4. *'The wanderer . . . moon'*: See Section 184, note 1.

293   I was sitting one day with Bishop Ryūen's nurse Mama

1. *nurse Mama*: 'Mama' was an affectionate name commonly used for a nurse.
2. *To whom . . . tale of woe*: The man's speech is laughably ornate, in an attempt to speak elegantly.
3. *On that spring day . . . like kind*: The poem relies heavily on puns: *moyasu* ('to burn' and 'to sprout') and *hi* ('fire' and 'day'). Yodono ('the field of Yodo') is homophonous with the man's quaint term for 'bedroom'.
4. *this promissory note*: He leaps to the conclusion that the paper is a record of gifts promised, which is presented on a long narrow sheet of thick paper (*tanzaku*) similar to the one the poem is written on.

294   There was a man whose mother died

This seems to be the beginning of an uncompleted tale.

295   A certain gentlewoman was courted by the Governor of
Tōtōmi's son

1.   *Swear then . . . Hamana*: This poem hinges on a rather pedestrian
pun on *kami* ('governor' and 'god'). The Bridge of Hamana is in
Tōtōmi, and is poetically linked with it.

296   Stealing an illicit conversation with someone

1.   *At Ōsaka Pass . . . Hashiri Well*: The name of the barrier gate of
Ōsaka is poetically linked with lovers' meetings, and Hashiri
Well ('Racing Water Well') was also located there. The poem
hinges on the word *hashiru* (to race), with a pun on *mizu* (water)
embedded in *mitsukuru* (to find).

297   Can it be true

1.   *Who set the fire . . . plan*: The poem is a tangle of punning images,
the main ones are: the *hi* of *omohi* ('thought') is also 'fire', and
kakaranu ('did not plan') is also 'it is not so'. Mt Ibuki's *ibu* can
also be read *iu* ('to say'), and the name conjures up the associated
poetic image of the moxa grass said to grow there.

[s3]   Things that are hard on the ear

1.   *while they apply tooth-black*: Women of the upper echelons
customarily blackened their teeth with an oxidized iron paint.

[s4]   Things whose Chinese characters make no sense

1.   *Chinese characters . . . some reason to them*: See Section 147 and
headnote.
2.   *Table salt . . . Summer under-robe*: 'Board eye salt'; written with
the same character as that for 'curtain drapes'.

[s5]   Things that look lovely but are horrible inside

1.   *Screens decorated with Chinese paintings. A limed wall*: The
brilliance of a Chinese-style painting contrasts with the unimpressive backing paper which is revealed if a screen is torn. The
lime coating hides the rough internal wall.
2.   *The prostitutes of Kōjiri*: Kōjiri, at the mouth of the Yodo River,
was home to prostitutes who entertained travellers.

[s6]   Women's outer gowns

Here and in Sections [s7]–[s9], the colours referred to are *kasane*
combinations.

[s17]   Comb boxes

1. *Comb boxes ... foreign creatures*: Lacquer boxes containing items for hair-dressing and make-up. The 'foreign creatures' design (*ban'e*) consists of roundels composed of exotic-looking birds, animals, etc., curved to face each other.

[s22]   Palm-leaf carriages

1. *carriages*: This is an abbreviated version of Section 29.

[s23]   A grove of tall pines shades the mansion

The scene is of a great mansion where the mistress has fallen ill through spirit possession. The priest strives to transfer the spirit to a medium and force it to reveal itself and depart, a feat which is perceived to be the result of the powers of the Buddha acting through the priest's incantations.

[s24]   The best places for palace service

1. *an offence to Buddhism*: As an expression of the formal antipathy between Buddhism and Shintō, the Kamo High Priestess was forbidden any participation in the world of Buddhism.

[s25]   A dilapidated house

This section appears in other versions of *The Pillow Book* at the end of Section 114 'Moving things'. It is possible that it continues into Section [s26], which also follows Section 114 in the other versions.

[s27]   I found it most offensive

The final sentence seems to belong in Section 90 'Infuriating things', and it is possible that all of this section was originally conceived as part of 90. Compare also the description of the pilgrimage in Section 115.

[s28]   When gentlewomen come and go from the palace

1. *Lord Naritō's*: Takashina Naritō, a cousin of Teishi, Provincial Governor and later Acting Deputy in the Crown Prince Harunomiya's household. (The latter was Genshi's husband.)

[s29]   I have written in this book

This concluding section explains the origin and intention of *The Pillow Book*. The gift of paper to Teishi can be dated to 994–996, when Korechika was Palace Minister. Tsunefusa's visit was between 995 and 997, when he was Governor of Ise. See also the Introduction, pp. xx–xxii.

1. *a "pillow"*: Sei probably intends a pun (see the Introduction, pp. xxi and xxxi n.4.).

2. *or so it is written*: This last sentence is couched as though written by a later hand. Such an ending was a not uncommon convention.